The Hitler Book

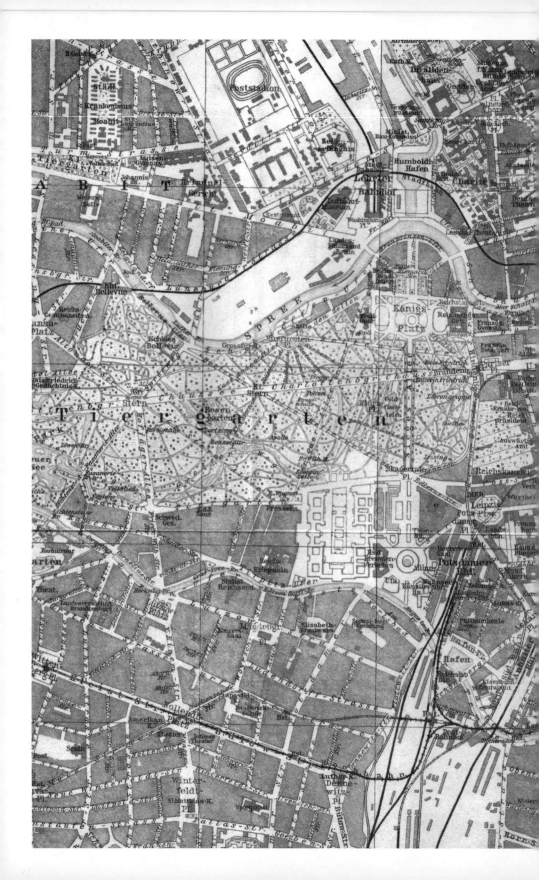

Berlin 1939: the beginning of the masterplan of 'Germania'.
In the centre (Vossstraße) is the new Reich Chancellery, the
scene of crucial decision-making and the place where the
Hitler regime collapsed

The Hitler Book

The Secret Dossier Prepared for Stalin

Edited by

Henrik Eberle and Matthias Uhl

Translated from German by

Giles MacDonogh

JOHN MURRAY

© Verlagsgruppe Lübbe GmbH & Co. KG, Bergisch Gladbach 2005
English translation © Giles MacDonogh 2005
Foreword © Richard Overy 2005

First published in Germany in 2005 by Verlagsgruppe Lübbe
This edition published in Great Britain in 2005 by John Murray (Publishers)
A division of Hodder Headline

The right of Henrik Eberle and Matthias Uhl to be identified as the Authors of the Work has
been asserted by them in accordance with the Copyright, Designs and Patents Act 1988.

1

A CIP catalogue record for this title is available from the British Library

Hardback ISBN 0 7195 5498 5
Trade paperback ISBN 0 7195 5500 0

Typeset in Monotype Bembo 10.75/13pt
by Servis Filmsetting Ltd, Manchester

Printed and bound by
Clays Ltd, St Ives plc

Hodder Headline policy is to use papers that are natural, renewable and recyclable products and
made from wood grown in sustainable forests. The logging and manufacturing processes are
expected to conform to the environmental regulations of the country of origin.

John Murray (Publishers)
338 Euston Road
London NW1 3BH

Contents

Foreword

Richard Overy

Despite everything that is now known about Adolf Hitler and Josef Stalin, there remains an intriguing gap in their history. Very little is known about what each thought about the other. Were they driven by profound hatred and mistrust? By a secret admiration, an unspoken regard for the historical giant whose public power each was committed to vilifying? What would have happened if Hitler had captured Stalin in Moscow in October 1941 as German troops pushed into the outer suburbs of the city? Or if Stalin had succeeded in taking Hitler alive inside his bunker in the last days of the war?

There are surprisingly few clues to answer these questions, though there is little evidence of open hatred between them. Stalin admired the Germans generally, not only because of the technical and administrative competence they displayed (which was borrowed widely by the Soviet Union in the 1920s in the form of advanced technology and engineering and planning advice), but because Germany 'gave the world such men as Marx and Engels'.[1] There is testimony of Stalin's reaction when he heard news that Hitler had ordered the murder of Ernst Röhm and other SA leaders in the famous Night of the Long Knives in June 1934: 'Hitler, what a great man! That is the way to deal with your political opponents.'[2] He is supposed to have said with a tinge of dictatorial regret that, side by side with Hitler's Reich, 'we would have been invincible',[3] and briefly, between September 1939 and June 1941, the two dictatorships were locked in a pact of friendship that the rest of the world found distinctly alarming. Hitler's remarks on Stalin are fewer and his obsessive hostility towards communism well known. Only in the last weeks of the war, when his reflections on past mistakes were obligingly recorded by Martin Bormann, his Chancellery chief, did Hitler ponder what the two men might have done between them if, 'in a spirit of implacable realism', the two had set out to build a 'durable entente'.[4] The historian should treat such remarks with caution, for the ideological gulf that separated the racist imperialism of Hitler's Reich from the revolutionary aspirations of Stalin's Soviet Union was enormous.

Nonetheless, it is difficult to imagine that the two dictators did not look closely at each other, gauging their different weaknesses and strengths, wondering what sustained the evident popularity and esteem publicly enjoyed by each man in his own system, or reflecting perhaps on what they might have in common.

It is against this background that this present volume should be judged. *The Hitler Book* is an extraordinary document, which owes its origin to the idea that after the defeat of Hitler in 1945 Stalin might want to know something in real detail about his fellow dictator. The immediate origins lie with the Soviet secret police. In 1945 and 1946 they were under direct instructions from Stalin to try to learn as precisely and truthfully as possible the circumstances of Hitler's death in the bunker on 30 April 1945, and to confirm that he was, indeed, dead. The report produced under the codename Operation Myth was based on extensive, often gruelling interrogation of the few eyewitnesses in Soviet hands, including Hitler's personal assistant and valet, Heinz Linge, and one of his military adjutants, Otto Günsche. Hitler's death was confirmed by a report finally produced in 1946 (the Soviet authorities indeed possessed the jawbones and dental work of both Hitler and Eva Braun, the mistress he married shortly before they killed themselves), but several years later the Information Committee of the Soviet security ministry decided to use this material as the starting point for a study of the Third Reich which could be presented to Stalin himself. A short account of the Battle of the Bulge was produced in April 1948 and given to Stalin and the members of the Politburo (the inner political 'cabinet' of the Soviet Communist Party). Stalin placed the account in his personal files and the committee decided to go ahead and authorise a complete survey of Hitler and the Third Reich based on further testimony wrung out of the unfortunate Linge and Günsche. The final document, 413 typewritten pages, under the innocuous title of 'Dossier' or 'File' (the Russian word *dyelo*), was sent to Stalin on 29 December 1949, just after his extensive seventieth-birthday celebrations. It was also filed away and eventually, after Stalin's death, a copy was deposited in a General Department archive, where it was discovered only two years ago by Matthias Uhl, who is the joint editor of this published edition.

The book itself was written by two security service officers, Fyodor Parparov and Igor Saleyev. It was not the first account of Hitler from first hand, but certainly the fullest. In 1945 British interrogators asked Albert Speer, Hitler's favourite architect and later Armaments Minister, to draft some long reports on Hitler's personality, on his entourage and on the course of German foreign and military policy. Speer obliged, but the resulting lengthy accounts were also filed in the archive and have resurfaced only in the past few years.[5] In 1943, the American psychiatrist Walter C. Langer was asked by General Donovan, head of the Office of Strategic Services in Washington, to produce a personality profile of Hitler to help American leaders understand what Hitler might do next. Langer's profile, based heavily on conventional psychological diagnosis, was eventually published in 1972 under the title *The Mind of Adolf Hitler*, though the full documentation has only recently been declassified by the United States National Archives.[6] Langer and the three colleagues who worked with him were able to base the profile on interviews with Germans who had known Hitler closely but had since fled from Germany. None of this secret material was available to the Soviet researchers. The richest source on Hitler, which they may well have consulted at some point, was the biography written by the émigré journalist Konrad Heiden under the title *Der Fuehrer*, published in 1944, but this account, for all its many merits, covered the story only as far as 1934.[7] The hard core of the Hitler dossier produced for Stalin lies in the years after 1935.

We can only speculate about what Stalin thought when he read the dossier prepared by his security ministry. Matthias Uhl found no jottings or marginalia in the version he uncovered, which for Stalin was unusual. The dictator covered his own books and papers with comments, exclamation marks and underlinings.[8] The former Soviet premier under Stalin, Vyacheslav Molotov, later recalled that if Stalin did decide to read something he did so with full and scrupulous attention.[9] It is possible that in this case he felt inhibited from writing given that at some point his colleagues might read his comments on his chief adversary. Or it may be that he only looked at it, knowing that this was not something that would ever see the light of day in his lifetime.

The dossier is significant not so much for the speculation that Stalin might have read it, but for what it might have told him about Hitler's personality and political behaviour. There were some obvious similarities between the two men, at least some of which Stalin must have already recognised long before the report. Both were populist politicians whose fortunes were transformed by a profound social and political crisis that helped them gravitate from the political margins to the political centre. Both were outsiders in another sense, Stalin from Georgia, annexed to the vast Russian Empire in 1806, Hitler from Austria, which was joined to its larger German neighbour only briefly, between 1938 and 1945. Both men were revolutionary in outlook, impatient to change the old order, critical of conventional bourgeois Europe, ambitious enough to want to reshape world history. Though propelled a good deal by individual good fortune and propitious historical circumstances, Stalin and Hitler achieved dictatorship because they each enjoyed an extravagant appetite for power and had the ruthlessness, political cunning and uncritical belief in their calling to be able to transform that ambition into reality. The techniques they each used to sustain the dictatorship, from the unscrupulous use of the security apparatus through to the overblown cults of personality, bore the same stamp. They both enjoyed, despite the terrible destruction that each unleashed, widespread and unrestrained public adulation. Soldiers really were heard to mutter Stalin's name as they dashed into battle; no other man in German history could ever have got his fellow countrymen to lift their arm and speak his name every time they greeted each other. Indeed so remarkable are these apparently trivial achievements that it compels the conclusion that in their different ways Stalin and Hitler exerted forms of direct personal authority unlike anything the modern age had yet seen.

The dossier presented Stalin with a picture consistent with the popular caricature of Hitler current throughout Europe in the 1930s. Some sense of the extraordinary character of the German dictator emerges, but the emphasis is on attempting to show Hitler as an abnormal individual. Allegations about his odd sexuality, or his habit of throwing unpredictable rages, or the assertion that he chewed the carpet in fits of hysterical anguish, was the stuff of contemporary gossip and hearsay, but is reproduced here to underline Hitler's uncertain mental state. The authors of the Hitler profile wanted to damn fascist leaders as licentious as well. At one point Hitler is described sniggering over photographs of naked Parisian dance-girls (a possibility quite out of step with everything else that is known about Hitler's prudishness and self-restraint); at another point the Italian dictator, Benito Mussolini, is said to spend his time at Salò, capital of the rump fascist republic set up with German support in 1943, indulging in orgies with a bevy of beautiful young Italian women.

The efforts to paint a lurid image of dictatorial indulgence were underpinned by the stock Marxist assumption that Hitler must have been the tool of German capitalism. This was the prevailing model in the 1930s and 1940s of a German big-business class thrown into crisis by the 1929 slump and forced to hire Hitler and his street rowdies to keep the working class under control and later to conquer markets in eastern Europe. There are a number of descriptions in the book where Hitler is host at lavish receptions for Germany's business elite, replete with every luxury and liquor; on one occasion, dated only 'autumn 1935' and apparently remembered by Linge more than a decade later, Hitler called wealthy bankers and industrialists together to demonstrate publicly the close links between regime and capitalism. The account contains a portentous remark by Hitler, overheard by Linge, which is clearly the product of a good deal of suggestion from his persistent interrogators. Hitler tells the armaments and iron and steel magnate, Gustav von Krupp, not to worry about the economic future when the riches of the 'east' lay before them. The idea that Germany under Hitler planned wars of capitalist imperialism was central to the Soviet worldview which was rooted in Leninist interpretations of the way the capitalist world was doomed to develop.

The thesis that Hitler could be understood as a tool of German capitalism is not presented stridently as so much propaganda, but is insinuated cleverly into the text. This is the case with a great many other assumptions and perspectives that are Soviet, not German, in origin. The text that follows is in this sense a political as much as a historical document. It tells us about the many things that coloured the Soviet worldview as well as Soviet interpretation of the very recent past. This was inevitable, given the fact that the document was written for Stalin and had, perforce, to observe both the party line and the historical legacy of the Soviet dictator. Neither Soviet author deliberately inserted falsehoods into their account – although the habit of putting remembered quotations in inverted commas gives the entirely misleading impression that this is exactly what Hitler said, rather than a vague recollection deliberately given more solid shape by the Soviet authors in order to convey the reliability of the testimony – but the calculated silence on some issues, or brief and dismissive comments on others, betray the priorities of the regime, not of the historian.

The most evident of these Soviet perspectives can be found in the treatment of the course of the Second World War. The account presented here is a refreshing alternative to those Western histories that give the Soviet front a supporting role and focus on the triumph of the West in defeating the Axis powers. Reading the story from the Soviet view, based only loosely on the interrogations of Linge and Günsche, the reader could be forgiven for thinking that the Soviet Union won the Second World War more or less on its own. There is almost no discussion of the Battle of Britain, but instead the claim, according to Linge, that in late June 1940 Hitler thought the western European issue over: 'All that remains for us now is to deal with the Soviet Union' (see below p.65). The idea that the real war for Hitler was always in the east was sown early in the dossier, and reaped in its later pages. Over and over again the authors stress not only how central war against the Soviet Union was in Hitler's strategy, but how significant the Soviet–German conflict was in deciding the outcome of the global war. This is not, of course, an entirely distorted assertion. War in the east was something that Hitler kept in mind as he planned the German remodelling of Europe; the destruction of Bolshevism was the dominant element of his worldview; and the exceptional conflict in the east, which cost over twenty-nine million Soviet military casualties (dead, wounded or taken prisoner), did blunt German military power and make possible Germany's defeat at Allied hands in 1945. In November 1943 Stalin told his Deputy Commander in Chief, Marshal Zhukov, that the Soviet Union could defeat Germany on its own, without the Western states.[10] Six years later, this had become conventional Soviet wisdom.

The hidden agenda in the Soviet account of the war also explains the treatment of other key episodes. The flight of Rudolf Hess to Scotland on 11 May 1941 is presented here as the product of collusion between Hitler and Hess to try to secure a separate compromise peace with Britain before invading the Soviet Union. At the time the flight had aroused serious suspicions in the Kremlin that Britain and Germany might broker an anti-Soviet agreement. Few historians now accept this version.[11] There was a fundamental implausibility in trying to secure agreement through an extravagant and risky gambit just weeks away from invading the Soviet Union, whose suspicions were bound to be aroused rather than lulled by the episode. Nevertheless the suggestion that Hitler might have done just this, implicit in the way the crisis is presented in the dossier, kept alive Soviet wartime speculation. British appeasement of fascism, allegedly based on Britain's imperial self-interest, features strongly in the discussion of the Munich crisis in the dossier. Soviet assumptions that Britain might have sought agreement with Hitler when it suited it derived from the established Soviet view that in the end all capitalist states had more in common with each other than with Soviet communism. Needless to say the Hitler dossier is entirely silent on the German–Soviet Pact signed in Moscow in August 1939 a few days before the outbreak of the Second World War.

The other factor that weighed heavily in wartime Moscow was the failure of the Western states to launch the 'Second Front' in Europe in 1942 or 1943. During these critical years on the Eastern Front, Stalin hoped that the Western states would do something substantial to distract German forces. He was largely impervious to the objections of Western leaders that the risks were very great, and the prevailing view in leading Soviet circles was that Western armies were afraid of the Germans (and of the high losses a tough invasion might entail). There was also the nagging impression that it suited the Western Powers for the Soviet Union and Germany to drain each other's fighting strength first before Western intervention. The discussion of fighting in the west is in general desultory (though the text does highlight an alleged quotation from Hitler indicating that if the West *had* attacked in early 1943 it would have been 'a catastrophe for Germany' – thus vindicating Stalin's urgent insistence on an early date for D-Day). The Normandy invasion of June 1944 is scarcely mentioned, and the fighting power of Western forces is denigrated by the occasional wry observation of their slow progress against the German enemy. The final rout of German armies in France is presented as a deliberate and orderly retreat to the German frontier in order to free up forces for the real war in the east against the Red Army. The account of the Battle of the Bulge, when Hitler massed a reserve for a final blow against the Western armies through the Ardennes forest in December 1944, is presented as a campaign that might have succeeded if it had not been for the need to transfer forces back again to stem the onrushing Soviet tide. Much of the rest of the war is simply ignored – the war at sea, in the Mediterranean theatre and Italy and in the Far East against Japan. So too are the Soviet Union's early campaigns against eastern Poland in September 1939 and against Finland in the winter of 1939/40. The Hitler dossier reduced everything to a gigantic duel between the Red Army and the Germans.

The most puzzling omission for a modern audience is the almost complete absence of discussion about the Holocaust. Although Soviet forces liberated both Majdanek and Auschwitz, with the storerooms full of shoes and human hair, the dossier only highlights the occasional atrocity perpetrated against Soviet civilians. There is one mention of mobile gassing vans but this has nothing to do with the system of camps and permanent gas chambers installed in eastern Poland to murder the Jews of Europe. Vans capable of operating as small gas chambers (in which their occupants were killed by carbon-monoxide poisoning) were used in the east to murder Soviet mental patients as well as some Jews. The exclusion of any mention of the systematic genocide was consistent with Soviet post-war policy. The victims of the German invasion were regarded as Soviet citizens of differing ethnic origin, not as particular national groups. The regime wanted to avoid giving the Jews a special place in the catalogue of victims because of a growing anti-Zionism and the difficulty of assimilating Jewish identity in the broader category of Soviet citizenship. When the Hitler dossier was produced, Soviet anti-Zionism was at its height and hundreds of prominent Soviet Jewish writers, doctors and academics were forced out of their professions or arrested or executed on trumped-up charges.[12] The Holocaust as a deliberate programme to exterminate the Jews of Europe was denied in Soviet writing down to the 1980s and even after the fall of communism has not been accepted unambiguously.

At the heart of the dossier lies the story with which the interrogations of Linge and Günsche began in 1945 – the final months in the bunker and Hitler's eventual suicide. More than 35 per cent of the dossier is devoted to the last five months of a regime that lasted twelve years. These were the events that the two prisoners could remember most vividly in 1945; both men were in closer physical proximity to their leader, and to the events that unfolded around him, than at any other time in the ten years they worked for him. The German historians Joachim Fest and Anton Joachimsthaler have recently published exhaustive accounts of the last days, based largely on eyewitness testimony. More material has been supplied with the publication of the memoirs of Hitler's secretary, Traudl Junge, written originally not long after the end of the war.[13] The dossier confirms much of what is now known, and adds many interesting details, including the recollection that in the bunker, in the last hours, the Hitler greeting was still used whenever Hitler appeared, and was even given by those present when his limp body was carried outside to be doused with petrol and incinerated. There is an ironic exchange between Linge and Hitler in April 1945 following a series of explosions above the bunker. 'What is the calibre?' asks a worried Hitler. Linge tells him it is the 'Stalin Organ', a rocket projectile known on the Soviet side as the Katyusha. 'What do you mean, Stalin organ?' asks a puzzled Hitler, mindful perhaps of the changed fortunes of the two men, the one huddled in a bunker, the other commanding a terrible vengeance on his crumpled enemy.

Hitler's final decision to kill himself was always treated by the Soviet side as evidence of his fundamental cowardice, 'an unworthy suicide' as the dossier tells it. For long the Soviet side insisted that Hitler had swallowed poison together with Eva Braun, whom he married a day before. But using Linge's evidence the dossier presents the story (already unearthed by the British secret service in 1945) that Hitler had shot himself in the head and only Eva Braun resorted to cyanide. Right through to the 1980s Soviet writers insisted that Hitler chose the easy way out by relying on poison. The dossier took a risk in exposing the mistake, for Stalin seems to have shared the view that Hitler was a coward. What Stalin would have done if the roles had been reversed is not entirely clear, but suicide was uncommon among the Soviet elite, whereas it was widespread among leading military and Party circles in Germany as defeat became a certainty. Stalin felt cheated by Hitler's death ('Now he's done it, the bastard,' he is said to have reacted on hearing the news. 'Too bad he could not have been taken alive').[14] But it was consistent with the stifling atmosphere of unavoidable doom spiced with moments of wild euphoria and disorientation that characterised life in the bunker and which the testimony of Linge and Günsche brings dramatically to life.

The Soviet dictatorship survived the war and lived on for a further forty-five years. *The Hitler Book* helps to explain that outcome despite the many advantages that German forces and the German economy enjoyed compared with its less developed and militarily unsophisticated enemy. Hitler's disdainful hostility towards his generals is evident over and over again; so too his extraordinary hubris. When he survived the bomb in his head-quarters on 20 July 1944 Günsche remembered him saying 'What luck! I am alive . . . That was the hand of providence.' Linge recalled another line: 'Only I am capable of saving the German people.' Hitler's obsessive self-belief consumed everything in its path, including the prospect of a more sensible strategy. German defeat was not just caused by Hitler; he ensured that defeat, when it came, would be total and devastating for the German population.

The Hitler Book is an unexpected and original perspective on the Third Reich and its leader. As a historical document it must be used with caution. There is much that is deliberately left out, much that its two Soviet authors did not know. The reconstruction of conversations and meetings relies on evidence from years of cross-examination in which the interrogators played a role in manipulating and selecting what they wanted to hear, just as the witnesses struggled to recall long-distant events which the usual tricks of memory must have distorted and disordered. The narrative is an approximation, not an exact replica of historical reality. But in terms of an overall historical truth it is no more and no less adequate than those many Western accounts of Hitler and the war that pretend that the Soviet Union was an adjunct to the war effort rather than a core element. *The Hitler Book* is a timely reminder that the heart of the terrible transformation wrought by the European crisis in the twentieth century was the contest between two extraordinary tyrants and the systems they dominated.

Translator's Preface

Giles MacDonogh

The year 2005 was a milestone for Adolf Hitler. In Germany the sixtieth anniversary of his death was heralded by a controversial new film, *Der Untergang* ('Downfall'); and March marked the publication of *Das Buch Hitler* ('The Hitler Book'), the previously mislaid text of an extensive dossier written for Stalin's edification and based upon the testimonies of German prisoners of war in Soviet captivity. *The Hitler Book* has since been proved one of the best primary sources on the inner workings of the Third Reich that we possess. It also called into question several scenes in *Downfall*.[1]

Downfall provoked a lively debate, above all in Germany. The Swiss actor Bruno Ganz's portrayal of a 'human' Hitler clashed with a convention which requires him to be cast as a carpet-biting devil. Audiences saw a worried, frightened and tearful Führer; they witnessed him kiss his new wife Eva on the mouth (*The Hitler Book* makes it clear that he kissed her – like a good Austrian – on the hand); they saw his concern for the well-being of his secretaries; and they saw the demon too, but one mitigated perhaps by human (rather than humane) emotions. They saw a *normal* woman love him, and excuse his conduct. More shocking perhaps (but this aroused far less outcry) the film turned a butcher like SS-Brigadeführer Wilhelm Mohnke into an honourable soldier and the SS doctor Ernst Günther Schenck into something approaching a Hollywood hero, despite the fact that he had carried out experiments on the prisoners in Nazi concentration camps.

That Hitler's demoniac side should be deconstructed one day was inevitable. From an historical point of view it had always stood in the way of objective appraisal. Hitler's munitions minister Albert Speer saw the danger of typecasting the Führer as early as 10 February 1947 when he wrote in his prison diary, 'I get the impression that people are increasingly representing Hitler as a dictator given to raging uncontrollably and biting the rug even on slight pretexts. This seems to me a false and dangerous course. If the human features are going to be missing from the portrait of

Hitler, if his persuasiveness, his engaging characteristics, and even the Austrian charm he could trot out are left out of the reckoning, no faithful picture of him will be achieved.'[2]

As Henrik Eberle and Matthias Uhl point out in their Afterword to this volume, there have been over a thousand biographies of Hitler to date.[3] Hitler had already been the subject of a handful of studies before war broke out in 1939. One of the earliest was written by the British writer, painter and fascist-sympathiser Wyndham Lewis, whose *Hitler* appeared in 1931. The future West German President Theodor Heuss's *Hitlers Weg* ('Hitler's Way') came out in 1932. Hitler's supporters voiced their opinion of it when they cast it on to the bonfire on Berlin's Opernplatz after their master came to power. Most of the others were written by Germans in exile: Rudolf Olden, whose book was published in Amsterdam in 1935, and Konrad Heiden, whose two volumes appeared in Zurich in 1936 and 1937. The recently republished *Germany – Jekyll and Hyde* was written by a third journalist, Sebastian Haffner, and published in London in 1940.

The most influential of these early biographies was Hermann Rauschning's *Hitler Speaks* of 1939 which – as Horst Möller points out in his introduction to the German edition of *The Hitler Book* – was partly a work of fiction: whole dialogues had been dreamed up by the author. Also important in framing the American view of Hitler were two émigrés who landed there: Ernst Fraenkel, the author of *The Dual State* of 1941 and Franz Neumann, whose *Behemoth* appeared the following year. All these books were perspicacious in their way; all of them took pains to warn their readers against Hitler, but none of them could have known the full scale of the disaster as it was revealed in May 1945.

The tone of Hitler biography changed with the peace. The war had left some fifty million dead and homes and lives all over the world shattered beyond repair; people needed to come to terms with the past. They needed to know who the men were who had brought this about. This meant the National Socialist Party leadership. Stalin, the dedicatee of *The Hitler Book*, was no less curious to learn about his adversaries – particularly the enemy in chief, Hitler. He was keenest of all to know *if* he was actually dead. His intelligence services were whipped into action to provide the answers.

Stalin was not alone among the Allied leaders. While Stalin's men were putting together the dossier that would become *The Hitler Book*, the historian Hugh Trevor-Roper had been seconded to British intelligence and was compiling the evidence that would become the core of *The Last Days of Hitler*. Trevor-Roper took a lofty, disdainful approach to the Nazi top brass: 'When a staid German general compared Göring to Elagabalus, he was not exaggerating. In the absolutism, the opulence and the degeneracy of the middle Roman Empire we can perhaps find the best parallel to the high noonday of the Nazi Reich. There, in the severe pages of Gibbon, we read of characters apparently wielding gigantic authority who, on closer examination, are found to be the pliant creatures of concubines and catamites, of eunuchs and freedmen; and here too we see the *élite* of the Thousand-Year Reich a set of flatulent clowns swayed by purely random influences.'[4]

Trevor-Roper's book had started out life much like *The Hitler Book*. It had been commissioned by Dick White, chief of counter-intelligence in the British Zone of occupied Germany (and later head of MI6), as a 'British Intelligence Report on the Death of Hitler'. The Russians were refusing to share their information with the Western Allies and the Anglo-Americans were obliged to reach their own conclusions based on interrogations carried out within their Zones. Trevor-Roper delivered the text on 1 November 1945, having reached the correct conclusion that Hitler had shot himself in the bunker on 30 April that year. It was released to the reading public only in March 1947. Such is curiosity about the twelve years of the Thousand-Year Reich that it has never been out of print.

Trevor-Roper longed to interview Otto Günsche and Heinz Linge for the original edition of *The Last Days of Hitler*. He was also looking for Hitler's pilot Hans Baur and the head of his police protection squad, Johann Rattenhuber, but none of them was to hand. They had all gone east after 2 May 1945, where they were helping Soviet investigators with their inquiries. He made a formal request for information. The Soviet authorities acknowledged it, but gave him nothing. He had not a clue that they were compiling their own book at the same time, and reaching much the same conclusions as him.

Indeed, in the preface to the third edition of 1956, written after the Soviet prisoners had been released and made their first statements to the press,[5] Trevor-Roper demanded to know why the Soviet authorities had never published the conclusions to their investigations: 'was it that they did not wish to discover the facts?'[6] To the best of my knowledge Trevor-Roper, by then Lord Dacre of Glanton, went to his grave in ignorance of the fact that the Russians had not only carried out the investigation, but that a report had been compiled that was every bit extensive as his own, if not more so.

The Soviet *Hitler Book* lacks the poise and Gibbonian turn of phrase that is the delight of *The Last Days of Hitler*. The Russians were also much more partial in their interpretation of the Second World War. Where *The Hitler*

Book has the advantage over Trevor-Roper, however, is in the more detailed study of the leaders of the Third Reich and in the testimony supplied by Linge and Günsche: men who were in general closer to Hitler – both physically and spiritually – than the high-ranking officers interviewed by British intelligence.

Neither man was well born, and both were members of the SS; and based on their statements *The Hitler Book* looks askance at the Wehrmacht generals who have generally received a better press in the West. The treatment of Field Marshal Erich von Manstein is a good example of this: his craven behaviour towards Hitler is shown to have disgusted even Martin Bormann. The Bavarian Sepp Dietrich, commander of the Leibstandarte 'Adolf Hitler' – a sort of Nazi Life Guards – comes across in a far more sympathetic light: a former coachman, he became a no-nonsense field commander; a brute perhaps, but one who fought alongside his men.

The Hitler Book is to some extent a portrait of Hitler by his servants; by the men standing behind the chairs of the Party officials and noble officers at meals and conferences. They were unshakeable in their loyalty even if they were perfectly aware of their master's faults. They had no sympathy whatsoever with the men of 20 July 1944, who rose up against Hitler and – in their opinion – contributed to Germany's defeat. Their disdain for Wehrmacht toadies, corrupt officials and medical quacks is clear. Hitler's doctor Morell is singled out for special treatment in *The Hitler Book*.

The combination of a jaundiced, Soviet account of the running of the war which is heavily critical of the West, together with more minute portraits of Hitler and his henchmen provided by the testimonies of German prisoners of war gives the text its unique character. The style is perplexing for that reason: it is a body with two souls – a Russian one and a German. Sometimes it appears inspired by cheap novels, as if the Soviet editors were striving unsuccessfully to reproduce the style of Ernest Hemingway. At others it reads like a military situation report, reflecting Otto Günsche's role in authenticating the minutes of Hitler's meetings with his generals. There are setpieces where you can feel the polish being applied – as in the description of Hitler's palaces, both in Berlin and the modern Berghof on the Obersalzberg, which the Soviet editors persist in describing as a 'castle'. And there is the gossip, provided because Stalin was evidently prurient about Hitler's unfathomable sex life, his mental instability and his dependence on drugs. This was Linge's unique area of expertise: what the butler saw.

The Hitler Book was published first in German, and the British and American editions have been taken from the text established by Henrik Eberle and Matthias Uhl and the Lübbe Verlag in Bergisch Gladbach in

March 2005. I have used their edition: a stunning piece of work in its detailed examination of the material and its extensive textual machinery. They present the 'file' in a succinct German translation by Helmut Ettinger. This I have rendered in entirety, although some repetitions have been edited out, particularly of ponderous Third Reich titles, offices and ranks. The foreword provided by Professor Horst Möller of the Institut für Zeitgeschichte in Munich and Berlin has been replaced by an essay by the distinguished British historian Professor Richard Overy. The Editors' Introduction remains much as it was, but the dictates of space have made it necessary to abridge the Afterword. Many of the bibliographical notes have been omitted. Virtually all of these referred to sources in German or Russian. Readers requiring this information will need to consult the German edition.

I have also had to drop the extensive biographical section, although where possible I have shortened the entries and recast them in the Notes at the back of the book. I have been at pains to do this in the case of the minor figures who have eluded biographical dictionaries and encyclopaedias before now, stressing which of them were Nazis, and which were Wehrmacht officers – some of whom were ready to question Hitler's authority, especially after the disastrous defeat at Stalingrad at the beginning of 1943. On the other hand figures like Mussolini, Chamberlain, Churchill, Hitler, Göring and Himmler I felt required little in the way of introduction.

Much of the remaining textual machinery has been shifted to the Notes at the back of the book in a desire to make it more readable. Where I have felt that the text requires immediate explanation, however, I have left the note at the foot of the page.

Although it is only sixty years since the defeat of Hitler's Reich, the book presents us with an unfamiliar world. Anyone who was anyone wore some sort of uniform in Nazi Germany: from the operatic costumes of a Hermann Göring, to Party chiefs and diplomats down to the soldier-servants who attended Hitler at his table. The sight of a nation in uniform was a garbled nod to the 'Prussianism' Hitler claimed to admire in Frederick the Great, as well as an affirmation of the 'nation in arms' and a trademark of twentieth-century fascist states. Outwardly there was only this militarised world. Hitler was briefed not only by his adjutants seconded from the three services and the SS, he had his personal adjutants too. At his HQ there were also permanent emissaries from the German Foreign Office and the Party – and all of them in uniform.

The Third Reich possessed a complicated infrastructure and a plethora of offices and titles. The competition between these institutions was deliberate:

it allowed the tyrant to divide and rule. The names can be confusing – particularly when it comes to the Party and the armed forces. Explanations have been provided where possible. I have retained the German ranks without translating them, but we have appended a table to show their equivalence to British and American ranks in the navy, army and air force.

The SS had its own ranks and structure, but instead of answering to High Command, it came under the aegis of the Reichsführer-SS, Heinrich Himmler. The Treaty of Versailles had destroyed the Prusso-German regimental traditions thereby weakening the Wehrmacht's claims to precedence over the upstart SS. As the war progressed the SS moved into a position where it could claim to be the new military elite. The pro-SS perspective of *The Hitler Book* makes the rivalry between the Wehrmacht and the SS abundantly clear.

The Russian editors of *The Hitler Book* are as damning in their condemnation of the Third Reich as Hugh Trevor-Roper was. Hitler dies a coward's death, shivering with fear in a hole in the ground. Unlike Trevor-Roper's *grand guignol*, however, something of the starker character of the time breaks through to show us why so many young men were prepared to fight and die for a man he condemned as a charlatan. Despite the gloss applied for Stalin, *The Hitler Book* is an impressive portrait, in flesh and blood.

Editors' Introduction

Henrik Eberle and Matthias Uhl

Adolf Hitler shot himself in the underground bunker of the Reich Chancellery shortly before half-past three on the afternoon of 30 April 1945. Advanced units of the Russian army were only a few hundred metres away. Under no circumstances would Hitler have allowed himself to fall into their hands. Towards the end of his life he had associated Bolshevism with his obsessive fear that he would be carried in a cage to Red Square and lynched by an angry mob.

Joseph Vissarionovich Stalin on the other hand had yet to escape from his Hitler nightmare, which had begun on 22 June 1941 with Germany's surprise attack on the Soviet Union. He doubted the report of the dictator's suicide. He believed that Hitler had fled and that the Western Allies had secretly granted him asylum. because they wanted, with his support, to continue the war against the Soviet Union. The accounts of Hitler's death sounded contradictory, and as more and more supposed Hitler corpses turned up, Stalin became ever more insecure. It was soon clear from reliable sources that several high-ranking members of the regime had got away. Stalin was unhappy with the results of the Soviet inquiry. At the end of 1945 he instructed the People's Commissariat of Internal Affairs (the NKVD) to reconstruct the last days in the bunker under the Reich Chancellery and prove that Hitler was dead.

People's Commissar Sergei Kruglov was put in charge and a working party of high-ranking officers was formed under him to carry out the inquiry, codenamed Operation Myth. This was its nerve-centre. Members of the NKVD hunted down all the available documents on Hitler and his regime, while officers in the department for prisoners of war searched the camps for Hitler's helpers, who had to undergo endless interrogations. The Ministry of the Interior (MVD; it became the more familiar KGB in 1960), the successor organisation to the NKVD, was also regularly involved with Operation Myth. Stalin demanded constant reports from his deputy in the Council of Ministers, the long-serving Minister of the Interior and Secret Police Chief Lavrenti Beria.

Eventually, on 29 December 1949, the dictator received something like a final report of 413 typed pages covering Hitler's life between 1933 and 1945. The title of the report was *The Hitler Book*. After he had read it, Stalin had the text placed in his personal collection of documents, the General Secretary's Archive. This copy is today preserved in the personal archive of the Russian President and may not be consulted by foreigners.

In 1959, Stalin's successor Nikita Khrushchev felt it opportune to step into the bitter debate over Hitler and the Second World War that was raging in West Germany. He gave instructions that certain material from the dossiers of Operation Myth should be made available to loyal Party historians. As a result a copy was taken of *The Hitler Book* for the Ideological Commission of the Secretariat of the Central Committee of the CPSU (the Communist Party of the Soviet Union) and handed over to Central Committee Secretary Leonid Ilychev on 20 April that year. But *The Hitler Book* did not really serve its purpose, because it presented a picture of the history of the Second World War that did not match official Party propaganda: there were various details concerning diplomacy in National Socialist Germany, the battles on the German–Soviet front and the downfall of the Third Reich that had been presented differently up till then. This was considered reason enough to put the documents back under lock and key. Secretary Ilychev prohibited access to them and had them transferred to the document collection in the General Department.

When the Party archives were opened in 1991, it became possible for foreign historians to examine the dossiers of the CPSU. Because *The Hitler Book* had been classified in the card index of the General Department's archive under an incomprehensible shelfmark, it was a long time before document no. 462a was discovered. Only when Matthias Uhl undertook a systematic examination of the papers of the General Department in the course of carrying out a research project for the Institute for Contemporary History in Munich did *The Hitler Book* finally come to light. A Russian colleague who had access to the presidential archive compared the copy to the original and confirmed the authenticity of the document: file no. 462a was a word-for-word copy of the 1949 NKVD/MVD dossier.

The most important basis for the later manuscript prepared by the working Party of the MVD were the statements and writings of two men who had lived in the closest proximity to Hitler for many years: Heinz Linge and Otto Günsche. Hitler had also ordered them to burn his body and that of his wife Eva. From 1935 Linge belonged to the Führer's Escort Command

and from 1939 was his manservant, and later he became the head of his personal household. Günsche entered the Escort Command in 1936 and in 1943 Hitler appointed him personal adjutant. After a short spell at the front he returned to Hitler's service as personal adjutant in February 1944. Both men went into Soviet captivity on the night of 2 May 1945.

For four long years, from 1946 to 1949, Linge and Günsche had to provide information about Hitler. Over and over again they had to give intimate details of the dictator's life, about his relations with the heads of the Wehrmacht, and about the goings-on at Führer HQ. Because there were strong doubts about Hitler's suicide, Linge and Günsche were taken to Berlin in 1946 where once again they had to give an exact description of the last hours of Hitler and point to the precise spot where he had been burned. After their return MVD officers requested that they – and others of Hitler's former underlings – commit their memories to paper. At the same time the pressure on prominent prisoners was increased when their status as prisoners of war was removed: the state prosecution threatened that, should they refuse to write their 'reminiscences', they would be charged as war criminals.

It was presumably Linge who was the first to agree to set down his 'memoirs'. His solitary cell was crawling with bugs, and he was humiliated and whipped many times. His interrogator treated him with a mixture of patience and pitilessness, which brought him, in Linge's words, 'almost to despair'. (Similar methods were used on Günsche.) By the spring of 1948 he declared himself ready to write a text on the German–British peace talks, which eventually found its way to Stalin.

The officers in the special commission later collated these writings in the files of Operation Myth and transferred the authors to a special court. Linge and Günsche were sentenced to twenty-five years' hard labour. In 1955 they were released from Soviet captivity with the last prisoners of war. Linge was allowed to proceed to West Germany. Günsche, however, was sent to East Germany and handed over to the Ministry for State Security (the Stasi, or secret police). Like many others who had been sentenced by Soviet courts he disappeared behind the gates of Bautzen Prison, in Bautzen, Saxony, in 1956.

Several officers, interpreters and female translators took part in collating *The Hitler Book*. The commission's head, Lieutenant Colonel Fyodor Karpovich Parparov, oversaw the progress of the work and edited the final text. He was certainly well qualified for the job, as he had studied law and since 1926 had worked for Soviet intelligence abroad. He cut his teeth in

Germany, where – disguised as a merchant from Costa Rica – he recruited several sources in the Nazi Party and the Foreign Office. His greatest coup was to recruit the (hitherto unidentified) agent 'Elsa' or 'Juna'. This was the wife of a high-ranking German diplomat in the immediate entourage of the Joachim von Ribbentrop, who was later Foreign Minister.

After short assignments in Turkey and the Netherlands, Parparov was caught up in Stalin's Purges, no doubt because his reports from Germany ran counter to the premises of the Hitler–Stalin Pact. He was rehabilitated immediately after the German attack on the Soviet Union, and after the end of 1941 he interrogated German prisoners of war behind the Russian lines as a member of the Fourth Administration of the People's Commissariat for State Security. His most important prisoner was Field Marshal Friedrich Paulus, who after weeks of talks was slowly but surely brought over to the Soviet side. Parparov later prepared him as a witness for the prosecution in the principal trial of war criminals at Nuremberg.

Although Parparov's knowledge of German is described as excellent he clearly found it difficult to transform the minutes of the interrogations and the writings of Linge and Günsche into the Russian-language *Hitler Book*. He had to reconcile two conflicting demands: the text had to feel authentic, as far as possible using Linge's and Günsche's own words, but he also had to take into account the reading habits and expectations of the 'client' – Josef Stalin. Between these two poles Parparov developed his own style: a remarkable blend of authenticity and compressed civil service Russian in which the pressure from without is plain for all to see.

Moreover, when the style and construction of the text make the origin of the material unrecognisable – the interrogation and report – it is evident that the MVD authors' collective could not resist the occasional temptation to heighten the more emotional situations. The most striking assault on the rules of sober and objective reportage can be found right at the beginning of *The Hitler Book*. The rehashing of a key scene from 1933 is obviously not authentic and is included to provide dramatic emphasis. The purpose is simply to introduce the character of Hitler and show the importance of his personal guard, the SS-Leibstandarte 'Adolf Hitler'. Only in the period after 1935 does the text take on the character of an eye-witness report. For many details from later years, including a number of one-to-one discussions with the Führer, the statements of Linge or Günsche are the only available sources. They report on situation briefings for which the minutes no longer exist and they recall scenes where others who were present kept quiet before the court or wisely held their tongues in their memoirs. They accurately register the mental and physical collapse of the dictator without having access to his medical records.

What differentiates *The Hitler Book* from other comparable documents is the existential, life-threatening circumstances in which it was created. Linge and Günsche had to be on their guard against saying anything that was wrong or imprecise lest they be hauled out the next day; and because they were kept in solitary confinement they could neither corroborate their statements nor work out a defence strategy. The interrogators, for their part, sought over the years of interviewing to remove memorised falsehoods and made Linge and Günsche go through their story over and over again.

Even if Linge and Günsche were the only sources for certain events, many details of life in the bunker were corroborated by other prisoners. When one considers that no documents were available either to the interrogators or to the prisoners, the results are all the more impressive. The facts and dates in *The Hitler Book* are overwhelmingly correct, scenes are exactly described and even documents precisely reproduced. A comparison between a document memorised by Günsche and the original which has since been published shows that he gives the word *erfolgt* rather than the *erhalten* in the original, and '*übernehme*' rather than '*übernehmen muss**'. Linge and Günsche had very precise recall when it came to Hitler's sayings. A comparison with the Führer's published speeches and writings and with the records of other contemporary witnesses reveals divergences, but nothing that is notably incorrect.

Linge's strength surely lies in his memory for incidents in everyday life and moods and in his descriptions of Hitler's immediate circle. Thus he was the source for most of the passages which seem particularly to have interested Stalin and which are best described as the tittle-tattle at Hitler's court. As a front-line soldier Günsche had a greater comprehension of the military situation. The events he recalls are recounted very coolly. He describes the arrest and execution of Hitler's brother-in-law Hermann Fegelein entirely without emotion; and it was he who convinced Hitler that it was necessary to hand him over to a court martial.

While the MVD team altered the style and content of the statements only in exceptional cases, their influence on terminology is much more striking. The text betrays the anxious desire of the writer both to comply with Stalin's request that the manuscript be utterly true to life and to suit the style of the General Secretary and Supreme Commander. Had the work

---

* 'Succeeds' rather than 'maintains'; 'takes over' rather than 'must take over'.

displeased him or even just raised questions it might have had unforesee-able consequences for the team. Passages that did not accord with Stalin's conception of events were struck out. As a result in the finished text there are only two hidden allusions to the Hitler–Stalin Pact of 1939. The obsequiousness of the team is manifest in the frequent repetitions of names, functions and so on, as well as in the many contextual explanations (which Stalin added to his own speeches and publications), where they use brackets and footnotes to gloss – often superfluously – aspects of German life or politics. This otiose material was meant to make it more approach-able for Stalin, but renders it odd to the contemporary reader.

What is noteworthy is the sparing use of official terms for National Socialist organisations. Terms that must have been used by the prisoners appear only rarely and then in paraphrase. There is much about Hitler's Bodyguard, but no mention of the Führer Escort Command and rarely do they speak of the Leibstandarte. The Nazi Party (or NSDAP) is never given its proper name or its appropriate abbreviation, but is referred to only as the national socialist Party (with the adjectives in the lower case). Official terms are given in parenthesis: 'Third Reich', 'Brown House', 'Wolfsschanze', 'Hitler Youth' or 'Volkssturm'.

The use of surnames without Christian names, rank or title creates dis-tance. This is no less true of the constantly used word *Schloss* or castle to describe Hitler's Berghof. Even if – in view of the size and substantial infra-structure of the residence on the Obersalzberg – this is not erroneous, it certainly does not come from Linge or Günsche. Instead of the more usual 'German greeting' or 'Hitler greeting', 'fascist greeting' is used, and the characterisation of the SD Chief Ernst Kaltenbrunner as a 'butcher' must have been written into the text by Parparov's editors.

The Hitler Book contains the accounts of two SS officers who dealt with Hitler daily without ever being close to him as a man. They admired him and were convinced Nazis, but – like most of their contemporaries – they did not understand what goals the dictator was really pursuing. In remembering him they have certainly distanced themselves from him by sharpening up their condemnation, but they never denied their proximity to him. The result in *The Hitler Book* is a document which is at once unique and strange: it rests on material culled from two SS-Sturmbannführers, and was written by an authors' collective made up of members of the Soviet internal secret police who spent four years writing a biography of Hitler until it conformed to the reading preferences of their client.

The text of file no. 462a from the former Party Archive not only contains many previously unknown details relating to Hitler's policies and leadership in war, it also gives an unretouched picture of how this was seen by his entourage. The document reflects with great vividness the falling out between the Führer of the Greater German Reich and the man who believed for a while that he could carve up Europe with him, but who then forced him into a murderous combat that cost the lives of millions of people. *The Hitler Book* thus throws light on the antagonism between Hitler and Stalin, a conflict that many historians from Alan Bullock to Richard Overy have seen as a key to the understanding of the history of the last century.

THE HITLER BOOK

NKVD Secret Dossier for Josef V. Stalin, based on the minutes of the interrogations of Hitler's Personal Adjutant, Otto Günsche, and his valet Heinz Linge, Moscow 1948–9.

Управ... ...оеннопленных
...... (..ПВИ)

ДЕЛО

№ 1-Г-23

№ Ф. 451
О-пи 5
ЕД. хр. 36

О Гитлере и его окружении —

Материалы расследования

(т. Гитлер)

Срок хранения 25 лет ц ЭК 4

НАЧАТО: 48 г

Окончено:
38 билов

I

Summer 1933 – Summer 1934

Summer 1933 – the sun was shining in Berlin's Wilhelmsplatz, the location of the Reich Chancellery. After Hitler came to power on 30 January 1933, the new era of the Third Reich began here. Behind the curtains of a window on the first floor stood a man of middling height, a lock of hair falling across his forehead. It was Hitler. He was leaning slightly forward watching the military parade taking place in the *cour d'honneur* below. The changing of the guard was being performed by soldiers of his bodyguard, known as the Leibstandarte 'Adolf Hitler'.[1] The SS men swung their legs high and made a tremendous noise as the soles of their boots hit the asphalt. The men stood to attention, their gaze fixed before them. The change-over was complete. Hitler stepped back from the window. It was already 2 p.m., time for his lunch.

Today he was lunching with his adjutants Wilhelm Brückner[2] and Julius Schaub[3] and the commander of the Leibstandarte Sepp Dietrich, together with the Reich Chief Press Officer Otto Dietrich.[4] Heinz Linge[5] was taking telephone calls in Hitler's dining room. He was able to hear the conversation at the table. It was not hard to recognise when it is the adjutants who are speaking; they wanted to profit as much as they could from their positions before it was too late. Hitler said sarcastically that he had no intention of giving up the post of Reich Chancellor so quickly. In a shrill voice he cried out, 'They predicted that I wouldn't last more than a few months. But they will be amazed: I am staying put!'

He then announced that he would crush any resistance with all means at his disposal: 'I am not a chancellor like Bismarck, who was just the Kaiser's minister. I have my own Party! I am the Führer! What qualities should a Führer possess? Above all a name that is constantly on everyone's lips. For that reason I have introduced the greeting "Heil Hitler!", which features my name. In the circumstances I am more than happy I was not born Oberhubinger or Unterkirchner!* The masses must always have

*Old Bavarian family names that surface in jokes and stories. (Russian note.)

the Führer before their eyes . . . All cameras must be directed towards me: the crowd follows my every move. The Führer needs to move the masses like an actor – his clothing, his mimicry and his gestures – they are all important.'

Lunch was over. Hitler rose in the best of moods. With his hands in his pockets he trilled to himself 'Schön ist jeder Tag, den du mir schenkst, Marie Luise' (Lovely is each day that you give me, Marie Louisa) – a hit from the Berlin music halls he loved.[6] Suddenly he fell silent and turning to his adjutants he said, 'How lucky I am that providence sent me to the desperate German people as a saviour in their hour of need.'

Meanwhile in the Gestapo's HQ in the cellars of the Prinz Albrecht Hotel in Berlin's Prinz Albrecht Strasse prisoners were locked up who were unable to believe in Hitler's divine mission.[7] In the Gestapo prison particularly important people were held. After the 'Enabling Law' hundreds of thousands of upright Germans were despatched to concentration camps – Oranienburg, Buchenwald or Dachau.* Prison buildings that had been boarded up for years because of their dilapidated condition returned to their original vocation on Himmler's authority, 'for the protection of the people and the Fatherland'. In the Chancellery it was known that new prisoners were delivered to penitentiaries and concentration camps on Hitler's personal orders.[8] He explained, 'We would have far too much to do if we wasted our time with legal processes. I can't rely on the Mr Justices of this world. It is therefore far more practical to arrest people . . . without the sticklers for legal niceties getting wind of it . . . This right I claim for myself. I am my own Minister of Justice!'

The cellars of the Hotel Prinz Albrecht were far too small to contain all the important 'political prisoners' of the Third Reich. They were also crammed into the infamous Columbia House in Berlin-Tempelhof, a dilapidated former factory where the Gestapo had set up another prison.[9] The gaolers in Berlin's Gestapo dungeons were selected Nazis who had 'specialised' in street fighting, ambushing and murdering communists before Hitler assumed power. Their guardrooms were emblazoned with posters bearing the legend 'Führer command, we will obey!' Prisoners

---

*The Enabling Law (Law to Remedy the Distress of People and Reich) came into force on 24 March 1933. It empowered the regime to pass laws altering the constitution over a period of four years without consulting the Reichstag or Reichsrat. The law was prolonged several times, and remained in force until May 1945. The concentration camps at Dachau (20 March 1933) and Oranienburg (21 March 1933) were the first two official camps to be created after the Reichstag fire in March of that year. Buchenwald was not opened until 15 July 1937.

were kicked, bestially mistreated and tortured. The gaolers explained with a grin, 'We have fun here . . . Himmler said, "The hardened cases will remain here until the cows come home . . . so we are charting the path to national rebirth."'

23 June 1934. Special orders were issued that the gates to the SS Leibstandarte Barracks in Berlin-Lichterfelde should be closed. No one could leave the buildings. The soldiers had orders to sleep in full kit; belts and steel helmets lay at the ready on the stools beside their beds, machine guns on the table. For a week now there had been practice scrambles every night. No one actually knew what was going on. Superior officers said nothing. Finally, on the evening of the 29th several units of the Leibstandarte entrained at Lichterfelde-Ost station and were taken to Munich. By the time they had boarded, rumours had seeped through that the SA's Chief of Staff, Ernst Röhm – one of Hitler's closest Allies – had been planning a Putsch.*

On the afternoon of the 30th the units of the Leibstandarte detrained in Munich Central station and marched to the Brown House.† Hitler stood on the balcony. The SS men paraded before him, goose-stepping by, four abreast. The so-called Röhm Putsch had already been put down. Röhm and his henchmen had been arrested – an operation led by Hitler in person. In the early hours of the morning of the 30th he had proceeded in a heavily armed motorised column towards Bad Wiessee (two hours' drive from Munich), where Röhm and his staff were to be found.

In Bad Wiessee Hitler caught Röhm, the Silesian SA-Obergruppen-führer Heines[10] and other SA leaders in bed with young homosexuals. He placed them all under arrest. Röhm was removed to the police prison in Munich. He was encouraged to take his own life, and a pistol was placed in his cell for that purpose. Röhm threw himself sobbing to the ground, and begged for his life. Only a miserable grovelling remained of the posturing and pomposity that the German people had hitherto seen in this leader of the National Socialist Party and the Third Reich.‡ Röhm was then shot.

---

*The SA (Sturmabteilung) stormtroopers, or Brown Shirts, were the Nazi Party's paramilitary arm. They had become too powerful, and were now effectively supplanted by the SS (Schutzstaffel), which had also grown out of the Party's need in the 1920s for protection squads.

†'Brown House' was the popular name for the Munich palace that was the seat of the Nazi leadership in Munich. (Russian note.)

‡Röhm did not grovel, but he refused to kill himself and was shot by two SS officers. His last words were 'My Führer! My Führer!'

The official version of the story was that Röhm had been executed for homosexuality, but Hitler concealed from the German people the fact that homosexuality was widely practised and tolerated in the higher echelons of the National Socialist Party and the Hitler Youth. Hitler revealed to his close circle the real reason why he had had his rival Röhm shot, when he said, 'No one plays around with me! That should serve as a warning to all my open and hidden enemies! I am not a chancellor of the old school. I am Hitler! In the Party and the state there is just one boss, and that's me!' In the days of the Röhm Putsch, the struggle for power between Hitler and Röhm, numerous innocent people were shot who were unacceptable to the Third Reich for one reason or another.[*]

SS men from the Leibstandarte who had remained behind in Lichterfelde and who had been involved in the shootings in Berlin were able to fill in the details for their comrades once they returned from Munich. Lorries loaded with prisoners had been driven to the barracks complex in Lichterfelde. Stripped to the waist the prisoners were put up against the chapel wall in the yard and shot.[11] The members of the firing squad reported, 'You could not imagine how sozzled we were. We were given endless amounts of schnapps to get us drunk.' At the same time the former Chancellor and Minister of War General von Schleicher was 'rendered harmless'. It was known in the army that Schleicher opposed Hitler and favoured a military dictatorship. On Himmler's orders two Gestapo men forced their way into the general's home. Schleicher's daughter, who opened the door to them, was shot on the spot. The Gestapo men stepped over her body and, as Schleicher reached for his pistol, shot both him and his wife.[†]

---

[*]On the Night of the Long Knives eighty-five high-ranking SA leaders and prominent opponents of the Nazi Party were shot. Several hundred, possibly as many as a thousand, people were killed between 30 June and 2 July 1934. The law issued on 3 July 1934 – 'Law Dealing with Measures for the Necessary Defence of the State' – made the killings retrospectively legal.

[†]The door was opened by the housekeeper, who survived the assassination of Schleicher and his wife. According to her testimony Schleicher did not reach for his gun, but simply replied affirmatively to the question posed by the Gestapo men whether he was General von Schleicher, whereupon they opened fire. The general was eliminated because he had attempted to split the Nazi Party and keep Hitler from power in 1932.

2

Summer 1934 – February 1936

Although Hitler had been able to remove his opponents and rivals in the Party, he was still not sole ruler in Germany. The aged President, Field Marshal Paul von Hindenburg, stood in his way. For the ambitious Hitler it was unbearable to have to stand in the shadow of a man like that. At last on 9 September 1934 Hindenburg died.[1] After his death Hitler appointed himself head of state and Commander in Chief of the armed forces. The position of president was incorporated into his own office. Now he had all the reins of power in his hands. In his first Reichstag speech following Hindenburg's death, he declared that he would not claim the salary due to him as President.* This declaration represented the same sort of demagogic wizardry as Goebbels's propaganda and was designed to convince the German people that Hitler was a selfless being who served only his countrymen.

With the assumption of power, Hitler became one of the richest men in Germany. He was earning millions and naturally had no need of the presidential salary. His book *Mein Kampf* was compulsory reading,† and made him an enormous profit.[2] He was also co-owner of Eher, the Party publishing house, which mopped up one publisher after another to become one of the largest presses in Germany.[3] Because of its monopoly status, it was able to pay out colossal dividends and Hitler received the lion's share.‡ He had unrestricted access to the funds of the National Socialist Party,§ which was basically a massive capitalist concern. Together with membership fees and large donations from German bankers and industrialists, income from

---

*In February 1933 Hitler had already declined to accept the chancellor's salary of 47,200 marks. When he stopped paying taxes to the Reich on 12 March 1935 he began to pay himself both the salary due to the Chancellor and the President's.
†*Mein Kampf* was compulsory only for Party members, but married couples often received it at their weddings.
‡The money did not all go into Hitler's pocket. It was largely used to finance the Party apparatus and political activities.
§In truth he disposed of both the Nazi Party's funds and the entire state treasury.

various businesses including estates in Mecklenburg and Bavaria flowed into the Party purse. In addition, a chain of Party hotels was founded, scattered throughout Germany and called Parteihotel-Konzern Färber. The director was the long-standing Nazi Färber[4], a friend of Martin Bormann's.

Hitler, however, was not satisfied even by this enormous income. Flying in the face of the rules established at the time of his takeover of power, he decreed that both state funds and representative funds should be excluded from control by the treasury in order to allow him to use money freely for his personal purposes.[5] At the same time he declared; 'I am not having it that some old cripple should tell me how I should spend my money!'

On the Obersalzberg near Berchtesgaden Hitler bought a huge plot of land and had a luxurious country house* built there that we know by the name Berghof. An orgy of demolition was required before the mansion could be built. In order to prepare the site, houses, hotels and even a sanatorium for handicapped children from all over Germany had to disappear.[6] Hitler's palace, with its landscaped parks and roads, cost around 100 million marks.† Its construction involved not only the squandering of the people's money, but also the sacrifice of human life. It was built on almost insurmountable cliff walls that rose to great heights. Explosives were used without sufficient care, causing avalanches and rock falls. Working conditions were similar to those imposed on prisoners, and there were a number of deaths.[7]

Schloss Berghof was built at an altitude of 1,000 metres on the slopes of the Obersalzberg in the resort of Berchtesgaden in the Bavarian Alps. It consisted of sixty rooms filled with expensive furniture, Gobelin tapestries and paintings by Dutch, Italian and German masters. Hitler bought the pictures from the dealers Frau Almers[8] in Munich and Haberstock[9] in Berlin, as well as from his photographer Hoffmann[10] and the director of the picture gallery in Dresden.[11]

On the ground floor was Hitler's dining room. The tables were made from light pine, and it was furnished with silver, expensive porcelain and crystal that cost millions. The service belonged to the state and before Hitler's accession it had been used for government receptions in Berlin. The table silver was not only stamped with the German eagle and the swastika but also engraved with the initials 'AH' (Adolf Hitler). The table was decorated with golden angels holding bowls for candles. On the same

---

*The word *Schloss* is used here, but its translation as 'castle' or even 'country house' hardly fits the bill in English.
†The equivalent of £5 million – the cost of building an airport in the 1930s.

floor were the great hall and the drawing room. The drawing room was dominated by an enormous stove, its brown tiles decorated with reliefs of girls carrying Nazi flags and of young drummers. In that room hung a valuable old Italian painting depicting the Colosseum in Rome.

On one side the drawing room opened on to a conservatory and terrace; on the other it led into the giant, 200-square-metre great hall, separated from the drawing room by an archway. A few steps led down to the drawing room, next to the lowest of which a head of Zeus excavated in Italy stood on a pedestal. The chief feature of this great hall was a 32-metre giant panoramic window that could be fully opened. Hitler directed all his guests' attentions towards this feature, which offered a splendid view of the Alps and of the Austrian city of Salzburg. He proudly declared that it was for this window that he had had the mansion built. In front of it was a long marble table, at which during the war years Hitler held his situation conferences in the periods spent on the Obersalzberg. The walls were covered with Gobelins and canvases, including Titian's *Venus*,[*] while the floor was laid with red velvet and strewn with rare Persian carpets. On the Bechstein grand was a bust of Richard Wagner. Hitler liked to spend his evenings here by the big fireplace in the company of his intimate circle, drinking tea and listening to gramophone records.

In the entrance hall of the mansion was a portrait of Bismarck that was lit up at dusk. From here a wide marble staircase led up to the first floor, to Hitler's private suite, which adjoined the rooms of his lover, Eva Braun. One of the rooms in Hitler's apartment was a picture gallery. Here stood a cupboard of immense value, inlaid with different rare woods, that had once belonged to Frederick II.[†] Hitler's study had a light-brown table and furniture made of polished maple; over the chimney hung a portrait of Moltke.[‡] Eva Braun's suite was especially luxurious.

The mansion owned three square kilometres of the neighbouring slopes that included the 1,800-metre Mount Kehlstein. The Kehlstein House, a tea-pavilion fashioned from grey granite, had been built at the top of the mountain, its size and construction reminiscent of a medieval castle. In the tea-pavilion there was a knights'-hall fifteen metres in diameter. Between its tall windows, sunk into deep niches, had been fitted golden candelabra that burned great wax candles. There were also a roomy dining room, a drawing

---

[*] Actually *Venus et amor* by Paris Bordone. It had been acquired by Haberstock using Party funds.

[†] They mean Frederick the Great, not the medieval emperor.

[‡] Helmuth von Moltke (1800–91), Prussian General Staff Chief and architect of German victories in the Wars of Unification.

room and rooms for Hitler's bodyguard and staff, as well as service rooms. A paved road leading to the Kehlstein finished in a tunnel under the cliff. From there you reached the tea-pavilion by lift. That road alone cost thirteen million marks.[12]

In the park there were meadows and a red-deer reserve. The mansion had a home farm with all the latest technology that provided Hitler and his court with food. Hitler was of the opinion that 'cows have a better time of it here than people' and he added: 'It would be really nice to be a cow here, don't you think?'

In the autumn of 1935 Hitler gave his first official reception as head of state for Germany's industrial and financial magnates. In the Reich Chancellery they awaited the arrival of the guests. Hitler's rooms were embellished with gold, bronze and Gobelins of legendary worth, as the ostentatiousness of this reception was meant to put all the Kaiser's heady banquets in the shade. A grey-haired woman in an expensive evening dress approached the brightly lit halls in their festive guise, ancient diamonds sparkling at her wrinkled throat. She was the wife of Hjalmar Schacht, President of the Reichsbank and Minister of Finance. Today, she was to play hostess, as Schacht was the man of the feast. It was he who had initiated Hitler's meeting with the financiers and industrialists in a bid to demonstrate the common bond between capital and the Hitlerian regime.

While he waited for his guests, Hitler – dressed in tails and accompanied by his butler Linge – wandered through the halls filled with sweet-smelling hothouse flowers. The former Corporal Hitler was excited: he was tormented by doubts about whether he could cut the right sort of figure in this elegant society. He walked among the tables that had been set for the guests and here and there adjusted a knife or a fork. Just before the party began he stopped before a mirror to try out facial expressions again that he wanted to use in greeting 'their lordships'.

The guests arrived in their cars. Servants in blue liveries with gold braid helped them out of their limousines. Girls in brown silk dresses with lace aprons and bonnets took their coats. At a signal from Meissner, the chief of the so-called Presidential Chancellery, the master of ceremonies, Jungfer, who was standing at the ready with sword at his side and a three-cornered hat under his arm, beat the floor three times with a staff and called out the names of the guests as they entered.

Hitler greeted them with a deep bow. Finally he delivered a speech, in the course of which he detailed the promise he had made before his takeover of power that capital could feel secure. 'Now it is clear', he explained, 'that the state is the most important patron of industry and cares for its development. For me rearmament is now the first priority. I will invest such power in Germany as the world has never seen. Guns! That is my foreign policy!'[13]

When Hitler finished, the industrialists, bankers, members of Cabinets and political bosses applauded. Dinner was served. At the tables the captains of industry were to be seen: Krupp, Röchling, Kirdorf, Vögler, Poensgen, Stinnes, Schröder and Pferdmenges.[14] Hitler sat next to the armaments-king Krupp von Bohlen und Halbach. Linge was standing behind Hitler's chair and heard Krupp whisper to him, 'I have heard from Schacht that there are problems with foreign currency at the moment, which might have an effect on the importation of Swedish steel . . .' Hitler replied with self-assurance; 'Privy Councillor, there is foreign currency for that, even if I have to dig it out of the earth myself. We shall also acquire earth from which we will extract iron and coal. You know which earth I mean. Just think of what sort of race inhabits the territory that stretches out eastwards from our front door. They are people of the second class. We must remove from these people the responsibility for looking after such a huge area and put it to proper use.' Krupp agreed with him and developed his own theory that Germany had an historical right to an empire in the east.

The banquet ended late. Hitler withdrew to his private apartment in the best of moods. In the pantry the servants and ADCs polished off the wine.

In the first days of November 1935 Hitler, Hess and Goebbels inspected models of warships that were exhibited in the so-called congress hall of the Chancellery that was situated next to Hitler's private apartment. The models had been sent to Hitler by Naval High Command in connection with the naval construction programme after the conclusion of the Anglo-German Naval Agreement,* signed in London by Ribbentrop on 18 June. The Agreement filled Hitler with enthusiasm. He declared it his first great foreign policy success. According to his interpretation the Naval Agreement meant first and foremost that, despite the Versailles Treaty, Britain officially recognised German rearmament and secondly that the questions of disarmament and collective security had lost their meaning.

---

*The Agreement of 18 June 1935 allowed the German fleet to reach 35 per cent of the total British Imperial and Commonwealth tonnage. The British saw the Agreement as a cue to further treaties limiting rearmament, but Hitler saw it as the first step in the revision of the arms limitations enshrined in the Versailles Treaty.

While he looked at the model warships, Hitler avowed, 'We will fool them and build such a fleet as we deem necessary. When Ribbentrop set out for London I told him, "Paragraphs don't mean anything to us. The politicians of the Weimar Republic were fools who took such things seriously. We know how to hide the tonnage we need." '[15] Then Hitler, Hess and Goebbels left the congress hall accompanied by Adjutant Brückner and Linge and went into the smoking room opposite, where Hitler's pilot Baur[16] and the photographer Hoffmann were sitting by the fire.

Hitler announced self-importantly, 'Ribbentrop has proved himself a first-class diplomat. I noticed that immediately about him.' 'But Hindenburg didn't like him,' riposted Goebbels. Hitler sat down and, putting on a deep voice, quoted the dead Hindenburg: 'My Chancellor, I have heard that there is a young man you want to appoint Foreign Minister. I, however, do not wish to see him in this post.' There were peals of laughter all round. In Hindenburg's lifetime, Hitler had given the impression to the people that the two of them enjoyed a father-and-son relationship. But now he turned to Goebbels and continued in a mocking tone, 'Do you remember the story of the swastika flag, doctor?' And once again in Hindenburg's deep voice: 'Flying over Goebbels's ministry there is a new flag. I don't like it.'

The mood was a happy one. Goebbels told one joke after another. This unprepossessing fellow – he was lame to boot – had once again cast his wife aside for a pretty starlet and preferred to spend his evenings away from home.* Goebbels told the latest story about Göring: that he worshipped fantastic uniforms and orders to such a degree that he had even pinned a medal on his pyjamas. Hitler loved it. As a joke he commissioned Hoffmann to make a splendid medal out of gold and silver paper and to hand it to Göring together with a florid citation. Hoffmann laughed himself sick. This deformed man, who enjoyed a monopoly in taking photographs of Hitler and who earned immense sums from state functions, was drunk every night. Hitler, the head of the National Socialist state, was unconcerned about all that. Before Hoffmann put in an appearance he used to ask, 'So, what sort of state is he in?' On this occasion he warned his court photographer – who was basking in a haze of schnapps – not to go too close to the fire, or he might explode.

Hoffmann began to recite a satirical poem about the mass arrests of innocent people in the Third Reich, and was half dead from mirth as

---

* Goebbels had recently fallen for the Czech soubrette Lida Baarova. His wife Magda had left the house and gone off to take a cure in Dresden. It was Hitler who brought them back together.

a result. It was about ten brothers who arrive one after the other in a concentration camp. The joke was that they had committed typical misdemeanours such as playing Mendelssohn sonatas or owning books by Heine. Breathing heavily, Hoffmann recited:

> 'The fourth one told jokes about Ley[*]
> Oh, my Lord, then there were but three . . .'

They all roared with laughter, Hitler slapping his thighs with admiration. In high spirits he declared, 'The British believe that I sit in the Chancellery like some vicious bulldog who is never happy with his lot. It is a good thing they can't see us now. Today we should call the restaurant in the Chancellery 'At the Sign of the Merry Chancellor'.

On 9 November 1923 Hitler had organised a Putsch in Munich. With a handful of National Socialists he wanted to seize power in Bavaria and from there spread out into the rest of Germany. The night before – 8 November – the plotters gathered in the Bürgerbräukeller. Hitler loved theatrical entrances. He appeared in the beer hall with a pistol in his hand, fired a bullet into the ceiling and declared that the 'revolution' had begun. The following day, the 9th, Munich's National Socialists tried to occupy the administrative buildings under Hitler's leadership. The plotters were scattered by government troops in front of the Feldherrnhalle, a monument on the Odeonsplatz. Fifteen National Socialists died in the mêlée[†].

After Hitler came to power the anniversary of the Putsch was celebrated every year. On 8 November 1935 he accordingly drove from Berlin to Munich for the celebrations. As always he stopped at his flat at 16 Prinzregentenplatz, where he had lived until he came to power. He was wearing mufti, with a suede hat pulled down over his eyes. When he drew up in front of his door he got out of the car. From a tin attached to the dashboard he took out a dog-whip that he always carried around with him in those days. A crowd had gathered outside the building. A bedraggled figure, clearly a working woman, emerged from the front row and tried to approach the Führer. Hitler's SS bodyguard had in the meantime sprung from the car and pulled her back. She still managed to shout. 'Führer, have pity! My innocent husband has already been in a concentration camp for over two years.' Hitler heard the woman's cries, quickened his step and

---

[*]Ley was leader of the National Socialist Workers' Front (Russian note). The poem was based on the popular jingle 'Ten little niggers'.
[†]And four police officers.

disappeared through the door. As he walked up the stairs he flourished his whip and screamed at his bodyguard, 'I don't want that to happen again! Or you too will end up in a concentration camp!'

In the flat Hitler was welcomed by his housekeeper, Frau Winter[17]. The place had a secret. One of its fifteen rooms had been locked since 1932. It smelled musty and contained a moth-eaten sofa covered with a thick coat of dust. Before 1932 Hitler's young niece Nicki, who had also been his mistress, had lived here, only for the relationship between uncle and niece to end with the girl's suicide. For years after Nicki's death – before he met Eva Braun – on the anniversary of her death Hitler opened the door to the room with a key he carried on him and spent several hours there. Why Nicki took her own life remained a mystery. In order to cover up the suicide, Hitler's staff put it around that she had detonated a bullet while cleaning her pistol.[*]

On the evening of 8 November Hitler, dressed in a National Socialist brown shirt and the Blood Order[†] on his chest, went to the Bürgerbräukeller, where the former plotters were assembled. The Blood Order was consecrated after Hitler came to power. It was awarded to those who had taken part in the uprising. At the door of the beer hall Hitler was welcomed by the 'Alte Kämpfer'[‡] Christian Weber[18] on behalf of all those present. This National Socialist – hated by everyone in Munich – was now a Bavarian State Councillor and owned horses, stables and race tracks, bus companies and garages. The gathering gave Hitler a noisy greeting. After the old German custom they raised their beer steins in memory of their dead comrades.

Hitler gave a speech. In the world of old Party members he was under no pressure to do so. He bellowed as he struck his fist on the table, his face distorted, his head bobbing wildly up and down, the lock of hair falling low across his forehead. His speech was reminiscent of those days when he was still a big-mouthed political gambler. His oration was greatly to the taste of the gathering. They were people from obscure backgrounds who, now that they had achieved wealth and power, led unbridled, dissipated lives. As Hitler remembered the conspirators who had died in the 1923 Putsch, he declared in a mystical tone that he had seized power through

---

[*]The story of Hitler's relations with his niece Angela 'Geli' Raubal, Linge and Günsche would have learned second hand. They do not appear to have known her pet name. It is interesting that both believed that Hitler's relationship with her was sexual.

[†]Founded March 1934 for all those who had taken part in the Putsch.

[‡] Alte Kämpfer was the name given to Nazis who had joined the Party before the takeover of power. (Russian note.)

blood sacrifices, which had been offered on the 'Altar of the People's Struggle'. He spoke of the rebirth of German militarism; of the purity of the German race; of the prosperous peasant, who was the carrier of German blood; of his determination to extinguish democratic ideas; and of the communists who were languishing in prisons and concentration camps.

With a hysterical cry of 'Heil!' Hitler ended his speech and quit the gathering of Alte Kämpfer with their Blood Orders. Sweat poured from his blood-red face. He was hoarse and scarcely able to utter another sound. With a shaking hand he straightened his Sam Browne belt. His brown shirt was stuck to his back. Linge helped him into his leather coat and escorted him to his car. As soon as Hitler sat down in the pre-heated car a blanket was wrapped around his legs, his coat buttoned up to his chin and the collar turned up. He was taken as quickly as possible back to his flat, where servants brought the completely debilitated man out of his trance using hot baths and tranquillisers.

The next day, the 9th, the National Socialist Party myth, which had been born in a Munich beer hall twelve years before, reached its apogee. With muffled drum-rolls and gun salutes the old soldiers of the Hitler Putsch marched beneath swastika flags through the streets of Munich. At the head of the procession was Julius Streicher,[19] the Gauleiter of Franconia who had numerous convictions for rape to his name.* The front row was made up of Hitler, Göring, Rosenberg and Himmler in brown shirts all decorated with their Blood Orders. Only one Old Fighter was absent: Röhm. His place among the insurgents was taken by the Minister of War, Blomberg. That year the coffins of the fifteen dead men who had taken part in the Putsch were carried on gun-carriages from the cemetery to the 'Hall of Honour' that been built under Hitler's directions on the Königsplatz.[20]

The city of Munich was hung with red-brown banners symbolising the martyrs' blood, emblazoned with three golden runes dedicated to the Old German god Wotan. The flames that issued from bowls filled with oil reposing on pylons were supposed to represent the sacrificial fire of German priests, from which – according to the testimony of the Nordic sagas – heroes rose to Valhalla, the Arcadia of the ancient Germans. The National Socialist Party recreated in this way the myths of a cult that had disappeared thousands of years before – and this in strictly Catholic Munich.

---

*Streicher's conviction was not for rape but for defamation.

3

March 1936 – October 1937

At the end of February 1936 Hitler had a series of meetings in the Reich Chancellery with Hess, Goebbels, Göring, the Minister of War Blomberg and the Foreign Minister Neurath – who was replaced by Ribbentrop in 1938. They discussed the remilitarisation of the Rhineland.[*] Blomberg pointed out that it would be a risky undertaking. At the time Germany did not have enough troops had the Western Powers chosen to attack. A document prepared by the German General Staff and presented by Blomberg expressed the following reservations: that the statute created for the Rhineland by the 1925 Treaty of Locarno described the French position as necessary for France's security. Moreover, since the time of Richelieu a neutralised left bank of the Rhine had been an important element in French policy, which aimed at hegemony in central Europe.[1] The remilitarisation of the Rhineland would therefore be a blow to two of the salient features of French policy: the striving for security, which had become even more urgent since the First World War, and military supremacy in central Europe.

The German General Staff estimated the relative strengths of Germany and the Western Powers, partners in the Locarno Treaty, as wholly disadvantageous to Germany. In their view, the French army alone possessed forces clearly superior to those available to Germany at this time. On the other hand, in the opinion of the Foreign Minister Neurath the diplomatic conditions for the remilitarisation of the Rhineland were favourable, and he told Hitler that it was 'now or never'. Hitler was beside himself with rage about the attitude of Blomberg and the General Staff and roared, 'What a preposterous situation! In a National Socialist state the army must be on the fighting side!'[2]

Hitler decided on the remilitarisation of the Rhineland on the basis of the following assumptions. First, France would not take any decisive action

---

[*] The Versailles Treaty had decreed that no fortifications could be built or troops stationed on the left bank of the Rhine or within a fifty-kilometre strip on the right bank.

if it was not certain that Britain would come to its aid. Secondly, Britain would not enter into any form of armed conflict with Germany because the Rhineland Question essentially concerned France alone. Thirdly, Britain would, however, support a peaceful resolution of the Rhineland Question because a conflict with Germany would unavoidably force France to remember the French–Soviet Assistance Treaty, concluded by the French Popular Front government in 1935. That would fully open European politics up to Soviet influence, something that would be repugnant to the British Cabinet. Goebbels cried out dramatically, 'My Führer, we are a young nation. The French have had their day and the British have grown old. The right of youth speaks for us, and it is the sole valid right; that of the mightier!'

The remilitarisation of the Rhine began in the early hours of Sunday 7 March 1936.[*] The General Staff presented Hitler with a compilation of the reactions to these developments by foreign military attachés. It was based on official talks with the departmental chief of the General Staff, the former military attaché Rabe von Pappenheim.[3] From the records of the discussions that took place on the 7th it emerged that the French military attaché General Renondeau – who, like his Ambassador, François-Poncet, was keen to reach a compromise with Nazi Germany – was extremely irritated by the German move. The conversation between Renondeau and Pappenheim came close to high drama. Replying to Pappenheim's question how he judged the resulting position, Renondeau insisted that in such highly tense situations the opinions of ambassadors and military attachés had no importance; in this case the government had to speak. To Pappenheim's next question as to how in his opinion the French government would react or what he would do if he were in the French leader's place, Renondeau rose and announced with truly Gallic pathos, 'I, my dear friend, would declare war on you!'

The British military attaché Colonel Hotblack[4] opened the discussion with a sarcastic remark. He told Pappenheim that he was grateful to the German government for making such a 'lovely Sunday' for him as a result of its actions.[†] Hotblack's reaction to events was notably calmer than that of his French counterpart. Especially striking was Hotblack's statement that everything should be done to avoid rash and unconsidered actions that could not be put right afterwards. From this remark it could be concluded the British Embassy saw the possibility of a mediating role.

[*] The 7th was actually a Saturday.
[†] The remilitarisation of the Rhineland began on a Sunday morning. (Russian Note.)

The American military attaché Major Truman[5] and his assistant Major Crockett had always displayed a profound understanding of the internal, external and, in particular, military affairs of Hitler's Germany. They expressed their total approval of the action in the Rhineland and congratulated Pappenheim. At the same time they expressed their fears of possible reprisals by other powers. In their opinion the states that had formed the Locarno Pact would, out of principle – to say nothing of the military aspects of the situation – refuse to come to terms with the fact that Germany had breached its obligations. As the British military attaché Hotblack told Truman, it was important that a mediator should intervene in order to introduce some form of détente. Pappenheim came to the firm conclusion that on the question of mediation Truman was echoing the opinion of Dodd, the American Ambassador in Berlin. From what Truman had said he inferred that the remilitarisation of the Rhineland troubled the American Ambassador hardly at all. Truman was only worried that 'the German act of force had damaged the general principal of the inviolability of treaties.'

The military attachés of the smaller states, which continued to see France as a victorious power with a first-class army, were of the opinion that Paris should and would contest the occupation of the Rhineland, and with force. The Belgian military attaché General Schmitt was infuriated. He declared most emphatically that the Western Powers would not accept Germany's contravention of the Locarno Treaty. In particular he raised the point that the remilitarisation of the Rhineland would damage Belgian national interests. Schmitt ended his meeting with Pappenheim with thinly veiled threats.

On the evening of the 7th the remilitarisation of the Rhineland had been completed by a risibly small force. From a military point of view it was total bluff. On the western border (Aachen, Trier, Saarbrücken), a force of just three battalions was deployed. It was assisted by police units which were stationed on the left bank of the Rhine and subsequently merged into the army.[6]

A few days before, Hitler had issued orders that soldiers who were themselves of Rhineland origin should be sent home on leave in mufti. In their suitcases they carried their arms and uniforms. They were given the job of parading through towns and villages on the 7th in order to convince the French that 'German troops had marched in.' At the same time Goebbels announced on the radio to the German people and to the world that 'German troops were crossing the Rhine bridges in an uninterrupted stream. The endless passing of aircraft squadrons had darkened the skies . . .' Hitler and Göring listened to Goebbels's speech on the Siemens receiver in the music room of the Chancellery. Hitler slapped Göring on the shoulder and said, 'Göring, we are really complete chancers.'

Britain took on the mediating role. The German General Staff informed Hitler that the British military attaché Hotblack required Germany to make 'a conciliatory gesture' so that the French could save face. The American military attaché Truman advised making such a gesture with unusual insistence. The General Staff concluded from the conversations with Truman that he had the full backing of his Ambassador, possibly even of the American General Staff, to support Britain's mediating role through military channels. But Hitler made no concessions whatsoever. Indeed, he sent the Western Powers packing with, as he put it, 'sedatives'. In a hypocritical speech before the Reichstag he offered France and Belgium a twenty-five-year non-aggression pact with Germany.

The Rhineland bluff was a complete success.

Hitler travelled to the Rhineland after its remilitarisation in order to show himself to the people as a simple citizen in a worn-out leather coat. Then he drove to Munich and his lover Eva Braun.

Eva Braun was a teacher's daughter who had worked in Hoffmann's photographic studio. After Hitler's niece Nicki committed suicide in such mysterious circumstances in 1932, Hoffmann brought the Führer and Eva together. Twenty years old at the time, she became Hitler's lover. He gave orders for a villa to be built for her in the Wasserburger Strasse, not far from his Munich residence.[7] He visited her there rarely, however, preferring to receive her at his own place in the Prinzregentenplatz in order to keep his relationship a secret from the people.

As soon as he reached Munich he summoned Eva to his side. While he waited for her he talked in Bavarian dialect to his housekeeper Frau Winter, who told him the latest Munich gossip. Hitler liked listening to this sly person. She had considerable influence on him and played an important role in the appointment of state offices in Bavaria, drawing his attention to friends of hers who coveted posts, titles or honours. Above all Anni Winter protected criminal elements in her own Party circle.

Eva arrived with a little suitcase. She was the sporty sort, with a slim figure and a fresh complexion, and she dressed tastefully. She ran quickly up the stairs and Linge opened the door to her. When Hitler heard his mistress's voice, he went to meet her with a smile on his face. He made a joke about her new little hat and took her into the study, where he had hot chocolate and tea, cognac, pralines, fruit and cold champagne ready. For hours the two of them walked around the room hand in hand. Then Hitler read the evening papers, while Eva made herself comfortable at the fireside table, pecking at this and that. That was how they usually spent their time together. Only after midnight did Hitler withdraw to his bedroom, where Linge had, as usual, prepared him tea, fruit and stimulants prescribed for him by his new personal physician, Dr Morell. Eva took herself off to a room prepared for her, or Linge escorted her home.

Dr Morell was a quack in a white coat, who made hormone mixtures for the rakes of the Kurfürstendamm.* Hoffmann recommended him to Hitler after he had treated Hoffmann for a venereal disease. Very soon the Führer invested him with a professorial title and the Gold Party Badge for 'special services to research in sexual hormones'.[8] Morell gave him injections of stimulants and Hitler called Morell his saviour, especially during the war when he couldn't go a single day without a jab.

Hitler's relationship with Eva Braun was clearly abnormal. In the Berghof she wandered around with dewy eyes and a tortured expression. In the evenings she retired early to bed, while Hitler liked to conduct endless conversations with his closest collaborators until the early hours. The chambermaid frequently found Eva dissolved in tears. When Hitler was not there, she came back to life with a vengeance, seeming relaxed and gay, and she would even dance. Hitler's circle saw her as a 'bird in a gilded cage' who had as Hitler's bedfellow condemned herself to a life of self-denial.

In May 1937 Hitler drove to an agricultural exhibition in Munich.[9] During the tour his naval liaison officer, Captain Albrecht,[10] stepped up to him and gave him a report. Hitler broke off his tour and drove back to his flat on the Prinzregentenplatz. There he disappeared into his study with Albrecht to await the arrival of the Supreme Commander of the navy, Admiral Raeder.[11] Hitler was furious. The Spanish Republican air force had attacked the cruiser *Deutschland*, which had been operating in Spanish waters on Franco's side,[12] and he wanted revenge. After half an hour's conversation with Raeder, Hitler ordered his bodyguard to return to Berlin.

It was a warm May evening when Hitler's limousine brought him from Berlin-Tempelhof airport to the Reich Chancellery. The Führer did not enter the building though the main door as usual, but slipped in unnoticed though the park on the Göringstrasse. His return to Berlin was to remain a secret. Blomberg, Göring and Raeder, who had also flown back to

*A smart street in west Berlin. (Russian note.)

Berlin, arrived in the conservatory for the meeting. Neurath entered a little later. Hitler angrily laid into the commander of the *Deutschland*,[13] calling him spineless, because despite first-class anti-aircraft guns he had been unable to bring down a single enemy plane. Even as he spoke, coded signals were being transmitted to German warships in the Mediterranean. These rapidly brought death to the inhabitants of the Spanish port of Almería.[14] Hitler asked Linge to spread out on the conservatory table a large map of the Iberian Peninsula that he kept in his study and used to chart the progress of the Spanish Civil War.

Hitler fancied himself as a field commander. He explained to Blomberg, Göring and Raeder what steps needed to be taken in his opinion to end the blockade of Madrid. He directed slanderous abuse at Franco: 'From a military point of view Franco is wholly useless. He is a typical sergeant and nothing more. Why on earth did I send him Faupel?[15] Where are his eyes? He has certainly not managed to gain the upper hand with Franco.' Hitler had sent Faupel to Burgos in the autumn of 1936, in theory as his Ambassador, but in reality as a military adviser attached to Franco's staff. The elderly general had worked as a military instructor in Peru after the First World War and gained experience of civil war there.

Hitler's meddling in the Spanish Civil War began in July 1936 while he was attending the Bayreuth Wagner Festival. The old German themes that Wagner set to music fitted in with Hitler's peculiar ideas on the purity of the German race. As a result he took care to make friends with Wagner's descendants. Wagner's daughter-in-law Winifred[16] called him Wolf, which pleased him as he liked being compared to a bloodthirsty animal. On one of the last days of the festival Hitler received the German Ambassador to Spain, Count Welczeck.[17] Welczeck came to see him in secret, in the company of members of the Spanish Falange. From that point on, aircraft from German Lufthansa* began to bomb cities in the Spanish Republic as well as transporting Franco's Moroccan units to Spain. At that precise moment the devoted fan Hitler was listening to Wagner's opera *Die Walküre* in the company of the select audience of Europeans and Americans attending the festival.

Franco didn't win his battle against the Spanish Republic with foreign troops from Morocco. Although he was able to invest the suburbs of Madrid his forces were incapable of taking the city. After a meeting with Hitler in the Reich Chancellery in July 1937, it was decided to strengthen

---

*The Luftwaffe was formed in 1935. Until then it had operated under the disguise of a civil aviation company, and continued to do so in Spain.

the military assistance granted to Spain. Powerful Luftwaffe and Panzer squadrons were put at Franco's disposal. The Luftwaffe operated in the skies over the Spanish Republic as the 'Condor Legion' under the command of the air force general Sperrle,[18] who was promoted to the rank of field marshal in the Second World War.

In addition to the support from the Luftwaffe and motorised squadrons, Germany made regular deliveries of weapons, munitions and other military supplies to Franco. To conceal them the arms were taken to a distant quay in Hamburg docks, the entry to which was guarded by the police, and loaded on to merchant ships. They sailed with an escort of German warships, which nonetheless kept a certain distance until they reached the Spanish coast. To organise the technical and military assistance accorded to Franco, and to co-ordinate the various units operating in Spain, the German High Command created a Special Staff W under the command of General Jaenecke.[19] He reported directly to Hitler on the course of the Civil War and about the experience gained by German troops in the fight against the Spanish Republic. Hitler insisted that the fronts should be expanded to their maximum extent, declaring that he would give Franco everything he needed in order to bring all of Spain under his control as quickly as he could.

The summer of 1937 passed and Germany worked feverishly at rearmament. For the autumn of that year it was decreed there would be manoeuvres for every part of the newly equipped German army. In the course of these all the modern weapons and formations forbidden by the Versailles Treaty were tried out on a large scale for the first time: heavy artillery, tanks, anti-tank guns, motorised units, planes and anti-aircraft guns.[20] 'The front to the east!' was the motto for the autumn manoeuvres in Mecklenburg and Pomerania.* The exercise was to simulate war with two opponents in the Baltic, a contingency which played a major role in the plans made by the German High Command for war in the east. It was clear that the Soviet Union was seen as a future enemy. The manoeuvres were in contravention of the Treaty of Versailles and were intended to demonstrate Germany's military strength. The presence of Mussolini at these war games was meant to stress the military significance of the Berlin–Rome Axis that had been created a year before.

From a political and military point of view the aggressive character of the manoeuvres was so clear that it could not be misunderstood, even in

---

*The manoeuvres took place from 19 to 30 September 1937. For the first time all three branches of the Wehrmacht took part. There was no motto.

Britain. Despite that, shortly before they got under way Major Haig, the assistant British military attaché in Berlin, transmitted the British General Staff's desire to be invited to attend them. Permission was granted and the British General Staff received an invitation from the German army. This resulted in a piquant situation: in September 1937 Hitler, Mussolini and the representative of the British General Staff, Field Marshal Montgomery-Massingberd,[†] stood side by side at the manoeuvres. Hitler and Mussolini appeared radiant as they adopted victorious poses.[21] Montgomery-Massingberd also seemed happy – probably because everything was pointing east and British interests remained undisturbed.

In Hitler's circle the satisfaction was plain for all to see: the participation of a member of the British General Staff as Hitler's guest at the manoeuvres was clear proof that Britain not only accepted the rebuilding and strengthening of the German Army, it also bestowed its blessing. Britain did the world no service.

[†]Actually Field Marshal Cyril John Deverell, the then Chief of the Imperial General Staff.

4

November 1937 – February 1939

Hitler spent November 1937 in his Berghof mansion. Eva Braun had invited her lady-friends to stay. They were frivolous women, occasionally offensive in their behaviour, having the manners of their bohemian Munich world. At table they talked openly of the most intimate things. When an SS batman brought refreshments to their rooms they walked around half-naked without a thought. And when a film was shown in the evening they talked loudly about the actors' physiques. 'What a splendid manly specimen,' they said. They quite openly worked their way through the unusually tall soldiers in Hitler's bodyguard. They were particularly delighted when the photographer Hoffmann made one of his cynical jokes or the personal physician Morell talked about his Kurfürstendamm practice.

Hitler scarcely noticed the tittle-tattle of ladies in those days. He thought it was normal, as he adhered to the principle that a woman should be stupid. He was concerned with one question alone: Austria. As there were still clashes between National Socialists orchestrated in Berlin and supporters of Schuschnigg's government, many Austrian Nazis had taken refuge in Bavaria. The so-called Austrian Legion was recruited from these men, and they were drilled and trained in street-fighting by Austrian officers and NCOs from the Leibstandarte 'Adolf Hitler'. The HQ of the Austrian SA had been set up in Munich. Austria was infiltrated by fighters trained in sabotage by the Austrian Legion. It was Hitler's wish that that the Legion should be honoured with a parade before the Berghof. There he told them not to give up the fight for a Nazi Austria. When all was said and done it was his home, which one day would be attached to the German Reich.

On 14 November the German government was expecting a visit from Lord Halifax, Lord Privy Seal in Chamberlain's Cabinet and the man entrusted with the negotiations between Britain and Hitler over the union of Germany and Austria.[*] The tall, gaunt Halifax arrived at the Berghof

---

[*] The visit took place on the 19 November 1937. Viscount Halifax was Lord President of the Council.

around 3.00 p.m. The master of the house waited for him personally at the door, shook his hand warmly and accompanied him to the cloakroom. When Halifax had removed his coat and taken off two woollen pullovers he looked even thinner. He followed Hitler into his study where a discussion took place in the presence of Neurath and the interpreter Schmidt.[1] About an hour and a half later Hitler and Halifax re-emerged. Their faces showed total agreement. When Halifax left, Hitler remained behind in the best of moods. He rubbed his hands and slapped his thighs as if he had already concluded a good deal.

During their evening discussion, Eva Braun's friends poked fun at Halifax's garb and his long, wizened physique. Hitler defended him, praising him as a clever politician who fully supported Germany's claims. He stressed that Halifax had assured him that Britain would not stand in Germany's way in respect of its Austrian policy. Moreover, Halifax had declared that Britain wanted to sign a parallel treaty to the Rome–Berlin Axis. This was not in any way to affect German–Italian relations. Hitler exclaimed joyfully: 'I have always said that the British want to put me on a lead, because they make their policy from the same principles as I do: the first priority is the elimination of Bolshevism.'[2] After his meeting with Halifax Hitler summoned the Austrian Legionaries, who paraded again before the Berghof: 'The hour approaches when your wishes will be fulfilled.'

Nineteen-thirty-seven had hardly drawn to a close when the disturbances orchestrated by the Nazi Party in Vienna had reached the level Hitler required, but the good mood that had been engendered by the highly promising meeting with Halifax had vanished. The government in Vienna was manfully resisting the Anschluss, or union of the two countries. Schuschnigg and the leaders of Austria's big business concerns opposed the union because it robbed these last of their economic independence and ran counter to their own aggressive plans. They were attached to the idea that Austria was the second German state, and one with a special mission to fulfil in south-east Europe. The circle around Schuschnigg based their belief that an independent Austria could survive on the fact that in the 1914–18 War it had led Slavic peoples in the struggle for the German nation.

Furious about the behaviour of Schuschnigg's government, Hitler summoned the Austrian Chancellor to the Obersalzberg. On 11 February 1938 Schuschnigg arrived.* Hitler received him in his study with none of the

---

*Actually on the 12th.

customary protocol. His expression was dark, his brow furrowed. He wanted to make it clear to Schuschnigg what sort of storm he could expect from now on. The conversation was conducted without witnesses. It was not long before his thundering voice could be heard all over the first floor of the house: 'Merciful God! What are you actually thinking of? I, an Austrian by birth, have been sent by providence to create the Greater German State! And you stand in my way! I will crush you!'

Hitler rang for Linge, who was in attendance by the study door. As he walked in he observed the crumpled Schuschnigg and the Führer snorting with rage. With flashing eyes Hitler issued Linge with the command: 'Get me Keitel!'[3] As a result of Schuschnigg's visit Keitel had been present in the house since the early hours of the morning. Fully armed and wearing boots and spurs he looked like the god of war, Mars in person. Keitel was Hitler's most loyal general. He had replaced Blomberg, who had fallen from grace as a result of his lack of decisiveness over the remilitarisation of the Rhineland and whom Hitler often mentioned later: 'He is too soft for me. I cannot use him for my broader plans.'* When Hitler summoned him, Keitel was sitting in the conservatory. Buckling on his sword, he glanced at himself in the big mirror − as Hitler used to do − to see if he looked sufficiently warlike, then, with much clattering of weapons, hurried up the stairs to Hitler's study.

A while later Keitel accompanied Schuschnigg downstairs. The SS men posted all over the mansion thought that the Austrian Chancellor looked wretched. He departed with a bewildered air and made a distracted gesture which, in the opinion of the SS men, was meant to be a 'Hitler greeting'. At dinner Hitler recounted how he had 'laid into' the unhappy Chancellor: 'When Keitel entered I asked him, "How many divisions are mustered at the border, Keitel?" And then, "And what does our intelligence say of the opposing army, Keitel?" And Keitel answered with scorn, "Not worth mentioning, my Führer." There was only one scene in the drama − the appearance of the god of war, Wilhelm Keitel.' Hitler roared with laughter.

Soon after he had received Schuschnigg, the Führer travelled back to Berlin. Rumours were rife in the Reich Chancellery originating from Papen[4], the German Ambassador in Vienna: Schuschnigg was apparently not playing the game and had asked Britain for help. Now the Chancellery was plunged into hectic activity. Hitler received the British Ambassador, Henderson.[5] Apart from that he had a number of meetings with Göring,

---

*The pretext for Blomberg's dismissal was his marriage to a woman with a criminal record as a prostitute.

Keitel and the Commander in Chief of the army, Brauchitsch[6]. Feverish calls were made to Vienna. On the afternoon of 11 March Göring arrived to see Hitler. In the evening there was a call from Vienna. Hitler gave instruction that it should be put through to the music room, where it would be more secure. The leader of the Austrian Nazis, Seyss-Inquart,[7] was on the line. Before Hitler could have a word with him the connection was interrupted. Telephone conversations always distressed him, but now he was doubly nervous. He was almost at war with the telephone. There were often crossed lines which led to absurd situations. When someone asked him who he was, and he told them the truth, the voice at the other end replied, 'You* must be really crazy!' In Bayreuth someone called him to ask the time. Then on another occasion as he was speaking to Eva Braun, someone broke in to say: 'Private conversations are not allowed here.'

On 11 March the telephone operators in the Chancellery were clearly unaware of the importance of Seyss-Inquart's call. For some unknown reason there was insufficient power to bring the call to the private apartments of the Führer. Hitler and Göring were finally obliged to go directly to the switchboard, where Hitler took the receiver. After a long pause another voice came on the line, but it was only the telephone technician. Hitler completely lost his nerve and passed the 'difficult' task over to Göring. Göring, who was so corpulent that he needed practically the whole switchboard room to himself, finally managed to connect to Seyss-Inquart. He shouted into the receiver, 'Hello, Seyss, what is going on down there?' He listened for half a minute and then asked Hitler a question under his breath. Hitler was standing with one knee on the sofa, and excitedly twisting the curtain cord. In the end he pulled it so hard that the entire curtain came away and fell onto the sofa. Then he screamed, 'Yes, he should act!' Göring ended the discussion, saying, 'Yes, fine, we are in agreement. See you soon!' Hitler was incandescent with rage, however, because Schuschnigg had called a plebiscite to decide the question of union with Germany.

At 9.00 a.m. the following day, the 12th, Hitler left Berlin in an aircraft escorted by fighters and landed at Oberwiesenfeld airport near Munich. From there he drove by car to the staff of Army Group von Bock[8] at Mühldorf on the Austrian border. On that same day German troops marched into Austria. Hitler himself reached the forward units of his Leibstandarte in Linz that evening. From the balcony of the town hall he announced the Anschluss of Austria with the German Reich. Next

---

*The German uses the familiar *Du*, which made the remark all the more surprising. Virtually no one called Hitler *Du* (apart from Röhm).

to him stood the new Austrian Chancellor, his favourite, Seyss-Inquart. Schuschnigg had ceded the position to him in a hurry.

Hitler entered Vienna on 14 March. The Leibstandarte had already taken over responsibility for security in the city. Hitler stopped at the Hotel Imperial where Cardinal Innitzer[9] of the Catholic Church came to welcome 'his Führer'. In Vienna Hitler proclaimed the Greater German Reich. A day later the troops in the Viennese garrison were already sporting German eagles on their uniforms.

As a result of the Anschluss, Germany now had common borders with its Allies Italy and Hungary. Czechoslovakia, on the other hand, was now almost encircled, from the north, south and west. The incorporation of this peaceful state was now on the agenda. The German press spoke quite openly of its annexation as part of Hitler's aggressive plan for the east. The National Socialist leaders began whipping up the Sudeten Germans, who lived in the border areas of Czechoslovakia, urging them to carry out acts of provocation against the Czechs.[*]

This campaign of vilification reached its apogee at the Nazi Party Rally in Nuremberg in the first half of September 1938. The rally took place under the motto 'Greater Germany' and focused on the question of German expansion towards the east. Hitler played the role of protector of the Sudeten Germans, whom he made out had been enslaved by the Czechs. In his speech of 12 September Hitler declared, 'I will no longer stand for it, that the Czechs should treat three and a half million Germans like children!'[†] His hysterical speech was full of slander and denigration of the Czechs.

At the same time military preparations were under way. German troops under the command of General von Leeb[10] had gathered at the Czech border. The Austrian army – now incorporated into the German Wehrmacht[‡] – had been quickly introduced to Prussian drill. Hitler was unconcerned by France's treaty obligations to the Czechs. In his opinion, 'The French will not cross the Maginot Line.'[§]

---

[*]The Czechoslovak state created after the First World War contained around 3.5 million Germans. After 1933 the tension between the German minority and the state grew worse. Hitler used this as a pretext to demand cession of the Sudentenland to the German Reich.
[†]Hitler's actual words were, 'But I make the demand that the repression of the 3.5 million German in Czechoslovakia ceases and that from this moment they enter into their rights.'
[‡]The German armed forces had been collectively known as the Wehrmacht since March 1935; before that they were called the Reichswehr.
[§]A 150-km-long defensive wall along France's border with Germany containing thirty-nine forts, seventy bunkers, 500 artillery and infantry posts and 500 bastions. It was constructed between 1929 and 1932 and named after the Minister of War, André Maginot.

Hitler's speech at the Nuremberg Rally and news of German troops massing on the Czech border did not fail to have an effect in London. On 15 September the rally had only just come to an end when the British Prime Minister, Neville Chamberlain, landed at Salzburg airport, close to Hitler's mansion, the Berghof. The Foreign Minister, Ribbentrop, and the Chief of Protocol, Baron von Dörnberg,[11] were ready on the tarmac to welcome Chamberlain and his staff.* On the steps of the mansion Hitler stood waiting for Chamberlain in person, dressed in a Nazi uniform. Next to him were his adjutants Brückner and Schmundt,[12] as well as Counsellor Hewel,[13] Ribbentrop's permanent envoy to Hitler. The Führer greeted Chamberlain with an outstretched arm, and his visitor waved his hat in a friendly way. They shook hands, introduced one another to their colleagues and mounted the broad steps. At the entrance to the Berghof there was an SS troop with drums. The two leaders inspected the guard of honour, and Chamberlain waved his hat again, an umbrella hanging from his left arm. Hitler led the Prime Minister to the cloakroom and then to his study on the first floor, with Ribbentrop and the interpreter Schmidt in their wake. Chamberlain's team were conducted to the conservatory, where they were given coffee.

After a three-hour conversation with Hitler, Chamberlain took his leave, and was once again treated to drum-rolls from the guard of honour. Hitler accompanied him to his car, where they exchanged a warm handshake. Chamberlain returned to Salzburg in the company of Ribbentrop and spent the night there in the Hotel Österreichischer Hof. The next day he flew back to London. After Chamberlain had driven off Hitler paced up and down with Counsellor Hewel. Little by little the doors to the rooms opened where Eva Braun and her lady-friends had been waiting for the departure of the British delegation. Gradually the official atmosphere of the mansion evaporated.

Counsellor Hewel reported that the British government had been startled by the militant tone of the National Socialist Party Rally; for that reason Chamberlain had wanted to come to see Hitler in person to take stock of his demands. These currently amounted to a German claim to the Sudetenland. Chamberlain had led him to understand that London's attitude to this was benevolent. He was ready to travel one more time to

---

*Chamberlain landed in Munich and took a train to Berchtesgaden. He was accompanied by Nevile Henderson, the British Ambassador to Berlin, his economic adviser and the head of the central European Department of the Foreign Office. Their Salzburg hotel, the Österreichischer Hof, has been renamed the Sacher.

discuss how the transfer of the Czechoslovakian Sudetenland to Germany might be effected.

Linge looked at his watch: it was time for dinner. He told Hitler that everything was ready. In the dining room Hitler greeted the ladies who had come from their villas: the wives of Inspector-General Speer and Reichsleiter Martin Bormann. Hitler led Frau Speer to the table, whose husband would later be known as the man in charge of a massive slave-army of prisoners of war and peace-loving citizens. They were followed by Bormann with Eva Braun. The others came after and very soon the dining room was filled with a cacophony of table-talk. The women, who had observed Chamberlain through the window, made fun of the old-fashioned Englishman who was so attached to his umbrella. Hitler declared boastfully, 'The old man took an aeroplane for the first time in his life in order to come and see me.' He added sarcastically, 'He will have to be prepared to pay if he becomes a target for your mockery once more.'

In fact Chamberlain flew back to Germany just one week later, on 20 October*, this time with a whole brigade of colleagues. Bad Godesberg near Bonn in the Middle Rhine district was chosen as the place for the negotiations, a hundred minutes by air from London. The conversations took place in the Hotel Dreesen. The owners, Dreesen and his wife, were old Party friends of Hitler whom he used to stay with even before 1933. After Hitler's accession Dreesen became President of the National Socialist Hoteliers' League.[†] In the Briton's honour the Hotel Dreesen was fitted with new furniture and carpets. Hitler and his staff made that establishment their HQ, while Chamberlain was housed on the other side of the Rhine in the Hotel Petersberg.

On the evening of 22 September the British guests were transferred by motor-ferry to Bad Godesberg. Ribbentrop and Baron von Dörnberg accompanied Chamberlain to the hotel near by where Hitler was expect-ing him. To make a point and against all the rules of diplomacy, Ribbentrop was wearing a simple business suit, over a brown shirt.[‡] They passed through two rows of SS men to reach the hotel lobby and went upstairs to the first floor. The largest room in Hitler's suite served as the meeting

---

*Actually on 22 September 1938.

[†] Fritz Dreesen (1884–?) had allowed Hitler a free stay in the hotel after he came out of prison in 1925. He was rewarded with Nazi patronage, but was never head of the official hotel and innkeepers' association. He joined the Nazi Party in 1933. The hotel in Bad Godesberg still exists.

[‡] It was conventional for diplomats to wear morning dress.

room. Hitler was already there. An hour later Chamberlain appeared in the lobby once again. There were SS guards everywhere. He did not appear as happy as he had been before the talk. He then climbed into a car which took him to the ferry.

Hewel spoke to Brückner and Linge: 'The Führer and Ribbentrop know how to treat the British. They make their demands higher every time, and that way Chamberlain must dig ever deeper into his pockets. But the City of London is not interested in morality, they think only of business. The distinguished gentleman is well aware that they can have your head off before you can say knife.' In the evening Dörnberg, who was staying in the same hotel as the British, announced that the British Ambassador in Berlin, Henderson, had turned up. A little while later Henderson asked to speak to Hitler at the Hotel Dreesen on Chamberlain's behalf. He was taken to Hitler's study. Ribbentrop was standing in the doorway and said crudely, without beating about the bush, 'Now, Mr Henderson, what does Mr Chamberlain say?' Henderson pushed his way past him through the doorway. Hitler often proclaimed after discussions with Henderson that the Ambassador acted for the good of Germany and keenly and zealously transmitted German desires to London.

Once Henderson had left, Hewel was summoned to see Hitler and Ribbentrop and they formulated at great speed the Führer's demands in respect of Czechoslovakia that had to be handed to British the same day. A secretary took dictation from Ribbentrop – you could hear a typewriter clattering in his room. The typed pages were brought for Hitler to check then carried back to Ribbentrop. From time to time Ribbentrop himself could be seen hurrying to Hitler with the papers in his hand. Gaus,[14] the head of the legal department of the German Foreign Office, was also involved in formulating the demands. Finally the drafting seemed finished, but Hitler was still not happy. He called for Linge and ordered Hewel to bring him the last part of the text once again. So it went on late into the night. In the Hotel Petersberg, where Chamberlain was staying on the other side of the Rhine, they were also burning the midnight oil, and the ferry plied the Rhine back and forth.

Twenty hours later, on the evening of the 23rd, Chamberlain appeared once again in Hitler's hotel, and they spoke to one another at length in the presence of Ribbentrop and Schmidt. During the discussion, maps of Czechoslovakia were required, which Hewel brought in. When he re-emerged from Hitler's study he was of the happy opinion that things were going swimmingly. 'The Führer doesn't treat Chamberlain very graciously any more and is applying a hefty pressure. In Britain's name

Chamberlain had made unambiguous promises about the handover to the Sudetenland to Germany. He will have to give in to our other demands.'

Not long afterwards, the discussions were ended, and Hitler and Chamberlain came downstairs. Beside a palm tree in the lobby the Führer's photographer Hoffmann blocked their path. With a flash he took a significant picture: Hitler with the British Prime Minister under the palm of peace.

Chamberlain flew back to London, Hitler to Berlin, where he waited for the Czechoslovak answer to his demands that had been handed over by the British. Prague, however, wouldn't bend.[*] Hitler was livid. He said, 'We are not going to negotiate any more. We'll strike!' He gave his bodyguard the order to don grey Wehrmacht uniforms to replace the black SS ones in order to demonstrate his bellicose mood. At the time the Italian Ambassador to Berlin, Attolico, wearing the fascist uniform of the Italian Blackshirts, was a frequent visitor to Hitler. On 27 September 1938 he appeared four times. As he left the Reich Chancellery for the third time that day, Hitler told Linge – who was bringing him the papers – in a tone that mixed anger and contentment, 'He's shitting himself! If we took his advice we'd never see the end of this business.'

Later that evening the story ran round the Chancellery that Mussolini had persuaded Hitler to call a four-power conference between Germany, Britain, France and Italy to decide the Sudeten question.[†] In the early hours of 28 September Hitler prepared to travel to Munich, where the conference was to take place.[‡] In the evening Hitler's train left Anhalt station in Berlin and arrived the next morning in Kufstein in the Tyrol. Here he was going to meet the Duce on his way to Munich. There was not a soul on the platform – the station was closed. The train carrying the Duce drew to a halt alongside the opposite platform. Mussolini stepped down from the carriage and Hitler hurried to meet him. The Führer held both his ally's hands and looked at him meaningfully with wide-open eyes. Then they got into Hitler's saloon car and continued their journey to Munich together. In Munich Hitler and Mussolini drove together to the Prinz Carl

---

[*] The Czechs were supported by Britain and France. Chamberlain threatened Germany with 'offensive measures' and placed the fleet at the ready. France called up its reservists.
[†] He was acting on Chamberlain's wishes.
[‡] Attolico visited the Chancellery many times on the 28th rather than the 27th, as stated here. His purpose was to deliver Mussolini's suggestion to call a conference. At 3.00 p.m. he called to say that Hitler had agreed. The news of the Munich Conference was issued at 7.40 p.m. on 28 September 1938. Hitler left in the late afternoon of the 28th.

Palais where the Duce was staying together with his son-in-law and Italy's Foreign Minister, Count Ciano.

Munich's streets gave no inkling that a four-power conference was about to take place. On Hitler's orders all public demonstrations of enthusiasm were banned over the next few days. In this way he wanted to make the foreign statesmen understand that National Socialist Germany was not impressed by international conferences. He had just one word he used for both parliamentary sittings and conferences: 'talking shops'.

Chamberlain landed at Oberwiesenfeld airport near Munich, and was met by Ribbentrop and the Bavarian State Councillor Christian Weber in the uniform of an SS-Brigadeführer. This Munich entrepreneur and fanatical anti-Bolshevik was considered a suitable person to welcome His Britannic Majesty's Prime Minister. The Hotel Regina was reserved for Chamberlain and his staff. Göring met the French premier Edouard Daladier at the airport, and Daladier took up residence at the Hotel Vier Jahreszeiten. The conference was convened on 29 September in the Brown House, the headquarters of the National Socialist Party.*

Before the conference began, Hitler fetched Mussolini and drove with him to the Führer Building, where they waited in Hitler's study for the arrival of Chamberlain and Daladier. At about 1.00 p.m. drum-rolls from the parading SS guard of honour announced the arrival of Chamberlain, accompanied by Ribbentrop. Chamberlain handed over his coat and climbed a flower-bedecked staircase to Hitler's study. Along the corridors stood SS men with expressionless, rigid faces, who had been given orders to create the impression that they were ready to march. Chamberlain responded to their shouts of 'Heil Hitler!' with an amicable nod. Hitler tried to adopt a military bearing like his SS men. Each time he appeared he sought to impress upon Chamberlain that he had been enraged by the Czechs. Seated with Mussolini in the middle of the room, he waited for Chamberlain to approach him without rising from his seat before coldly and impassively offering him his hand in the flashlight of the photographer Hoffmann. Mussolini too showed reserve when greeting Chamberlain. Now the door opened and Daladier stepped in. Hitler received him in the same way as he had greeted Chamberlain.

Without further ado, Hitler asked the heads of government of Britain, France and Italy to take their places around the table near the fireplace. Hitler sat as always with his back to the window, so that his face appeared

---

*The conference took place in the so-called Führer Bau – or Führer Building – which had been completed for the Nazi Party in 1937.

in shadow. In the armchair to his left was Chamberlain, looking worried and confused. Daladier and Mussolini took their places on the sofa also to the left of Hitler's seat; both looked dignified and decisive. Thus began the infamous Munich Conference.

After the midday break the interpreter Schmidt emerged from Hitler's study and asked for General Keitel and Colonel Schmundt to be summoned and to bring a General Staff map with them. The delegates then stood at a long table where the map had been spread out. The conference now took on the character of a border commission. By the evening Hitler had reached the goal he had set for himself for that day. The international treaties that had guaranteed the territorial integrity of Czechoslovakia were now mere scraps of paper. To Hitler's rhetorical demand, 'And what if the Czechs won't co-operate?', Daladier replied sharply, 'If they won't co-operate, Excellency? They must co-operate!' – notwithstanding the fact that France and Czechoslovakia were Allies.

Hitler looked unusually fresh. He was in an excellent mood. He ordered Linge to bring him the guest book from the Brown House and, all four heads of government appended their signatures in 'friendly' commemoration under the date 29 September, a fateful day for peace-loving peoples.[*] Thus the Munich Conference drew to a close. Hitler and Mussolini drove to the station where Hitler bade the Italian leader goodbye. As his train had already arrived, Mussolini leaned out of an open window and once again shook both Hitler's hands. Hitler drove from the station to his flat on the Prinzregentenplatz.

Chamberlain and Daladier informed the Czech representatives staying in Munich of the results of the conference: the Sudetenland together with the areas bordering on Austria were to be ceded to Germany. The Czechs, who had not been allowed to take part in the conference that decided their country's fate, had been awaiting the outcome in the Hotel Regina, where the British delegation under Chamberlain's leadership was also lodged. When it was decided to put the Czechs in with the British, Ribbentrop had said with a grin, 'They won't do anything stupid there.'

Daladier flew back to Paris the next morning. On the same day, 30 September, Chamberlain asked for a further interview with Hitler. Counsellor Hewel took him to Hitler's private residence on the Prinzregentenplatz, a venue intended to stress the unofficial nature of the meeting. An hour later, Hitler asked his secretary Johanna Wolf[15] to come

[*]The negotiations had lasted thirteen hours. They had signed the so-called Munich Agreement at 2.30 a.m. on 30 September 1938.

in, and a few minutes later a typewriter could be heard from Eva Braun's room as the secretary typed a joint declaration by Adolf Hitler and Neville Chamberlain. Several copies were made of the finished memorandum. Both men signed the document which informed the world that Germano-British relations were of decisive importance in the guarantee of peace in Europe and that the Munich Agreement (relating to the partition of Czechoslovakia) would be seen 'as symbolic for the wishes of both our peoples never again to wage war on one another'.

Chamberlain looked happy as he stuck the document in the breast pocket of his suit and he shook Hitler's hand at length. When he walked out on to the street he raised his hat in a friendly way in response to the 'Hitler-greetings' of the SS men, who could not conceal their amazement at his evident satisfaction. That very day Chamberlain boarded the plane that had taken him to Hitler's Germany three times.

Only a day later, on 1 October 1938, German troops under the command of Colonel General von Leeb crossed the Czech border and passed unhindered through the line of defences built by the French fortress-builder Maginot,[16] opened for Hitler by the French premier Daladier and the British Prime Minister Chamberlain. The Sudetenland and a few areas near the former Austrian border were incorporated into the Third Reich. Munich, the fruit of Britain and France's quest to divert Hitler's aggression to the east, turned out to be the prologue to the Second World War.

In London and Paris the general public heard that as a result of Munich 'peace had been saved'. Ribbentrop reported to Hitler that Daladier had been received in triumph at Le Bourget airport when he returned from Munich. Members of the French Cabinet, Senators, representatives of the banks and business as well as members of the diplomatic corps had turned out to greet him and to congratulate him on a diplomatic victory. The American Ambassador Bullitt was also there and before all else wanted to smoke a cigarette — a 'pipe of peace' as he called it — with Bräuer, the German Chargé d'Affaires who was standing in for the Ambassador, Count Welczeck. Daladier was carried to his car amid cries of 'Long live Daladier! Long live Chamberlain!'"

The fateful year 1939 dawned. As Hitler returned from a birthday visit to Göring on 12 January he met Hess, Goebbels and SS-Gruppenführer Wilhelm Keppler[17] in the dimly lit smoking room. Keppler, who bore the title of 'Commissar for Economic Affairs', was one of the men most responsible for the economic expansion of the Hitlerian empire. He excused himself, telling the others that the Führer had quickly to instruct him on some matter and followed Hitler into the music room. Half an hour later Keppler left the music room and said, as he took his leave of Hess and Goebbels, 'I'm quite giddy. The Führer has just informed me we are going to get the rest of Czechoslovakia.* This is now the most important job for me: to prepare the incorporation of the industries in the Bohemian and Moravian basin. We really need this.' With that, a laughing Keppler hurriedly left the Chancellery.

In his unbridled megalomania, the old Chancellery was no longer big enough for Hitler, so he had ordered a new palace to be built in the Vossstrasse, the so-called New Reich Chancellery. When representatives of foreign powers came to the New Chancellery in the future they were to be overwhelmed by the greatness of Hitler and by his aura of limitless power. Looking ahead to the New Year reception of 1939 Hitler had told one of his adjutants, 'When these gentlemen enter the mosaic hall they must immediately sense the whole sublime nature of the Greater German Reich. The long corridors will reduce my visitors to humility.' True to his promise, in the New Year Hitler obliged the foreign diplomats to walk through the corridors of the New Chancellery before they could finally appear before him.† This was meant to heighten the tension as they made their way to a meeting with 'Europe's Pilot', as Hitler styled himself. On his special orders architects reset the palace of the railway king Borsig as a wing of the Reich Chancellery. From the Wilhelmstrasse to the Göringstrasse there was now a terrace of buildings of monstrous size and unimaginable luxury.

From the great *cour d'honneur* the visitor reached the entrance hall with its pink-grey marble columns and gilded candelabra. That was connected to the mosaic hall, decorated with an immense German eagle. From there one proceeded up marble steps to a granite hall under a cupola perfumed by exotic plants. Here began the gallery lined with red marble and mod-elled on Louis XIV's at Versailles.‡ Even the window niches were faced with marble that was made to glitter through indirect lighting. Italian specialist masons had covered the walls with polished marble that had been ground or mixed with cement so that everything shone and sparkled. The Gobelins came from Habsburg palaces and the Rothschild Palace in Vienna. The gallery ended in a great reception room that was bathed in

---

*Hitler gave orders to prepare to finish off the rest of the Czech state and to annex Memel on 21 October 1938.
†When the new building was officially opened with the New Year reception on 12 January 1939.
‡The Galerie des Glaces at Versailles measures eighty-six metres in length, including both antechambers. The marble gallery at the New Chancellery was 146 metres long.

dazzling light from massive chandeliers. The carpet covering the floor was so enormous that part of the wall had to be removed in order to bring it into the room. The halls were filled with expensive marquetry furniture and the doors too were decorated with inlaid wood. The study room adjoining the hall was panelled with rare woods.

Hitler's new study was twenty-five metres long.* On the walls and the fireplace there was marble of different hues. In one niche were hung valuable pictures, with a massive portrait of Bismarck over the colossal fireplace. On the giant marble table stood Frederick the Great on horseback in white marble. Another feature that caught the eye was the heavy curtains that hung to the ground in the eight windows. During the day you could see the columns and fountains in the park, as well as the glass tea-pavilion decorated with bronze and porphyry.

Because of the swampy subsoil, the Chancellery was built on a concrete raft. The building of the whole complex cost a total of 300 million marks.† When it was all finished Hitler did not find the palace magnificent enough and decided to let Hess have it one day and to move himself into a more imposing residence in the Tiergarten next to the Reichstag, but this lay on the drawing board. The future palace was to be so vast that at least 300 to 400 servants could be accommodated standing in a row.[18]

On the evening of 14 March 1939 the New Chancellery was brightly lit. Hitler had decided that the time had come to conclude the second round of his Munich policy. In the preceding weeks the halls of the Chancellery had buzzed with diplomats, advisers and experts of every description. One of them was the leader of the Slovakian Separatist Party, Tiso.[19] Diplomats from Budapest and Warsaw also frequently visited him during this time. After Munich they and their countries' leaders had a hunger for Czech territory, like Hitler himself.[20]

On this day there was an unusually lively atmosphere in the Chancellery. Keitel, Schmundt and officers of the General Staff disappeared into Hitler's apartments, and in the conservatory they spread out their plans for the invasion of Czechoslovakia. 'This time', said Hitler, 'I shan't need a conference. In Munich they said A, now they'll have to say B.' Hitler's train had orders to get up steam. His staff prepared to leave.

On Hitler's table lay a dossier containing a detailed biography of the President of the Czechoslovak Republic, Hácha. Hácha had replaced

---

*The study was 27 long by 14.5 wide by 9.75 metres high.
†The building cost 88.9 million marks.

Beneš, who had resigned over the Munich Accords and the cession of the Sudetenland. Hitler had ordered him to attend on him in Berlin and was waiting for his arrival at any moment.[21] A company of the Leibstandarte 'Adolf Hitler' entered the *cour d'honneur* to receive the Czech head of state. An hour later he was that no more. Hácha arrived in the company of his Foreign Minister, Chvalkovsky; after the endless journey through the entire New Chancellery building, they at last found themselves before Hitler. This time the Führer had not needed a mirror in order to rehearse the necessary facial expression, and was standing there with the demeanour of the greatest ruler of all time. The doors closed behind them.

After a frosty greeting, Hitler asked the two Czech leaders to sit at the table at which Ribbentrop, Göring and the State Secretary in the Reich Ministry of the Interior, Stuckart,[22] also took their places. Stuckart had been invested with the job of administering occupied territories. Hácha was faced with a demand that he should sign a pre-prepared document which rendered the Czech Republic a protectorate of Germany and which declared Slovakia to be an independent state. This time Hitler did not play the card of having Keitel enter in the guise of Mars, the god of war, as he had done when the Austrian Chancellor Schuschnigg visited him, to make it clear that German troops had mustered at the border. Without further ado he told Hácha that the Wehrmacht was ready to occupy Czechoslovakia.

Hácha refused to sign the document. The atmosphere in Hitler's study grew uglier. Ribbentrop jumped up and bore down on Hácha to get him to sign the paper that already carried Hitler's signature. Hitler threatened Hácha, 'If you don't sign, German bombers will reduce Prague to ruins!' Not long after midnight Hitler's personal physician was called to the study as well as members of Hitler's bodyguard, the SS men Bornhold, Hansen and Köster[23]. Soon afterwards they reappeared with Hácha's motionless body and carried him to a neighbouring room. He had fainted. Morell gave him an injection and after a few minutes managed to revive him.

Hácha was taken back to Hitler. A fountain-pen was pushed into his hand and he was assured that no one intended to Germanise his land. The Czech people would be allowed complete independence (exactly as they enjoyed at that time). Finally Hácha gave in and signed. After Hitler had wrung the signature out of Hácha, it occurred to him that the document required a raison d'être. An appeal from the Czechoslovak Republic was drafted there and then with a request to Germany to take it under its military wing and therefore to liberate it from 'inner disturbances' and 'pressure on its borders'. Hácha signed that too.

Panting, indeed heavily out of breath, Hácha informed the government in Prague of the documents he had signed. The Czech military received orders to lay down their arms.

The morning dawned on 15 March and Hácha left the Chancellery. Half an hour later Hitler's car was coming to a halt before Anhalt station. His train was already getting up steam, but he would not allow it to leave. Together with Keitel he was waiting for reports on how the occupation of Czechoslovakia was proceeding. Himmler was also on Hitler's train, looking pale but with a piercing look behind his round spectacles. He wanted personally to direct the liquidation of Czech patriots.

When Hitler was certain that a journey into Czechoslovakia would place him in no danger, the train left Anhalt station. He got out at a little station at Reichenberg in the Sudetenland. A column of vehicles was ready for him, and Hitler took the direct route to Prague. Around midnight the huge Mercedes limousines sped through the sleepy, peaceful capital of Czechoslovakia. Night lights glowed in the shop windows. There were practically no soldiers to be seen and no policemen either. The chauffeurs took a wrong turning, but when they finally located the Hradschin everyone was happy. The historic castle on a hill above Prague was the seat of the President of the Czechoslovak Republic.

Hitler climbed out. In the headlights he stood before the door of the venerable castle that floats above the roofs of Prague. He had reached his goal. He came in the footsteps of Kaiser Ferdinand, who had started the Thirty Years War here. The inhabitants of the castle were forced to make up a room for him, and he quickly settled himself in. Around him gathered his extensive entourage. Apart from the generals, almost all of them were wearing SS uniforms. Among them was Himmler with his staff, studying brief reports that he had been given. Leaning over him was Karl Frank,[24] one of the leaders of the 'Fifth Column' in Czechoslovakia and Himmler's plenipotentiary. That night he led an operation in Prague that would ruthlessly flush out all the enemies of the Greater German Reich.

Hitler wanted to feed those present, but there was nothing for the hospitable host to offer. That made him furious at a stroke. All the food and drink in the entire castle was to be brought to him as fast as possible and placed on the table. Hitler then spent almost all night in lively conversation, discussing what would be done the next day. SS-Gruppenführer Stuckart, State Secretary at the Ministry of the Interior, made notes together with Frank and Himmler on how the occupied country would be administered. The dim light of a small chandelier was not enough to dispel the half-darkness in the room, and the men's figures with their swastika armbands threw long shadows. Down in the streets and lanes of Prague meanwhile Himmler's and Frank's Gestapo men rushed around conducting mass arrests. Back at the castle Hitler returned to the basis for dealing with the Slavs. He declared, 'Whoever fails to heed the German as the representative of the master race must reckon with punishment by dispossession, prison and death. Villages that resist German dominion will be put to the torch and razed to the ground.' He philosophized too about German *Lebensraum*, or living space, and said that with the annexation of Czechoslovakia new political arrangements, new sources of wealth and new positions of importance now opened up for him.

When it was light and the Gestapo had performed the bulk of their task, the square in front of Prague Castle filled with German soldiers. The occupation was complete. Minister Frick[25] arrived with his advisers, and the old-school diplomat Neurath, appointed Reich Protector of Czechoslovakia, appeared with his own hurriedly assembled retinue. After lunch Hitler drove through the streets of Prague. As in a German city he stood up straight in his car so that the Czechs could see their new master. The following day he took a train back to Berlin via Vienna. He now governed two empires, and possessed the palaces of both the Hohenzollerns and the Habsburgs. On the way to Berlin he told his entourage, 'Marching into Prague pleased me more than all that shilly-shallying in Munich.'

5

March – November 1939

After the annexation of Czechoslovakia, the Baltic port of Memel was ceded by Lithuania to Germany on 22 March 1939 with the tacit consent of the Western Powers.[1] It had been particularly easy to solve the problem of annexing the Memel territory from Lithuania, and Hitler remarked to Linge: 'Yes, Linge, you are living in a great era. We now perform these trifles as a matter of course. You must know the fable of the elephant and the mouse, where the elephant eventually crushes the tiny mouse. It is a law of nature that the strong swallow the weak.'

With the incorporation of the Memel territory, Germany had made a further leap east. Koch,[2] Gauleiter of East Prussia, became lord of the region. A small man with the face of a bulldog, he was a fanatical enemy of Russia and liked to compare himself to a medieval Teutonic knight, proudly declaring that his Gau – East Prussia – would play a special role in the expansion to the east. In the middle ages the Teutonic knights had plundered the Slavic races that had settled on the Baltic coast and forced them into slavery. In Hitler's time, the twentieth century, Koch festooned official buildings with banners proclaiming the motto of the Teutonic knights: 'For Living Space in the East!'*

The next victim of German aggression after the annexation of Memel was Poland. In order to conceal his preparations for war with Poland Hitler brought up the problems of Danzig and the Corridor.† On 18 April, two days before Hitler's fiftieth birthday, the leader of Danzig's National Socialists, Albert Forster,[3] entered the Reich Chancellery. He was a frequent visitor. As Hitler normally didn't get up before twelve or one, Forster had to wait. He went into the so-called step room where Hitler's secretaries worked. Along with the secretaries Fräulein Daranowski and Fräulein

---

*The Teutonic knights had no such motto.

†Under the Versailles Treaty Danzig was declared a free state and placed under the constitutional supervision of the League of Nations. The territory was in Poland's customs area and Poland represented it abroad. In order to allow the Poles access to the sea, a part of German West Prussia was ceded to them too: the so-called Corridor.

Schroeder,[4] he met Linge there. Forster expounded on the difficulties he faced as Gauleiter of Danzig. 'If only war would come!' he exclaimed. 'Then I could stop arguing with these damned Poles. And I wouldn't be a mere Gauleiter of Danzig. No! I'd be Gauleiter of the whole of West Prussia as soon as we'd chased out all the Poles.'

On the evening of 19 April Hess and Forster sat together in the smoking room of the Chancellery. They were waiting for midnight to congratulate Hitler on his fiftieth birthday, which fell on 20 April. Around midnight Hitler appeared in the smoking room, and Hess congratulated him on behalf of the National Socialist Party. He was followed by Forster, who said, 'I am here, my Führer, to offer congratulations from the city of Danzig! Danzig looks on you full of hope and is waiting for the moment of truth.' Hitler expressed his gratitude for their good wishes. His breast filled with pride, he said: 'It is a pity that I did not come to power ten years earlier. Now I am already fifty. I can not longer delay my plans. I must find living space and sources of wealth for Germany. A genius is born only once a century and for that reason I cannot leave the fulfilment of these tasks to my successors. They will have only one duty – to retain what I have conquered. At the parade tomorrow I shall prove to the entire world that I fear no war.'

Hitler sat up with Hess and Forster until the early hours. The conversation turned to the reaction that had been unleashed by the annexation of Czechoslovakia. Hitler said sarcastically, 'I don't understand why London is so amazed. They must have known it was going to happen.' Referring to the negotiations that the British were conducting in Moscow at that time, Forster asked, 'Why are they spending such a long time talking about things? Are they really going to deal with the Russians?'[*] Hess said, 'These negotiations are another trick on the part of the British government to satisfy public opinion. Chamberlain and Halifax need to disarm the opposition. Neither Britain nor France is going to conclude a deal with the Soviets.' 'That is not the most important matter,' Hitler said. 'The talks in Moscow are a double game. The British want to frighten us with Moscow. We are clear about their position. They want to come to an agreement with us in the west without making too many alterations to the Versailles Treaty as regards Moscow. France is not worth discussing. They just do what London tells them.' 'The best antidote', Forster suggested, 'would be to give the British a proper fright.' Hess rejoined, 'The demonstration of

---

[*]Since March 1939 Britain and France had been negotiating an assistance treaty with the Soviet Union.

German military strength at the parade tomorrow will provide the British with an impressive warning.' Hitler added, 'The British are bad actors. Their tricks don't impress me one jot. With their manoeuvres in Moscow they are trying to convince me that they have a choice.'

The next day, 20 April, Linge woke Hitler as early as 8.00 a.m. The Führer donned his brown Party uniform, but instead of the usual Sam Browne he put on the golden dress belt of a German general as Supreme Commander of the Wehrmacht. He stood before the mirror in his bedroom for ages, feasting his eyes on his own image like a peacock and repeatedly adjusting his jacket. Then he assumed a solemn expression and went down the steps to the great hall.

The Reich Chancellery was a sea of flowers. The great hall was decorated with palms and exotic plants. Servants stood at the doors wearing magnificent uniforms with silver lanyards and medals on their chests. In the middle the adjutants and liaison officers were lined up, together with Hitler's bodyguard and the pilots from his own flight. Then there were soldiers from the Leibstandarte in their black SS uniforms, their new belts made in imitation of Kaiser Wilhelm II's guards. Officers from the Leibstandarte – like those from the Wehrmacht – wore silver lanyards and dress-uniform belts. In the great hall Hitler's adjutant Brückner congratulated him in the name of his personal staff, then the military band struck up in the *cour d'honneur*.

Linge handed Hitler his gold-embroidered cap and gloves. At a signal the band fell silent. A company of the historic 1st Battalion of the Berlin Garrison had arrived in the courtyard. Dressed in the dress uniform of the army, the commander gave the order to present arms. Hitler appeared in the doorway and the battalion commander responded with a fascist salute. The band now played 'Deutschland, Deutschland über alles', the Horst Wessel Song – the National Socialist anthem[5] – and Hitler's favourite piece, the Badenweiler March. Two limousines then drove up, bringing Himmler and his closest colleagues from the SS and the police, clad in SS dress uniforms with black steel helmets. Hitler received their tribute and went out with them from the courtyard on to the Wilhelmstrasse. Standing in his Mercedes he reviewed the parade of SS and police units.

He then returned to the Chancellery. Göring, Hess, Goebbels, Ribbentrop, Neurath, Keitel and the other grandees of Hitler's Germany had appeared meanwhile. Göring was hung with crosses from head to toe. He had added the best yet to his innumerable orders; one granted to him by the King of Sweden consisting of a thick gold chain hung over his shoulder. The Order of the Golden Fleece shone around his neck, awarded by Franco in gratitude for the help accorded by the German Luftwaffe in the war against the Spanish Republic. Everyone congratulated Hitler and assured him of their loyalty.

Now Hitler received his presents. Models – of tanks, field guns, aircraft, battleships and so on – sent to him by captains of industry found a special place, most of all a model of the Siegfried Line* equipped with electric lights. They were meant to personify the spirit of the Third Reich. Hitler valued these gifts highly and toyed with them for hours on end. After receiving his presents he left the Chancellery with all of his entourage and went to the Brandenburg Gate. His black, armour-plated limousine carried the 'Führer's Standard' with a swastika and an eagle in each corner. Behind the Brandenburg Gate the troops were lined up on parade. Hitler stood up in the car and, with his arm outstretched, drove past the troops lined up along the Tiergarten.[6] Tribunes had been built in the square in front of the Technical University. When Hitler got out of his car, the diplomats and military attachés present stood up. Hitler, Göring, Hess, Goebbels, Ribbentrop, Neurath, Keitel and the Führer's adjutants took their seats on a tribune covered with a red-velvet baldachin with golden tassels.[†]

The parade started. Hitler took a few paces forward. The march-past began with the standard-bearing battalion, who lowered their banners as they passed Hitler. All present rose. The orchestra played 'Deutschland über alles' and the Horst Wessel Song. After the standards came the infantry, marching in close formation and wearing camouflage,[‡] then Luftwaffe regiments and units of Marines. Onlookers were particularly struck by the paratroops in their marching kit and steel helmets, who were parading for the first time. Behind them followed a huge column of motorized infantry that filled the entire breadth of the street. Then the heavy artillery roared by, the noise of their motors mingling with the sound of the horn-players. After a short pause the cavalry appeared; then it was the turn of the tanks. As a finale, a squadron of the latest aircraft – planes Europe had not previously seen – flew over their heads.

Hitler's eyes glowed in triumph. He was in the best of moods when he returned to the Chancellery. In his wake came a column of cars bearing all

---

*The Allied name for the so-called West Wall built between 1938 and 1939. It was a 630-km line of defences along Germany's western border made up of 14,000 bunkers and so on. It cost 3.5 billion marks.

†It was pale grey, almost white, decorated with gold tassels and various party and state symbols – eagles, swastikas and iron crosses.

‡Only the paratroops wore camouflage; the rest were in dress uniforms.

the guests who had been invited to the banquet in the Chancellery − ministers, Reichsleiters, Gauleiters, SA and SS leaders, the chiefs of the air staff, and the motorised corps of the National Socialist Party, as well as representatives of the High Commands.

In the evening Hitler received private wellwishers. One of them was a woman of average height in her middle years with chestnut-brown hair. It was the film-maker Leni Riefensthal[7] whose star was on the wane. Hitler had passionately admired her since 1931, with the result that she had been commissioned to make films about the Party rally and the 1936 Berlin Olympiad. Leni Riefenstahl stood a few metres away from Hitler and stared at her Führer with a wide-eyed and steadfast gaze. Suddenly, from her painted lips came a piercing shriek, and, visibly shaken, she covered her face with her hands. When she had composed herself she stammered in a scarcely audible voice, 'My Führer!' Launching herself at her idol, with both hands she thrust an enormous bunch of carnations towards him. Hitler took the flowers with a self-satisfied air and handed them to Linge. Then he offered her his arm and led her into the music room.

After Leni Riefenstahl had left, Hitler received his sister Angela,* who was married to Professor Hammitzsch from Dresden. After the death of her first husband Raubal, Angela had become Hitler's housekeeper on the Obersalzberg. He threw her out when she pleaded for a victim of the mass-murder after the Röhm Putsch of 30 June 1934. Since then he had seen his sister but once a year − on his birthday.

On 21 April[†] Hitler travelled to the Obersalzberg to see Eva Braun. When he arrived he learned from Bormann that on the journey down the SS soldier servants Wibizek and Sander had purloined a number of the models he had received on his birthday. Hitler issued orders for their arrest. Mad with rage he shouted, 'Into the concentration camp with these toe-rags! Into the quarry! Yes, they can break rocks! And they will never come out!'

Hitler remained on the Obersalzberg the whole summer, spending much of his time as usual in the company of Eva and her lady-friends. He often left them on their own reading crime or adventure stories. As a result of this trash an oven-fitter who was working in Hitler's palace in the

---

*Angela Hammitzsch (1883–1949) née Hitler, first married to the tax official Leo Raubal whom she bore three children: Leo (b. 1906), Angela or 'Geli' (b. 1906) and Elfriede (b. 1910); after the death of her first husband, in charge of the kitchens in a Viennese girls' home; from 1926 Hitler's housekeeper on the Obersalzberg; dismissed after mocking Eva Braun's appearance in public; there is no evidence of her interceding for anyone at the time of the Röhm Putsch. She married the architect Martin Hammitzsch in 1936.

†He left on 3 May 1939.

summer of 1939 ended up in a concentration camp. He was building a tile-oven in Hitler's study that was being decorated by the Munich artist Sophie Stork[8] – a friend of Eva's – with scenes from the history of the National Socialist Party. The oven-fitter recounted to other workers at the Berghof that Hitler possessed an 'impressive' library, and the SD* got to hear about it. On Hitler's orders the man disappeared into Dachau concentration camp.

It was 29 August 1939. There was a warlike mood in the Reich Chancellery. Hitler's closest circle was aware that the war against Poland had been decided upon and that Germany would launch an attack on its neighbour at any moment. Hitler's bodyguard were issued with machine guns. The Führer Column, made up of heavy general-purpose vehicles manufactured by Krupp that were generally used for manoeuvres,† had been transferred to the German–Polish border from whence Hitler would observe the progress of military operations in Poland a few days later. The French and British ambassadors, Henderson and Coulondre, had sought an audience with Hitler, but in vain. He had ordered that they be taken to Ribbentrop. 'I don't want to see them any more,' he said. 'Ribbentrop can deal with them. I have no intention of solving the Polish problem through negotiations with Poles, Britons or Frenchmen.'[9]

On 31 August Hitler suddenly summoned the Reichstag. On the night of 1 September he dictated a Reichstag speech to the secretaries in his study in which he would declare war on Poland. At this time the German–Polish war had *de facto* already begun, because that night German troops had already crossed the border into Poland.‡ At 10.00 a.m. on 1 September Hitler drove to the Reichstag session held in the former Kroll Opera House.[10] Before he left, Morell injected him with a stimulant. On this day Hitler had for the first time put on a field-grey jacket in preference to the brown Party uniform. Linge had ordered it for him a few days before.

---

* The SD (Sicherheitsdienst), the SS security police.

† Hitler used only Mercedes cars. For journeys to the front and to his HQs he used the cross-country model 770G4 W31. The suggestion that he used Krupp vehicles was made by the Soviet editors to demonstrate a close connection to 'monopoly capital'.

‡ At 4.45 a.m. on 1 September 1939 the ship *Schleswig-Holstein*, lying at anchor in Danzig, opened fire on the Polish side of the harbour. This was the official beginning of the war. German dive-bombers had, however, already attacked the Polish town of Wielun, 100 kilometres from Breslau, at 4.40 and destroyed 60 percent of it. There was an even earlier attack: on 26 August 1939 a German–Slovakian unit had occupied the Jablonka Pass. No one had remembered to tell the commander that the date for beginning operations had been postponed.

As the session had been convened so abruptly, many Reichstag members from the provinces had been unable to attend. Their places were taken by SS men from Hitler's and Göring's bodyguard, who played the role of members and voted for the war against Poland. The National Socialists in the Kroll Opera House had prepared a rousing welcome for Hitler. Göring opened the session as President and Hitler spoke. He portrayed himself as a lover of peace and blamed Poland for attacking Germany. He declared that he was now forced to fight a war for the survival of the German people. During his speech, Hitler frequently glanced at the box opposite where the foreign diplomats were gathered. On the way back to the Chancellery, he told his adjutants what simple pleasure he had derived from seeing the faces of the British and the French growing longer and longer.

Hitler's speech and Germany's declaration of war on Poland were greeted by a stormy ovation, with hearty applause from the Japanese and Italian ambassadors in the diplomatic box. As a sign of their approval for the war, the deputies as well as the members of Hitler's and Göring's bodyguard all rose to their feet. As President of the assembly, Göring declared unanimous support. On the Führer's way back from the Kroll Opera House to the Chancellery large crowds on Unter den Linden and the Wilhelmstrasse proclaimed their enthusiasm for the war with Poland. As always after a big speech, Hitler returned to the Chancellery exhausted and bathed in sweat. He took a hot bath and swallowed an Ultraseptyl sedative prescribed by Morell.[*] That same evening Ribbentrop brought him notes from the British and French ambassadors demanding an immediate cessation of hostilities against Poland and the withdrawal of German troops. Hitler commented, 'We will now see if they come to Poland's aid. They'll chicken out again.'

On the morning of 3 September Henderson and Coulondre handed in notes to Ribbentrop to inform him that Britain and France found themselves in a state of war with Germany.[†] Hitler threw a tantrum. In the presence of Ribbentrop, Hess, Goebbels, Himmler and the others who were gathered there, he ran about the conservatory roaring and foaming at the mouth: 'The Poles are a miserable, good-for-nothing, loud-mouthed rabble. The British understand that as well as we do; the British gentlemen understand that might is right. When it comes to inferior races they were our first schoolmasters. It is disgraceful to present Czechs and Poles as

---

[*]Ultraseptyl was not a sedative but a common chemical product for the relief of inflammation. Morell frequently prescribed this sulphonamide.
[†]The British declaration of war was handed not to Ribbentrop, but to the interpreter Paul Schmidt at 9.00 a.m., as the Foreign Minister claimed he was detained. Ribbentrop received the French declaration at 12.20.

sovereign states when this rabble is not a jot better than the Sudanese or the Indians – and only because, on this occasion, it is about German interests and not British ones. My entire policy towards Britain has been based on recognising the natural realities as they exist on both sides, and now they want to put me in the pillory. That is an unspeakable vilification!'

At around 8.00 Hitler's cavalcade stopped before the station. Hitler boarded a train that from now on would be called the Führer HQ. He went off to war with Poland,[11] setting up his staff on the military exercise field at Gross-Born in Pomerania on the German-Polish border.[12] The Polish campaign was carried out according to plans worked out by the Chief of the General Staff, Halder.[13] After three weeks of war Poland was no more than the ruins of Warsaw, charred towns and villages, devastated fields and POW camps, with the surviving population suffering from hunger and other privations. Their government had left them in the lurch and fled to London.*

Like all German soldiers, the SS men in Hitler's camp felt themselves to be the lords of the manor, but they had to be on their guard against isolated resistance from Polish patriots. Despite grotesque acts of repression carried out by punishment squads, the Polish people would not give in and fought for their independence. One day when Hitler was returning to his mobile HQ in Gross-Born from a tour of inspection in Poland, a group of Polish patriots fired on vehicles in the Führer Column carrying Hitler's bodyguard. As a result of this Högl,[14] the Police Chief attached to Hitler's staff, called a meeting attended by Himmler's Chief of Staff, Baron von Alvensleben.[15] This resulted in Alvensleben inviting Högl, Linge and other SS men from Hitler's staff to visit a POW camp near Gross-Born to have a look at the 'Polish beasts'. The major commanding the camp guided them through the huts where Polish prisoners lay huddled in filth. Those prisoners whose faces did not appeal to Alvensleben he ordered to be whipped there and then by the camp guards. Alvensleben joined in himself. An aristocrat and estate-owner, he kicked the semi-conscious prisoners and bellowed that 'These creatures should be treated in such a way that they learn who their masters are.' As they left, the commandant asked them to come by more often. He would then organise some 'exciting scenes' for them.

Once the Germans had conquered Poland a colonial government was established under 'Generalgouverneur' Hans Frank.[16] Frank, an old

---

*The Polish government fled first to Romania on 17 September 1939. On 30 September, a government was formed in Paris under General Wladyslaw Sikorski. It moved to London in 1940.

accomplice of Hitler's from the time the National Socialist Party was founded, was a lawyer by profession and had defended Hitler in court when he was tried for organising the National Socialist Putsch in Munich in 1923. Before 1933 Frank defended SA men who had been arraigned before the courts for murdering communists and other progressive Germans. After Hitler came to power Frank was rewarded for his 'services' by being made President of the Academy of German Law. His activities in Poland consisted above all in holding orgies in the Royal Castle in Cracow and exterminating people in Auschwitz and Majdanek.

When Hitler's special train returned from the Polish campaign it came to a halt in a station where a hospital train was standing at the opposite platform. With a hypocritical, grieving expression the Führer passed among the wounded soldiers. For the rest of the war he never once visited a hospital train. He justified his attitude by saying that a warlord could not afford to be sentimental.

The 1939 anniversary of the Munich Putsch took place under war conditions – though it has to be said that, even if France and Britain were now at war with Germany, neither of them had done anything so far that could be interpreted as an act of war.[17] For the annual meeting with the Alte Kämpfer in Munich's Bürgerbräukeller, Hitler discarded his usual brown shirt and put on his grey military tunic instead, to which he pinned the Blood Order. As he had to get back to Berlin urgently, the evening began an hour earlier than usual.* He gave a short speech to those assembled in the beer hall, declaring how happy he was to have the chance to lead the German nation in their struggle. He left the celebration to a thunderous chorus of 'Heils' and drove to the station, where his train was already getting up steam.

The train had yet to reach Nuremberg when a telegraph message came in that there had been an explosion at the Bürgerbräukeller after Hitler's departure. There were no other details. Liebel, Bürgermeister of Nuremberg,[18] together with Martin,[19] the City Police Chief, were waiting eagerly on Nuremberg station for Hitler's train. They climbed up into his carriage where they were received by Linge. Martin asked that he might be announced without delay, as he had urgent news to report to Hitler. Hitler, who had just received the telegram, went out into the corridor and immediately asked Liebel and Martin, 'What's happened?' 'My Führer,' Martin

---

*The occasion began half an hour early at 8.00 p.m. as Hitler's train left at 9.31 which meant leaving the Bürgerbräukeller at 9.07. Elser's bomb went off at 9.20 p.m.

answered, 'I have just received a report from Munich that an attempt has been made on your life. Roughly an hour after you left the Bürgerbräukeller there was a powerful explosion. The people who were still there in the hall were buried under the falling ceiling.'*

Hitler went pale. Gasping for air he asked, 'Where is Himmler?' Martin replied that Himmler had stayed behind in Munich and was personally leading the investigation. Hitler became even more excited and commanded that Himmler was to remain in Munich for as long as it took to put all those criminals involved in the business behind bars. He composed himself and added angrily, 'Tell him that he should proceed ruthlessly and exterminate the whole pack of them – root and branch.' Liebel and Martin left the train. The news of the failed attempt on Hitler's life travelled like wildfire through the train. Hitler was congratulated on his amazing escape. He replied that he was under the special protective hand of providence.

Reports showed that an explosive device had been concealed in one of the columns in front of the stage at the Bürgerbräukeller. The waiters testified that in the last few days before the attack a man unknown to them had been seen in the beer hall several times. His description was urgently despatched to the border posts, which finally led to the arrest of a certain Elser, who was trying to enter Switzerland. During his interrogation Elser confessed to having put the explosive device in the column. He had done it without accomplices and had planned to kill Hitler because he wanted to change the political order in Germany. Although there was no further evidence, Hitler – not wanting to believe that Elser had organised the attempt on his own – issued orders for mass arrests.[20]

The SD was of the opinion that the British secret service was behind the plot. To this end SD operatives devised a little game by establishing radio contact with a British secret service station in Holland and making out that they represented a German anti-fascist group. In the course of this operation German SD managed to lure the British spy Captain Best to the Dutch–German border. The SD men shot the hapless Dutch border guards and dragged Best on to German territory.[21] No involvement in Elser's attempt on Hitler's life could be established in the course of Best's interrogation, and he disappeared into a concentration camp.[22] Elser, however, was retained by the SD and put to work making bombs.

---

*Elser had concealed the bomb in a column beside the speaker's rostrum. Eight men were killed by the falling ceiling and sixty were injured.

6

December 1939 – May 1941

In December 1939 Hitler returned once again to the Berghof.* One evening he summoned Göring, Hess, Keitel, Funk[1] and Todt,[2] the Reich Minister for Armaments and Munitions, to a meeting in the great hall. Linge hung a sign on the door saying 'Please do not disturb', so that Eva Braun and her coterie would keep clear of the room that evening, as it was separated from the drawing room only by a curtain. When Göring appeared, the servants rushed towards him from the cloakroom, because he never bothered to go in there. Instead, always wishing to appear a very busy man, he would throw his coat, hat and marshal's staff to the servants as he passed. With great swinging strides, his cylindrical legs crammed into spurred boots, he stormed into the hall. A few minutes later he was joined by Hess, Funk, Todt and Keitel. When Linge announced Hitler, all the others were at their places.

Hitler was sunk in thought as he came down the short staircase followed by Linge. The Führer straightened his back and walked in with firm, quick steps. Those present raised their arms in salute. Hitler greeted Göring, Hess, Funk, Keitel and Todt affably and they all went over to the giant marble table. Hitler opened the discussion by confirming that Göring would take over the running of the entire war economy. He received full powers to secure the economic foundations of the war. When Hitler had finished, Göring's rasping voice was to be heard. He spoke about the state of supplies and painted a glowing picture of a permanently expanding, gigantic arms industry. His description attested to boundless optimism.

Hitler leaned with his entire weight on the table so that his fingers bent. He declared that the favourable military position of Germany and the victorious mood of Germany's troops should be comprehensively harnessed, that fate itself called for further action. The German military machine was going full throttle and could not be halted. The French must come out and fight. 'We'll soon lure them out from behind the Maginot Line. What do

*For two days, 20–22 December.

you think, Keitel?' Keitel laughed in a self-satisfied way and said, 'That will mean a massive spring-clean.' 'Germany is full of determination,' Göring said, adding, in agreement with Hitler, 'We are in a position to pick up the gauntlet. The Western Powers will have to pay the price for declaring war on us.'

On 23 December Hitler left the Obersalzberg to spend Christmas in the Rhineland to boost morale among the troops massed on the Rhine and on the Belgian frontier. On 24 December, his special train stopped at a freight siding near Aachen. Hitler drove to a troop position. In the houses of the little town one could hear the voices of children singing – the greatest religious feast of the year was being celebrated. Families were divided, however, as many fathers and brothers were away with the forces: they were in Poland, they lay in bunkers along the Siegfried Line, or they were standing in readiness in the Rhineland.

An SS patrol walked slowly up the fourteen carriages of Hitler's train. The railway police were also on duty. Behind the locomotive and right at the end of the train there were carriages equipped with two four-barrelled anti-aircraft guns to deal with any possible air attack. These carriages remained in use on Hitler's train for the duration of the war. The gunners in their warm coats looked into the darkness of the frosty night and hopped from one foot to the other to keep warm.

On the road leading to Hitler's train you could hear the motors of six-wheeler all-purpose vehicles approaching with dimmed headlights. Linge emerged from the carriage at the same time as Hitler's car came to a halt on the platform. Suddenly Linge heard a loud voice. On the wing of the second vehicle, the one following Hitler's, sat a drunken Bormann with his face turned backwards bawling some hit song from the Rhineland Carnival. Linge opened the door to help Hitler out of the car. Bormann climbed down from the wing of the second car and swayed towards the train. He walked into Hitler's path. 'My Führer, that is not your carriage,' he mumbled. 'No, my Führer, of course that isn't your compartment. Yours is further back.' Linge declared that they were standing in front of Hitler's carriage. 'So', said Hitler, 'I was right after all. Of course it's my carriage.' Bormann pulled his cap straight. It was sitting cocked on the back of his head. He required a great effort to climb into the neighbouring carriage.

A little while later Bormann appeared in the corridor of Hitler's carriage. With a stupid grin on his face, he walked towards the Führer's compartment. In his hands he held a little Christmas tree which Eva Braun had decorated on the Obersalzberg and which she had asked Bormann to give to Hitler for Christmas. Screwing up his face, he intimated to Linge that it was meant to be a surprise for Hitler. All of a sudden the little tree fell from his hands. Nuts and glass balls rolled from its branches. As if struck dumb, he stood there wide-eyed. He was seized with fear. 'Quick, quick!' he hissed at Linge, who leaped over to pick up the tree. Bormann now carefully approached Hitler's compartment. He gave the Führer a letter from Eva and the tree. At the same time the Secretary of the National Socialist Party[*] − who was so drunk he could hardly stand − wished the Führer a happy Christmas on behalf of the Party.

Hitler's train started out in the direction of Bad Ems. The motorised infantry regiment of the SS Leibstandarte 'Adolf Hitler' was garrisoned in the spa. Once they had arrived in Bad Ems, Hitler took his car to the pump room where the men of the Leibstandarte were celebrating Christmas. He was welcomed by the commander of the Leibstandarte, Sepp Dietrich.[3] When Hitler entered the room Dietrich gave the command, in a slightly familiar manner, 'Quiet, men!' The Führer permitted the more relaxed tone to demonstrate that he and the Leibstandarte belonged to one another. Accompanied by Dietrich, he walked along the long rows of SS men standing stiffly to attention with their arms raised in salute. He took a seat at the tables covered with white cloths that had been arranged in a horseshoe in the middle of the room. The officers and men of the Leibstandarte sat down in their turn, and every SS man received a present from Hitler of sweets and cognac. Before the tables there was a stage on which the Leibstandarte orchestra was playing. On the right next to the stage stood a Christmas tree, festively decorated and sparkling in the candlelight. In front of the stage a rostrum had been set up.

After the orchestra had played a few marches, Sepp Dietrich said some words of greeting. In response to his three cheers for Hitler, the SS men gave three shouted 'Heils!' Then Hitler went over to the rostrum. He said, 'You soldiers of the Leibstandarte are now standing at the West Wall[†] to conquer new living space for Germany. It is our right in life to step out of our narrow confines. Now it pleases Britain suddenly to stand in our way and declare war on us. The real reason for that was not the Polish campaign. It is in fact the English plutocrats who are madly jealous when they see how the German economy has developed. The nation that has conquered

[*]Bormann was currently personal secretary and Chief of the Chancellery to Hitler's deputy, Rudolf Hess.
[†]He means the Maginot Line. (Russian note.) The Russians are wrong: Hitler meant the West Wall, or Siegfried Line.

a vast living space for itself is Britain. I shall break these English gentlemen! The future belongs to the Germans, not the British, who are already show- ing signs of senility. You soldiers of my Leibstandarte are fate's elite and guarantors of German victory!'

Hitler's speech was crowned with thunderous applause. There were more and more cries of 'Sieg Heil, Sieg Heil!' Afterwards Hitler once more took his place among the SS men. The orchestra played merry marches while punch was served to the SS men. After that some sketches were performed in which members of the British Cabinet were lampooned. Chamberlain appeared with a foolish, morose face and with an umbrella on his arm. Hitler said goodbye to the SS men in a fine mood. From Bad Ems he travelled back to the Obersalzberg, where he celebrated the New Year together with Eva Braun.[*]

At the end of March 1940 the commanders of the army, air force and navy were summoned to a meeting in the Reich Chancellery. The situation in the west was unchanged. French and British troops remained passive. Their skirmishes consisted of the occasional verse from their victory song 'We're going to hang out the washing on the Siegfried Line!' Göring, Keitel, Halder, Jodl, Brauchitsch, Raeder and General Falkenhorst[4] took part in the meeting with Hitler, in the course of which the plans for an invasion of Norway and Denmark were discussed. Falkenhorst was there because he had been given command of the forces which were to occupy Scandinavia.

After the meeting Hitler invited Göring and Raeder to a meal in his dining room. Its purpose was to sound out Raeder, who was critical of plans to occupy Norway because he feared that the powerful British fleet would inflict heavy losses. Hitler replied, 'If the German fleet has ever needed to justify its existence, it is now. I am not going to stand for it that the fleet rusts in its harbours as it did under Wilhelm II.[5] It is better to risk losing it. Even when our cruisers go down, they will still be fulfilling an important mission. You will be writing a glorious chapter in the history of the German navy!' Göring gave Hitler his support and stressed how important it was to invade Norway. As he expressed it, it would be a German aircraft carrier in the fight against Britain.

At the end of the meal, Hitler was in a splendid mood. He was not being entirely serious when he recounted a story from before his rise to power. In 1925 he had noticed a crowd gathered around his car that was waiting for him outside Munich station. The people were laughing at a horse that

[*]He was there from 31 December 1939 to 5 January 1940.

was tearing straw out of the split and worn-out seat of Hitler's car and enjoying a good meal. Hitler found it so humiliating that he walked home. Everybody had to laugh at his story.

Over the next few days – this was in April 1940 – during the operation to land troops in Denmark and Norway, Hitler devoured pounds of pralines. 'They are nerve food,' he told Linge. A meteorologist from the Air Ministry recommended by Göring brought a weather report to the Chancellery every day. After he had made his prognostications, the date for the beginning of the Norwegian campaign was decided. The man, who had no idea why his weather reports were so important, died soon after the invasion of Norway.[6] Hitler joked about it, 'He had a stroke when it became clear to him how important his weather forecasts were.'

Hitler's plans paid off. Norway and Denmark were occupied.* At the same time the British fleet appeared off the Norwegian coast. Although it encountered only a risibly weak German force, consisting mostly of minelayers and torpedo boats, it did not engage and sailed back to Britain. When it reappeared near the coast of Norway again, the bridgeheads were already secure and the Germans could land troops in Norway with impunity.

Later the British themselves sought to land troops in Norway, putting down an insignificant force in Trondheim that was wiped out by the Germans.† The secret plans for the landings were found on the body of a dead officer. They contained highly detailed instructions, such as in which direction the British soldiers should march after the landing on the Norwegian coast – left or right – and how they should carry their weapons. The orders gave details of the equipment assigned to the British force, chiefly rations and sporting gear. When these secret orders were put before Hitler he laughed and said sarcastically that the British had landed in Norway to play games, not to fight.

The Wehrmacht attacked France in May 1940, after it had occupied Denmark and Norway. On the first day of the offensive, 10 May, Hitler left Berlin for the headquarters they called 'Felsennest' (or Rocky Lair) which

---

*Denmark put up little resistance, but there was heavy fighting in Norway. Only on 9 July 1940 did King Haakon VII order his army to lay down their arms.
†From 14 to 20 April 1940, British, French and Polish forces landed at Andalsnes, Harstadt, Namsos and Narvik. The first two landings were meant to create a pincer movement towards Trondheim. The attack failed, however, and the Allied forces were evacuated at the beginning of May. The Allies managed to occupy Narvik for the time being, but because of the critical situation in France their forces were withdrawn at the beginning of June.

had been built into a hill near Euskirchen.[7] Hitler's bunker was completely underground, so no trace of it could be seen from the surface. A screen was set up to disguise the entrance. Hitler's rooms − bed and study − were furnished in campaign order. The bunker also served as a home for Keitel and the adjutants Schmundt and Schaub as well as for Linge. Thirty or forty metres away there was the mess with its concrete walls, and two hundred metres further on, behind a copse, was a wooden meeting room, also disguised behind netting. Jodl[8] was lodged here. The area on the hill containing the three buildings was encircled with barbed wire and was called 'Restricted Area 1'. The rest of Hitler's HQ was in the village at the bottom of the hill.

The German army marched quickly through Belgium and Holland into northern France. The attacking forces cut off important elements of the enemy's strength, including units of the British Expeditionary Force, which was caught in a pincer-movement at Dunkirk.[9] The British retreated fast, letting the French cover their backs, but the noose around Dunkirk grew ever tighter. It was like tracking an animal, and German artillery and tanks fired on the British streaming in mad panic towards the coast.

On the flat shore at Dunkirk, the British built pontoons by driving lorries into the water in an attempt to reach their boats. In order to escape from the horror of Dunkirk, they threw away a good deal of clothing and weapons and jumped in the water to swim to the vessels. The hell of Dunkirk reached its hottest point when the Luftwaffe, which enjoyed total control of the skies, began a constant harrying. German bombers hit the fleeing British not only on land, but also in the water. Ships filled to the brim with soldiers were sunk in a hail of German bombs.[10] The whole stock of weapons and equipment that the British left behind fell into the hands of the German army. In their attempt to save their skins the British abandoned their French allies to their fate. The French fought and fell for them in battle.*

When the commander of the Expeditionary Force returned to British Isles with the pathetic remains of his army, Churchill decorated him with

---

*Operation Dynamo, the evacuation of Dunkirk, managed to take out 338,000 soldiers including 123,000 Frenchmen, and bring them to England. The British saved the bulk of their Expeditionary Force and were not obliged to capitulate. The evacuation was assisted by Hitler's 'Stop Order' that immediately halted the German tanks 18 kilometres from Dunkirk. There is no proof that he did this to reach an understanding with Great Britain. The cause of the order was the fear of an attack on his flank by the French army and the assurances he had received from Göring that he would deal with the British.

the Order of the Bath for this 'stunning' victory of British arms. This caused a good deal of mirth at German High Command where they deemed it right and fitting that Wavell should receive this honour after the 'cold bath' he had received in the waters of the English Channel.* The flight of the British from France gave the German High Command the opportunity to transfer substantial forces from the area around Dunkirk to the Somme–Oise Front without further ado. On 5 June they broke through the French defences on the south banks of both rivers, and on 14 June they captured Paris. French prisoners of war showed in no uncertain terms what they thought of British behaviour at Dunkirk. When they ran into Britons in the POW camps, they beat them up, calling them selfish cowards and traitors. At the outset this obliged the Germans to separate the French and the British and keep them in different huts.

Hitler was quite out his mind with joy, and travelled to Dunkirk.† When he returned he reported that he had found field telephones in perfect condition in the staff quarters so hurriedly abandoned by the British. He was full of contempt when he told Göring that the British had left their entire baggage train behind in Dunkirk. 'They thought only of their skins,' he said. 'They can certainly beat their colonial subjects with whips, but on the battlefield they are miserable cowards.'

Göring was also in an excellent mood. While they were waiting for the car outside their lodgings, he told Hitler his most recent 'adventure'. A few days before, he had gone into a tavern on the Rhine, and all the customers had risen to their feet. The only ones who had not were a couple of Catholic priests. 'I showed them what for – I had them packed off to a concentration camp,' Göring said laughing. 'And I gave orders for a pole to be set up and one of my old caps to be put on top of it. Now they have to walk past it every day and give it a National Socialist salute.' Hitler laughed and gave Göring a benevolent clap on the shoulder. As the fun was over, Göring shook his hand, gave a self-important wave with his baton, sat down in his car and drove off to his HQ.

Before May was out, France's complete defeat was already evident. Around this time Hitler received a letter from his Axis partner Mussolini.‡ Hitler flew into a fury because Italy, which for six long months had procrastinated

---

* The BEF was commanded by Field Marshal Lord Gort. Wavell was in the Near East. Gort received the Order on 2 June 1940.
† As part of a general tour of the front, Hitler visited Dunkirk on 26 June 1940.
‡ Alfieri handed him the letter on 30 May 1940.

about entering the war, now wanted to come in at any price. In order not to have to share the spoils with Mussolini, Hitler said he didn't need Italy for the present: France already lay at his feet. In reply to Mussolini's letter he wrote that Italy's entrance into the war should be put off until the Luftwaffe had destroyed the French airfields in the south, which would make military operations easier for the Italians. But they took no notice of Hitler's 'convincing' arguments and soon after that they declared war on France.* The partners in the Berlin–Rome Axis acted 'with one accord'.

Hitler was vexed by the question of what other secret goals Mussolini might be pursuing – apart from securing his share of the loot in France. Was it Gibraltar or Malta? Or did the Italian navy want to launch an attack on Suez? At the end of May Ribbentrop was given the job of ordering the Italian Ambassador Alfieri from Berlin to the Hotel Dreesen in Bad Ems. Hitler gave instructions that Alfieri's visit should be made to look like an enemy envoy seeking peace. That day the signposts were removed on Alfieri's route, so that he would not figure out that Hitler's HQ was in Euskirchen, one and a half hour's drive from Bad Ems. On the way to his meeting with Alfieri, Hitler seemed extremely irritable. He really was determined to find out what the Italians had in mind, because, since their declaration of war, the Italian High Command had done precisely nothing about joining in the fighting.

Hitler's talks with Alfieri in the Hotel Dreesen lasted about an hour. Soon the Führer's raised voice could be heard from the room where they were taking place. He threw angry accusations at Alfieri. He gave full rein to his fury and roared that he could not understand why Italy was being so passive. 'Can you explain that to me? In the end can you give me a clear answer? This cannot go on!' he screamed. His underlings knew that he was angry not about Italy's passivity but because Mussolini had declared war on France against his will. Alfieri drove away from the hotel crushed and distraught. Hitler left soon after.

He sat through dinner at HQ in grumpy silence. Keitel, Jodl, Bormann, Dietrich, Hewel, Hoffmann, Morell and the adjutants secretly exchanged glances. Hitler voiced his fury once again in front of them. 'The Italian declaration of war that we so drastically needed last autumn,' he explained, 'Vittorio Emanuele† initially made conditional on Mussolini appointing the Crown Prince commander of the army. The Duce naturally refused.'

---

*Hitler gave his answer on 31 May 1940. Italy declared war on Britain and France on 10 June. It employed thirty-two divisions in its reannexation of Upper Savoy.
†The Italian king. (Russian note.)

Those present knew what Hitler meant. Crown Prince Umberto was a known Anglophile. Jodl zealously agreed with Hitler: 'Of course, my Führer, but you have always said, "Why doesn't the Duce send the whole Savoy dynasty packing?"' 'Look', Hitler opined, 'Mussolini doesn't have an easy time of it. The army supports the King, the Church is on the King's side, the court is riddled with intrigue and there are a lot of strange elements in the Fascist Party.'

In Jodl's opinion the Italians should at least make life difficult for the British fleet in the Mediterranean. Hitler continued, 'I asked Alfieri what sort of plans Italy had. We keep waiting for an offensive from the Italian army. Alfieri was not forthcoming. It is obvious that they have no serious plans. When I categorically demanded to be informed why the Italians were so inactive, Alfieri replied with utter cheek: it was raining at the front.' Keitel exclaimed angrily, 'What is going on with Mussolini?' Bormann also uttered astonished and contemptuous interjections. At the end of the conversation Hitler suggested that the passivity of the Italians might have its good side, as it meant that their appetite for France could be properly curbed.

At the beginning of June Hitler's HQ was transferred from Euskirchen to Brûly-de-Pesche, north of Rocroy on the French–Belgian border.* Hitler instructed that it was to be given the name of Wolfsschlucht, or Wolf's Ravine. So Hitler's nickname 'Wolf' appeared for the first time in the title of an HQ. The Wolfsschlucht lay in a little wood. The HQ had been quickly constructed and had a temporary feel to it. Hitler lived in a solitary-standing wooden hut along with Brückner, Schmundt and Linge. Next door was a concrete building consisting of a single room. The mess was eighty to a hundred metres away. Keitel, Jodl and Bormann together with the rest of the staff were quartered in the school and in the evacuated houses of the Franco-Belgian village of Brûly-de-Pesche. Situation reports were delivered in the schoolhouse, where both Göring and Brauchitsch had their staffs. Around this time Himmler's chauffeur managed to kill himself in his car by handling a machine gun with insufficient care. He was buried in Brûly-de-Pesche. At his funeral Himmler said, 'He rests in German earth. This land will belong to us for ever.'[11]

In the first half of July 1940 Hitler invited Reichsleiter Amann[12] to his HQ. The former First World War sergeant had been Hitler's superior in the Regiment 'List'. After Hitler came to power he was made General Director of the Eher Publishing Group, of which Hitler was co-owner. After Amann's visit to HQ came Wiedemann,[13] another old comrade in

*On 6 June 1940.

arms from the Regiment 'List'.* He had emigrated to America, but in 1933 Hitler had called him back. As an eyewitness to the Führer's 'heroism' in the First World War he had to heap praise on him. Together with Amann and Wiedemann Hitler wanted to visit the former positions of the Regiment 'List' in France during the First World War.† Under armed escort they left HQ in a Krupp general-purpose vehicle. Hitler's cavalcade raced down French roads, through towns and villages, past ruins, freshly dug graves and fields furrowed by grenades. Refugees returning home fell to one side as Hitler's vehicle with its howling siren appeared. It also ran into groups of exhausted French POWs.

With map in hand, Hitler tried to find the place where the Regiment 'List' had fought or been stationed. Somewhere near the Chemin des Dames, he gave the order to halt. The entire crew got out. Hitler strode quickly across the field and came to a stop before some trenches that had partially collapsed. With the sort of joy that comes from seeing someone again, he pointed to the ditches piled up with rubbish and rusting barbed wire. Full of pride he remembered how he had been a messenger near here. Hitler really livened up. No one had seen him like this for ages.

On the evening of 15 June 1940 the first report circulated in Hitler's HQ that the French government was about to sue for a truce. It came from Stohrer,[14] the German Ambassador in Madrid, who had been contacted by the French Chargé d'Affaires there. The news spread like wildfire through the camp. Everybody congratulated one another and recalled Hitler's words that the railway carriage in the woods at Compiègne in which the Germans had sued for an armistice in 1918 would now be the scene of German triumph. Hitler gave instructions for hefty celebrations. Soon his entire staff was drunk.

On the basis of the report from Madrid, the army High Command set to work drawing up a draft peace treaty with France. It was founded on France's total capitulation. It envisaged the French army laying down its arms and the occupation of the whole country. Officers and men would be taken captive and all their equipment turned over to the German army as booty. Hitler rejected the draft.

On 17 June he gave Keitel and Jodl the broad outlines and conditions for a new draft truce with France. At the time he listed the following considerations: Britain would try to stop the French government from

---

*The Bavarian Reserve Regiment 18 was created in September 1914 from various battalions. After the death of its commander, Colonel Julius List, it was awarded his name. Hitler served in it from 16 August 1914 to 14 October 1918, chiefly as a messenger.
†The visits took place on 25 and 26 June 1940.

signing a truce and would encourage them to continue the fight. For that reason Churchill had suggested a Franco-British alliance on the principle of a comprehensive legal amalgamation of the two countries. It was therefore important for German policy to drive a wedge between France and Britain. This could not be achieved by a demand for unconditional surrender or by the occupation of the whole territory. That would run the risk that the French government would refuse a truce, flee to North Africa and continue the fight from there, together with Britain. A golden bridge had therefore to be built so that the French regime would accept the conditions for the armistice. The goal was to take France out of the war – possibly its colonies as well – and to isolate Britain.

Meanwhile on 16 June, as the French government's official request for a truce became known, negotiations began in Rome between the German and Italian governments. It was arranged that Hitler and Mussolini should meet in Munich on 18 June to agree the conditions for an armistice with France. On the evening of the 17th Hitler, with Keitel, Ribbentrop and his assistants, flew to Frankfurt am Main, where his special train was in readiness. When this arrived in Munich on the morning of the 18th, Hitler and company drove through the jubilant crowds to the Führerbau on the Königsplatz.

That same morning he welcomed Mussolini at Munich station. After lunch at the Führerbau they conferred in Hitler's study. In the same room, barely two years before, on 29 September 1938, the 'historic' conference between Hitler, Mussolini, Chamberlain and Daladier had taken place. The consequences of the Munich Conference were plain: Hitler now occupied Czechoslovakia, Memel, Poland, Holland, Belgium, Denmark, and Norway and had annihilated France. These conquests had resulted in the deaths of hundreds of thousands of soldiers on the battlefields, in the ruin of countless buildings and in the hunger and misery of nations.

At the start of the conversations between Hitler and Mussolini a small group of officials were present: on the German side Ribbentrop and Keitel, on the Italian, Ciano. The second part of the conversations was conducted by the two of them alone. Immediately after the talks Hitler took Mussolini to the station and the latter left Munich. That very same evening Hitler returned to his HQ. After dinner on the train he gave a run-down of his dealings with Mussolini. He pointed to the exaggerated ambition of the Italian: the Duce was demanding the cession of Savoy, Nice, Corsica and Tunisia. With that he could secure hegemony over the Mediterranean. Hitler declared that he had been able to dampen Mussolini's ardour. He seemed content that the other had given in.

At midday on 19 June Hitler was in Frankfurt am Main again, whence he flew to his HQ at Brûly-de-Pesche. There he gave Keitel immediate orders to prepare the Monument to the Armistice for the coming negotiations with France. Already at the beginning of June 1940, when France's military collapse had become apparent, Hitler had expressed the idea of concluding the new armistice in the very place where Germany had been forced to capitulate on 7 November 1918, and thereby publicly annul the 1918 proceedings.*

On 20 June the text for the armistice with France was ready. Hitler personally dictated the so-called preamble to the document. As he conceived it, this had a double purpose: in the first place the French should psychologically agree to German demands because the courage and 'heroic struggle' of the French army was properly and respectfully acknowledged. Secondly, in his preamble, Hitler based German demands on the need to continue the war against Britain – so the thrust of the treaty was not against France, but against Britain.

On the evening of the same day Günsche† received an order from Hitler to be present at the negotiations in the woods of Compiègne in order to oversee his personal security. Günsche was to stand at the door of the glass partition between the compartments so that his height of almost two metres could be seen from all sides. He had orders to shoot any member of the French delegation who should dare to conduct himself in an improper manner towards Hitler. The start of the negotiations in Compiègne Woods was set for the morning of 21 June. It had to be adjourned, however, as the French delegation failed to reach Paris in time because the roads were crammed with troops and refugees.

On the morning of 21 June Keitel and Jodl drove in their car to the Monument to the Armistice. This historic site had been specially prepared for the negotiations. The railway carriage in which, following the German defeat in 1918, the Armistice with France had been signed had been fetched from the museum the French had built for it and taken to the same spot

---

*Negotiations had begun in Compiègne Woods on 7 November 1918 and were concluded with the Armistice on the 11th.

†Otto Günsche (1917–2003), 1931, entered Hitler Youth; 1934, Leibstandarte 'Adolf Hitler'; 1935, joined the Nazi Party; 1936, NCO in the Führer Escort Command; 1941–2, officers' school in Bad Tölz; January to August 1943, Hitler's personal adjutant; front-line service as company commander in the Leibstandarte 'Adolf Hilter'; February 1944–April 1945, Hitler's personal adjutant; taken prisoner by the Russians; 1950, sentenced to twenty-five years in a labour camp; 1955, released; delivered to the East Germans and imprisoned in Bautzen; 1956, released; fled to West Germany.

where it had been in November 1918. There it was placed on the tracks that were still maintained in the centre of the clearing. A second set of rails, on which the train of the German delegation had once stood, was now empty.

Nothing had been changed in the carriage itself. It was an ordinary dining car belonging to an international Pullman company that had been turned into a conference room. It contained a big table with chairs on both sides. Before the alley that led to the Monument to the Armistice there was a victory column that had been set up by the French featuring a fallen German eagle. This was now hung with swastikas. A guard of honour was stationed on the alley. Tents were erected containing an office, a telephone exchange and a telegraph station and were dotted around the woods.

Göring, Brauchitsch, Raeder, Ribbentrop and Hess arrived at midday. Hitler had summoned them to witness the solemn handing over of the other armistice conditions. Finally Hitler appeared in person. Posing like a monarch he strode up and down the guard of honour, inspected the monument draped with swastikas and a plaque announcing the French victory over Germany in November 1918. When it was learned that the French delegation was now approaching on the Paris road, Hitler, Göring, Brauchitsch, Raeder, Ribbentrop, Keitel, Hess and Jodl got into the carriage and took their seats at the table. The other side of the table was left free for the French delegation. Wearing a steel helmet and carrying a loaded pistol in his pocket, Günsche took up his post at the door leading to the neighbouring compartment. On his right stood Schmidt the interpreter.

At around 2.00 p.m. the French delegation appeared, accompanied by General von Tippelskirch.[15] It consisted of the leader of the delegation, army General Huntziger, General Parisot, of the land army, General Bergeret of the air force, Vice Admiral Le-Luc of the navy and Ambassador Noël. At the entrance to the alley, the French delegation got out of their car. They were led past the covered victory monument and the guard of honour to the carriage. When the delegation arrived, Hitler and his followers rose silently from their seats. The French were shocked: they had not expected to see the entire German leadership deployed before them. Silently and with a stern expression Hitler abruptly gestured that they should take their seats.

When they had all sat down, Keitel rose. Slowly and deliberately he fixed his monocle in his eye and began to read the preamble to the treaty. Schmidt translated it into French. Then Keitel gave the leader of the French delegation, General Huntziger, the text of the Armistice in German and French as well as a map of France on which the demarcation line between occupied and unoccupied French territory had been drawn. Now the ceremonial handing over of the Armistice conditions had come to an end. Hitler, Göring, Brauchitsch, Raeder, Ribbentrop and Hess rose and left the carriage. Keitel and Jodl remained behind in order to carry on the negotiations with the French delegation; with them were a few others and the interpreter Schmidt.

As Hitler stepped down from the carriage, an orchestra struck up the German national anthem. Keitel and the others in the carriage jumped up and raised their arms in the fascist salute. Keitel sang along loudly and the remaining Germans in the carriage also joined in. The French stood up too. A member of the French delegation had tears in his eyes. Hitler did not wait for the results of the negotiations but flew back to his HQ that very day.

After Hitler had left, Keitel asked the French to approve the text of the Armistice. At this Huntziger asked if he might be put in contact by telephone with the French government in Bordeaux. Keitel feared at this point that the negotiations might be protracted and he reacted evasively. He declared that the French delegation must be invested with the necessary powers to conclude the treaty itself. Huntziger stated that the French delegation possessed this authority but the conditions for the Armistice decided the fate of the French nation, and as a result it was necessary to inform the French government. He then reminded him that the German delegation in 1918 had been accorded permission to consult its government, and Keitel gave in.

Huntziger called the French Commander in Chief, General Weygand, in Bordeaux. Interpreter Schmidt listened in to the conversation. Weygand first asked where Huntziger was, and Huntziger replied, 'You can imagine.' Weygand replied, 'My poor friend!' Then Weygand inquired about the Armistice conditions. Huntziger answered that they were hard, and delivered them point by point. Weygand promised to give a clear answer as soon as he had informed Marshal Pétain.[16] The negotiations in the carriage continued.

In the course of these Huntziger asked Keitel what peace conditions Italy planned to impose. He expressed the fear that the Italian conditions might be difficult and unjust. Keitel was evasive in his reply: he didn't know the Italian conditions. The Franco-Italian negotiations would follow immediately after the signing of the Franco-German treaty. Heatedly, Huntziger replied that France didn't actually require a truce with Italy as one had existed *de facto* since Italy had declared war. Should Italian conditions damage France's honour the French regime would not accept them. At this General Huntziger's tone became particularly aggressive, and he stressed each word: 'We would not agree.' A piquant scene now took place. The Italian military attaché in Berlin turned up unexpectedly at the

Monument to the Armistice in Compiègne Woods and began to ask a German officer how the negotiations with the French were proceeding. Every effort was made to ensure that the Italian general was not seen by the French delegation.

On the evening of the 22nd, Keitel presented the French with an ultimatum. In a short memorandum he allotted General Huntziger an hour at the outside to inform him whether the French delegation was prepared to accept the Armistice conditions. In the event of their not accepting, the German delegation would conclude that the negotiations had been for naught, and the war would start up again in full measure. Huntziger relayed the contents of the memorandum to Pétain in Bordeaux. Half an hour passed before Huntziger declared that the French delegation was ready to sign the Armistice.

On 24 June Hitler invited Keitel, Jodl, Bormann, Hewel, his adjutants and a few other people from HQ to a dinner in the mess. He was in a splendid mood. He expressed his satisfaction at the way the war had gone so far, and displayed optimism on the subject of Britain. 'The western European problem has now been solved. All that remains for us now is to deal with the Soviet Union,' Hitler declared, rubbing his hands. Around midnight, Hitler's guests listened to a broadcast from Goebbels on the wireless that was enlivened from beginning to end by the sounds of battle. Listeners believed that it had been recorded at the front. In reality the noises had been produced in a recording studio in Berlin.

In October 1940, Hitler decided to meet Franco to discuss the possibility of Spanish participation in the war. The meeting was held in Hitler's train in the station at Hendaye near Biarritz. Hitler, Keitel, Franco, the Spanish Foreign Minister Serrano Súñer and the interpreter Schmidt took part in the discussions, which lasted around two hours.[*]

There were detailed discussions of a plan codenamed Isabella/Felix[†] worked out by the German General Staff for the conquest of the British fortress of Gibraltar. The following plans were aired:

- Two staffs would be formed: a technical staff under the command of the German General Lanz[17] and a supply staff led by the German General Jaenecke.

[*]The meeting took place on 23 October 1940.
[†]Felix foresaw a Spanish occupation of Gibraltar with German help; Isabella was conceived as a response to a possible British landing on the Iberian Peninsula. The goal was to drive the British from the European continent and to occupy Spain's and Portugal's harbours.

 — Fifteen German officers in mufti equipped with false passports and
   Spanish visas would be despatched to Spanish Morocco. Their mis-
   sion on behalf of the German General Staff would be to find out
   about the network of roads around Gibraltar and learn how suitable
   it was for German motorised units and artillery.
 — A Spanish division under the command of General Asensio would
   practise storming Gibraltar near Algeciras.
 — German gunnery crews in France would train north-west of
   Besançon by shelling cliffs similar to those in Gibraltar. The Spanish
   General Staff was to send its German counterpart samples of the
   stone from the Gibraltar fortress to be analysed by the army weapons
   office in Military High Command.

Keitel waxed lyrical about a gigantic gun from Krupp with a range of
almost 200 kilometres.[18] Hitler had decided to make it available to Franco
for the destruction of Gibraltar.

Isabella/Felix was supposed to be launched in January or February 1941,
but Hitler quickly threw out the plan and decided against Spain's open participation in the war because he had made up his mind to attack the Soviet
Union at the first opportunity.[*] Hitler declared that Spanish entry into the
war would make it necessary to defend the long coastline of the Iberian
peninsula against Anglo-American landings, which would tie down large
numbers of German forces. Besides this, Germany would be forced to
supply Spain with war material, fuel and food. After he took the decision
to attack Russia according to the Barbarossa Plan,[19] Hitler clearly had no
more interest in opening a new theatre on the Iberian peninsula. A policy
of benevolent neutrality towards Spain seemed preferable.

Behind the mask of neutrality Franco's Spain allowed German U-boats
and other warships to be repaired and refuelled in Spanish ports. Spain gave
support to the German Luftwaffe, which was attacking Anglo-American
ships in the Atlantic, and made its airfields and transmitting stations available. As far as the war economy was concerned, Spanish wolfram and
molybdenum ore played an important role in the German war effort. Apart
from that, Spain helped Germany circumvent the economic blockade by
importing deficit raw materials from America and sending them to
Germany. Reports from Admiral Canaris, the head of the Abwehr or military intelligence in the High Command, highlighted the assistance that the

[*]It was Franco who rejected Felix, as he did not want to be overly bound to Germany; nor
did he like the sound of Isabella.

Spanish regime gave: the Abwehr had been able to set up stations in many places in Spain with the connivance of Franco's government. German intelligence in Spain transmitted useful information to Berlin on the make-up of British land and sea forces and on the activities of British and American secret services in Spain and Spanish Morocco, on the ties between English and American circles to the highest echelons of Vichy France* and on the political mood among the Arab races in French Morocco.

After France had capitulated, the German High Command issued orders that plans were to be prepared for Operation Sea Lion, the invasion of Britain. The navy received the task of mustering and transferring the necessary material and of holding itself in readiness. To this end the army commanders were to collect all available sea and river craft in their areas.[20] The troops practised landings, and naval officers were attached to the Army High Command as advisers. At this time both air fleets – those commanded by Field Marshals Sperrle and Kesselring[21] – were concentrated in the west. While they worked out plans for Operation Sea Lion, the German High Command came to the conclusion that the most important factor in a successful landing in Britain would be German air superiority.[22] In Hitler's view and that of the German High Command, British naval superiority and German superiority in the air cancelled each other out. For that reason it was thought to be particularly important that the Luftwaffe should operate against the Royal Navy in the narrow English Channel, which is not more than 30 kilometres wide between Dover and Calais.

Hitler put off the date of the landings again and again, because he hoped that the threat of an invasion alone would persuade the English to conclude peace. He was of the opinion that the French defeat and the blow the British must have received at Dunkirk, together with the threat of an invasion, the U-boat war and a German Blitz would be enough to force the British to make peace. He said that if Churchill proved stubborn, however, he would bring Britain to its knees. But first he had to deal with the Soviet Union. When in the autumn of 1940 the preparations for an attack on Russia were intensified, Operation Sea Lion was used to conceal the imminent attack in the east and the realignment of forces there. Hitler

---

*France's Vichy government, based in the spa town of that name from 10 July 1940 and headed by Marshal Pétain, was formally independent under the Franco-German Armistice, though in reality it was careful to accommodate Germany. It controlled some 40 per cent of (unoccupied) France and introduced a number of fascist features to the state.

issued orders to continue with Operation Sea Lion throughout the winter in order to give the impression that the invasion of Britain would take place in the first months of 1941.

The day after Hitler's meeting with Franco, the Führer's train stopped at a small coaling station fifty kilometres north of Tours in southern France for a meeting with the Vichy French head of state, Pétain, and his premier, Laval.* In contrast to the arrogance with which Hitler had treated the French in Compiègne, he wanted to demonstrate his desire to co-operate politically with the Vichy regime. He drove off to meet Pétain and Laval in his car down a short stretch of road. He got out to wait for them, but Pétain and Laval were not slow in coming – the latter with his inevitable white tie.

Hitler was deferential towards the elderly Pétain in the same way as he had been towards Hindenburg in his time. Laval he treated like an ally. He asked Pétain amiably to get into his car. Pétain climbed in. He was already rather frail, but he nonetheless tried to look dashing and erect. Hitler joined him. Keitel and Laval took the second car, and they all drove to the station where Hitler's train was to be found. In Pétain's and Laval's honour a company of soldiers was standing waiting. Hitler and his French guests inspected them and then boarded the train. In Hitler's saloon car they settled down to talk. As well as Pétain and Laval, Keitel and the interpreter Schmidt took part. The discussion revolved around the problem of absorbing the whole of French industry into the German war effort and the question whether the Pétain regime would support Germany in its war against Britain. The talk lasted around two hours.

Hitler, Pétain and Laval reviewed the guard of honour once more. As he said goodbye, Hitler shook Pétain's hand heartily. An affable smile appeared on Laval's face. After their departure, Hitler went back to his carriage. He was in excellent spirits. At dinner he seemed especially proud that Laval, in the course of their talks, had compared him to Napoleon. As regards war with Britain, Laval had assured him of full support, but at the same time he declared that the common enemy, Soviet Russia, should not be forgotten and that the guns needed to be directed against this enemy straightaway. He then alluded to Napoleon's Russian campaign of 1812 and gave Hitler to understand that he would succeed where Napoleon had failed. Hitler described Laval as a shrewd politician and a loyal friend of the

*The meeting took place on 24 October 1940 at Montoire-sur-le-Loir, which is in the northern half of France.

German people. As a joke he said it might be better not to examine his racial purity: as a typical southern European he certainly would not pass. According to Hitler, Pétain had behaved like a 'defeated hero', which pleased him greatly. Around midnight Hitler's train started up on its journey across France to Munich.

In March 1941 Hitler had conversations with Göring in his Munich flat on the Prinzregentenplatz. Afterwards he wanted to drive to the Führerbau and asked Göring to accompany him. Since the attempt on Hitler's life in the Bürgerbräukeller in November 1939 they normally no longer drove together in the same car. Göring and Hitler were complicit in these security measures, which had the aim of making sure that 'Führer I' and 'Führer II' could not be liquidated simultaneously. Linge accompanied them on the drive to the Führerbau. In the car Hitler and Göring talked about the war with Russia. They were clearly continuing the conversation they had started in the flat. Hitler said that they should not wait any longer for the Russian war. Göring, on the other hand, was of the opinion that they needed to protect their backs against Britain first. Hitler declared categorically that the war with Russia was already decided, and as far as Britain was concerned, 'we'll deal with them later, if the stubborn Churchill fails to see sense'.

In March and April 1941 preparations for the attack on the Soviet Union were in full swing. Powerfully equipped troop formations from France, Belgium, Holland, Denmark and Norway that had been earmarked for Operation Sea Lion and the invasion of Britain were transferred to the Soviet border in the east. Elite Panzer divisions that had taken part in the occupation of Yugoslavia and Greece were hastily reformed and immediately set in motion towards the east where they were to play their part in the Blitzkrieg against the Soviets.*

In May 1941 Hitler returned to the Berghof from Mönichkirchen, south of Vienna, where he had been to observe the operations of German troops against Yugoslavia and Greece.† At around 10.00 a.m. his adjutant Albert Bormann[23] – the brother of Martin Bormann – and Hess's adjutant SA-Oberführer Pintsch[24] appeared in the antechamber to Hitler's study.

---

*To protect the Italians who were failing in their attempts to conquer Greece, Hitler ordered an attack in south-east Europe. Between April and June 1941 German troops invaded Yugoslavia and Greece.
†From 12 to 25 April 1941 Hitler was at his Frühlingssturm HQ near Mönichskirchen where, from his special train *Amerika*, he directed the Balkan campaign. After a short spell in Berlin he arrived at the Berghof on 10 May.

Pintsch was holding a sealed white envelope in his hand. Albert Bormann asked Linge to wake Hitler and to announce him, as he had an urgent letter from Hess to deliver. Linge knocked on the bedroom door. Hitler's sleepy voice could be heard asking, 'What is going on then?' Linge reported. Hitler answered, 'I am just coming.'

A few minutes later Hitler emerged unshaved from his study, which was connected to his bedroom. He walked up to Pintsch and asked him for Hess's letter. With the latter in his hand he hurried downstairs to the great hall. Linge, Pintsch and Bormann were still on the stairs when Hitler rang the bell. When Linge entered the hall Hitler was standing at the door with the open letter in his hand. 'Where is the man?' he snarled. Linge fetched Pintsch. Hitler asked him, 'Do you know what this letter contains?' Pintsch said yes. As he left the room, Linge saw Hitler and Pintsch go over to the big marble table. A few minutes later the bell rang again, Hitler was still standing at the table with Pintsch at his side. Hitler said, 'Bring Högl here.'

Högl was Chief of Police on Hitler's staff. Hitler ordered him to arrest Pintsch. Högl, who knew Pintsch well, seized him. Pintsch was aghast. As it later transpired, Pintsch told Högl that he had been convinced that Hess had flown to Britain with Hitler's knowledge and consent. As a result he could not fathom why he had been arrested. Hess had already taken Pintsch into his confidence at the end of January, revealing that he intended to fly to Britain in order to conclude the negotiations that had begun in August 1940. Pintsch knew from Hess that in August 1940 a meeting of British plenipotentiaries with the German Professor Haushofer had taken place in Geneva on the initiative of the Duke of Bedford and other influential British politicians.[25] Haushofer had been sent by Hess for preliminary talks.

During these talks the Britons had declared that their country was ready to begin peace talks with Germany. As a precondition they demanded the revocation of the non-aggression pact that Germany had concluded with the Soviet Union. Hess told Pintsch that he and Hitler were prepared to accept these British conditions; on the other hand, Hitler had postponed the start of proper negotiations with Britain until he had occupied the Balkans. From his talk with Hess, Pintsch was aware that Germany's policy at that time was concentrated on the preparations for war with Russia.

After Pintsch's arrest Hitler summoned Martin Bormann. He was Hess's chief of staff at the time. It was soon known that Hitler had appointed Bormann to Hess's position as his deputy in the Party. Those who knew Bormann well were aware that behind the deeply mournful face which he put on for appearances' sake he was extremely happy that his hour had come. 'What a hypocrite!' said one SS man to another. 'A vegetarian who feeds himself on smoked sausage' they called the freshly appointed successor to Hess, because he talked to Hitler about his vegetarian diet and when he went back to his villa he stuffed himself with fatty smoked sausage.

Following his talk with Bormann, Hitler summoned Göring and Ribbentrop to the Berghof. In the meantime, the Reich Press Chief Otto Dietrich, who was also staying there, was ordered to report to Hitler. Hitler directed Dietrich to inform him of everything the British had to say about Hess's flight. At the same time he forbade him to mention anything to the press. On the evening of 11 May, after Göring, Ribbentrop and Bormann had arrived at the Berghof, Hitler spoke to them. They sat together for a long time, ordering Dietrich to come to them several times to ask him whether he had heard anything from Britain. Nothing had been said about Hess. Late that evening Dietrich told them that British radio had announced that Hess had landed by parachute in a distant part of northern England.* He had told the policemen who took him into custody that he had come to pay a visit on his friend the Duke of Hamilton. Hitler quickly inquired whether the British had made any mention of the purpose of Hess's visit. Dietrich answered that there had been no talk of that. At that Hitler directed Dietrich to describe the flight in the German press as an act of insanity. It seeped out to Hitler's officials that the decision to declare Hess insane had come up in the course of Hitler's conversation with Göring, Ribbentrop and Bormann. When the announcement came from London that the Duke of Hamilton claimed to be unacquainted with Hess, Hitler blew up: 'What hypocrisy! Now he doesn't even want to know him!'

During discussions among Hitler's staff about Hess's flight it was said − under an oath of silence − that Hess had been carrying with him a memorandum outlining peace terms. Hess had drawn them up, and Hitler had approved them. The most important was that Britain would grant Germany a free hand in the Soviet Union, and in return would be guaranteed its colonial possessions and its hegemony in the Mediterranean. Apart from that the memorandum laid down plans for an alliance between the 'great continental power of Germany' and the 'great sea power of Britain' that would rule the whole world. In connection with this it was known that since February 1941 Hess had been working on economic and political proposals that would form the basis for negotiations with Britain. Other people involved were Bohle, head of the foreign organisation of the National Socialist Party, and Jagwitz, head of department in the Ministry

---

*Scotland.

of Finance, General Karl Haushofer and Hess's brother Alfred, who was Bohle's assistant.[26]

Adjutant Pintsch, whom Hitler had had arrested, was handed over to the Gestapo in Berlin. There he was asked to make a statement to the effect that he had noticed that Hess had shown signs of being psychologically disturbed in the days before his flight. After Pintsch had signed a written undertaking that he would say nothing about anything connected with Hess's flight to Britain, he was released – as the Gestapo told him – on Hitler's orders. After his release Pintsch, who had the equivalent rank of a general, was degraded to a simple soldier and sent to a punishment company in the east. It was clearly hoped in this way to get rid of a witness to this delicate affair. Pintsch, however, survived, and in December 1944 Hitler even consented to his being promoted from soldier to lieutenant.

Hess's wife was not arrested, but remained living on her estate. Hitler decreed that she be paid a considerable sum of money. She nonetheless corresponded with her husband. The letters passed under the eyes of Martin Bormann.

7

June 1941 – January 1942

In the first months of 1941 Hitler had put the entire heavy industry of France, Belgium, Holland, Czechoslovakia, Italy, Romania and the Balkans to work in preparation for the invasion of the Soviet Union. The industries of these countries were subordinated to Germany's planned aggression against Russia. After he had mobilised the enormous industrial and human resources of conquered Europe, Hitler dictated a speech in the Reich Chancellery on 22 June 1941 to mark the summoning of the Reichstag on the day of the attack on Russia. The secretaries Fräulein Daranowski and Fräulein Schroeder took shifts in Hitler's study. Hitler dictated until 5.00 a.m. The speech was copied for the press in the adjutants' room. Linge brought the pages out of Hitler's study every fifteen minutes. At five o'clock Hitler lay down to sleep. He rose again at 8.30 a.m.

Before his official performance, with raw voice and red eyes, Hitler delivered the weightiest passages out loud – those calculated to appeal to the German psyche – while he looked for the best intonation, gestures and mimicry. During this speech Hitler declared war on the Soviet Union. At about 10.00 in the morning of 22 June, Hitler, dressed in a grey military tunic, drove to the session of the Reichstag in the Kroll Opera House. Before he left the Chancellery, Morell administered an injection of stimulants. Around 11.00 a.m Berlin time, the world learned of the German attack on Soviet Russia, despite the non-aggression pact concluded between the two countries. Hitler hypocritically declared before the Reichstag that, after long reflection, he had reached the decision to anticipate the threat from the east.

That same day Hitler travelled from the Stettin station to East Prussia and his specially commissioned headquarters in a wood near Rastenburg. On his orders once again it had been baptised with the name of the savage animal – Wolfsschanze or Wolf's Lair. Hitler, who had so suddenly exposed the 'danger of an attack from the east', found in an area of two square kilometres near Rastenburg numerous concrete bunkers and wooden huts, which had been already standing for a year and a half. The construction of the HQ near Rastenburg had been decided before the French campaign, as part of the preparations for attacking the Soviet Union.[1] Hitler's staff happily took up residence in their new home. On the way they had received a stream of reports on how the attack on their wholly unwitting[*] Russian neighbours was proceeding.

Everyone expected a lightning victory. Hitler's regime tried to drive it home to every German that the Russian campaign was a Blitzkrieg. Hitler's officials had attended special lectures in which the Red Army had been portrayed as weak, cumbersome and inadequately equipped. The Soviet staff was characterised as inexperienced. When Hitler received the situation reports on German troop movements in the Soviet Union he hurried over to the mess where a map of Russia was hanging on the wall. With a victorious expression and a thick red pencil in his hand he drew in the positions of the Wehrmacht. He then spent a long time with the generals and officers at his HQ.

At the end of August 1941 Mussolini accepted Hitler's invitation to come to the Wolfsschanze.[†] He was received with great pomp. Hitler almost exploded with pride and self-satisfaction, and Mussolini congratulated him exuberantly. At the time Mussolini had sent Italian troops to the Eastern Front, who were then on the march near Uman. Hitler and Mussolini flew east[‡] in a Focke-Wulf 200[2] and landed at a military airport near Uman. A long table had been set up for them in the open air. In a hangar near by the position of the armies was explained to Hitler on big operational maps by Rundstedt, Chief of Army Group South, the Panzer commander Kleist and the commander of the Luftwaffe in the Ukraine, Löhr.[3]

After the report Hitler and Mussolini wanted to see the Italian Blackshirts. They set out in ten Krupp all-purpose vehicles. In the first was Hitler's army adjutant, Major Engel,[4] who showed them the way. He had a photo-reporter with him, sent by Hoffmann. The second vehicle was decorated with the standards of the Führer and the Duce. Here sat Hitler and Mussolini, together with Schmundt, Linge and Dollmann. The latter was employed as an interpreter with Mussolini and permanently stationed in Italy, where he had been sent by the German Foreign Office. On the way Hitler presented his 'new possessions'. 'Look, Duce,' he said, and pointed to the fields of black earth. 'Here is the most fertile soil on earth.

---

[*]Unwitting they were not: they had received plenty of indications from their intelligence.
[†]He arrived on 25 August 1941.
[‡]On 28 August 1941.

Your Italians must toil to work their stony soils. Here, however, are huge regions with this kind of rich earth. This is going to be the breadbasket of the new Europe.'

Hitler's cavalcade reached a point where two wide roads crossed. The Italian division was supposed to march past Hitler and Mussolini here,[5] but it was late. They decided to drive towards it, and soon they could make out in the distance the forward units of the Italian Blackshirts. Hitler and Mussolini prepared themselves for the encounter, parking their vehicle at the side of the road. The commander seated in the car at the front and the first lorries filled with Italian troops, however, assumed that Hitler and Mussolini would be waiting at the agreed place and drove past them without noticing. Soon, however, soldiers recognised Mussolini and greeted him with loud cries. The divisional commander sprang from his vehicle and ran over to Hitler and Mussolini, holding on to his steel helmet that was bouncing up and down on his head. He was completely out of breath when he finally stood to attention before Hitler's car. It was clear that he was too flustered to know to whom he should report, Hitler or Mussolini. Hitler gestured towards Mussolini. While the SS men from Hitler's bodyguard in the background grinned at the 'elegant' Italian general's confusion, Mussolini listened to the stammered report with a serious expression on his face.

The division set out anew. The Italian soldiers in their lorries sang a sort of tarantella. 'Just look at the Duce,' Hitler's bodyguards said to one another with a wink, 'he stands there like Caesar in person.' Visibly moved by the inspection of his troops, with extravagant gestures Mussolini assured Hitler on the way back that he would send more Italian divisions to the Eastern Front, and naturally only the best ones.

The SS Leibstandarte 'Adolf Hitler' had been on the Eastern Front since the beginning of the Soviet–German campaign. Before marching east it had been hastily transferred from Greece to Brno in Czechoslovakia, where it was brought up to strength and prepared for the attack on Russia. At the end of June 1941, the Leibstandarte crossed the German–Soviet frontier east of the city of Lublin. As a motorised infantry division, it was incorporated in the Panzer army commanded by General von Kleist and had the task, with one Panzer corps, of breaking through in the direction of Rovno–Zhitomir.

The Leibstandarte had been issued with special orders for the Russian war, which the company commanders had read during training for crossing the Russian border. According to these orders the Russian campaign was to be fought under the slogans: 'Bash the Russians' brains in, then you will be absolutely sure of them!'; 'You are the absolute lords of these lands! The life and death of the population lie in your hands'; 'We need the Russian expanses without Russians!'

The SS men in the Leibstandarte were ordered to level Russian towns and villages. They would acquire such a terrible reputation that the Leibstandarte's very name would inspire dread and horror in the Russian mind. It was drummed into them that the Leibstandarte should leave only scorched earth behind as it marched through Russia. Should the Führer arrive in the area, it should be immediately clear to him that his Leibstandarte had been through. In a village near Rovno on the march to Kiev, the Leibstandarte encountered strong resistance from a unit of Russian guards.* The place could be taken only when all the division's tanks and artillery were brought to bear. In reprisal for the Russian resistance, around twenty old men, women and children who had been left behind were executed. They were herded together and shot from the armoured cars of the reconnaissance battalion. The village was burned to the ground.

As the Leibstandarte proceeded in the middle of July it came up against a heavy Russian counter-attack that threatened its left wing. The battle raged for a whole week and was fought with great ferocity on both sides. Already on the first day the Leibstandarte commander, Sepp Dietrich, issued orders that no prisoners were to be taken – they were to be shot on the spot. Everywhere special commando units were trained in the task of systematically putting every house in conquered villages to the torch and 'smoking out' any inhabitants who were hidden in cellars or shelters.

At the beginning of August, the Leibstandarte swung into Uman. Although hardly six weeks had gone by since the attack on Soviet Russia, the regiment had already suffered heavy losses that exceeded its casualties in the campaigns in Poland, France and Greece. In the companies there was a dearth of munitions carriers and, under threat of death, Russian POWs and civilians replaced them. On Dietrich's orders, the Russian carriers had to be of a certain racial type, as they had to move among SS men; in other words they had to be blond and blue-eyed. In battle they had the task of bringing up ammunition, and many of them were killed by enemy fire. With malicious pleasure the SS men said, 'These Ivans have died for the Greater Germany.' In the fighting near Kherson, the dog belonging to Sturmbannführer Meyer, commander of the Reconnaissance Battalion,

---

*Elite units were constituted only after 18 September 1941. These were not 'guards'.

was killed by shrapnel. To avenge the dead creature, Meyer assembled thirty peaceful inhabitants and shot them with his own hands.

When at the beginning of September German troops reached the Dnieper on a wide front, the Leibstandarte was transferred to fill in an area south of Dnepropetrovsk. Where their units marched in, those inhabitants who had survived the artillery barrage were herded into barns like cattle. Every day they were sent out to perform the most menial jobs and were horribly beaten. All that they possessed the SS men took away with them.

In the middle of September, Günsche, who was serving with the SS on the Eastern Front, travelled from the Dnepropetrovsk region back to the SS Officer School at Bad Tölz in Bavaria. On the way he made a detour to Hitler's HQ at the Wolfsschanze, as he wanted to visit his friends in Hitler's bodyguard, in which he had served from 1936 to 1941 before he was transferred to a unit of the Leibstandarte. To Schaub and other comrades he expressed his astonishment at how massive and grandiose this HQ was in comparison to the others in the west. Günsche asked whether Hitler planned to spend the winter there. Everybody had to laugh. Schaub declared pompously, 'Spend the winter? What are you thinking of? We are fighting a Blitzkrieg against Russia. Christmas we will certainly be celebrating on the Obersalzberg as usual.'

When Hitler heard that Günsche had arrived from the Eastern Front, he had him brought to his bunker, where he received him in his conference room. As Günsche came in, Hitler walked straight up to him with giant strides, whistling gently to himself. He was in a magnificent mood. He offered Günsche his hand and said, 'So, Günsche, how are you? What are Dietrich and my Leibstandarte up to?' Günsche gave his report, declaring that morale among the SS men was excellent, that they enjoyed making war in Russia, but that the Russians were stubbornly resisting. 'We will break them soon, it is only a question of time,' replied Hitler. 'I have ordered Panzer armies with over two thousand tanks to group before Moscow. Moscow will be attacked and will fall, then we will have won the war.'

Hitler told Günsche that he did not intend conquering the whole of Russia. The first priority was to annihilate active forces and to occupy fertile areas. When the German forces reached the Urals the signal to stop would be given. The rest of Russia could starve. Should the Russians try to reassemble their forces on the far side of the Urals he had a powerful Luftwaffe to deal with them. Hitler concluded: 'As the reformer of Europe I shall make sure that a new order is imposed on this land according to my laws!' With these last words his face had turned red. He dismissed Günsche with a fascist salute.

★

In November 1941, with the Russian bombardments the position of the German troops dug in before Moscow had become more critical with every day that passed. In the reports from the Eastern Front that Linge delivered to Hitler, there was ever more talk of stubborn resistance on the part of the enemy. Linge, who knew Hitler's moods, observed that he had become increasingly irritable. During the situation reports in particular, he laid into Halder, Brauchitsch and Keitel. These meetings took place daily at midday in Keitel's bunker at the Wolfsschanze.

On one of the first days of December Hitler's voice could be heard coming from the conference room. He was speaking on the telephone to Guderian[6], the general commanding the Panzer army before Moscow. Hitler bellowed into the receiver, 'Guderian! Maintain your positions at any price! I shall send you reinforcements! I will mobilise everything I have! Just stick it out, whatever you do – stick it out!' A few minutes later reports came in that Guderian was retreating. The story went round the officers of Hitler's bodyguard that the Führer was not happy with his General Staff.

The conferences on the situation on the Eastern Front became ever stormier. Hitler screamed, thumped his fists on the table and accused the generals of being incapable of fighting. The latter often lurched out of the conference room into the corridor of the bunker in order to pull themselves together after a broadside of curses from Hitler. Once the Supreme Commander of the Northern Army Group, Field Marshal von Leeb, appeared in the corridor in the middle of a conference. He strode back and forth in a visible state of agitation. Linge and Keitel's adjutant Gabriel were in the next-door room, awaiting Hitler's orders as usual. Leeb stood in the door and said to Gabriel, 'What am I supposed to do, then, if the Führer no longer believes me?'

The defeat before Moscow and the unsuccessful blockade of Leningrad led to a worsening of relations between the Waffen SS and the Wehrmacht. SS men accused the Wehrmacht of lacking real aggression and using officer-school methods. From the Wehrmacht's side, they complained that the SS units had the pick of the weaponry and equipment and enjoyed a special position in the armed forces. On both sides there were accusations of arrogance.

The steadfast defence of Leningrad made Hitler livid. He had wanted to win by attrition. Spitting with rage he shouted, 'I shall reduce this city to its foundations and wipe out its population! Leningrad will never rise again! I swear a holy oath on this!' When he had calmed down a little, he repeated many times over this period, 'Anyone can deal with victory. Only the mighty can bear defeat!' The Supreme Commander of the Army,

Brauchitsch, was no longer to be seen in the Führer HQ after the Moscow débâcle. He was meant to be ill, but no one was taken in by that.* Schmundt informed officials at HQ ambiguously that Brauchitsch was on leave for health reasons and that the Führer had taken over command of the army himself. Apart from Brauchitsch, Hitler dismissed at this time the Chiefs of the Panzer armies, Guderian and Hoepner[7], the Supreme Commander of the Northern Army Group, Leeb, and other generals.

When the Japanese attacked the American fleet at Pearl Harbor on 7 December 1941, Hitler's HQ took heart again. The defeats of the German armies before Moscow and Leningrad were forgotten. Germany declared war on the United States of America.† On this day the discussion at lunch revolved around America's fighting abilities. Halder was scornful, drawing from his experiences in the First World War. American officers could stand no comparison to Prussians – they were businessmen in uniform who shivered for their lives. In the art of war they had a long way to go.

A few days later Schmundt turned up in Linge's room to drink a little glass of schnapps with him, as was his wont. A few minutes later Hitler appeared. He occasionally dropped in on Linge to listen to popular music on his radio. Hitler received the latest report from the fronts, then sat down at the desk and asked for his spectacles. It was reported that German submarines had sunk American ships. 'Read that, Schmundt,' Hitler told his military adjutant. 'Do you see how good this open war against America is for us? Now we can really strike.' He pointed out that the Americans were tied down in the Pacific theatre. This led one to hope that German submarines could even more effectively disturb the provisioning of Britain from the US. Hitler leaned right back and poured out his contempt for the Americans. He pointed out that an American car had never won an international tournament; that American aircraft looked fine, but their motors were worthless. This was proof for him that the much lauded industries of America were terribly overestimated. They didn't really have to perform well, only in an average way, and benefited from lots of discounting.

After Hitler and Schmundt had left, the head of Hitler's personal protection squad, Schädle,[8] popped in to see Linge. He began to talk about the situation on the Eastern Front and about how bad it was. He remarked that it had been a long time since Hitler had been at the front. The troops should see their Führer. 'For the hundredth time, what does the boss get

---

*He was dismissed on 19 December 1941.
†On 11 December 1941.

up to the whole time?' asked Schädle. Linge knew what Hitler got up to, but he held his tongue. Hitler spent his time hearing situation reports, gossiping with the photographer Hoffmann and his chums, reading adventure stories, drawing incomprehensible designs, because he saw himself as a great artist, skiving off in the evenings with Schaub, because the latter showed him colour slides of naked French dancers, or taking his dog – the Scottish terrier Burli, which Bormann had acquired for him – for walks. In the HQ the little dog was known as 'the Greater German Imperial Hound' because of its diminutive size.

At the beginning of December 1941 Hitler's bodyguard saw their wish finally fulfilled: Schmundt gave orders that a plane be prepared to fly to the front at Taganrog. That was almost 2,000 kilometres from HQ. The weather was cold and misty and Hitler's pilot Baur thought conditions unfavourable for such a journey. Keitel visited the Führer in his bunker and began to plead with him, in the submissive tone that he always adopted when speaking to him, to cancel his flight to the front because of the bad weather. 'No! No!' Hitler interrupted him. 'It is now very important that they hold their positions in the south. Even my Leibstandarte is retreating. I absolutely must fly.' In a servile voice, Keitel tried to explain to Hitler that he feared that something might happen to him. 'You are the only man, my Führer – it all depends on you!' Hitler was flattered and replied, 'All right, let's see what the weather is like tomorrow.'

Hitler decided to fly to Taganrog the next day.* At around midday his plane landed in Poltava. He, Schmundt, Morell and Linge got into a Heinkel bomber and flew to Mariupol escorted by fighters. The aircraft shook terribly, and Hitler looked pale and miserable. He was received at the airfield by Reichenau[9] and Kleist. They drove from there to a barracks where the army staff was housed.

In a dimly lit corridor in the staff building Linge ran into a man wearing a sheepskin and a fur hat ornamented with an SS deathshead. 'Comrades, you have finally come!' he exclaimed. It was Sepp Dietrich, the commander of the SS Leibstandarte 'Adolf Hitler'. He asked where the Führer was, and was taken straight to him. The SS men who had come with Dietrich told Linge that the Russians gave them no peace. They vented their fury on Wehrmacht Command and expressed the hope that Hitler would show himself to the troops to raise morale.

---

*He flew to Mariupol on 2 December 1941 and drove with Sepp Dietrich to Taganrog.

But Hitler contented himself with a visit to the army staff. He left orders that the Donetz basin be held at all cost and the following morning flew back to Poltava. As a result of bad weather, there was an unavoidable delay. Reichenau, who left Mariupol at the same time as Hitler and whose staff was based in Poltava, was nowhere to be seen. There was no available telephone connection with the Wolfsschanze near Rastenburg, and Hitler was plainly nervous. For a whole hour he waited in great excitement in the over-heated office of the airfield commander. Finally Reichenau walked in. His pilot had been unable to find the airfield, he explained, and the weather was frightful – zero visibility – and extremely cold. Hitler immediately accepted Reichenau's invitation to his home.

The next day he returned to his comfortable HQ where he was happily greeted by Keitel. Hitler was very pleased with his act of heroism.

8

February 1942 – February 1943

After a meeting with Hitler at the Wolfsschanze in early 1942 Fritz Todt, the Reich Minister for Armaments and Munitions, lost his life in mysterious circumstances.* The minister's aircraft exploded at a height of around thirty metres after taking off from Rastenburg airfield. Todt and the crew were burned to death. The cause of the explosion remained unexplained. In Hitler's HQ a number of rumours circulated that it had been the work of foreign secret agents.

Hitler named the architect Albert Speer as Todt's successor. It was a job for a liaison man between the captains of industry and the High Command. Speer was often to be seen at the Führer's HQ. When he arrived on the courier train that shuttled backwards and forwards between the capital and an HQ, he often waited in Linge's room until Hitler awoke. He also made telephone calls while he was there, speaking to his assistant Saur or with the Army Weapons Office. There were often angry exchanges between his ministry, the military leadership and the industrial concerns over the division of the spoils in the east.

Once when Schaub was in Linge's room, he complained of the difficulties in distributing captured industrial companies and sources of raw materials in occupied Russia. Speer said the industrialists were chiefly concerned with their own profits. Representatives of big business followed behind the armies and requested that plundered companies and materials be handed over to them. Krupp, Röchling and the other heavy-industry magnates demanded the lion's share for themselves because they wished to turn it over to the service of the Fatherland. In Speer's opinion Hitler needed to call a meeting with the industrialists immediately, at the very least to bring a little order to the war economy. It was particularly necessary that the German High Command should attack the Caucasus in order to capture the oil fields at Baku. At Speer's suggestion, Hitler invited

*He died on 8 February 1942.

the major industrialists to his HQ in May 1942.* The following came: Dr Hermann Röchling, Chief of the Reich Iron Organisation, Dr Albert Vögler, President of the board of the United Steelworks, Dr Walter Rohland, leader of the Main Panzer Committee, Erich Müller, Managing Director of Krupps and the right hand of Krupp, the armaments king, Paul Pleiger, Chairman of the board of the Hermann-Göring Works, as well as President of the United Coal board, and others.[1]

Hitler invited his guests to lunch before the meeting . The table groaned under the weight of rare delicacies, products that Reichskommissar Koch – the former Gauleiter of East Prussia – had procured in the Ukraine for the HQ. When the subject of production capacities in the armaments industry came up at lunch, the industrialists began to complain of a lack of manpower. Hitler asked what impression the French workers sent by Pétain's government had made. The industrialists answered that the French worked well, but that there were too few of them. Then the discussion turned to the use of Russian POWs as labour. Hitler asked how well the Russians worked. The industrialists replied that the Russians tried to dodge work: they had to be treated with force and closely watched.

One of them observed that the Russians smoked heavily and that tobacco should be handed out as an encouragement. Hitler replied that he would issue instructions immediately that 'tobacco' would be produced out of weeds from the fields and woods as a prize for good work among Russian POWs. The industrialists demanded an augmentation in the number of Russian POWs assigned to businesses. Hitler assured them that he would personally look into it, that industry should receive enough POWs and peaceful citizens from Russia as manpower. He declared conceitedly that the next offensive on the Eastern Front would yield so many prisoners that industry wouldn't know what to do with them all.

After the meal, Hitler went with them to the tea-house where there was a large conference room. Wine, champagne, cognac and Havana cigars were laid out for the industrialists. The discussion took place behind closed doors in the strictest secrecy.

That same month Hitler invited Antonescu to his HQ.[†] He was put up in the solitary guest bunker, and Hitler had his talks with him there, with Schmidt acting as interpreter (Antonescu spoke French). Schmundt and

*On 6 May 1942 Speer created an Armaments Council on which officers and industrialists sat. Hitler received them at the Wolfsschanze on 18 May.
[†]The Romanian dictator Ion Antonescu came on 11 February 1942.

Linge waited on Hitler at the door while the discussion, which was very lively, took place. It concerned the use of Romanian troops at the siege of Stalingrad. Antonescu promised Hitler that he would make a large contingent available, but pointed out that Romanian units were badly armed.[2] Hitler asked the exact number of weapons the Romanians required. Antonescu replied that he did not have the precise figures on him, but would transmit them immediately on his return to Bucharest. After the meeting, Antonescu took part in Hitler's conference. The next day Hitler accompanied him to the airport, where he said goodbye to him with particular warmth.

Soon after Antonescu flew home the Romanian requests for armaments arrived at HQ. During lunch in the mess Hitler told Keitel and Jodl that the Romanians had made outrageous demands. He had no intention of satisfying them. 'I need those weapons myself,' said Hitler. 'I will pay for their petrol with cars, motorbikes, bicycles and possibly even with prams, but not with weapons. They wouldn't know what to do with German weapons.' Keitel told Hitler what he wanted to hear, that the Romanians would have asked for far more weapons than they needed. Hitler opined that they wanted either to make a profit or perhaps to create reserves so that they could attack the Hungarians after the war. In this connection Hitler made fun of the Vienna Accord[3] that had obliged Romania to cede Transylvania to Hungary. Hitler made no bones about it: the dispute between Hungary and Romania over Transylvania played into his hands. It gave him the opportunity to act as umpire and to stir them up in the war against the Soviet Union, because the Hungarians wanted Transylvania and the Romanians a revision of the Vienna Accord.

In the same conversation, Hitler recounted his talk with the Hungarian Regent Horthy before the war with Soviet Russia and imitated the latter's Viennese dialect. When Hitler had requested that Horthy join the war against the Soviet Union, the other replied, 'We are armed in spirit, but not in *matériel*.' Everybody laughed.

As the southern sector of the Eastern Front became the focal point of the war at the end of June 1942, Hitler's HQ was transferred to the Ukraine.[*] It was now located several kilometres away from Vinnitsa in a strip of wood. At Hitler's direction it was named Wehrwolf (or Armed Wolf).[4] In the immediate neighbourhood were both Göring's and the Army High Command's staffs. Himmler had set up his HQ on the outskirts of Zhitomir.

---

[*]Hitler moved his HQ to Vinnitsa on 16 July 1942.

When Hitler arrived at Wehrwolf Colonel Thomas,[5] the HQ commander, was waiting for him. Hitler, Thomas, Schmundt and Linge went into the antechamber of the house. There hung here a map of the European part of the Soviet Union painted on wood. The positions reached by German forces were marked with arrows. Hitler liked the way the map was made and went up close to get a better view. With his finger pointing at Rostov and Stalingrad he told Thomas, 'You will soon need to make some corrections to this map. We are going to give them a blow that brings them to their knees! The whole world will sit up!'

Thomas took Hitler over the terrain around the HQ and showed him the security measures. The area was surrounded by a defensive strip of bunkers, anti-aircraft guns and tanks, as well as anti-tank ditches and minefields. Rattenhuber,[6] Hitler's head of security, had formed a special group of RSD* men whose job was to watch the approaches to the HQ and to keep an eye on the local population. Thomas continued his report: in order to increase the vigilance of the headquarters personnel, a rumour had circulated the night before Hitler's arrival that a Russian wearing the uniform of a German major had managed to get into the camp with the idea of murdering Hitler. Hitler gave an approving nod and asked, 'Who built the camp?' Thomas answered, 'Mostly Russians prisoners from the camps.' Hitler's face darkened. He told Thomas, 'They must all be shot. There is not a moment to lose. They know too much about my HQ.'† Thomas clicked his heels and answered, 'At your command, my Führer.' He turned on his heels and went.

As a supplementary security measure at HQ, Himmler had formed a special unit called 'Reichsführer SS' at his HQ in Zhitomir which regularly combed the area for partisans.‡ In autumn 1942 partisans ambushed the car of Sturmbahnführer Schnäbele, Himmler's pilot. Schnäbele was sitting in the car together with another officer and two Russian women whom they were driving back to their quarters. The partisans killed Himmler's pilot and the other officer. When their bodies were found, Himmler ordered that the whole area be searched. The partisans were never found. Himmler reported to Hitler, who instructed that all the innocent inhabitants of the villages around should be shot. One of Himmler's units undertook the shooting of

*The RSD (Reichssicherheitsdienst), the Reich security service, had been formed under Rattenhuber to protect the Nazi top brass. It answered to the Gestapa, not to the SD.
†Eight thousand members of the Todt Organisation and 2,000 Russian forced labourers were used in the construction of the camp. There is no report of a mass extermination.
‡Begleitbataillon Reichsführer-SS. It later became the 16th SS Panzergrenadier Division and was responsible for numerous war crimes in Italy.

the Russian citizens. There were heart-wrenching scenes: women who begged for mercy were beaten back with rifle butts and then shot; children who buried their heads in their mothers' skirts were torn away from them and shot before their mothers' eyes. The bodies of the murdered men, women and children were thrown into ditches that had been dug for that purpose. SS men from Hitler's bodyguard came over from Vinnitsa to witness this orgy of retribution.

On the first day after his arrival at Vinnitsa HQ Hitler was in a victorious mood again. He ordered Linge to bring him writing equipment, drawing instruments and atlas, a magnifying glass and a coloured map showing Russia's mineral deposits. He was very excited. He pointed to Rostov and said to his ADC Schmundt, 'Yes, Schmundt, when we possess this area then I can carry on with the war without worry.' His finger wandered further towards the Caucasus: 'And we shall get our oil from here, which we so urgently need.' With his finger, he pointed to an area around Astrakhan on the Caspian. 'This is where I shall cut the Russia aorta, and then it is over,' Hitler finally said, placing particular stress on the word 'over'.

In the last June days of 1942 the Germans began their offensive in the Causcasus and in the direction of Stalingrad. There was an optimistic atmosphere at Hitler's HQ. A lot of schnapps was drunk and the rich food played its role. This was down to the Reichskommissar for the Ukraine, Koch, who filled the pantries of Hitler's HQ with provisions he had stolen from the Ukrainian people. The roads leading to Vinnitsa were constantly plied by lorries carrying provisions. Under German guard, Ukrainian peasants brought flour, butter, bacon, eggs, poultry and cattle into the HQ camp. Hitler's adjutant Schaub administered a special supply of provisions that in accordance with the Führer's directions was sent to his friends and old National Socialists in Germany. Hitler had given Linge the job of providing for Eva Braun in Munich, and food was sent to her by special courier. Above all she wanted more Ukrainian bacon, which she particularly liked. Koch not only looked after the Führer's HQ with his deliveries, but also serviced the Reich Chancellery in Berlin and Hitler's Berghof mansion on the Obersalzberg. An enormous quantity of flour, sugar, butter, bacon, meat, eggs and poultry went to those two places.

In July 1942 Alfred Rosenberg, the newly appointed Reichsminister for Occupied Territory in the East, arrived at Hitler's HQ near Vinnitsa in an operatic brown uniform with lots of gold trimmings. Rosenberg was a German Balt. As the 'ideologist' of the National Socialist Party he had unlimited power in the field of fascist thought. His practical and organisational abilities, however, were not greatly respected by his entourage.

After Rosenberg it was the turn of the puffed-up 'lords' of occupied Soviet Russia, who were all jealous of one another: Erich Koch, known as 'The Emperor of the Ukraine', Wilhelm Kube, a drunken lecher who had been Gauleiter of the Mark Brandenburg and was now Hauptkommissar for White Ruthenia, and Hinrich Lohse, the portly former Gauleiter of Schleswig-Holstein, who was now Reichskommissar for the Eastern Territories. They were followed by the Reichsminister for Agriculture and Provisions, Backe, and the State Secretary in the Reich Transport Ministry, Ganzenmüller.[7] The last to come – as pompous as ever – was Göring. He wore a dove-blue field marshal's uniform that was hung with innumerable medals and waved a gold and ivory marshal's baton.

Hitler had called them together to talk about the food situation in Germany. He wanted to stop transporting provisions from Germany to troops at the Eastern Front and to feed them from supplies garnered in occupied Russia. The assembly waited to be allowed in to Hitler's presence. They were joined by Bormann, and got talking about the black market in Germany that had grown larger and larger in recent times. Göring told Backe, 'Everything is trafficked. If they sent you to prison for trafficking they would have to put the whole of Germany in gaol. That is not the problem. The problem is getting everything from Russia. Then we would have no more worries about the black market.'

After a little while Linge, who was standing with them, was summoned to see Hitler. He came back quickly and announced, 'The Führer is waiting for you.' Göring tumbled into Hitler's blockhouse first. Rosenberg was right behind, but Koch caught up with him and overtook his minister. The last man in was Bormann, who significantly took up his place next to Hitler in order to show all those present the power he had acquired since Hess's flight to Britain.

After they had dealt with the question of provisions, Hitler demanded an increase in the number of workers from occupied territories that were to be sent to German industry – he said he had promised the industrialists that he would deliver manpower. He directed Bormann to call Sauckel, who had arrived at Führer HQ that day and on Hitler's instructions was waiting in Bormann's house. Fritz Sauckel, the Gauleiter of Thuringia, had built the concentration camp at Buchenwald near Weimar and already possessed sufficient experience of forced labour.[8] Hitler made him responsible for the mass deportation of the populations of the Soviet Union and occupied Europe to Germany.

Once Sauckel had arrived, Bormann left to prepare his letter of appointment. Hitler corrected the text twice before signing it. From this moment onward the fate of millions of people – Russians, Ukrainians, White Russians, Latvians, Lithuanians, Estonians, Poles, Czechs, Frenchmen, Belgians, Dutch, Serbs and Greeks – lay in the hands of the Lord of Buchenwald. As Bormann collected Sauckel's signed letter of appointment from Hitler he declared, 'This is a triumph for the National Socialist Party.'

In the autumn of 1942 morale was very low at HQ. As a result of the stubborn resistance of the Russians, the troops commanded by General Paulus[9] at Stalingrad had ground to a halt. List's tank offensive in the Causcasus had fizzled out: [10] after some initial success, he remained stuck in the hills and so was unable to carry out Hitler's order to proceed along the Black Sea coast to Tiflis and to take the oil fields in Baku. When Hitler reported in the course of a briefing that units of List's forces had reached the to the peak of Mount Elbrus and raised the swastika, he added with bitter mockery, 'Did they want to match the sporting prowess of the British?'[11] Hitler relieved List of his command without even receiving him in person. Next he summoned the Chief of the General Staff, Halder, and asked him whether he should not take extended leave for the sake of his health. Halder was with Hitler for ten minutes, then he went on 'leave'.[12]

Hitler now completely withdrew himself from the generals and spent his time in isolation. He would not go to the mess with them any more, and ate his lunch alone in his study. In the evenings he asked Linge to put on gramophone records of funeral music. He picked up books like *I Claudius, Emperor and God*,[13] which described the gruesome struggles around the throne of the Roman emperor, or a work on the campaigns of the Holy Roman Emperor Friedrich Hohenstaufen in the thirteenth century. Besides he was in a highly irritable state. A fly on the wall could send him into a rage and he would be beside himself with fury at the appearance of a harmless butterfly. Everything was done to prevent flies, midges or butterflies from coming near him. His quarters were fitted with mosquito nets, while every morning soldier-servants did the rounds with fly-swatters and killed every insect they could find. On the table there were glasses filled with honey, and fly-papers hung from the ceiling. In the corridor and outside the house there were high-powered blue lamps wrapped in wire netting designed to destroy the insects.

Hitler asked Bormann to acquire a German shepherd dog for him, having sent his Scottish terrier to Eva Braun's mother in Munich. He named the new German shepherd 'Blondi' like her predecessor, whom he had had shot at the Berghof because she had grown too old.

Hitler directed Bormann to prepare typed minutes of the situation reports. As he no longer trusted the generals, every word that was spoken had to be recorded. To this end stenographers and other personnel were brought in* who had previously taken the minutes in the Reichstag, in ministerial Cabinets or in the offices of the National Socialist Party. In Bormann's presence they swore a personal oath to Hitler to maintain the strictest silence over the contents of the minutes. There were always two stenographers on duty at any time, who wrote down Hitler's every word and those of the other participants. The stenographers and other personnel were lodged in a special house in the camp that was strictly guarded, and the minutes were kept there under lock and key. Only Bormann, Scherff,[14] a colonel on the General Staff to whom Hitler had given the job of writing the history of the war, and the Führer's adjutants were allowed access. Hitler feared that the minutes might be stolen or altered.

Hitler promoted his ADC Schmundt to general major and named him head of the Army Personnel Office. One September Schmundt came into Linge's room in a joyful frame of mind. 'Let's raise a glass,' he declared. 'I have something to celebrate. The Führer has just invested me with the Gold Party Badge.' For a non-Party member like Schmundt it was indeed a great sign of trust, because only old National Socialists who had been with the Party since its foundation day, 24 February 1920, received the badge. As they raised a toast, Schmundt said, 'Yes, being head of the Army Personnel Office is not going to be easy. The Führer wants the highest commands to be given only to those who are, first of all, personally devoted to him, and secondly sufficiently flexible to approve of all his brilliant ideas and plans, and thirdly show no pity in war. A good replacement for Halder has already been found. The Führer always said that Halder was a feeble-minded village schoolmaster. By the time he has said his bit the position has already changed. General Zeitzler,[15] who was former chief of staff to Field Marshals von Kleist and von Rundstedt, will be here in a few days. He is the sort of man the Führer likes. He is spry and, besides, he knows your Sepp Dietrich well. I am sure the Führer will get on with him. The generals have betrayed the Führer. They were not up to putting his plans into action at the front. The Führer says that it is only now that he really understands Frederick the Great. When he felt himself deceived in

*From 12 September 1942.

the Seven Years War he drew himself away from his generals and his brother Prince Henry and only lived with his dogs.'

It was long after midnight, and Schmundt had drunk a good deal. When he struck up a soldier's song – 'Es reiten die blauen Dragoner' ('The blue dragoons are riding'), Linge firmly shut his door so that Hitler would not be woken. One song followed another. In the grey light of dawn Schmundt nailed up the door to Schaub's room – which was next to Linge's – as a joke. Schaub was still tippling with the photographer Hoffmann in the mess.

At the beginning of October 1942 Günsche arrived at Hitler's HQ from France. He had graduated from the officer school in Bad Tölz in May 1942 and, returning as an officer to the Leibstandarte, was assigned to special duties on the staff. At the time the Leibstandarte was in Normandy, but was transferred from there to the Eastern Front in June. It was meant to make up for the heavy losses sustained in the battles on the River Mius and the Sea of Asov. Sepp Dietrich had sent Günsche to Führer HQ to learn about morale there and to find out what further plans Hitler had for the Leibstandarte.

When Hitler received Günsche, he was very pale and had dark rings under his eyes. He waved his visitor towards him, quickly shook his hand and asked him about the state of the Leibstandarte. Günsche reported that the peaceful atmosphere of France had suited it well. It was being brought up to strength with newly trained recruits without a hitch and the Leibstandarte was ready to fight again. Hitler smiled.

At the time the Atlantic coast was only weakly defended. The impregnability of the Atlantic Wall had been heavily exaggerated by German propaganda.[16] It offered no real protection, as it was made up of scanty field defences, some coastal artillery and a limited number of refuges for submarines at Saint-Nazaire and Lorient. In order to give the impression that many troops were concentrated in western France, a great number of HQ flags had been run up. It was meant to signify that there were many staffs, which in reality did not exist at all. For the same reason the Leibstandarte paraded through Paris from time to time with full kit and baggage and with new tanks. The columns would be extended to the maximum to give the impression of a powerful offensive force. Tanks would drive at high speed down the Champs Elysées and through the Arc de Triomphe, where Field Marshal von Rundstedt, the Supreme Commander of Army Group West, would take the Leibstandarte's salute. Photographers and reporters relayed these propaganda manoeuvres to cinemas and newspapers as a proof of German strength in the west.

In his talks with Günsche, Hitler said he had run the risk of denuding the Western Front in order to hit harder in the east. It was already autumn, and the sea was stormy. The British had missed the best moment and could not carry out any landings before spring the following year. He was not going to shy away from throwing all his strength at the Eastern Front, the Leibstandarte included. Stalingrad must and would fall. The outcome of the war would be decided in Russia. The war would end in German victory. As they said goodbye, he ordered Günsche to tell the commander of the Leibstandarte, Sepp Dietrich, to begin preparations immediately for transfer to the Eastern Front. At this meeting, Hitler treated Günsche very coolly and gave the impression of a deeply embittered man. At this time in fact those in Hitler's immediate circle tried as hard as they could to avoid running into him. 'What's he like today?' the SS sentries in his house would ask one another at the changing of the guard.

When Russian troops became ever more active in November 1942, Hitler no longer felt safe in Vinnitsa and transferred his HQ back to Rastenburg.* On 8 November he flew to Munich in order to take part in the anniversary celebrations of the National Socialist Putsch. He made a solemn speech in the Bürgerbräukeller, where the survivors of the Putsch met as usual: 'I will never give back earth a German soldier has trodden on.'[17] From Munich he returned to the Wolfsschanze.

Normandy at the beginning of January 1943: units of the Leibstandarte together with other German divisions were travelling together from France towards the Eastern Front. Hitler had rapidly turned the plans he had mentioned to Günsche in October 1942 into reality. In France the Leibstandarte had been attached to a powerful Panzer division of 20,000 men and 200 tanks. The main part of the division was thrown at the Eastern Front by express transports. By the beginning of January all that was left were a few staff and other small units. The divisional commander Sepp Dietrich ordered Günsche to report to him. Dietrich, who called his SS men 'Du,'† said, 'Günsche, you must leave us. You have orders to report to the Führer.' Günsche showed surprise at this unexpected order. Dietrich slapped him on the back and said, 'Make sure you do your job well. Look after the Führer.'

---

*On 1 November 1942.
†The use of *Du* was largely confined to families and very close friends. Hitler's only *Dutzfreund* was Röhm. Dietrich's use of *Du* is to stress the close bond and radical structure of the Leibstandarte.

On 12 January 1943, Günsche arrived at Hitler's Wolfsschanze HQ. Schaub took him directly to the Führer. On the way he said with a sour look, 'Bad times, old fellow. We have long since kissed goodbye to the idea of a Blitzkrieg against Russia. We are all very worried about Stalingrad.' Hitler received Günsche in the camp hut. Around 105 metres square, it had several large windows on one side, and a long map table. Between the windows there were telephones on wires with additional headsets. Besides Hitler's desk, the room contained a round fireside table and two safes, one set in the wall, the other free standing. On the walls there were large topographical maps.

Hitler stood with Bormann at the low, round table. Next to him was his German shepherd dog Blondi, who began to growl softly and bare her teeth when Günsche appeared. Günsche looked Hitler up and down as he stood waiting at the door. The Führer's appearance had greatly changed since the last time he had seen him, three months before in Vinnitsa. He looked a very sick man. His face was earth-brown, his cheeks had fallen in, and there were heavy bags under his eyes. With a brooding look, Hitler asked Günsche to come closer. He held out his hand and said in an unusually soft voice, 'Günsche, from today you are my personal adjutant. I have chosen you because I want no more new people around me. We will talk about your duties tomorrow. Everything else you shall learn from Bormann and Schaub.' Günsche replied, 'My Führer! I will prove myself worthy of your trust!'

In the antechamber Günsche ran into Schaub, who was already waiting for him. When Schaub congratulated Günsche, he had a worried look once again. In the HQ it had long been held that you could read Hitler's mood in Schaub's face. For that reason he was also known as 'Hitler's barometer'. When Günsche asked him whether Hitler was ill, Schaub shook his head. No, since the situation at Stalingrad had become so bad, he had just deteriorated considerably.

Schaub took Günsche round the HQ and introduced him to his colleagues. Next to the Führer's bunker in Restricted Area I was the bunker of Martin Bormann, where an assistant and four secretaries were also lodged. The telegraph equipment was housed there too so that, according to Schaub, Bormann could be in direct contact with every Gauleiter in Germany, as well as with the staff in the Party offices in Berlin and Munich. Next to Bormann's bunker was the house of the secret stenographic service. With a conspiratorial look Schaub reported that nowadays every word of the situation reports was written down by the stenographers. 'The Führer', Schaub said, 'no longer trusts the generals. He wants everything in black and white. You are going to have a lot of work to do with these stenographers, because one of your duties is to read through the minutes of the situation reports.'

The next-door bunker was inhabited by Keitel and Jodl with their staffs, the Reich Press Chief Dietrich, General Bodenschatz, Göring's liaison officer at HQ, Ribbentrop's representative Hewel, the liaison officer from Naval High Command, Admiral Krancke, Himmler's liaison officer, SS-Übergruppenführer Wolff,[18] together with Morell, Hoffmann and Scherff. Hitler's longstanding surgeon Brandt was lodged in a bunker with the adjutants.[19] The secretaries Schroeder, Wolf and Junge lived at the inn.[20] Apart from the bunkers for Hitler's bodyguard and security service in Restricted Area I there was a tea-house, two messes, the cinema, the bathhouse and the garages.

In Restricted Area II of the HQ there was the commander of the Führer's Escort Battalion, the administration of the household and the new railway station where three trains stood, one each for Hitler, Keitel and Warlimont[21] – with his Wehrmacht Operations Staff. The Staff Quarters for Army High Command and the Chief of the General Staff Colonel General Zeitzler lay about twenty kilometres south-east of the Wolfsschanze in Lötzen Wood. Göring had his staff quarters in an old hunting lodge of Wilhelm II's in Rominten near the German–Soviet border, two hours by car from the Wolfsschanze.[22] When he came to the Wolfsschanze on a short visit he spent the night in a large bunker constructed for him alone in Restricted Area I. Himmler's staff HQ was near Angerburg. To reach the Wolfsschanze from there took only forty-five minutes. He called it the Field Command Position of the Reichsführer SS. Ribbentrop was lodged with his small staff on a country estate east of Rastenburg, one and a half hours by car from the Wolfsschanze. Grossadmiral Dönitz remained in Berlin.

At 1.00 p.m. the next day, 13 January 1943, a few minutes before the beginning of the situation report, Hitler emerged from his living quarters accompanied by his Waffen-SS adjutant Günsche and went to the conference room. When he had entered the room, the Führer said, 'All right, Günsche, these are your duties: during the conference you stand on my right. Pay full attention to what is said. I have reasons to be distrustful. Don't be influenced by anyone. You need to have correct information about the positions of the SS divisions. Rely, however, only on information from their staffs.' Now Linge entered and announced, 'My Führer! The gentlemen are here.' Hitler nodded. A few seconds later entered the representatives of the highest echelons of the military: Keitel, Jodl, Zeitzler, Warlimont, Buhle,[23] Jeschonnek,[24] Bodenschatz, Krancke, Christian,[25] Counseller Hewel and the military historian Scherff, together with Hitler's military attachés Schmundt, Below,[26] Engel[27] and Puttkamer.[28]

In the last few weeks of the Battle of Stalingrad, Göring had ceased to take part in the briefings at Hitler's HQ. After he had solemnly promised Hitler that his Luftwaffe would get supplies to Paulus's encircled army at Stalingrad, the Führer had seen neither hide nor hair of him.[*] He preferred to wait until the dark clouds had parted and went hunting on his Rominten estate instead.

That day Hitler offered only Zeitzler his hand. He wouldn't give the others – Keitel included – so much as a glance. His adjutants quickly spread out on the table three big maps that had been brought by Zeitzler showing the positions of Army Groups South, Centre and North on the Eastern Front. In addition there was a special map giving the positions of the encircled Sixth Army at Stalingrad. Hitler put on his spectacles and leaned over the maps.

With characteristically rapid gestures, Zeitzler began to explain the situation at Stalingrad. He said the Sixth Army's predicament had worsened again, and that the Russian army had made deep incursions into the German positions, which he showed on the map. Paulus had had to retreat. The Russians were stubbornly continuing their attack. There were over 40,000 wounded in the Sixth Army, and munitions and provisions had run out. Paulus was urgently requesting the promised support from the air, but German planes had trouble getting through the Russian anti-aircraft barrage.[†] When Colonel Christian, the Lufwaffe Chief of Staff, saw how Hitler's face was darkening, he corrected Zeitzler with the remark that provision from the air had been hampered by bad weather.

Zeitzler continued his report. He communicated Paulus's request for permission to break out of the Russian pocket with the battleworthy elements of his army. Hearing these words Hitler went red with anger. Keitel gave Zeitzler a signal to be quiet, but it was already too late. Hitler pushed his spectacles across the table, something that always presaged an outbreak of fury, and roared, 'Paulus should certainly not dare come to me with such things! He can't come out of there! I refuse his request!' Hitler was now in a state. Breathing heavily he continued, 'Can't Manstein get through there either? It is not conclusive that Stalingrad cannot be taken. The divisions

---

[*]Göring had assured Hitler on 24 November 1942 that he could supply the Sixth Army from the air. Army command required 700 tons a day. Göring promised 500; the Luftwaffe were more cautious and said 350; on average never more than 100 tons were delivered.
[†]The Luftwaffe lost 488 transport planes over Stalingrad, almost two-thirds of all they possessed.

are already there from the west. I will lead the attack on Stalingrad with them!' There was dead quiet in the conference room. All those present feared uttering an ill-considered word that might irritate the furious Hitler yet more. Finally Keitel decided to break the silence. He put his hand on the map and said, agreeing with Hitler, and speaking with a loud voice, 'Yes, my Führer! Stalingrad must he held at all costs! In the First World War we had even greater difficulties.'

Hitler's anger gradually abated. He ordered Zeitzler to inform Paulus by telegraph that his decision was inalterable. Stalingrad must be held, whatever the cost. Milch[29] and Hube[30] would be despatched to Rostov, where they would ensure the provisioning of the army from the air. Paulus must not lose courage: the Führer and the entire German people were proudly following the heroic struggle of his army.

After Zeitzler's report it was the turn of the Chief of the Wehrmacht Operations Staff, Jodl. He spread a map of the Western Front on the table with notable calm. From the western theatre there was practically nothing to report. The Anglo-Americans remained passive in their fight with Germany, and for the time being the Western Front was a place where worn-down German divisions could rest and be reformed. Jodl spoke very softly and slowly of the situation in France, Norway and the Balkans. It was easy to see that he carefully weighed up every word so that Hitler's wrath might not be stirred up once again.

At the next briefing Zeitzler reported that the situation of the Sixth Army had worsened even more. Paulus's radio messages revealed only one thing – the hopeless position of the beleaguered units, with tens of thousands of wounded, a complete lack of provisions and relentless attacks from the Russians. Milch and Hube reported from Rostov that Soviet fighters and anti-aircraft fire made it impossible to drop munitions and provisions into the Stalingrad area. In their report it was said that 'The flak over Stalingrad has created an impenetrable wall of fire. All our planes would be annihilated. We can't get through.' But Hitler would not relent.

After Paulus's radio messages came another from General von Seydlitz, the commander of LI Army Corps of the Sixth Army,[31] who radioed that in the current situation he could no longer take responsibility for his corps. Hitler threw a fit: 'Reject responsibility – that is cowardice! I will not freely give up Stalingrad, even if the whole Sixth Army perishes in the act!'

The tenth anniversary of Hitler's takeover of power fell on 30 January 1943. On this day Hitler was particularly pale. He had slept all night. Before the briefing, Morell injected him with a higher dose of stimulants, as had become customary in recent months. In the room were the usual conference participants. Keitel delivered a short speech. He said, 'Today, on the tenth anniversary of your coming to power, my Führer, we and the whole army stand closely rallied round you and think of the great victories to which you have led us and to which you will lead us again. In these difficult days, my Führer, we want to continue the struggle under your brilliant leadership, with constancy, until the final victory.' Hitler was moved, and offered Keitel his hand. It was the first time this had happened since autumn the previous year, when Halder went.

At 10.00 in the evening on 1 February, Zeitzler telephoned Hitler. Accompanied by Schmundt and Günsche, the Führer went to the telephone in the conference room, shuffling in and dropping feebly into an armchair by the table on which the map of Stalingrad was spread out. Hitler cast an angry look at it and with a rough movement of his hand swept it off the table. Günsche gave him the telephone, while he himself took the headphones to listen in to the conversation with Zeitzler. Zeitzler gave a brief report: the Russian noose around Stalingrad was growing ever tighter. Paulus could not be expected to survive the night. Hitler asked where Paulus was. Zeitzler answered that he didn't know for sure – he thought he was in his command post. Apart from this, Zeitzler informed Hitler of a radio message from Strecker,[32] the commander of XI Army Corps, that when the Russians appeared the Germans intended to blow themselves up.* 'Thank you,' Hitler replied and put down the receiver. He immediately ordered Schmundt to inform Paulus that he had been promoted to field marshal.

With a dragging gait Hitler left with the room with Blondi and said to Linge, who was waiting for him in the corridor, 'Get Hoffmann to come and keep me company for a bit.' When Hoffmann entered the bunker he went straight to Linge. He was tipsy, despite the fact that Hitler had banned alcohol at HQ for two weeks as a result of the terrible developments at Stalingrad. Hoffmann had his own supplies of champagne and had no problem circumventing this ban. He told Linge that he would play a joke on Hitler, and for this he asked Linge to serve him apple juice topped up with mineral water in a champagne glass.

When Linge brought Hitler his tea, he ordered the soldier-servant to put down Hoffmann's glass of champagne. Hitler stared at the glass and looked furiously at Linge. Hoffmann quickly explained that it was only a joke. Hitler's face brightened, and he and Hoffmann had a good laugh.

*The Sixth Army had already surrendered on 31 January 1943. Two days later Strecker gave himself up – in one piece.

Hoffmann exploited Hitler's improved mood by asking him to provide labour for his country estate. What a smooth operator! thought Linge as he left the room.

At 4.00 in the morning of 2 February, the bell rang from Hitler's bedroom. Linge put on a dressing gown and knocked on the door. Hitler's bass voice sounded from within: 'Linge, find out from the Press Department whether Paulus's promotion to field marshal has already been announced. If it hasn't the announcement should be withdrawn.'* Linge rang the assistant Press Chief Lorenz straightaway. Lorenz answered that the announcement had already been made and could not be withdrawn. Linge relayed this to Hitler. He replied in a discontented tone, 'Thanks,' and added, 'If other news comes in bring it to me at once. I can't sleep anyway.'

At around 6.00 a.m. Jodl's secretary, Sergeant Dänicke, brought over two uncoded radio messages from Stalingrad. The first announced, 'The enemy is right in front of our positions. We are surrendering.' And the second: 'The Russians are breaking through our positions. We are destroying everything.'[33] Linge delivered both messages, the last signs of life from Paulus's army, to Hitler's door and knocked. A quarter of an hour later Hitler came out into the corridor wearing a military coat with the collar turned up. Pale, stooping and with swollen eyes, he was completely despondent and said to Linge, 'I am going to take Blondi out, then I shall lie down again. Find out whether the briefing can be put forward an hour. Wake me an hour before it starts.'

The conference was brought forward to 11.30. When Hitler entered the room the participants greeted him in silence with arms outstretched in a fascist salute. The room remained silent as a tomb. Hitler crossed to the table and glanced fleetingly at the maps, then slid into an armchair. He asked those present to leave him alone with Keitel, Jodl and Zeitzler. 'Zeitzler, is anything known about Paulus?' he asked. 'No, nothing,' Zeitzler answered. In a weak voice, Hitler gasped out, 'Last night I had a premonition that the Russians had taken Paulus prisoner. As a result I wanted to rescind his promotion to field marshal. The German people should not know that a German field marshal is in Russian captivity. The story of Sixth Army's struggle and collapse must be told to the German people with the generals fighting shoulder to shoulder with their men in the trenches and dying with them at the end. I need a million new soldiers.'

*The German Press Agency had been informed on the 30th.

97

At these words Hitler rose. He walked slowly up and down the room. Then he returned to the table and asked, 'Is there anything else on Stalingrad besides these two messages? What are the Russians saying?' 'No, my Führer, nothing,' Zeitzler answered, 'but in Kharkov and the Lower Don the position of our troops has become highly critical.' Hitler dragged himself from the room accompanied by Günsche.

On 29 December 1949 Josef V. Stalin (*top*) received the final report in the Ministry of the Interior's investigation into the life and suicide of Adolf Hitler. *The Hitler Book* was compiled by a team of authors headed by Feodor Karpovitch Parparov (*below left*). It was based on the statements of Hitler's personal adjutants, the SS officers Heinz Linge (*below centre*) and Otto Günsche (*below right*). Both were captured on 2 May 1945 and handed over to the NKVD, or Soviet secret police

Reich President von Hindenburg and Hitler on 1 May 1933 on their way to make an announcement

November 1933: Hitler inspects his newly formed Leibstandarte 'Adolf Hitler' guard on the parade ground of the former Cadet School in Berlin Lichterfelde. Standing to his right is Sepp Dietrich, the Commander of the Leibstandarte

Holidays together in the Baltic in 1935: Hitler with the Goebbelses in Heiligendamm

Until his murder in 1934, the SA Chief of Staff Ernst Röhm was Himmler's superior

Hitler and Göring on the Obersalzberg in 1938: the Reich Chancellor and the Prussian Minister President enjoying an informal meeting

Berlin 1938: the Leibstandarte 'Adolf Hitler' on parade

Hitler visits workers building the Siegfried Line in the Saar, 1938

Before the conversion of Haus Wachenfeld into the Berghof, Hitler worked in the parlour of his home

A propaganda postcard shows the Reich Chancellor with a 'status-symbol' desk. It is entitled 'The Führer at home on the Obersalzberg'

In 1928 Hitler bought Haus Wachenfeld near Berchtesgaden. After his accession to power he had his favourite holiday home transformed into his residence and rechristened it the Berghof. Various ministries erected offices in Berchtesgaden, and Schloss Klessheim served for diplomatic receptions. Hitler's guests landed at the airfield in Ainring. The Platterhof was the SS barracks

Top left: The people were kept at a distance by barbed-wire fences and SS guardposts

Top right: The great hall was not only used for receptions, it was also where films were screened for Hitler's entourage

Hitler in Alpine pose

1939: the New Reich Chancellery (*top*) forms the stage for Hitler's performances. The great study of nearly 400 square metres played just as formal a role as the so-called *cour d'honneur* (*bottom*), the entrances to which were guarded by SS men

9

February – Summer 1943

The obliteration of the German army at Stalingrad had a dreadful effect on Hitler. He certainly would not have survived it had it not been for the stimulating injections of his personal physician Morell, administered every second day after breakfast. He began to have nervous stomach cramps. Because he was in extreme pain he had to keep to his bed for several hours a day. Linge, who administered the opium prescribed by Morell, could not help seeing that he was writhing in agony.[1]

The attacks of nervous irritation increased. One moment Hitler's collar was too tight and was stopping his circulation; the next his trousers were too long. He complained that his skin itched. He suspected poison everywhere, in the lavatory cistern, on the soap, in the shaving cream or in the toothpaste, and demanded that these be minutely analysed. The water used for cooking his food had to be investigated as well. Hitler chewed his fingernails and scratched his ears and neck until they bled. Because he suffered from insomnia, he took every possible sleeping pill. His bed was warmed with electric blankets and cushions. He was short of breath, and as a result he asked that an oxygen cylinder be set up in his bedroom from which he frequently inhaled. He ordered that the temperature in his room be kept at a constant 12 degrees, because he believed that low temperatures had a refreshing effect on him. Participants at his briefings often left the room because they were cold and went somewhere to warm up.

He scarcely ever left his bunker now. Only in the morning before break-fast would he take his German shepherd Blondi out for ten minutes, when she would stay at his side. This huge, trained animal obeyed him alone, growling at everybody else, and guarding him day and night. Even during conferences she lay at his feet. After lunch Hitler would stretch out in his clothes on his bed and stay there until the evening. Then he would go to the evening situation report that took place at 9.00 every day. When it was finished he would remain in the room and play ball with his dog. He found it funny when Blondi stood up on her hind legs and batted the ball back with her front paws outstretched like a hare. On such occasions Hitler ordered her, 'Go on, Blondi, be a hare for me!' Around midnight Hitler would ask Linge to put on records of stately music, just as he had done in his Wehrwolf HQ in Vinnitsa when he first began to distance himself from the generals.

Göring had no scruples about using Hitler's condition for his own ends. Now he came to him daily. By means of these tactics he hoped to achieve a special position for himself. Now that Hitler had come to detest his generals, he sought Göring's company. At breakfast he would tell Linge, 'I am having lunch with the Reichsmarschall. They could cook something special for him. His favourite dish, for example, fried chicken and an apple turnover for dessert.' At this time too there was a rapprochement between Hitler and Eva Braun, who was living either in Munich or at the Berghof on the Obersalzberg. In the past months he had rarely written to her. Now he called her almost every day.

After the catastrophe at Stalingrad, a few weeks had to pass before Hitler once again spent time with his secretaries, with Bormann, Hoffmann and Morell and with the adjutants. He remarked to Linge that their company took his mind off the failure on the Russian front and calmed his nerves.

The situation on the Lower Don worsened yet again. Kursk, Kharkov and Rostov were under immediate threat. The Kuban position looked extremely critical. Zeitzler reported at Hitler's conferences in the first half of February 1943 that German troops in the Caucasus ran the risk of being cut off. On the operations maps that he brought with him, red arrows marked the points where the Russians had strengthened their attacks.[2] In order to see better, Keitel, Jodl, Warlimont, Buhle, Scherff, Schmundt and Günsche, who were standing around the table, leaned over the maps as Zeitzler conducted his briefing. One could scarcely make out the German front line: the German positions were encircled or penetrated by the enemy. In many places the Russians had actually broken through.

Hitler sat at the table with his face towards the window and looked totally exhausted. Before Stalingrad he had always stood for situation reports. Now his back and legs gave him pain if he did so. He interrupted Zeitzler and told him in a tired voice, 'It cannot go on like this. Our industry cannot survive without the coal from the Donetsk. No! We have got to hold our positions! My generals must finally understand that!' He ran his right hand over the map and pointed to a point south of Kharkov where advance units of Russian tanks had been drawn in. He was amazed that the Russians had advanced so quickly. 'From Stalingrad to this point is a distance of around 500 kilometres. Where are the Russians getting their strength from? By my reckoning they should be completely out of breath by now. I don't understand it.' Hitler shook his head and fell silent. Suddenly his face coloured. He roared, 'These generals! When they retreat they could at the very least blow everything sky high! I have the impression that they run away without so much as looking behind them and leave a good deal to fall intact into the hands of the Russians. I want everything destroyed and burned! Every house!'[3]

Zeitzler sought to calm him by pointing out that there were orders to destroy everything in the event of retreat and they were carried out to the letter. After this comment Hitler once again stared impassively into the middle distance. At the end of the meeting he declared that it was necessary for him to fly to the front in person to see Field Marshal von Weichs, the Supreme Commander of Army Group South.[4] That very evening Hitler ordered his pilot Baur to prepare a plane to fly to Zaporozhe, where Weichs had his HQ.

On the morning of 10 February Hitler flew to Zaporozhe in his Condor, escorted by a squadron of fighters.[*] He was accompanied by Jodl, Buhle, his adjutants, Morell and Linge. Apart from these, he took his secretary Fräulein Schroeder with him and two stenographers to write the minutes of the meetings in Zaporozhe.

In Zaporozhe Hitler moved with his staff into the former Russian Fliers' House, where Weichs had his HQ; but only a day after his arrival he had to leave the town again in a hurry. At around 11.00 a.m. he received the engineer Brugmann,[5] who had come over especially from Dnepropetrovsk where he was directing the work to make the Dnieper dam function again. Brugmann was known in Germany because he had built the Party rally building in Nuremberg for the National Socialist Party. In Dnepropetrovsk he was the so-called O-T-Führer, the leading representative of the Todt Organisation. Hitler directed Brugmann to destroy the dam if the Germans had to abandon their positions.

He then went into the meeting with Weichs.[†] A few moments later the adjutant Below burst excitedly into Hitler's study to look for Linge. 'We need to pack straightaway!' he exclaimed. 'Russian tanks have appeared at Zaporozhe airfield. We must hurry!'[‡] Linge feverishly threw

---

[*] Hitler did not leave until 17 February 1943. He took off at 2.00 p.m. from the airstrip in Wilhelmsdorf and arrived at the HQ of Army Group South at 6.00 p.m.

[†] He had a meeting with the new commander of Army Group South, Manstein, and Field Marshal Wolfram von Richthofen. It is not known if Weichs was also present.

[‡] Hitler flew back on 19 February 1943. The Soviet army was some sixty kilometres away.

all the essentials together. Hitler arrived shortly afterwards. He was very nervous and gave Linge *carte blanche* to pack what he wanted. When the cases had been taken down to the car, Below reported to Hitler that the Russian tanks had not advanced to the airfield where Hitler's aircraft was standing, but to another, further east of Zaporozhe, and they had been driven away again. Hitler breathed a sigh of relief. He summoned Field Marshal Weichs and Colonel General von Richthofen, who commanded the Luftwaffe in this sector.[6] In a great hurry and while he was on the point of going, he invested Weichs with the oak leaves to his Knight's Cross and promoted Richthofen to field marshal, then he drove off. No meeting took place.*

On the way to the airfield Hitler passed a column of peaceful Russian citizens who were carrying out street work under German guard. Filled with loathing Hitler remarked, 'It is quite right to make Slavs do this, these robots! Otherwise they would have no right to their share of the sun!'

Hitler flew from Zaporozhe to his HQ at Vinnitsa. There he summoned General Major Stahel.[7] Stahel had distinguished himself in the defence of 'difficult sectors of the front' that Hitler had ordered maintained to the last soldier. Apart from this he was known for his merciless dealings with the Russian population. Below and Günsche were present during the meeting with Stahel. Hitler appointed Stahel commander of the Zaporozhe Fortress. He commanded him, 'Fly there at once! You must hold Zaporozhe! Put every soldier in firing positions! Gather up the whole Russian population and force them to build fortifications until the blood spurts from their fingernails!' 'What sort of power do I possess?' Stahel asked. 'All!' Hitler answered. 'Do whatever you want; and no stupidity about sentiment!'

In the second half of February 1943 Field Marshal Rommel arrived at the Wehrwolf HQ from the African Front. Rommel had commanded Hitler's HQ during the 1939 German–Polish war. In the French campaign of 1940, he had commanded a Panzer division that was the first to reach the French coast. After this he was appointed commander of the German Afrika Korps. He was Germany's best-loved general and Hitler had a very high opinion of him.[8] When Rommel arrived at Wehrwolf his mission in Africa had ended.† His corps had had to retreat, because the reserves promised by

---

*Weichs only received the oak leaves on 5 February 1945; Richthofen had been promoted field marshal on 31 January 1943 together with Paulus, Weichs and Kleist.
†On 10 March 1943. He was given not only oak leaves, but swords and diamonds to his Knight's Cross. This was as good as it got.

Hitler had not materialised as they had been thrown at the Eastern Front. In Africa only one secure point remained in German hands. It was in a suburb of Tunis, defended by Rommel's successor, Colonel General Mackensen.[9]

Hitler accorded Rommel a very friendly reception and gave him the highest honour: oak leaves to his Knight's Cross. But Rommel was dejected. He told Hitler that he would without doubt have been able to advance to Alexandria had Hitler sent him the promised reinforcements. At the same time he pointed out that the Italian troops could not be relied on. In his words, they ran away like rabbits. Hitler countered Rommel, insisting that he had had no other choice – Rommel would understand that they could not dwell on the secondary African theatre when they were in danger of losing the war in Russia. 'I had to bring together all our strength', Hitler explained, 'to stop up the gap that had been made at Stalingrad.'

Hitler continued by saying that he had great worries in the west. If a second front were to be opened there it would have a devastating effect on the Eastern Front: 'A landing in France would be a catastrophe for Germany,' he opined. He told Rommel that the Atlantic Wall was very poorly defended and needed to be strengthened urgently. At present only in the regions of Pas de Calais and Cap Gris Nez on the French coast was there any concentration of heavy artillery with high-performance guns. Apart from those the so-called Atlantic Wall consisted of field defences that in one place had been strengthened by minefields. The artillery on the coast was using mostly guns plundered in France, Poland, Czechoslovakia and Belgium and they were of an antiquated sort with very limited supplies of munitions. The coast was only lightly defended and there were practically no reserves as every able-bodied man had been thrown on to the Russian Front long ago. Hitler announced that Rommel would take over the business of strengthening the Atlantic Wall and ordered him assume command of the troops in France.

The importance of the Atlantic Wall might be measured by the fact that immediately after Rommel's reception at Hitler HQ, he went on leave.

The situation on the Eastern Front worsened from one day to the next. Russian attacks grew ever more destructive. Only at the cost of a heavy loss of life and equipment did the Germans manage to fight off Russian pressure and to some degree stabilise the German Front around Kharkov–Poltava.[*]

---

[*] In March 1943 Manstein had retaken Kharkov.

Once the dark clouds had parted a little at the front Göring reappeared at Hitler's HQ in Vinnitsa. In a theatrical gesture he embraced Zeitzler and exclaimed, 'Zeitzler, it is simply a miracle that you have managed to stabilise the front!' Zeitzler, who was invariably known to his underlings as 'General Kugelblitz' (lightning-cannonball) because of his round form, rapid movement and shiny pate, glowed at the Reichsmarschall's encomium. Even Hitler livened up a bit and said, 'A short while ago I still believed I would have a stroke if anyone were to bring me good news.'

Hitler decided to use the sudden calm at the front to travel to the Obersalzberg. Among his staff this caused great joy, as it was hoped that his condition might improve in Eva Braun's company. In the first days of March Hitler flew from Vinnitsa to the Wolfsschanze near Rastenburg, where he spent a few days before leaving for the Obersalzberg.

While he was here he received a report from Werner von Braun,[10] the inventor of the long-range guided missile later known as the V2. Braun's briefing was top secret and took place in the cinema at the Wolfsschanze. Only Keitel, Jodl, Buhle, Schmundt, Günsche and the attendant adjutants were allowed in, while the building was surrounded by SS men from Hitler's bodyguard. Braun illustrated his talk with slides. These showed a powerful rocket that could ascend to a height of eighty kilometres. The body was filled with a tonne of explosive, travelled to its target with colossal speed and had a range of 200 to 300 kilometres. The explosion was so powerful that it could destroy an entire area of a city and its inhabitants. Hitler heartily applauded during the briefing and abandoned himself to imagining the horrible scenes among the population when such a bomb went off. He was inspired by the lecture and immediately invested Braun with the title of professor and promised to visit him in his labours at Peenemünde.*

At this time Hitler summoned Keitel and Himmler. Once again he directed that his orders should be strictly observed and that everything was to be destroyed when the Germans retreated from Russia. Hitler stressed that the Russian army should find only scorched earth and unin-habited desert. It was his opinion that this would stave off Russian attacks. Hitler spoke of stepping up reprisals in those areas of Russia still occupied by Germany. He asked Himmler to use more sealed lorries containing mobile gas chambers so as not to squander munitions desperately needed by the army for shooting Russians.[11] Referring to a report by

---

*The lecture took place on 7 March 1943. Werner von Braun was accompanied by General Walter Dornberger. They showed a film of the take-off of the first V2 on 3 October 1942.

SS Gruppenführer Hennicke,[12] the Police Chief in Rostov, Himmler announced that mobile gas chambers had proved their worth. With a cynical smile, he added that this method of killing was 'more considerate' and 'more silent' than shooting.*

For his own part, Hitler had taken a personal interest in the development of gas chambers. He thoroughly examined the development of projects of this sort when they were presented to him by Himmler. Hitler decreed that the man who built the gas chambers, an engineer from Eisenach, should be given comprehensive support and the best technical assistance. On Hitler's personal orders gas chambers were first operated in Kharkov.[13]

Shortly before Hitler had decided to leave for the Obersalzberg, Göring arrived from his Rominten HQ with a mournful look on his face. He told Hitler that Colonel General Jeschonnek, the Luftwaffe Chief of Staff, had unexpectedly died of appendicitis. No one believed this story in Hitler's retinue, as it had been known for a long time that there were tense relations between Göring and Jeschonnek.† The reason for this was that Jeschonnek had allowed Hitler to see material that contradicted the boastful information that Göring had fed him on the growth and fighting capacity of the German air force. In Jeschonnek's argument the priority given to constructing bombers rather than fighters detracted from German strength in the air. Besides this, he pointed out that there was a dearth of production of finished aircraft. The differences of opinion between Göring and Jeschonnek had begun when Göring openly announced at every opportunity, 'If an enemy aircraft should ever cross the German border my name is Meier.' And as far as the German people were concerned Hermann Göring's real name was Hermann Meier.‡

Hitler preferred Göring's style of report to Jeschonnek's. Göring's bombast appealed more to the Führer, who had long since been divorced from reality. In his diseased conceit Hitler could not bear to hear truth that conflicted with his own visions. As a result he was irritated by Jeschonnek's behaviour and the man became ever more unpleasant for him. The true cause of Jeschonnek's death was soon clear. Hitler's Luftwaffe adjutant swore his comrades to silence when he told them that Jeschonnek had shot himself in his staff HQ. In order to cover up the suicide, the general was

---

*For the reasons why the text does not mention the Jews here, see Editors' Afterword, p. 301.

†He killed himself on the night of 18 August 1943 in Goldap in East Prussia.

‡ Meier is a common family name in Germany. (Russian note.)

buried with full military honours. Flattering obituaries appeared in the press. In place of Jeschonnek, the post of Luftwaffe Chief of Staff went to Air Force General Korten.[14]

Shortly before Jeschonnek, the well-known fighter pilot Colonel General Udet had committed suicide as well.[15] He was the head of the technical office of the Air Ministry, a job he owed to Göring, who was a personal friend. Udet was a heavy drinker and was constantly in debt. Göring always bailed him out. Udet shot himself while he was personally flying his aircraft, and the plane smashed to smithereens on the ground.[*] In the official version, Udet lost his life in a flying accident. Hitler told his adjutants that the reason for Udet's suicide were factual errors. In the Führer's words, erroneous decisions on aircraft construction were responsible: to the detriment of other aircraft types, Udet had pushed through the construction of dive-bombers, because he believed this to be the future. All those who were in the know at Hitler's HQ were aware that the false turn in aircraft production was above all Göring's fault. The programme was based on his ideas and directives, and not on Udet's. As the mistake was clear, Göring needed a scapegoat. Rumour had it that Göring had used the debts incurred by Udet's frivolous lifestyle and had recommended he 'draw conclusions'. It was not difficult to attribute faults to the dead Udet that more properly belonged to Göring.

After 10 May 1943 Hitler moved back to his Berghof mansion on the Obersalzberg, where he was awaited by Eva Braun and her coterie.[†] At the same time Hitler's HQ, along with the staff quarters of Göring, Himmler and Ribbentrop, were transferred to the area around Berchtesgaden–Salzburg–Bad Reichenhall. Keitel and Jodl were lodged in the Lammers' house, Chief of the Reich Chancellery, between Berchtesgaden and Bischofswiesen. Warlimont and his Wehrmacht Operations Staff moved into the barracks at Strub near Berchtesgaden. Göring lived either at his Obersalzberg villa or at his castle near Nuremberg. His new staff chief, Korten, who had replaced Jeschonnek after his suicide, was put up with his staff in a Berchtesgaden hotel. Himmler's Field Commando Postion was housed in a big villa near Salzburg. Nearby Dönitz and Ribbentrop established their staffs – Dönitz in a villa and Ribbentrop

[*]Udet shot himself in his Berlin flat on 17 November 1941. He was Quartermaster General for the Luftwaffe. The cause of his suicide was the loss of the Battle of Britain and the failure to provide sufficient aircraft for the Soviet campaign.
[†]Hitler stopped off briefly in Berlin where he attended the Heroes' Memorial Day and escaped another attempt on his life on 21 March 1943.

in Schloss Füschl, which was his own property. From now on the war would be directed from Berghof on the Obersalzberg.

Eva Braun took over the role of lady of the house. Only Hitler's closest circle were aware of this, however, and as soon as unfamiliar faces appeared Hitler directed Eva to retire to her rooms. After a wartime incident in Munich he drew the veil of secrecy concerning his relationship ever tighter. One evening some unknown women insulted Eva outside her villa and called her 'Hitler's whore'. When Hitler heard about this he ordered that the police guard on her house be strengthened. At the same time he took even stricter care that officers who were not part of his personal staff should not see Eva or her lady-friends at the Berghof. He did not want to lose his reputation as a recluse.

The horrors of the war troubled Eva but little. She had her own worries. There were then thirty people working in the kitchen at the Berghof. Eva wanted to have ten more women, but as a result of total mobilisation they were not immediately available. When she complained about this to Hitler, he was furious and angrily barked at Bormann, 'I conjure entire divisions out of the earth − it must be an easy task to find a few girls for my Berghof! Organise it!'

As a rule Hitler rose at midday on the Obsersalzberg. Then Dr Morell administered his now daily stimulant. Hitler had his breakfast alone at his desk in his study and remained there until the beginning of the military situation report. This took place twice − at around 1.00 p.m. or 1.30 p.m. and at around 10.00 in the evening. Shortly before it began, the cars of Keitel, Jodl, Warlimont, Korten and other participants would drive up to Berchtesgaden. When they had gathered in the great hall Hitler would be told that everything was ready. He would come down the stairs and go into the hall where, after the fascist salute, he would give every one of them his hand. Then he would sit down in his preappointed chair at the table with the stenographers sitting along the wall and the others standing around the table. The situation reports lasted around two hours. When Zeitzler was absent, Colonel Brandt, the Leader of the Operations Department of the General Staff, would report on the state of the Eastern Front. Zeitzler normally stayed in his staff quarters in Lötzen in East Prussia and came to the Obersalzberg just once a week.

When the participants in the midday conference had left the building lunch would be served. Hitler would generally remain in the hall speaking to his adjutants or reading the reports from the German News Agency.

The inhabitants of the Berghof would meanwhile gather for lunch: Dr Morell and his wife, Hitler's surgeon Brandt with his wife, Hoffmann, Dietrich, Hewel, Lorenz, Frentz,[16] the HQ film reporter, Hitler's secretaries with their wives. Bormann and his wife would join them, together with the wives of Dietrich and Speer. When everyone was present, Hitler would be told they were ready to eat, and only now would he join them, greeting the women by kissing their hands. Then he would escort one of the women to the table. There was a distinct order of precedence. He usually placed the wives of Bormann, Brandt, Speer or Dietrich or Eva Braun's friend Frau Schönmann on his right.[17] Hitler didn't much like having Frau Dietrich next to him, because she dressed in an old-fashioned way and didn't have anything to say to him. Eva always sat on his left, with Bormann on her other side.

At table they always talked about the most banal things: the war and its horrors were never mentioned. They spoke of ladies' clothes and the difficulties that they had to surmount because, with total mobilisation, there were no more cold perms or manicures to be had from hairdressers; or they complained that officers behaved in an improper way towards women on the railways. Eva put so much pressure on Hitler that he directed that hairdressers should permit cold perms and manicures. When there was talk of ladies' make-up, Hitler joked about Eva's lipstick, which left marks on her napkin. He laughed when he remarked that now, in wartime, ersatz-lipstick was being produced from dead animals. Theatre and cinema were also favourite themes, especially American colour films. Frau Schönmann, a Viennese lady married to a civil engineer from Munich, was very vivacious and launched a battle of words with Hitler at the table. Her Viennese charm had an effect on him. They talked about Viennese actors and directors, about the sayings of Frederick the Great, about recipes, or about how much a hen's egg weighed. Hitler was so enchanted that he had the Brockhaus* or books on Frederick the Great brought to him so that he could look things up. These 'nourishing' conversations accompanied lunches at the Berghof.

After lunch the ladies would retire to their rooms in order to change for the walk. Hitler would meanwhile feed his German shepherd Blondi, before being handed his cap and walking stick. The whole party would then go out into the park and wander in the direction of the tea-house on the Mooslahner Kopf. Before Hitler set out the entire area would be regularly combed by members of the SD. The guards were posted in such a way that

---

*The standard multi-volume German encyclopaedia.

they could not be seen by Hitler. On the walk he spoke mostly to Schmundt or Below. Högl, the chief of his police command, the RSD Chief Rattenhuber and Linge would walk behind him, with the others following.

It would take about twenty minutes to walk from the Berghof to the tea-house, a round pavilion standing on a great cliff promontory. There was a meadow before it that was fenced off from the slope. A bench had been set up here where Hitler would have a rest on the way. He was often photographed here by Eva Braun, Hoffmann or Frentz, happily posing for them with Blondi. Then they would all go on to the pavilion, where soldier-servants poured them coffee. They would either continue the conversations from lunch or talk about Blondi or Eva's dogs – she had two little black terriers called Negus and Stasi. Hitler, who would make himself comfortable by the open fire, occasionally nodded off during these conversations. Then the talk would continue in a whisper. At around seven the entire party would go back to the Berghof by car and Hitler would disappear into his study until dinner time to read newspapers or reports from the German News Agency. When the weather was bad Hitler stayed at home and had a nap on the sofa or in his study.

Dinner would be served at 8.00 or 8.30. It was similar to lunch – that is, dominated by banal talk. At 10.00 was the evening situation report. After that Hitler would sign documents granting decorations to officers and industrialists, permission for officers to marry foreigners or death sentences for others accused of defeatism. While he was busy, Eva and her friends would watch American colour films in the bowling alley. When they came back to the drawing room next to the hall where Hitler was, they would draw attention to themselves by laughing and talking loudly. This was to make him see that he had concentrated enough on the war and that he should give some thought to them. Eva's little dogs Negus and Stasi would bark and frolic on the carpet.

When Hitler at last joined the ladies, his dark looks would brighten. In the adjoining hall the servants would light a fire in the fireplace, and Hitler, Eva, her sister Gretl,[18] Eva's companion Fräulein Kastrup,[19] Eva's lady-friends, Morell, Hoffmann, Dietrich, Brandt, Bormann, the adjutants and the secretaries would assemble once again in the hall. Hitler would sit by the fire next to Eva, while the other women sat in groups or reclined on the sofa or in heavy armchairs that formed a semi-circle around the fireplace.

These were the so-called tea evenings. Servants would serve champagne, liqueurs, tea, coffee and a snack. Eva would sit wrapped in a fur cape with her legs drawn up in an armchair. In Hitler's presence she was silent and preferred listening to her friends talking about the film they had just seen. Hitler would ask Günsche to hand him a gramophone record from a collection of thousands stacked in a large cupboard. On the Obersalzberg Hitler preferred light music, always listening to the same operetta melodies from Lehár and Suppé. The end of the evening was always signalled by the overture to *The Merry Widow*. Hitler could listen to two or three hours of gramophone records every night before he retired to his private apartments. Generally Eva would say goodnight earlier.

As soon as Hitler left, Bormann because unrecognisable. In Hitler's presence he played a man overburdened with work. Now, however, he would let the mask drop and take the whole gathering off to a party in his villa, bringing the cars round to the side entrance of the Berghof. Evan's friends, Hoffmann, Morell, Lorenz, the adjutants and Hitler's secretaries would get in quickly and drive to Bormann's place. His house was brightly lit. SS soldier-servants served champagne, cognac, liqueurs and sweetmeats as wild American dance music issued from a huge record player. Bormann would grab his beloved, an actress from Dresden who lived in his villa, and swing her round the drawing room.[20] Bormann's wife would help serve the guests, after he had got her out of bed for that purpose. She had borne Bormann eleven children and was like a slave to him. He had forced her to come to terms with having his lover live under the same roof as her. The dance nights of Hitler's deputy in the National Socialist Party, Martin Bormann, were well known for their wildness. These nighttime parties took place frequently on the Obersalzberg in the year of war 1943.

The death sentences that Hitler signed during those days on the Obersalzberg concerned officers accused of defeatism. In the face of the German army's defeat on the Eastern Front, Hitler had given the order that officers suspected of defeatism should be court-martialled. The same accusation was thrown at officers who saw themselves forced to retreat from a hopeless position. Hitler ordered them to be executed without pity.

The verdicts of the courts martial went first to Keitel, who handed them over to Hitler's adjutants with purely formal annotations as Hitler had to approve them as Supreme Commander of the Wehrmacht. The sentences were read out to Hitler by Rear Admiral von Puttkamer, his naval adjutant. Hitler approved them without examining one single case in detail. He never exercised his right of reprieve. Only once in 1944 did he commute a death sentence. General Lieutenant Feuchtinger, the commander of a Panzer division in France, had been sentenced to death for massive embezzlement. Hitler commuted it and reduced it to a short prison sentence.[21]

Hitler always maintained that his generals were alone responsible for his defeats, but he called none of them to account. Brauchitsch, Halder and others he pensioned off, giving them high honours when they left and allowing them to retire peacefully to their country estates. On the other hand he signed death warrants for junior officers without mercy.

In those days on the Obersalzberg Hitler had to approve marriages between officers and foreign women. Such requests came in from German soldiers stationed in conquered lands – France, Belgium, Holland, Denmark or Norway – who wished to marry native women. They concerned above all German sailors. Puttkamer brought the requests every two or three weeks, and Hitler would examine them minutely. Above all he would take a long look at the photos of the women attached to the requests.

According to the regulations laid down by Military High Command a portrait photograph in profile, another showing head and shoulders and a full-length picture had to be provided. Hitler liked to draw comparisons with people he knew. One candidate had a nose like Winifred Wagner's daughter Verena,[22] another looked like Hess's wife. Most of the women in the photos were not particularly pretty. Laughing, Hitler would remark that when the soldiers, who had fallen in love with these women, sobered up again, they would curse him because he had allowed them to marry them. He studied all the accompanying paperwork – the careers of the supplicant, police reports on the foreigners and their parents and the SD's evaluation of the political position of the families. He rarely signed straightaway. Most often he asked Linge if he might look at the request a second time. He declared that it was important to look at these things carefully so that no racially inferior blood should come to Germany as a result of these marriages. For that reason he retained the right to approve such requests personally.

Hitler and the High Command did everything to prevent the general public from learning of the failures on the Eastern Front. Press and radio hammered home to the German people morning, noon and night that the war would be won. Goebbels wrote a weekly column in the newspaper *Das Reich* extolling the great victories that had occurred during the 'planned retreat' of German troops from the east. In the broadcasts he delivered on Berlin radio, Hans Fritzsche from the Ministry of Propaganda falsified the actual position at the front and demanded ever greater sacrifice from the German people in the name of victory. In this spirit press reports were prepared from the front. Keitel and Jodl had to present them to Hitler first and he would correct them so that the people had no clear idea of what was happening at the front.

The newsreels recorded at the front were likewise worked on by Hitler in person on the Obersalzberg. Without his corrections the films could not be shown. He would change pictures and texts that had been written by Goebbels. First of all he would watch the film almost without a word, viewing it together with Keitel, Bormann, Jodl, Dietrich and his adjutants in the hall of the Berghof. Scenes that showed retreating German troops, burned-out tanks or wounded soldiers – in short anything that might point to defeat – Hitler would have cut. They would be replaced by footage from old newsreels from the 'glorious' year of 1941 which showed only images of exhausted Soviet POWs, Germany artillery fire, German Stuka attacks or happy moments in the field mess – anything that brought to mind the triumphal march of Hitler's promised Blitzkrieg. During the screening Günsche would read out Goebbels's accompanying script and take down Hitler's corrections. The Führer was particularly attentive to scenes filmed at his HQ, allowing only pictures that displayed him in the victorious pose of the first years of the war. Shots taken in recent times, which showed him frail and stooping, were excised at his categorical order and destroyed. In his opinion the German people would be horrified to see him thus.

While Hitler spent March to June 1944 on the Obersalzberg, ever more frequent reports from Zeitzler and Himmler came in of anti-fascist acts among German soldiers and officers. The National Committee for Free Germany and the German Officers' League had been founded in Russian captivity.* When the first reports of this sort came in, Hitler opined that it could only represent individual prisoners who had been drugged to make them co-operate with the Russians. Further reports from Zeitzler and Himmler showed clearly, however, that the National Committee for Free Germany was founded on a broad-based movement in the POW camps that was opposed to Hitler and the war. For good or evil Hitler had to put out of his mind the notion that only individual prisoners opposed him.

The activities of the National Committee had a noticeable effect on the soldiers at the front. First of all, they contradicted the assertions of German propaganda that the Russians took no prisoners. The appeals

*Created respectively 13 July and 12 September 1943 on Stalin's orders and made up of soldiers and political refugees. They were used chiefly as propaganda and had little effect of German morale.

of the National Committee that were dropped on German positions had been signed by thousands of POWs. Secondly, German soldiers saw that POWs were able to indulge in political activity in the Soviet Union. Thirdly, they received a more truthful idea of what Hitler's war had so far brought them and of what the future had in store. All that put Hitler in a blind rage. He gave orders to the Wehrmacht that the leaflets dropped by the National Committee should be destroyed immediately and that any soldier or officer found in possession of one was to be put before a firing squad. The families of German POWs who fought against Hitler on the Russian side would be thrown into prison or concentration camps.[*]

In the last phase of the war, Hitler feared above all that the Russians would arm anti-fascist-inclined German POWs and give them the chance to fight against him. Hitler himself was the first to speak of the Seydlitz army that the Russians were apparently forming from anti-fascist POWs under the command of the captured German General Seydlitz.[†] One can only express amazement that Hitler's babble about the Seydlitz army should have been taken up by British and American politicians.

Even before Hitler's move from Rastenburg to the Obersalzberg there was often talk that Germany's Allies had been disturbed by the heavy defeats on the Eastern Front. They demanded to speak to Hitler. The first to request an audience was Antonescu. Hitler kept postponing the visit. 'If I see him I'll have to see the others,' was what he said. As the requests of the Allies became ever more urgent, Hitler directed Ribbentrop to organ-ise meetings with Antonescu, Mussolini and Horthy. For these visits he chose the old bishop's palace of Klessheim near Salzburg, which was about an hour's drive away from the Obersalzberg. Restored in 1942 and fur-nished with magnificent furniture from France, Schloss Klessheim was to serve as the venue for visits from foreign statesmen.

The meetings with the Allies in Klessheim began at the end of March. Hitler had come to an understanding with Keitel and Jodl that they should present the situation on the Eastern Front in a favourable light for Germany. On his orders, Jodl had had a map prepared on a scale of 1:1,000,000 which gave a false perspective of the situation at the front. With this map Hitler illustrated the talks with Antonescu, Mussolini and Horthy. The front line

---

[*] Fifty-three relatives of members of the National Committee were dragged off to Schierlichmühle in the Riesengebirge after the bomb plot of 20 July 1944.

[†] Seydlitz had made the suggestion, but the Soviet authorities were distinctly cool.

was far from being correctly drawn in – indeed, in some sectors it had been incompletely reproduced. The strength of the enemy, Germany's strength and the direction of operations were not recognisable. That way the situation looked much more positive than it actually was. Among Hitler's staff the conversations with Antonescu, Mussolini and Horthy were referred to jokingly as discussions about the 'alleged positions'.

Antonescu came first.[*] Before he arrived Hitler declared, 'I will give Antonescu the enema he requires.' Together with Ribbentrop Hitler greeted him on Liefering station near Salzburg, which had been refurbished for guests travelling to Klessheim. For Antonescu's visit Hitler spent a whole day at Klessheim, when the usual situation reports took place there and not on the Obersalzberg. Even so Anonescu was not invited to them, but remained in his suite. When the first briefing was over, they prepared themselves for the talk with Antonescu. The 1:300,000 maps that exactly reproduced the positions at the front were cleared away and the maps with the 'alleged positions' were laid out in their place.

With a wink Linge announced to Hitler that they were ready with the 'alleged situation report'. Hitler went to Antonescu's suite and returned with him to the conference room. This now looked completely different to half an hour before. It hummed with Romanian officers and Foreign Office officials. Ribbentrop, Meissner,[23] Keitel, Jodl and others were present. In a storm of flashlights Hitler made theatrical gestures and in a victorious tone offered an overview of the position on the Eastern Front. A few modest observations on Antonescu's part were swept aside by Hitler with a reference to Germany's inexhaustible resources and plans for a grandiose new offensive that promised certain victory. Keitel, Jodl and Zeitzler sang the same tune. Antonescu flew back to Romania in good humour. Hitler went back to the Obersalzberg.

A few days later Hitler received Mussolini,[†] who was very impressed by the 'alleged positions'. At the end of the meeting he exclaimed, 'Führer! The Berlin–Rome Axis will win!'

Next came Horthy.[‡] He was little interested in Hitler's briefing on the positions on the Eastern Front. Instead he complained to Hitler about the provocative appearance of Germans in Hungary and the scandalous behaviour of German soldiers towards Hungarian civilians. Hitler made every

[*] Antonescu came on 12 April 1943. Mussolini had been before him.
[†] Mussolini's visit lasted from 7 to 10 April 1943.
[‡] He arrived on 17 April 1943. He also complained about the measures against the Jews. Hitler shouted, 'The Jews must either be annihilated or be thrown into a concentration camp.'

effort to calm him down by dealing with him amicably and promising to put a stop to it.

At the same time the President of Slovakia, Tiso, paid a call.[*] He received no briefing on the 'alleged positions'. Hitler was of the opinion that a good lunch was sufficient. With a laugh he said, 'To everything I say, he replies yes and amen.'

After Hitler had received his Allies in this friendly way, he immediately began to shower them with horrible curses. The cause was Keitel's suggestion that he decorate with the Knight's Cross the Italian General Gariboldi, who had commanded the Third Italian Army at Stalingrad.[†] Now all Hitler's pent-up fury about the defeat at Stalingrad was released. He cursed the day he had asked Mussolini to send Italian troops to the Eastern Front. He called the Romanians and the Italians in particular a cowardly rabble. In his eyes they bore the principal responsibility for the defeat at Stalingrad. Keitel immediately began backtracking. Absolutely true to form, he demonstrated by nodding vigorously that he entirely shared the Führer's opinion. He declared that his suggestion did not mean that that he wanted to honour the Italian general for bravery, only that the Führer might wish to make a gesture in connection with Mussolini's visit. With much argument and counter-argument Hitler finally gave in and proposed that General Gariboldi should be honoured with the Black Eagle, which was given to foreigners in peacetime. However, it soon became clear that the general already had this honour. Eventually Hitler talked himself into giving him the Knight's Cross.

Gariboldi was ordered to present himself at the Berghof, because only Hitler could hand out the award. The general appeared, accompanied by General Marras, the Italian military attaché in Berlin. Both men were led into the great hall where the Führer was. The adjutants gathered in the drawing room next door to watch the ceremony through the curtain, as they knew with what ill will Hitler had consented to grant this honour.

The Italians looked very intimidated when they came in. Hitler stood ostentatiously facing the wall. Gariboldi and Marras remained dithering in the doorway. Hitler made a half-turn and, with a nod, gestured to Gariboldi to approach. Without so much as honouring him with a look, he handed him the closed case containing the order. At the same time he hissed between his teeth that he was very busy, and quickly left the hall. Gariboldi stood there with the order in his hand as if struck by lightning.

[*] On 23 April 1943.
[†] He commanded the Eighth Army. He was granted the Knight's Cross on 1 April 1943.

As Hitler walked across the drawing room where the adjutants were standing, he shouted out to them that it had been the most disagreeable moment of his life.

Once a week Zeitzler and Heusinger, the Chief of the Operations Department of Army High Command, arrived from East Prussia for the Obersalzberg briefing. At the beginning of April, Hitler summoned Zeitzler to attend a special briefing. All the usual participants were present. After Zeitzler's report on the situation at the front Hitler referred to a conversation he had had with Keitel and Jodl the night before and declared something like the following: 'The situation on the Eastern Front permits no large scale multi-directional offensive. We need to pull a few important pieces out of the Russian Front in order to gain the initiative again. We must finally be able to talk of success again. The sops I threw at the Allies at Klessheim will not keep them sweet for ever. Neutral foreign nations are also reacting unpleasantly and we have to hang on to the Turks for dear life.'[*] Hitler put on his spectacles and looked at the map, then continued in a shrill voice: 'Here, at Kursk, we have the opportunity of giving the Russians a blow and threatening Moscow again.'

Hitler held out his hand and Günsche quickly gave him a coloured pencil. Hitler drew two green arrows on the map. One went in the direction of Orel and the other towards Belgorod. Both cut deep into Russian positions and ended up way behind Kursk. Hitler continued, 'Zeitzler, in my opinion, we should launch the main offensive here, at the centre of the Kursk Salient that leads out of the areas of Belgorod and Orel. I am hoping for a great success. Work the plan out! Send your best staff officers out to have a look straightaway. They need to examine the area properly. We are going to use the Ferdinand[†] for the first time in this operation. The monster will be the pile driver with which we shall smash the Russian positions. No T-34[‡] will stop it.' The Ferdinand, a self-propelling, over-heavy gun, had been just introduced in great numbers for use on the Eastern Front.

Hitler was wholly absorbed by the preparations for the Kursk offensive. A little while later Zeitzler presented him with the plans worked out by

[*] The Turks provided Germany with non-ferrous metals, vanadium in particular.
[†] A heavily armoured self-propelled 8.8cm gun that in battle proved itself poorly conceived, especially at close quarters. An improved version was called the Elephant.
[‡] The T-34 was a thirty-ton Soviet tank armed with a 7.6cm cannon (8.5cms from 1944). It could reach fifty kilometres an hour and had a range of 300–400 kilometres. About 40,000 were built. It proved itself far superior to German tanks.

the General Staff. In his briefing he pointed out that the Russians had concentrated forces in the area of the German attack. Intelligence from the air
and on the ground had indicated that they had greatly strengthened their
positions at the centre of the Kursk Salient. Moreover, two Russian tank
armies had suddenly disappeared from the Kursk Salient but had not reappeared in any other sector of the front. Zeitzler supposed that they had
been taken from the front and put in reserve; from that he concluded that
the preparations for the attack were no secret to the Russians and that there
would be no element of surprise here.*

Hitler suggested another variant in the attack: the main thrust should be
directed not against the centre of the Salient, but much further west. So he
persisted with his plans. In his opinion the attack should be a concentrated
blow on a sector of the front no wider than four to five kilometres. The
operation should begin with an artillery firestorm, whereupon pioneer
units and infantry could destroy the Russian fortifications. He would send
in the tanks only when a breakthrough had been effected, the minefields
cleared and the Russian anti-tank guns silenced.

During later meetings Hitler became more and more insistent that the
Battle of the Kursk Salient could decide the war. He ordered that the entire
tank production for May and June be handed over to the armies of Model
and Hoth.[24] In that way the number of tanks available to these armies at
the beginning of the attack rose to around 3,000.[†] At Kursk the elite Panzer
divisions SS Leibstandarte 'Adolf Hitler', 'Das Reich', 'Totenkopf' and
'Gross-Deutschland' were assembled and equipped with the newest Tiger
tanks[‡] and Ferdinand guns. Besides this, Hitler directed Göring to concentrate practically the whole of the Luftwaffe in the area of the Kursk
operations and give the offensive comprehensive support from the air.

At a situation report before to the Battle of Kursk, aerial photographs
were shown bearing the legend 'Russian positions north-east of Belgorod:
Top secret'. From these one could discern a system of intensely defended
trenches, artillery positions and observation points. When Hitler saw them,
he said, 'That won't save them either this time!'

In preparation for the Battle of the Kursk Salient, Hitler transferred his HQ
from the Obersalzberg back to the Wolfsschanze in East Prussia in the

---

*The Soviet agent Sandor Rado had warned them of the plan on 1 April 1943. Later he
was able to report on the postponement as well.
†The Germans had around 2,700 tanks, Russia 3,300.
‡A fifty-five-ton tank with an 8.8cm cannon.

middle of June 1943. At the same time a delegation of generals and staff officers arrived from Turkey.[*] They came on the initiative and at the invitation of the High Command. The Turks were to observe the strength of the Germans on the Eastern Front during manoeuvres of the Panzer divisions concentrated in the region of Kharkov–Belgorod, which were preparing for the Battle of Kursk. After the manoeuvres, the Turks came back to the HQ to meet Hitler. They then had extensive discussions with Keitel and Jodl before returning to Hitler for tea. After their meeting with Hitler, they visited France at the invitation of the High Command. Hitler was very pleased with his talks with the Turks. 'We can rely on the Turks. The demonstration of our Panzer divisions at Kharkov made a big impression on them.'

In France the Turkish delegation was received by Field Marshal von Rundstedt, the Supreme Commander of Army Group West. He had been given orders from Führer HQ not to spoil the impression the Turks had been given at the Panzer-division manoeuvres on the Eastern Front and to show the guests only the strongly fortified parts of the Atlantic Wall. So the Turks visited the heavy battery 'Fritz Todt' on Cap Gris Nez.[25] They were naturally not shown the coastal artillery made up of antiquated plundered guns.

On 5 July 1943 the offensive in the sector Belgorod–Kursk–Orel began. On the morning of the first day Hitler badgered his adjutants incessantly to find out from Zeitzler what progress had been made. At around 12.30 Zeitzler appeared before Hitler in person. The latter launched himself at him and asked him excitedly, 'Zeitzler, how is it going at Kursk?' Zeitzler answered vaguely and evasively. He said that he had only scanty information from the front so far. The Russians were resisting manfully. He added carefully, 'The element of surprise was clearly not there.' Hitler lost control: 'The Ferdinand! The Ferdinand must immediately be thrown at the front! We have to break through, whatever the cost!'

On 6 July Zeitzler reported that the infantry and pioneers had not been able to penetrate the Russian defensive positions and had sustained heavy losses. After that they had had to send most of the Panzer squadrons into the attack. Hitler exploded. He ordered the Panzers to be kept in reserve and, no matter what the sacrifice, to use the strength of the infantry and the pioneer units to reduce the Russian positions. New reserves should be thrown into the fight. He reiterated his order that concentrated blows should be inflicted. At the time Hitler was like a man suffering from a fever.

---

[*]They arrived in Berlin on 24 June 1943 and in Rastenburg on 6 July.

Every hour he issued orders that Zeitzler should be asked whether the Russian positions had finally fallen and how much territory his SS Leibstandarte had won.

After a few days Zeitzler reported that the attack had stagnated. The German divisions had had to go over to the defence, and in some areas the Russians were carrying out quick counter-attacks. The Ferdinand and the Tiger were being knocked out of the battle one by one by Russian anti-tank guns and embedded T-34s. Hitler simply didn't want to believe it. He threw a fit, beat his fists on the table and screamed, 'This all comes from not carrying out my orders!'

Günsche received orders from Hitler to fly out to the Leibstandarte right away, find out the position on the ground and report to him in person. Günsche flew to the area north of Belgorod, where Sepp Dietrich, commander of the Leibstandarte, had his HQ. Immediately before landing, he could see heavily manned Russian positions. Everywhere were the remains of burned-out German heavy tanks and self-propelled guns. Dietrich told Günsche, 'Over there are ten kilometres of what I was supposed to be able to take, but at what price! Of the more than 150 tanks I started out with, not even twenty are still battleworthy. The infantry has sustained heavy losses. The neighbouring division has fared no better. Who knows how deeply manned the Russians lines are? It is easy to talk when you are in East Prussia, but here it looks different. We are not going to break through.'

The following evening Günsche was back with Hitler. As he tried to report on what he had seen, Hitler interrupted him with a tired, helpless gesture and said, 'Forget it. I know . . . Even Dietrich has been repelled. With the Kursk offensive I wanted to reverse fate. I would never have believed the Russians were so strong . . .'

10

Summer 1943 – February 1944

At the end of June 1943, even before the Battle of the Kursk Salient, Field Marshal Kesselring, Supreme Commander of the German army in Italy, arrived at the Wolfsschanze to report to Hitler. Göring, Keitel, Warlimont, Below and Günsche were present for Kesselring's briefing. Jodl was indisposed. The conference turned on the danger of an Anglo-American landing in Italy after the capitulation of German and Italian forces in Tunisia at the end of May. Kesselring pointed out that after the fall of Tunis the Italian High Command had sabotaged measures for the reinforcement and defence of Italy. Under the pretext that they lacked fuel, the Italian navy had been confined to port. Kesselring proposed that he should himself takeover the command of Italian forces in order to foil the plots of the Italian High Command.

Hitler reacted calmly to Kesselring's briefing. He declared that he would rather see an Anglo-American landing in Italy than one in France. As to the behaviour of the Italian High Command, he suggested withdrawing Italian troops from the regions where fighting with Anglo-American troops was expected and using them entirely for coastal defence. After the meeting Kesselring flew back to Italy.

That same night Hitler ordered Günsche to find out whether Göring was already asleep. The latter was staying in his bunker at the Wolfsschanze at the time, which was less than a hundred metres from Hitler's. Günsche was told on the telephone that Göring was on the point of going to bed. In the company of Günsche and Linge, Hitler hurried over to Göring's bunker. The Reichsmarschall received Hitler in his nightclothes, a colourful dressing gown tied with a blue belt and a silk shawl around his neck, and lacquered slippers with silver buckles on his feet. He looked like a maharaja and reeked of expensive scent. Hitler remained for around half an hour. He talked about the situation in Italy as described by Kesselring and about his own plan to meet Mussolini.

The next morning Hitler gave Ribbentrop the job of organising a meeting with Mussolini. That same morning he flew from Rastenburg to

Salzburg in the company of Keitel, Warlimont, Bormann, Hewel and his adjutants and personal bodyguards. Warlimont was representing the indisposed Jodl.* The Führer and his retinue drove in a cavalcade from Salzburg to the Obersalzberg to see Eva Braun. There he also met Eva's parents, who were not generally to be seen at the Berghof when he was in residence, and he ate with them all that evening. Eva's father wore the uniform of a captain in the administrative service.

The following day at about 7.00 a.m., Hitler and his staff returned to Salzburg airport. An hour later he flew to Italy with a fighter escort, landing on the military airfield of Belluno, north of Venice. He was greeted by Mussolini, Cavalero, the Italian Chief of Staff, and Kesselring. From the airfield it was a rather long trip by train and car to a villa in a remote spot in the mountains where the discussions were to take place.† Hitler was maddened by the protracted journey, as he wanted to return to Germany the same day.

Worse still, the car bringing Warlimont failed to turn up, having lost contact with the others when the driver took a wrong turning. The Italian officers accompanying him explained that they didn't know the way. Their car halted at a crossroads and Warlimont, his right-hand man Major Waizenegger and Günsche got out to look for tyre marks in the dusty earth in order to determine which direction Hitler and Mussolini's cavalcade had taken. Warlimont could hardly conceal his anger. He was convinced that the mishap was deliberate cheek on the part of the Italians. They wanted to treat him as a nobody. He absolutely had to be at the conference from the beginning, because he had the required documentation in his briefcase. What was more, Keitel could not deal with the Italians. While the Italian officers wandered to and fro gesticulating, Warlimont grew more and more furious. He described the whole business as a devious plot on the part of the Italian military who wanted to ambush him so as to prevent negotiations. 'They don't want to fight, and they don't want Kesselring to be their Supreme Commander,' he said. At last a car appeared that had been sent by Keitel to look for Warlimont. He eventually arrived at the meeting an hour late.

Hitler's bodyguard were suspicious of the endless journey from the airfield and were further unsettled by Warlimont's long absence. During Hitler's previous visits to Mussolini only Italian guards had been used. This time Hitler's own escort, armed with machine guns, was stationed around the villa and outside the door of the conference room. Not surprisingly,

*He flew on 18 July 1943.
†The talks were held at the Villa Gaggià in Feltre near Belluno in northern Italy.

the atmosphere was not as it had been on earlier occasions. That could be seen at the buffet that had been set up in the park of the villa, and where the Germans and Italians stood in starkly separate groups.

After a meeting lasting more than three hours, Hitler and Mussolini retired for a one-to-one lunch. They then drove with their retinues back to the airfield in Belluno, and Hitler flew back to Germany. When he had sat down in the aircraft he told Bormann that the day had had a very unpleasant feel to it. 'Mussolini is my loyal friend,' Hitler said. 'He is the only real Roman among the Italians. As we parted he told me, "Führer, once I am no longer here Italian fascism will collapse like a house of cards."' Hitler spent the night on the Obersalzberg. The next morning he flew back to his HQ in Rastenburg.

In the days that followed, Hitler's concern about the reliability of his Allies in the Italian royal family grew. The SD reported from Rome that the royal family was engaged in secret negotiations with the British. At the beginning of July Hitler summoned to his HQ Prince Philipp of Hessen,[1] who was married to Princess Mafalda, a daughter of King Vittorio Emanuele. At the time Prince Philipp was an SA-Obergruppenführer, wore the Gold Party Badge of the National Socialist Party and was Oberpräsident of the Province of Hesse. He resided in Cassel.

Hitler thought he would learn from the Prince what his royal relatives in Rome were up to. As the Prince spent a lot of time in Rome Hitler believed that he would have been initiated into the plans of the Italian court. In the Führer's opinion, the Italian royal family, Crown Prince Umberto in particular, was capable of any sort of infamy towards Germany. 'Umberto', he said, 'is a personal enemy of the Duce, because he is striving to rule alone in Italy.' When the Prince of Hessen arrived at the HQ he was put up in the guest bunker. Hitler lunched with him every day and invited him to his tea evenings. Together they looked at illustrated books and at photographs of excavations in Rome. In his conversations with the Prince, Hitler sought to ascertain the views of the Italian royal family. He also ordered that the Prince's correspondence be vetted.

On 10 July 1943 Anglo-American troops landed in Sicily. On the 25th Keitel and Jodl appeared in Hitler's bunker together with SS-Obergruppenführer Karl Wolff, Himmler's liaison officer at HQ. They were flustered and asked to be announced immediately. They were asked to come to the conference room, and few minutes later Hitler appeared in the company of Günsche. He looked distraught. Since the failure of the Kursk offensive he had lived in constant fear of fresh bad tidings.

Keitel stepped up to Hitler and stuttered, 'My Führer, the Duce—'

'What's wrong with him?' Hitler snapped, interrupting him.

'—has been deposed.'

Keitel handed Hitler a letter from the Italian High Command. Hitler tore the letter out of his hand, quickly put on his spectacles and read half out loud, 'Mussolini's regime has been dismissed. His Majesty has asked Marshal Badoglio to form a new Cabinet. Italy will loyally fulfil its duties to its Allies and will continue the battle on Germany's side until the victorious end.'

Hitler had turned pale. He gasped for air. 'Where is the Duce now? What is known about him?' he finally asked.

'Nothing,' they all answered simultaneously.

Hitler screwed up the letter and shouted angrily, 'They are going to kill him, these Italians! This pack of traitors! That blackguard Roatta has become Chief of Staff!'* Hitler had for years hated the Italian General Roatta like the plague. He knew that Roatta, who had commanded the Italian troops in the Balkans, and whose mission it was to fight the Greek, Albanian and Yugoslav partisans, had made a fortune selling arms to them instead. 'They are all in cahoots with the British!' Hitler continued to roar. 'This damned royal family! And this Prince Philipp, the King's son-in-law, sits around here with me and acts as if butter wouldn't melt in his mouth. He knew all about it! And he's going to pay for it!' (Prince Philipp was handed over to the Gestapo in Königsberg for interrogation. His wife, the Italian Princess Mafalda, was put into a concentration camp.)

Hitler beat the table with his fists and continued in a paroxysm of rage, 'I'll show them! The Italian army will be disarmed! Jodl, which regiments can do that? ' Jodl answered in a soft voice, 'My Führer, we can send in the reserves from the Styrian and Tyrolean Mountain Rifle Regiments. They are not far from the Italian border. And although they are just freshly made recruits, for the cowardly Italians they will be quite enough.' After a short pause Hitler said that the Mountain Rifle Regiments suggested by Jodl were not best fitted to disarm the Italians. 'That is a job for my Leibstandarte,' he declared. 'They need to be brought up to strength anyway.'

He immediately gave orders to transfer the Leibstandarte 'Adolf Hitler' from the Eastern Front to the Innsbruck area on the German-Italian border. Then Jodl briefed him on the fighting against the Anglo-Americans in Sicily. With an abrupt movement, Hitler removed his spectacles and began to rotate them in his hands behind his back, until finally

---

*Lieutenant General Mario Roatta had been appointed on 1 June 1943.

one of the lenses broke. That often happened when he was angry and over-wrought. He threw the splintered glass and frames on to the table and said contemptuously, 'What a bunch of cowards, this Churchill and this Eisenhower! In their place I would have landed in Genoa, or even in Hamburg, certainly not in Sicily, which isn't in the least dangerous for us. That drunkard Churchill is really happy that we are bleeding to death in Russia and is waiting his moment . . .'

From General Staff reports Hitler knew that the British had deliberately put off the opening of a second front. These reports relied above all on information the German General Staff regularly received from official British sources via Spanish diplomats in London. They were transmitted by the Duke of Alba, the Spanish Ambassador in London, and his military attaché Colonel Alfonso Barra to the Spanish General Staff in Madrid, whence they were relayed to the German military attaché. They included details of the evaluation of the military situation by the British High Command and of British troop movements. From the information they presented to Hitler, the German General Staff drew the conclusion that Britain was still fighting a defensive war for the time being. London had carefully let slip this information, so that Germany would continue to keep all its forces on the Eastern Front. In the German General Staff this infor-mation from Spanish sources was codenamed the Alba Reports.

Himmler entered the conference room. Hitler was in such a state that he didn't notice him. When Günsche pointed him out, he turned quickly and gave Himmler a hurried greeting before asking him, 'Himmler, how could that have happened? The Duce certainly did not resign voluntarily. That's a joke. He was fired.' Himmler reported that up to now he had only incom-plete information on the events in Italy. From these, however, a conclusion could be drawn that the majority of leading Italian fascists, Mussolini's son-in-law Ciano included, were opposed to the Duce. They supported the royal house's action, which was aimed at taking Italy out of the war.

Hitler leaned against the table and told Keitel, Himmler, Jodl, Wolff and Günsche, who were standing around him, that he had always seen Ciano as a charlatan. He knew that, during the invasion of Albania, Ciano had appropriated important mining concerns. As Foreign Minister he had led the 'trust' that had run brothels throughout Italy. Hitler called Ciano's wife Edda, Mussolini's daughter, a slut. When she came to Germany, especially powerful SS officers had to be 'seconded' to her for 'maintenance'. Hitler sighed. 'I am sorry for the Duce. Himmler, find out if he is still alive, then find out where he is holed up. We must save him!'

★

Only a few days later General Marras, the Italian military attaché in Berlin, appeared at Führer HQ. After Mussolini's fall he had been appointed Ambassador to Germany by the Badoglio government, and he had now come to present his credentials to Hitler. Keitel and the Head of Protocol at the German Foreign Office, Dörnberg, led Marras and the accompanying officials from the Italian Embassy to Hitler's bunker. They had to wait in the corridor of the conference room, where Hitler was sitting at the time. The servants took their coats, and Linge announced Marras's arrival to Hitler. The latter got up from the table and assumed the grim expression he thought best fitted the occasion. Linge opened the door and bade Marras enter. Marras wavered a little and wanted Keitel to take precedence. Keitel observed that he was at home, and let Marras pass before him. When Marras saw Hitler, he turned to his officials in fear, before stepping forward with his credentials in his hand and clicking his heels before the Führer. Before Marras could utter a word, Hitler roared at him, 'General, I could have you arrested immediately! Your behaviour is tantamount to treason!'

Marras turned pale, and the hand holding his credentials shook. Linge had to leave the room. Twenty minutes later Hitler rang for him. When Linge returned, the Führer's face was still livid. On the table lay the credentials where they had been tossed without a glance. With a movement of his hand, Hitler indicated to Marras that he was to go. The Italian made a military about-turn and left the room in a hurry. In the corridor he tore his coat from the servant's hand and ran so fast from the bunker that Keitel, Dörnberg and Marras's escort could hardly keep up with him. He leaped into his car and fled from the HQ.

Hitler looked among the Italian fascists for a man fit to replace the vanished Mussolini. To this end he received at his HQ representatives of the Italian Fascist Party, who had fled to Germany after Mussolini's fall. The candidates for replacing Mussolini were presented by Bormann. Hitler wanted to speak to them personally. None of them, however, made the right pugnacious impression. They all mourned first and foremost the lost pleasures of life which they had enjoyed in Italy. The former Secretary of the Italian Fascist Party, Pavolini, complained above all of the loss of his fortune. Not once did he mention Italy's fate. Hitler was outraged. He said, 'They are all venal through and through, the whole lot of them. You can't rely on them to carry on the war.'*

★

*He nonetheless allowed Alessandro Pavolini to form a government in German-controlled Italy on 9 September 1943.

At the beginning of August 1943 Himmler appeared at the Wolfsschanze unannounced. He asked Günsche if he could see Hitler at once and was received immediately. With a radiant expression Himmler proclaimed, 'My Führer, the Duce lives!' Hitler didn't want to believe him. He felt that if Mussolini were still alive the British secret service would long since have taken him to England. Himmler had brought a map of the Abruzzi with him, to which he now drew Hitler's attention: 'My Führer, we have unimpeachable information that the Duce is being held prisoner in a remote house in these mountains.'*

Hitler paced up and down the room in high excitement, scratching a sore spot on his neck. He ordered Günsche, Keitel and Jodl to be summoned. With them and Himmler, he discussed how they might spirit Mussolini out. They decided to liberate him by means of a special commando unit that would parachute into the area near the house where he was being held prisoner. Himmler told Hitler that he had the very man, a proper daredevil. Hitler wanted to see him.

Later that very evening, Himmler returned from his HQ near Angerburg, forty-five minutes' drive from the Wolfsschanze, accompanied by a tall, broad-shouldered SS officer with a duelling scar on his cheek. On the left sleeve of his uniform tunic the letters SD had been embroidered in silver braid. It was the Austrian Skorzeny, who had worked as a Nazi agent before the Anschluss and had organised political murders.[2] Skorzeny made a good impression on Hitler, who ordered Jodl to outline to Skorzeny the plans to liberate Mussolini. Jodl was to tell General Student,[3] the Supreme Commander of the Parachute Units in Italy, to provide Skorzeny with the necessary paratroops. As Skorzeny left, Hitler said to him, 'Fly directly to Italy! Find out the lie of the land. Do whatever you think is right.'[4]

In the meantime the Italian army had been disarmed by the Germans. To this end, the SS Leibstandarte 'Adolf Hitler' had been transferred from its positions near Kharkov to the German–Italian border. They were no longer commanded by Sepp Dietrich, but by Theodor Wisch.[5] After the Battle of Kursk, Sepp Dietrich had been appointed commander of I SS Panzer Corps that had been made up of the Leibstandarte and another Panzer division recently formed in Belgium called 'Hitlerjugend' and consisting of sixteen- and seventeen-year-old SS men.

At the beginning of August the Leibstandarte entered the Tyrol and drove over the Brenner Pass to the Milan area. Its job was to disarm the

*Mussolini was being held in a hotel on the Gran Sasso in the Abruzzi.

Italian army, which was based in the triangle between Milan, Turin and Como and amounted to about an army in strength. The SS men had orders to treat the Italians like enemies and traitors and to suppress all resistance with an iron hand. At the beginning of the operation Günsche rejoined the Leibstandarte, after Hitler at his own wish had sent him to Italy as a company commander. As he took his leave, Hitler laughed and said, 'Don't frighten the Italians too much with your size.'

Most of the Italian soldiers were holed up in their barracks, and many of the officers had abandoned their uniforms for mufti and disappeared. The disarming went ahead as follows. An SS officer appeared at the barracks and asked the Italians to lay down their arms and give themselves up. The answer was always the same: 'Never. We will defend ourselves to the last drop of blood.' It was enough, however, to toss in a hand grenade for a white flag to go up and the soldiers to allow themselves to be disarmed without resistance. Then these 'allies' would be marched in long columns to work camps in Italy and Germany. These had been Hitler's orders: if the Italians don't want to fight, then they can come and work for us, until they drop.[6]

That was how the Leibstandarte fought in Italy. The SS men often spoke about it, how very different this 'pleasant war' in Italy had been from the horrors of Russia. When the Leibstandarte had finished its work, their confiscated booty — massive quantities of plunder — was transported to Germany. The work done, the various units headed for spas on Lakes Maggiore, Garda and Como, and there they relaxed after the heavy fighting in Russia and licked the fresh wounds they had received at the Battle of Kursk.

Here the Leibstandarte was once again completely brought up to strength and rearmed. Above all it received new vehicles from Fiat and Alfa Romeo. Besides this it was given a new section equipped with Panther tanks. Now the Leibstandarte had at its disposal nearly 300 tanks of the Tiger, Panther and Type IV models.[7] At the end of October 1943 the peaceful life of the Leibstandarte in Italy came to an end. Together with other German divisions it was thrown back on to the southern sector of the Eastern Front, where the situation had become threatening. Depressed, the SS men found themselves driving back to Russia and the horrors of real war.

In the second half of August Wolff reported that Skorzeny's mission had been a success.[*] Wolff had been Himmler's liaison man at Führer HQ, but

---

[*]Mussolini was freed on 12 September 1943.

after Mussolini's fall he had been appointed Chief SS and Police Führer in
Italy. Mussolini was liberated by General Student's paratroops, who had
landed near the house where he was being held. Skorzeny spirited
Mussolini away in a small aircraft of the Fieseler-Storch type.[8] Hitler
immediately sent his own pilot Baur with his own Condor to the place
where Mussolini was now being sheltered in Italy, and Baur brought
him safe and sound to Hitler's HQ. The Führer waited for him on the
airstrip at Rastenburg and, when the aircraft landed, walked towards to it.
Mussolini, wearing mufti and with a hat pulled down over his forehead,
was recognisable through the window at the front. The plane came to a
halt, the airport staff brought up the steps, and Hitler stood at the bottom.
Soon Mussolini appeared at the door, hat in hand, looking pale and gaunt,
and came down the steps with difficulty. Hitler took both his hands and
pressed them for a long while. But Mussolini appeared wholly apathetic.
So Hitler put his arm round his shoulder, shook him and spoke a few
words. Then they both laughed. Keitel, Bormann, Dietrich and the others,
who had been standing at a distance, came up and congratulated Mussolini
on his rescue. In the meantime both Skorzeny and Mussolini's son came
down from the aircraft, and they all drove together to Führer HQ.
Mussolini and his son were put up in Göring's luxurious bunker. For lib-
erating Mussolini, Skorzeny received the Knight's Cross, Germany's highest order. From the Wolfsschanze, Mussolini drove to Munich. There he
was put up in a castle belonging to the Wittelsbachs, the Bavarian royal
family, together with his son and his wife, who had travelled up from Italy.

At the beginning of September 1943, Mussolini formed a new government from the group of fascists who had fled from Italy to Germany and
who had remained loyal to him.* In Italy itself, the Germans fought the
Anglo-American troops who had landed in Sicily on 10 July. At the end of
August the German armies had to retreat across the Straits of Messina in
to southern Italy.† On 8 September the Italian King and the Badoglio government flew to the Anglo-Americans in Sicily and announced Italy's
capitulation. That was basically their own capitulation, as virtually all Italy
was in German hands and the Italian army had been disarmed by the
Germans. The Anglo-Americans held Sicily and a tiny piece of southern
Italy.‡ At the capitulation all Badoglio could give the Anglo-American

*Mussolini's puppet regime was formed on 15 September 1943.
†The Germans withdrew some 100,000 troops by the night of 17 August 1943.
‡The British had landed on the south-west tip of Calabria on 3 September 1943. On the
day of the Italian capitulation American and British forces landed in the Gulf of Salerno
and at Taranto.

High Command was the main force of the Italian navy. Because of the well-known fighting morale of the Italian navy, however, the German High Command attributed little significance to this.[*]

After the flight of the Italian King Vittorio Emanuele and his premier, Badoglio, Mussolini and his government returned to northern Italy, where they set themselves up on Lake Garda. But it was no more than a puppet regime, as the German occupying forces had the last say. Mussolini's government was restricted to civil matters and to finding manpower for Germany. These limitations of power were the result of Hitler's attitude to the Italians. He declared that he would in no circumstances allow them to have political power again, because they had betrayed him. He had created the Mussolini government only to show the world that Italian fascism was still alive. As a result he allowed Mussolini to recruit an army of four or five divisions, consisting of soldiers from the Italian army who had been disarmed by the Germans and who were in German labour camps. Marshal Graziani, who had remained loyal to Mussolini, was appointed their commander. The Graziani army was not intended for the front, but carried out purely police functions, most importantly suppressing anti-fascist revolts and fighting Italian patriots who attacked the German armies of occupation. For these police duties the Graziani army was equipped only with carbines and light machine guns.

Hitler no longer had confidence in Mussolini, whom he had once called 'the only true Roman'. After everything this man had experienced since his imprisonment, Italy's fate interested him no longer. SS-Obergruppenführer Wolff, the highest SS and Police Führer in Italy, had his agents watching Mussolini. He reported that the Duce was now entirely indifferent to the military and political situation in the country and was interested only in pleasure. The SD reported from Italy that Mussolini was leading a wild life and was surrounded by women with whom he enjoyed nightly orgies. On this subject Hitler told his adjutants, 'The Duce is interested only in his harem of young, pretty Italian women. They occupy all his attention.'

The Russian counter-attacks at Kursk had meanwhile grown into a major offensive. The situation reports of the German High Command spoke constantly of a 'planned' withdrawal of German troops in order to 'straighten the line' but it cost tens of thousands of dead and wounded on the German

---

[*]The Italian fleet went over to the Allies on 9 September 1943. On the way to Malta the Luftwaffe damaged the battleship *Italia* and sank the *Roma* with 1,500 men on board.

side. Hitler, however, unwaveringly repeated after every briefing on the situation on the Eastern Front, 'It will finally end in German victory.' In the meantime German troops on the Eastern Front daily retreated further and further under Russian pressure. The dreams of Ukrainian wheat, coal and ore and of Caucasian oil now belonged to history.

Industrialists turned up at Führer HQ and had long conversations with Hitler. In his immediate circle there was talk that Germany's lords were worried. The first to arrive was Dr Röchling, the head of the Reich Iron Combine, followed by the armaments king Krupp in a private train.[9] At this time Göring also popped into the HQ. Normally he gave himself up to a carefree life of hunting at Rominten. The agonies and the terrible loss of German troops on the Eastern Front worried him but little. With him he brought game and strong beer that had been specially brewed for him. At lunch Hitler read Göring a letter he had received from Schacht. Schacht had written that in industrial circles the situation on the Eastern Front was seen as a great danger to Germany. People believed that in these circumstances it would be wise to seek a separate peace in the west. Schacht indicated that he had private contacts and knew they could bring such negotiations to a completely successful conclusion.

Hitler was outraged by Schacht's letter, directing a torrent of abuse against him and roaring that Schacht wanted to bypass him and make policy behind his back. Any conversations with the Anglo-Americans that took place without his knowledge he saw as high treason. He threatened to pack Schacht off to a concentration camp.[10]

Göring kept quiet while Hitler foamed at the mouth. He tried to distract the Führer and at last managed to do so by telling him the news that old Schacht had divorced his wife and married his young secretary.

When the German armies were forced to retreat behind the Dnieper, Hitler summoned the Supreme Commanders of the army groups on the Eastern Front. They met in the dining room of the mess, 500 metres from the Führer's bunker. Hitler drove to the mess with Bormann, Schaub, Schmundt and Linge, and as he entered he greeted the field marshals and generals gathered there with a fascist salute. Then he delivered a speech in which he demanded that the front be held, whatever the cost.* At the same time he indicated that the situation was favourable for further military operations in the east because the opening of a second front in France was clearly still being postponed. He read those present two reports from the

---

*The meeting took place on 27 January 1944.

German Information Bureau which pointed out differences between the Anglo-Americans and the Russians.

At the end of his speech, Hitler spoke stirringly: 'Gentlemen! When the hour of danger strikes for Germany, I hope that you, my generals, will stand with me on the barricades! And you, my field marshals, will be at my side with your swords drawn!' At these words Field Marshal von Manstein, who was then commanding Army Group South, sprang to his feet and cried, 'Führer, command and we shall obey!' Hitler fell silent and looked at Manstein with displeasure. He couldn't believe he meant it. Manstein was a typical general of the school of Kaiser Wilhelm II, and was known to be a hardened monarchist who had merely played along with National Socialism. Then Keitel also cried out, 'To our greatly honoured Führer, a triple Heil! Heil! Heil!'

The field marshals and generals leaped up and raised their right arms high. Keitel bellowed three times, 'Sieg Heil! Sieg Heil! Sieg Heil!' and everyone joined in. Then he began singing the national anthem 'Deutschland, Deutschland über alles' and the Horst Wessel Song. The others sang along too. This choir roared out the national anthem with one voice, but when it came to the Horst-Wessel Song it was audibly out of step, as the field marshals and generals had little acquaintance with the music and words of this National Socialist anthem. They were still trilling when Hitler left the room.

Icy silence reigned in the car on the way back to the bunker. Bormann hissed through his teeth, 'Outrageous!' When they arrived at the bunker, Hitler went straight into the conference room. As Schmundt, Schaub and Linge disappeared into the adjutants' room, Schaub had a worried look on his face and hung his head, which meant that a storm was brewing. Just at that moment Bormann stepped into the room and said to Schmundt, 'Manstein must report to the Führer immediately!'

Schmundt went to fetch Manstein and brought him to Hitler. Immediately, bellowing could be heard. The Führer shouted at Manstein so much that the field marshal did not once dare interrupt him. He had been guilty of indiscipline, and Hitler insulted him for ten long minutes. He eventually came out like a schoolboy who has broken something and has received his just punishment.

In the first days of December Günsche was summoned to Hitler's HQ from the Eastern Front. He arrived as the SS Leibstandarte 'Adolf Hitler' was being thrown once again into the Russian theatre from Italy. Immediately after his arrival Hitler asked him to lunch. As Günsche sat down opposite him, Hitler said, 'Günsche, I have decided to call you back from Russia. I have received reports that the Russians inject their prisoners with special drugs to make them co-operate. I don't want to risk anything with you. You have been an active member of my staff for a long time and you know too much.' He added he had given orders that all those should be withdrawn from the Eastern Front who had served on his personal staff or had been with his bodyguard.

Although he had been away for only a short while, Günsche had the impression that he had become even more stooping and that his left hand had begun to shake. In recent times the Führer had said that he was always freezing. The shake had begun after the defeat at Stalingrad, but it was hardly noticeable then. Hitler was also gradually turning grey, and his movements seemed jerky and nervous. At lunch he knocked back a full glass of slivovitz, which was a complete change for him. In the past he had occasionally been served a schnapps for his digestion's sake, and he had always made a face when he drank it and had shivered, had even held his nose, because he didn't like the smell of alcohol. Now, however, with lunch and dinner he drank a considerable quantity of schnapps or cognac.

After the meal Hitler asked Günsche to tell him of his experiences at the front. Günsche knew that he liked to hear good news, so from the outset he proceeded cautiously, anxious as he was to let the Führer know that the German troops in Russia had lost heart. He did not mention the violent power of the Russian offensive, but spoke instead of the steadfastness of the Russians during the German counter-attacks. This was all too much for Hitler, however. He angrily motioned to him to stop and said, 'These are individual cases. I have completely different information.' He added heatedly that he was soon going over to the attack; he was advancing on the Dnieper and would retake Kiev. Then he stood up, gave Günsche his hand and said he had to feed Blondi. Grabbing the dog bowl that the servant had brought to him, he went slowly out of the dining room.

In the middle of February 1944 Zeitzler briefed Hitler on the situation on the Eastern Front. He had long ceased to be the bundle of energy he had once been. He still spoke as quickly as ever, but now he gave the impression of wanting to finish the briefing as quickly as possible. As always in recent times, he began with the situation of Army Group South. He reported that the position of German troops on the lower reaches of the Dnieper had got so bad that they would have to withdraw from the industrial area of Nikopol, and in this connection he said that the Army Group High Command wanted to retreat à few kilometres westwards in order to straighten out the line. At these words Hitler leaped up, threw himself across the table, screwed up the map in his left hand and screamed, 'If only the generals could finally understand why I cling to this area so much! We urgently need Nikopol manganese! They simply don't want to understand this. And as soon as they are a few tanks short, they go immediately to their radios and say, "Without tanks we can't hold on. We ask for permission to retreat!"'* Hitler had pointed out many times that Nikopol manganese was particularly important in the making of stainless steel. That was why sources of raw materials had to be retained at all costs. For that reason the Nikopol area had to be turned into a fortress that could not be taken by the Russians.

Hitler fell into an armchair. He stared at Zeitzler with wide-open eyes as if he wanted his support. Zeitzler, however, said nothing. He knew that to be the best policy at such moments. When Hitler's wrath had abated a little, Zeitzler continued. He reported on the difficult position of the Eighth Army in the Korsun–Shevchenkovsky pocket. The operation launched a few days before to relieve the Eighth Army was getting no-where thanks to the powerful opposition of the Russians.[11] Of the central sector of the front, along the line Bobruisk–Mogilev–Orsha–Vitebsk, Zeitzler had little to say. At the time the fighting was of merely local significance. In the northern sector of the front, according to Zeitzler, the German army had been pushed back into Estonian territory by the offensive launched by the Russians in the middle of January around Leningrad and Volkhov.

When Zeitzler had finished, Hitler ordered that the map of the south-ern sector be opened again. He studied it excitedly. Then, in a calmer voice, he declared that the war against Russia had entered a phase that would decide its outcome – victory or defeat. Any army can lose and be repulsed, but there is irrefutably a moment when all these blows come together to create a catastrophe. This was the current position on the German Eastern Front. As a result it was absolutely vital to demonstrate an iron will. Any further withdrawal ultimately meant defeat for Germany. From now on a general or officer who suggested to him that there should be further retreat he would punish severely or simply shoot. It was not pri-marily about operational experience any more, but about the firmness and steadfastness of commanders. As a result he would give the post of com-mander to young generals and officers who possessed these qualities. Officers of this sort he would promote by two or three grades. These last

---

*The Wehrmacht was forced to withdraw from Nikopol on 8 February 1944.

words Hitler spoke with a hoarse voice, having completely over-exerted himself. Standing up, he left the room by the side door and went back to his private quarters.

'Get me Morell!' he shouted to Linge, who had hurried after him. A few minutes later Morell appeared. As ever, Linge helped him prepare the injections. Hitler pulled off his jacket and offered his arm, which Morell immediately took.

11

February – June 1944

In the second half of February 1944 Hitler ordered several buildings at his Wolfsschanze HQ to be covered by an additional layer of concrete seven metres thick – his own bunker, the so-called guest bunker for Party leaders and ministers who came to report, the bunker containing the telephone exchange, telegraph office and radio station and some other buildings. The previous thickness of two metres Hitler now deemed insufficient because he feared Russian air attacks. The work was going to take several months, and during this time Hitler wanted to transfer his HQ to the Obersalzberg. Only Zeitzler and his assistants in the Army General Staff remained at Lötzen in East Prussia.

On 23 February Hitler travelled on his special train from Rastenburg in the direction of the Obersalzberg. In Munich he broke the journey briefly. From there Eva Braun, her sister Gretl and her friend Frau Schneider[1] accompanied him to the Obersalzberg. This time Eva had not asked Frau Schönmann to the Berghof. She was jealous of her, because Hitler had paid so much attention to her during her first visit in 1943. A few days later Eva's mother arrived at the Berghof. Eva had used her growing influence over Hitler to receive permission for this. In addition to her lady-friends, the wives of Hitler's personal physician Morell, of the surgeon Brandt and of the adjutant Below and Hitler's secretaries were also staying at the Berghof.

Keitel, Jodl, Buhle and Scherff were lodged in the Reich Chancellery department which was situated on the Obersalzberg between Berchtesgaden and Bischofswiesen, half an hour's drive from the Berghof. This time Admiral Voss[2] was also staying there. He had replaced Admiral Krancke as Dönitz's liaison officer at Hitler's HQ after Krancke had been appointed Supreme Commander of the Naval Group Command on the Atlantic coast. Göring moved into his Obersalzberg villa again with his wife and seven-year-old daughter. Himmler and Dönitz were in Salzburg. Not far from there Ribbentrop lived in his Schloss Fuschl. Colonel Streve,[3] the commander of Hitler's HQ, and his staff and Warlimont from the Army

Operations Staff moved into the barracks in Strub. Streve had replaced Thomas in autumn 1942. The latter had been transferred to the North African Front, where he had been killed.

The daily schedule at the Berghof was similar to that established between March and June 1943. Hitler rose at about noon. After breakfast, at around 1.00 or 1.30 p.m., he conducted his midday conference. When this was finished Eva Braun, her mother and her sister Gretl, Eva's companion Frau Schneider, Fräulein Kastrup, Bormann, Morell, Below, Brandt and their wives, Otto Dietrich, Hewel and Lorenz, as well as Hitler's secretaries and adjutants, gathered in the drawing room that adjoined the hall. Here they waited for lunch. At around 3.30 p.m. Hitler offered one of the ladies his arm and led the entire party to the table. That lady had to sit next to him. As in the previous year, really banal conversations were held at table. Not one word was uttered about the war. If the weather was good after lunch, Hitler and the others went for a walk to the tea-house on the Mooslahner Kopf. When the weather was bad he remained at home and passed the time in Eva's apartment. Together they leafed through old copies of German illustrated magazines from the years 1933 to 1939 and enjoyed looking at photographs of Hitler in his glory days. Hitler had dinner at around 8.00 p.m. with the same cast. After that there was the evening briefing, during which his military adjutants Below, Puttkamer and Borgmann[4] gave quick résumés of the present situation at the fronts. After the briefing there began the usual tea evening in the great hall with the inevitable champagne and gramophone music.

Cocktails wrought the change this year, mixed to Eva's recipes. She and the SS servants gave them funny names. When Hitler was served a new cocktail on one occasion, he asked what it was called. The answer was 'Omnibus'. When he inquired how they had hit on this name, it was explained that the cocktail was like a bus, in that it took everything on board and, like a bus, it got you there quickly. He broke into noisy laughter and praised Eva for her ingenuity. After midnight she would direct that there should be another light snack of turtle soup, sandwiches and sausages. At around 3.30 a.m. Hitler usually retired and went to bed.

In contrast to 1943, the daily routine was interrupted by air-raid warnings provoked by the passing of Anglo-American bombers. This generally happened between 9.00 and 10.00 in the morning, when the house Party was still in bed. When enemy planes approached Germany's southern border, the so-called pre-alarm sounded. The announcement was made by the operations room of the Luftwaffe Operations Staff, codenamed

Robinson,* to Hitler's Luftwaffe adjutant Below. He informed Linge, who woke Hitler and told the rest of the Party of the pre-alarm. Now there was a great to-do. Chambermaids dragged a huge number of baskets containing Eva's and the other ladies' clothes into the air-raid shelter. The ladies themselves came tumbling out of their rooms, sleepy eyed and without make-up. Their clothes had been hurriedly thrown on and their heads wrapped in shawls.

If the enemy aircraft reached south German airspace the sirens announced a full alarm and everyone threw themselves into the air-raid shelter. When the full alarm sounded, Hitler got dressed quickly without having breakfast, and in the company of his adjutants went out on to the terrace. There he learned the circumstances from Below and where the aircraft were located, and if there was an immediate danger he would make his way to the shelter.

Hitler's air-raid shelter had taken a year and a half to build. When he arrived at the Berghof, the work was nearly finished. It was composed of a system of tunnels under the rock of the Obersalzberg connected to one another by narrow corridors, so that the whole Obersalzberg was mined like a gigantic molehill. The entrance was in Hitler's subterranean rooms and was secured by an armour-plated door. A hundred steps led down to a passage under the earth. At the end of the steps a machine-gun post had been built. From this entrance a whole labyrinth of corridors led to Hitler's comfortably furnished rooms. Among them were great food storerooms that had been laid out in case the war required the Führer HQ to spend a prolonged period in the system of bunkers. For this reason the bunkers were expanded at the beginning of 1945 and new sleeping quarters added.

Whenever the air-raid warning sounded, the entire area around the Obersalzberg would at once be shrouded in artificial fog. To this end, a special unit had been split into small squads and issued with canisters of milk-coloured gas. They were sent up the mountains around the Berghof. The various anti-aircraft batteries around the Obersalzberg were ready for action. The SS battalion in the barracks less than 500 metres from the mansion reinforced the guardposts in and around the grounds. During the alarm Hitler remained on the terrace with his adjutants and made sure that the Obersalzberg was properly shrouded in fog. If the wind blew the fog away, he would lose his temper and order more canisters to be opened.

---

*Codename for Luftwaffe Operations HQ in Bartenstein, East Prussia. In the spring of 1945 Göring baptised his train with the same name.

Usually an alarm lasted one and a half to two hours. Not one bomb fell on the Berghof area.[5] The usual target for British and American bombers was Munich. During the attacks, in which the population suffered heavily, Hitler worried chiefly about the villa he had had built for Eva Braun, the Palace of the National Socialist Party on the Königsplatz and the restaurant Osteria Bavaria which had been his haunt in his first days in Munich.[6] When Hitler's flat on the Prinzregentenplatz was slightly damaged by the vibrations of an air raid, he declared proudly, 'Now I have also been bombed out!'*

Eva Braun was furious about the air-raid sirens, because she couldn't get a good night's sleep. Besides, she complained of the boredom, as the days seemed to be without end. She made Hitler pore over catalogues of porcelain and crystal with her and help her choose the loveliest for the Berghof. The catalogues were sent to her as the lady of the Berghof by Himmler and delivered by his officers. He in turn received the catalogues because the services were produced by prisoners from Dachau concentration camp working in the porcelain factory in Allach and other factories in Czechoslovakia. These depended on the SS administration main office.[7] Following a special order from Hitler and Eva, prisoners in Dachau concentration camp prepared porcelain lamps and a series of figures that showed Frederick the Great on horseback as well as generals and soldiers in the regiments and uniforms of the Seven Years War.

In order to bring some variety to life on the Obersalzberg, in April 1944 Eva Braun exerted pressure to have the magician Schreiber[8] invited from Berlin. Schreiber came with his wife, who assisted him in his performances. They were put up at Bormann's villa and were invited to come to Hitler's mansion for lunch and dinner. They would arrived with Bormann and his wife, and nearly every evening for two weeks Schreiber performed tricks for Hitler and his household. The performances took place in the great hall, after Hitler had finished with the situation reports. In general they began after the gathering for evening tea. The audience consisted of Hitler, Eva, her mother, her sister Gretl, Eva's friend Frau Schneider, her companion Fräulein Kastrup, Bormann, Morell and Brandt with his wife, Hewel, Otto Dietrich, Lorenz, Hitler's secretaries and the adjutants. Hitler sat in the front row; to the right and left of him were Eva and her mother, and in the same row Bormann and Otto Dietrich. The others sat behind.

---

*An echo of Queen Elizabeth's similar sentiment after Buckingham Palace was bombed in September 1940, 'Now I can look the East End in the face.'

To dance music (the records were selected by Eva and Bormann) Schreiber busied himself with trained doves which flew about the air or he made every imaginable thing about the audience disappear. Loud laugher would rock the hall as all of a sudden Bormann's gold watch or Eva's diamond-studded platinum watch — a gift from Hitler — vanished. Hitler livened up when he watched Schreiber's tricks, laughing and clapping a good deal. He told Schreiber what a good thing it would be if he could make the Russian armies vanish in this way.

In the first months of 1944 losses among the German armies fighting on the Eastern Front increased unimaginably. The soil of Russia was soaked in the blood of German soldiers, whose graves could no longer be counted. The railways brought tens of thousands of wounded to Germany day in, day out, and the hospitals were bursting at the seams. In German towns and villages, more and more blind or crippled soldiers appeared on crutches.

The scale of the losses was nonetheless concealed from the German people. The High Command continued to claim that a planned withdrawal was being staged on the Eastern Front and that the Russians were sustaining huge losses. Its own casualties were said to be insignificant. The German public were also unaware that hundreds of thousands of German officers and soldiers had ended up in Russian captivity. In order to make good the enormous loss of men in battle against the Russians, in keeping with the policy of total war announced after the defeat at Stalingrad, hundreds of thousands of men were conscripted who had previously been exempted as essential for production, as well as sixteen- and seventeen-year-old youths.[9] New divisions were formed from them and thrown at the Eastern Front. The remains of decimated divisions were transferred to France, Belgium or Holland to be made up and rearmed. In the German-occupied countries of western Europe there were therefore a certain number of German units that were basically the pathetic remnants of divisions pulverised in Russia.

Even with all these reserves, the ever greater holes on the Eastern Front could not be plugged. As a result Luftwaffe groundcrews were launched into the fray. From them they made the so-called Luftwaffe field divisions, which were incorporated into the army.[10] Waffen-SS units that had previously been composed of volunteers were also replenished with Luftwaffe and naval personnel as a result of losses on the Eastern Front and owing to the lack of reserves. These measures were not enough to stop the Russian army from pushing ever further west.

After the heavy defeats the Germans had sustained in the Ukraine in the autumn and winter of 1943–4, Hitler placed all his hopes on the spring.

He declared that the Russians would lose their initiative and that that would bring the Russian offensive to a halt, allowing the Germans to catch their breath and regroup their forces to organise their defence. But Hitler and the German High Command had another think coming. At the beginning of March 1944, as the spring weather was beginning to set in, Russian troops south of Sheptukhovka and on the Inhul, launched a massive new offensive and within days broke though German positions on a wide front and at great depth.[11] As a result Zeitzler appeared from East Prussia to give Hitler a special briefing in the middle of March. It was known that he had remained behind when the HQ had decamped from the Wolfsschanze and stayed with his staff in Lötzen in East Prussia. As a rule he came only once a week to the Berghof. On other days he was represented at Hitler's briefings by Colonel Brandt from the Operations Department of the Army Supreme Command. At the meeting which was specially convened for Zeitzler's briefing, Keitel, Jodl, Korten, Brandt, Schmundt, Hewel and Günsche were present. Hitler arrived late and, with a sombre look, took his place at the table on which the operations map of the Eastern Front had been spread out. The others stood on both sides of the table.

Zeitzler began his briefing. He announced that, in the course of the Russian offensive in the southern Ukraine, Germany had lost Kherson, Uman, Berislav and a host of other towns. The speed of the Russian advance to the west, coupled with muddy roads, he explained, had made it completely impossible to hold the front line in all places. He pointed to various spots on the map and named German divisions that had been surrounded or already wiped out. One of these was the Sixth Army, which had been reformed to replace Paulus's army destroyed at Stalingrad.[12]

Hitler drew his shaky hand over the map. With one finger he measured the breadth of the breakthrough at the front and said, 'The Sixth Army is our destiny. I should never have given the new army the name of the one beaten at Stalingrad. This number is unlucky for me.' He continued with growing fervour: he could not understand how the Russians could advance along muddy tracks, and the Germans must sink into the slime. In total fury he bellowed, 'My generals have forgotten how to command, that is the problem! They should learn from the Russians how to hand out orders!' Zeitzler wanted to take up a point, but in the end thought better of it and merely sighed deeply several times. For the first time in the war, Hitler had revealed his view that German generals should learn how to command from the Russians. In times to come he would repeat this often, that German generals could learn something from the Russians.

Zeitzler continued his briefing and expressed the fear that Army Group South might, in this situation, be cut off from Army Group Centre. As a result, he explained, Army High Command had suggested that the Crimea be abandoned to release the necessary forces to reform the front and take up new positions behind the Bug. At this point Hitler jumped to his feet and screamed, 'I have had enough now. I am not going to listen to any more of these gentlemen's suggestions for withdrawal for operational reasons. They keep talking of redrawing the line, but they always retreat! They have completely forgotten to look forward!' He turned to Schmundt and continued, 'Find me some generals who will advance to redraw the front line!' Then he fell silent and, with nervous movements, scratched his neck until it was bloody, chewed his nails and tore at his cuticles with his teeth.

Günsche was summoned to the telephone. In the conservatory he ran into Eva Braun, who was playing with her little dogs. 'Tell me, please, what have we got today: ku-La or la-La?' she asked. Günsche had to smile. He knew what these abbreviations meant. They meant short briefing or long briefing. Because she and her lady-friends were bored rigid by the military discussions at the Berghof, she had thought up the abbreviations in order to express her impatience for the end of the meeting. Hitler found the abbreviations appropriate. When Günsche returned to the meeting, Hitler had calmed down a little and was sitting in the armchair again. He was saying categorically that in no circumstances could the Crimea be given up. At every word Keitel gave a nod, and then he said, 'Yes indeed, my Führer, you are spot on. If we give up the Crimea the Turks will immediately go over to the other side.'

When the maps of the Eastern Front were removed from the table, Jodl began his briefing by spreading out the maps of the positions of the 'secondary theatres', known as the Western Front in Hitler's HQ. These included France, Italy, Holland, Belgium, Denmark, Norway and the Balkans. Jodl had a massive advantage over Zeitzler. He smiled as he reported on the campaign against Anglo-American forces in Italy. Pointing at the map, Jodl said, 'Here, my Führer, an American advance guard was annihilated. And here the Americans have advanced 500 metres.'

Hitler smiled. That made him happy. The Anglo-American forces that had landed in Sicily on 10 July 1943 — more than eight months before — had so far achieved no decisive success, although they were faced by only weak German forces. The Anglo-American armies pushed forward metre by metre with a tremendous effort and became bogged down with every step. Even the units which had landed behind the German front on the western Italian coast south of Rome had so far failed to reach their desired objectives. They could not break through the German Montalbo Line at the monastery of Monte Cassino.[13] It is known that the German front remained firm and unshakeable over the following months and in the Apennines and north of Florence in the winter of 1944–5. The Anglo-Americans were able to occupy the whole of Italy only when Germany surrendered in May 1945, something they had failed to achieve in nearly two years of fighting.

The army of the Polish General Anders was also with the Anglo-American troops that had landed in Italy.[14] In Hitler's opinion these corrupt troops had been purchased by the British; if the Germans were to offer them more, they would come over to their side. He joked that it would be better not to do so, because the English would simply up the ante and these venal subjects would go running back to them. Jodl proceeded to explain what German troops had been doing against Serbian, Greek, Slovenian, Macedonian and Albanian partisans in the Balkans. He reported that some 300 partisans were being killed daily. Hitler was very pleased with this news. As regards France, Jodl reported that more transport units of German divisions that had been recuperating and brought up to strength after the heavy fighting in Russia were being sent back to the Eastern Front.

To conclude the briefing, Hitler gave a short résumé of the political situation, dwelling exclusively on the differences between the Anglo-Americans and the Russians. This had been his hobby horse for some time and he returned to it at the end of every situation report. He read out secret reports from the German ambassadors in Madrid, Lisbon, Ankara and Stockholm which he had received from Ribbentrop. They were marked with the letter R (for Ribbentrop) and were covered in the Foreign Minister's marginalia relating to the growing anti-Soviet feeling in leading circles in Britain and America.

After these memos, Hitler read out excerpts from the reports of the German and foreign news agencies, also dealing with relations between the Anglo-Americans and the Russians. It was clear that the most highly regarded people in Britain were talking more loudly of the danger of Russia when they observed the rapid advance of the Soviet army. They demanded that Anglo-American forces launch a quick offensive in the west. Hitler believed these reports to be extraordinarily important. At conferences he maintained that in the present circumstances the danger of an attack in the west was the lesser evil, because the hostile relations between the Anglo-American camp and the Soviet Union could lead to a rupture, which would greatly influence the course and conclusion of the war in Germany's favour.

★

After heavy fighting German troops evacuated Odessa in April 1944 and Russian troops occupied the Crimea. In the middle of May they took Sebastopol, the last German strongpoint on the peninsula. The news made Hitler so livid that he had to take to his bed for a few days. He dismissed Kleist and Manstein as supreme commanders in the southern sector of the front, despite the fact that he held Manstein in high esteem at the time because of the brutality he had shown on the Eastern Front.[*] Once the Russians had taken the Crimea, they advanced to the Dniester with quick thrusts, crossed it and established several bridgeheads on its west bank.

In the course of Zeitzler's briefing at the end of May, Hitler had another fierce argument with him. This time it was sparked off by his report that the Russians had restarted their attacks in the area of Kishinev–Iaşi and pushed the German line further westwards. Hitler was completely beside himself. He bellowed at Zeitzler that there should be no retreat allowed in this sector and not one metre of territory should be given up. Once he had recovered from his fulmination he continued in a weak voice, 'From there is a straight road to Ploieşti. When we lose access to Romanian oil we will have well and truly lost the war. Then everything will be finished.'

In the days that followed Hitler was more and more uneasy. Finally he ordered Zeitzler, who had remained behind at HQ, to fly to the sector of the front in question and to appraise the situation in person. He said to him, 'For God's sake make every effort to stabilise the position so that there are no more surprises.' Early one morning in those first June days, Zeitzler flew to the staff of Army Group South. That same day he called Hitler after lunch from the Army Group South HQ, but the connection was very bad, as it was 1,500 kilometres away from the Obersalzberg. Hitler could understand virtually nothing. Enervated, he finally hissed into the receiver, 'Hold the line at all costs! Hold on at all costs!'

Günsche took the receiver out of his shaking hand. Hitler was so worked up that he was on the verge of fainting. Giddily he left the hall, and Morell was called for. Linge helped him prepare the injections. Hitler came out of his bedroom in his shirtsleeves, tired and stooping, with heavy bags under his eyes. He turned to Morell and said in a feeble voice, 'Professor, I believe the mountain air does not agree with me. My heart can't take it any more.' By now exhausted, he lay down on the sofa. Then he continued, 'You had better listen to my heart.' Morell replied that he would fetch the cardiogram immediately. On the table four syringes had been prepared. Hitler rolled up his sleeve for the injections.

[*]Both were dismissed on 30 March 1944.

The next day Zeitzler was already back from the front. He drove from Salzburg airport directly to the Berghof, in his tired and unshaven state. On the table in the great hall the operations maps were spread out, and he began his report on his visit to the southern sector of the front. In the guise of an introduction he assured his listeners that the High Command of Army Group South was doing everything in its power to maintain position. Then he began to speak of his personal impressions of the front and declared that he thought it a good idea to realign the front further back to account for the Russian breakthrough.

At this, Hitler sat up and howled that Zeitzler had allowed himself to be talked round by the generals. He had had the impression for a long time that Zeitzler was making common cause with them. Zeitzler wanted to reply, but Hitler continue to hurl accusations at him: 'Zeitzler, you have not properly appraised the situation!' Zeitzler turned as red as a beetroot, choked and suddenly fell forward with his torso on the map table. Günsche and Zeitzler's adjutant, Colonel Smend,[15] unbuttoned his tunic and laid him out in an armchair. In the meantime Morell arrived. He diagnosed a heart attack, and Zeitzler was immediately transferred to the hospital in Berchtesgaden.

Smend was shaken by these events and told Günsche that the Führer had treated Zeitzler improperly. He had worked like a madman and done everything possible to hold the front. For the time being the position of Chief of the General Staff was taken over by General Heusinger,[16] the Chief of the Operations Section of the General Staff.*

At this time an event took place at the Berghof that did not exactly fit in with the war and its horrors. In May 1944 a wedding was celebrated with all pomp and circumstance, between Eva Braun's sister Gretl and SS-Gruppenführer Hermann Fegelein, Himmler's liaison man at Führer HQ.[17] Fegelein had taken over the position from Wolff at the end of 1943, when the latter was sent to Italy as Chief SS and Police Führer.† His duties consisted in reading out Himmler's personal reports to Hitler. The themes were the activities of the police, SS and Gestapo; the use of police units to punish partisans in Russia; the construction and maintenance of SS divisions; and the special situation reports dealing with SS units on the Eastern Front which Hitler examined in comparison with the operations reports

---

* Zeitzler collapsed on 9 June. Heusinger replaced him from 10 June to 21 July 1944, when Guderian took over.
† The wedding took place on 3 June 1944. Fegelein was promoted Gruppenführer on 21 July.

of the General Staff. Now thirty-eight years old, Fegelein had been head of the central SS cavalry school in Munich before the war. More recently he had commanded the 8th SS Cavalry Division that had been active in fighting partisans in the Pripet Marshes.

After the occupation of Poland the cunning Fegelein had founded a workshop in Warsaw where gentlemen's and ladies' suits, fur coats, shoes, handbags and brief cases were made from plundered materials, using Poles as forced labour. He developed a thriving business and supplied Hitler's staff and Eva Braun with these articles.

At the Berghof, Fegelein quickly befriended Eva. At her bidding Hitler took him into his closest circle and also invited him to the tea evenings around the fire. Soon he was going in and out of her apartment – something she had never allowed anyone on Hitler's staff to do before. She had fallen under Fegelein's spell and with time became increasingly influenced by him. In her conversations with Hitler she couldn't heap enough praise on his manly, elegant appearance. He was a 'real man'. Hitler himself was not immune. He told Himmler, 'Himmler, with Fegelein you have sent us the right man.'

After only a month's acquaintance, Fegelein and Eva's sister Gretl were betrothed, thereby guaranteeing his position with Hitler. Eva made sure that the wedding would be celebrated with a magnificent party at the Berghof. There was no midday briefing that day. Hitler explained that he did not want to mar the wedding celebrations with bad news from the front. At the time there were bloody battles raging at Sebastopol. The ceremony took place in Salzburg, with Hitler and Bormann as witnesses. Thence the newlyweds drove to the Berghof, where Hitler received them solemnly at the gate. He was wearing the grey tunic of the Supreme Commander of the Wehrmacht, on his breast the Gold Party Badge, the Iron Cross First Class and the Medal of the Wounded from the First World War. After escorting the young couple into the great hall, he handed Gretl a present of a platinum handbag. Then he walked with the newlyweds into the drawing room, where the following were to be found waiting for the wedding breakfast: Eva Braun, her parents, Eva's elder sister Ilse[18] with her second husband, Fegelein's parents, his younger brother, the SS officer Waldemar Fegelein,[19] Eva's lady-friends, Himmler, Morell, Hoffmann, the wife of Hitler's surgeon Brandt, Below and his wife and Günsche.

Hitler led the entire party into the dining room, where the table was laid. The morning coats and uniforms of the gentlemen and the luxurious evening dresses of the ladies gave the Berghof a particularly festive allure. A state service that had been previously used for government banquets was set out on the table, which was decorated with vast flower arrangements and lighted candles in gold candelabra. The SS servants were clad in white jackets for the occasion. After they had served the calves' brain soup Hitler clinked his glass and all talk ceased. Rising from his seat he uttered a short toast and expressed his joy that Fegelein's marriage to Gretl Braun should be celebrated under his roof. As head of state he had one wish above all, that the young couple should be blessed with many children. He then raised his glass to the young bride and groom. After Hitler's speech, the servants brought in an endless succession of choice dishes and replenished the glasses with champagne and French wine, which lay in great quantity in the cellars under the Berghof. At the table the party was going with a swing. The fun reached its highest point when the servants brought in ice-cream bombes on silver plates that had been decorated with female figurines dressed in eighteenth-century costumes made of spun sugar.

After the meal the party moved to the great hall, where Hoffmann's photographers took pictures of Hitler posing with the young couple and other guests. Then Hitler remained behind as a cavalcade took the wedding party over to Bormann's villa where the celebrations continued with the Munich artistes invited by Fegelein. Hitler had not wanted them in the house. Later the guests drove to Hitler's tea-house on the Kehlstein where everything was prepared for the continuation of the party. There was merriment in all the rooms as a band played dance music non-stop and servants brought round champagne, liqueurs and the most refined delicacies. Because Hitler was not there, Eva Braun bloomed – dancing, flirting and enjoying the feast more than anyone. Indeed, the uninitiated person might well have believed that she was the happy bride. Himmler and Bormann joined in. There was nothing here to recall the suffering and terrible deprivations, the millions of dead and the destruction that the war had brought to so many peoples of the world.

In the evening the wedding party returned to Bormann's villa from the Kehlstein. They were all very merry by now and Hoffmann was as drunk as a lord. Bormann's house had been transformed into a pleasure palace for the occasion: there were rooms for dancing, for eating and for sitting out. One room was a cocktail bar, another had been decked out as a photographic studio. The musicians were dressed in white tailcoats and played tangos and foxtrots without a break. In the cocktail bar a military jazz quartet played lewd music-hall songs from the Viennese demi-monde as best they could.

At around 11.00 p.m. Hitler's adjutants Puttkamer, Below and Günsche drove back to the Berghof for the evening briefing. On Hitler's orders it was given by Colonel Brandt this time, as the adjutants had been at the

Party in Bormann's villa. Brandt reported on the latest fighting around Sebastopol and the heavy losses that the troops had sustained in combat there. That night thousands of German soldiers fell while great celebrations sounded on the Obersalzberg.

After Brandt's briefing, Puttkamer, Below and Günsche returned to Bormann's villa. The party was still in full swing, and lasted until the early hours of the morning. The next day Linge learned from the servants who had been at the feast that Bormann had sent his wife to bed as early as midnight, so that she might not spoil the party. When towards morning he had soiled his third dress shirt with sweat, he sent for her to bring him clean shirts. 'Believe it or not,' the servants reported, 'Bormann hauled his wife out of bed at four in the morning and ordered her to fetch clean shirts from another villa in Pullach near Munich. It is a good 200 kilometres there and back.'

Speer, Minister for Armaments and War Production, who made frequent tours of inspection at arms factories, maintained close relations with the captains of industry. When the German army sustained heavy losses on the Eastern Front, he reported with mounting frequency that the industrialists were increasingly dissatisfied with the military leadership. His information on their negative attitude was supported by the reports of Himmler, whose SD covered the whole country with a thick network of agents and informants permanently listening out for the slightest sign of criticism of Hitler. Speer strongly recommended that the Führer receive the major industrialists to raise their morale.

For this reason in the middle of June 1944 Hitler invited around 200 industrialists to the Obersalzberg.[*] They were put up at the Hotel Platterhof, which belonged to the National Socialist hotel concern. Hitler spoke for around an hour on this occasion. In his speech he tried to hit on the most convincing notions possible, but it was clear that he did not do much for the industrialists' morale. Above all he told them to continue standing at his side, as a fierce enemy might only be beaten by unwavering constancy. He stressed that his generals, fighting on the Eastern Front, did not understand the significance for German industry of the Donetz basin, the Ukraine and the manganese of Nikopol. They were always too myopic to see beyond mere military strategy.

Hitler continued by saying that, despite the loss of Russian territory and raw materials, armaments production was experiencing no particular

---

[*]The conference for 200 invited guests took place on 4 July 1944.

difficulties. There was still a considerable stock of raw materials that allowed manufacturers to get through bottlenecks and even to increase armaments production. After the war the Wehrmacht would be splendidly equipped with all sorts of arms and the armaments industry could look forward to making enormous profits. The world had been impressed by the quality of victorious German weaponry and Germany would deliver arms to the whole world. Hitler declared that after this war there would be more conflicts: Hungary would fight Romania, and Greece, Italy. Whether war or peace reigned between these nations would be Germany's decision. The rebuilding of bombed cities and the production of daily necessities would proceed at full pelt. Industrialists could expect to fetch high prices for their products.

In conclusion Hitler issued a rousing call to the major industrialists to give him their complete trust and do everything for victory. The hour was not far off when the great change would come. He left the room to loud applause and cries of 'Heil!'

On 6 June 1944 Linge woke Hitler early because Jodl urgently wanted to speak to him on the telephone. He informed Hitler that the Anglo-Americans had landed in France at dawn. Less than an hour later Keitel and Jodl arrived at the Berghof. Hitler received them in the great hall, looking on this occasion considerably better than usual. 'So it has happened on the Atlantic, Jodl?' Hitler asked quickly. 'Where exactly? Do you have any precise information?'

Jodl opened a map of the Atlantic coast on the marble table and pointed to the places where Anglo-American forces had landed. 'Here, south of Le Havre, my Führer, landing craft have dropped soldiers off. In many places they have already been driven back. Behind the German lines paratroops have been dropped. It is not easy to see where they are concentrated, but we can already say that the enemy has not brought off a surprise attack. The paratroops were expected.' Hitler sat up. His eyes twinkled. 'Gentlemen,' he said excitedly, 'I am glad that the Anglo-Americans have finally decided to land in France, and exactly where they were expected. Now we know where we are. We will see how things go from now on.'

Supplied with information from Ribbentrop, Himmler and Jodl, Hitler had anticipated an imminent invasion of France for the previous few weeks, but the uncertainty about not knowing when it was going to happen had tortured him. He had often discussed with Jodl how the exiguous mobile reserves in France – that is to say Panzer divisions – would be divided up. He declared that in the coming battle everything would be decided by the proper deployment of tank divisions. Several times they were repositioned before being finally concentrated in Normandy.

While Hitler and Jodl were speaking, it was announced that Göring had arrived. Hitler hurried out to meet him, to find the Reichsmarschall already in the entrance hall. Hitler was radiant when he took Göring's right hand in both of his and cried out with great animation, 'Göring, have you heard already? This morning the Anglo-Americans have finally landed in France, and right in the place where we expected them! We shall throw them out again!' Keitel and Jodl went to join them. Hitler took the map out of Jodl's hand and spread it out on the little table. Hitler and Göring leaned over it and looked for the places where the Anglo-American forces had landed. Then the four of them discussed what measures should be taken to deal with the enemy paratroops.

A few days later, however, the events in France were still playing a secondary role for Hitler. The battles around Army Group Centre on the Eastern Front seized his attention. At a briefing in the middle of June 1944, Heusinger reported on the position of the sector of the front controlled by Army Group Centre. He told Hitler that intelligence reports and the increased activity of Russian partisans – above all the destruction of railway lines behind the army group's positions – indicated that the Russians were preparing a major offensive in the central section of the front. Hitler said angrily that he had ordered long before that the partisan areas should be transformed into an unpopulated desert: 'They are all bandits! Enemies of the Germans and bandits – it is one and the same! They must all be exterminated!' With a worried look he examined the map for a long time and said, 'Transmit to Field Marshal Busch[20] that he should pay particular attention. The road to Germany leads directly through his army group! We must not retreat a single step here!'

On 23 June, only a few days after the meeting, the huge Russian offensive against the positions of Army Group Centre began in White Russia.* In this sector of the front the Russians had undertaken no great attack for several months. In the Vitebsk–Orsha–Mogilev region the Germans had erected a heavily manned system of fortresses that they called the Fatherland Line.[21] At the situation report of 25 June, however, Heusinger reported that the Russians had already penetrated the front

---

* Operation Bagration was launched 22 June 1944, the third anniversary of the attack on the Soviet Union. By the end of the operation the Russians had obliterated twenty-eight German divisions and 350,000 men.

southwest and south of Vitebsk to a considerable depth, and were carrying out heavy attacks right along Army Group Centre's line. In a few places they had already broken though. Heusinger made special mention of the devastating effect of the firestorm inflicted by the Russian artillery.

Hitler almost fell over the table and groaned, 'How could this have happened? Our best divisions are stationed there! Where is the Feldherrnhalle Division? Where is the 12th Infantry Division?' Heusinger's answer was muted: they had no clear picture of the positions of the Feldherrnhalle Division or other units yet. All the command staffs of Army Group Centre had changed their positions. Communication between the armies and the corps and between the corps and the divisions was very poor.

In the days to come it became clear that Army Group Centre was the very image of catastrophe. Heusinger reported that Vitebsk and Orsha and then Mogilev and Bobruisk had been given up. In the sector controlled by Army Group Centre the front had been broken across a width of nearly 300 kilometres. Large contingents had been cut off by the Russians and surrounded. Hitler directed that the front be held at any price. On his orders divisions were transferred from more peaceful sectors of the front and all the combat units of the Replacement Army* were thrown in. These reinforcements, however, were soon mauled in the same manner by the powerful blows of the Russians. Army Group Centre suffered terrible losses. Tens of thousands of soldiers and officers ended up in captivity. The advance units of Russian tanks travelled with lightning speed to threaten the borders of East Prussia. This was reported by Heusinger in his briefing on the situation on the Eastern Front.

Hitler sat at the table in a total daze and stared at the map of the Eastern Front. The excitements of the past few days and the experience of hearing of the destruction of the central sector of the front had caused his stomach cramps to reappear. Sitting at the table, he buckled up from time to time, his face contorted in agony. Then he sat up straight again and with shaking hands measured the distance of the advance units of the Soviet army to the borders of East Prussia. With a blue pencil he drew an arrow on the map that dug into the flank of the advancing Russians. Suddenly he cast a wild look around him, jumped up from the chair, threw the pencil on to the table and yelled, 'Treason! Treason!'

*The Replacement Army comprised troops being recruited and trained in Germany.

12

July 1944 – January 1945

Faced with the menacing situation on the Eastern Front, Heusinger and Schmundt asked Hitler several times to move his HQ back to East Prussia in order to conduct operations directly from there. Hitler, however, resisted. He said that he would not move back into the Wolfsschanze before the refurbishment of his bunker was ready. Only when he was shown photographs of the already complete so-called guest bunker, where he was to be temporarily housed, did he decide to go back to Rastenburg. At the beginning of July 1944 he gave orders to transfer his HQ there.[*] Eva Braun wanted to talk Hitler into staying at the Berghof, because she was frightened that something would happen to him. Hitler sought to console her: 'It is not for long my child. I shall soon be back.'

Hitler and the whole of his HQ boarded several aircraft at Salzburg airport and flew to East Prussia. In the five months of his absence, from February to June 1944, the Wolfsschanze had changed a good deal. The old bunkers had received seven-metre-thick concrete roofs, and the new constructions rose out of the woods like so many Egyptian pyramids. Hitler was lodged in a well-disguised bunker. After his arrival the first thing he did was to visit the Führer Bunker. The work of reinforcing the outside of the building had already been completed. Now workers from the Todt Organisation were busy with the interior.

There was a real maze inside the bunker. From the entrance one could reach the living rooms only through two so-called 'locks' or compression chambers in the corridor. The locks must be seen as two antechambers that were separated from one another and from the corridor by armour-plated doors. Here Hitler's personal bodyguard was on duty. In the first corridor were the secretaries' bedrooms: Fräulein Wolf, Fräulein Schroeder, Frau Junge and Frau Christian.

Frau Christian, née Daranowski, had married Colonel Christian of the Wehrmacht Operations Staff of the OKW at the end of 1942. A vivacious,

---

[*]He returned on 9 July 1944.

fun-loving person, her unstinting energy appealed greatly to Hitler and he satisfied her every wish. She had an obvious influence on him, borne out – if by nothing else – by the fact that her husband Colonel Christian was promoted general major and appointed Chief of the Operations Staff of the Luftwaffe.

From the first corridor there was a tortuous route to the second floor and the adjutants' rooms, those of Morell, Linge and the soldier-servants. From here corridors went zigzagging towards Hitler's study and bedroom. Hitler's dining room and the storeroom were also to be found in his bunker. There were pipes leading into his bedroom which could be made to discharge oxygen. This came from oxygen canisters that were kept outside the bunker in a ditch because Hitler was afraid they might blow up. The contents of the canisters had been tested in a laboratory in Lötzen after Hitler had argued that poison gas might have been mixed with the oxygen.

When he visited the bunker, Hitler ordered the entrance to be obscured by a thick concrete wall and for a machine-gun nest to be set up between the wall and the bunker in case of a Russian airborne attack. He also decreed that a machine-gun nest be created on the roof of the bunker to protect the approach. Hitler had become visibly more frightened and had had ditches dug in front of the guest bunker, where he was staying for the time being, and filled them with machine gunners. He gave Linge a new order: 'Ask Speer to deliver to us some of the new machine guns that are being introduced to the troops. I am going to carry a weapon.' Linge looked at Hitler in astonishment, as if to say that he didn't need a gun and that the SS men were there to protect their Führer. When Hitler saw the expression on Linge's face, he declared theatrically, 'Don't believe that I am going to sit idly by in this bunker. If it is necessary I shall take up arms and fight. Make sure the soldier-servants have regular shooting practice.'

On the day of Hitler's arrival at the Wolfsschanze there was a situation report with the usual participants. Heusinger briefed them on the central sector of the Eastern Front. Hitler sat bowed over at the table. His jittery left hand hung impotently at his side as he ran his right nervously over the map on the table. Heusinger reported that although they had concentrated strong forces from other sectors of the front and mounted tenacious counter-attacks, it had not been possible to prevent the Russian advance into Army Group Centre's territory. Minsk had fallen, and the Russians had crossed the Beresina on a broad front. Their battle reconnaissance troops were heading towards Vilnius and Grodno and southwards in the direction of Baranovichy and Brest-Litovsk. In a muted tone, Heusinger added that it would hardly be possible to bring the Russians to a halt before they reached the borders of East Prussia. In fact a thick red arrow had been drawn on the operations map, to show that Russian advanced units were approaching East Prussia. Staff HQ of Army Group Centre was already located on German soil in East Prussia. The former Supreme Commander of the army group, Field Marshal Busch, had been dismissed for 'inflexibility' and replaced by Colonel General Reinhardt,[1] who had commanded the Third Army of the army group until then.[*]

Despite the disastrous state of affairs in the central sector of the front, Hitler unexpectedly flew with his entire staff back from East Prussia to the Obersalzberg. He declared that he felt exhausted, that it was too hot in East Prussia and he could not take the climate. A little while before at the Berghof, he had said the mountain climate on the Obersalzberg was unbearable for him. Now he didn't like the weather in East Prussia.

On Hitler's orders, Heusinger remained at the Wolfsschanze, but only a few days later he came to the Berghof and requested the Führer urgently return as the menacing situation on the East Prussian border made his presence necessary: rapid decisions had to be made. Hitler gave in to Heusinger's pressure and on 10 July he returned to East Prussia.[†] The Führer Bunker was still not ready and the briefings took place in a wooden hut fifty metres from the guest bunker where Hitler lived. It was covered with only a light, sixty-centimetre-thick concrete roof. A few days after Hitler's return to the Wolfsschanze on 20 July there was an attempt on his life during a meeting here.

That day Hitler left the guest bunker at around 1.00 p.m. and went to the briefing. It was very hot. All the windows in the meeting room, which were on the left of the entrance, had been thrown open. At the beginning of the discussion the following were present besides Hitler: Jodl, Korten, Heusinger, Warlimont, Fegelein, Scherff, Bodenschatz, Voss, Brandt, Schmundt, Günsche, Puttkamer, Borgmann, Below, Keitel's adjutant John von Freyend,[2] Jodl's assistant Waizenegger, Büchs[3] and Assmann,[4] as well as Counsellor Sonnleithner[5] from Ribbentrop's staff, who was standing in for Hewel.[‡]

The discussion began with Heusinger's briefing on the situation on the Eastern Front. In the middle sector it was as follows: Vitebsk, Orsha, Mogilev, Bobruisk and Minsk now lay way behind the Russian lines.

---

[*]Busch had been replaced by Model on 28 June 1944. In August Model gave way to Colonel General Georg-Hans Reinhardt.
[†]Hitler returned on the 16th.
[‡]Also present were the stenographers Heinz Buchholz and Heinrich Berger.

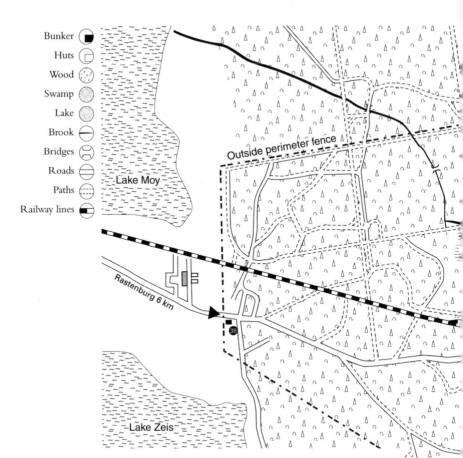

Bunker
Huts
Wood
Swamp
Lake
Brook
Bridges
Roads
Paths
Railway lines

Outside perimeter fence

Lake Moy

Rastenburg 6 km

Lake Zeis

1 The Führer's bunker
2 Guest Bunker
3 Briefing Bunker
4 Intelligence Bunker
5 Reich Press Chief
6 Stenographers and SD (Security Service)
7 Servants' quarters
8 Sauna
9 Common bunker or common room
10 Bormann
11 Guests, barber
12 Personal adjutants and physicians
13 Wehrmacht adjutants and the Army Personnel Office
14 Garages
15 Boiler house
16 Mess
17 Chief of the Wehrmacht Leadership Staff
18 Chief of the OKW
19 Mess
20 New Tea House
21 Old Tea House
22 Göring
23 Supreme Commander of the Navy
24 Luftwaffe Supreme Command
25 Supreme Command of the Navy
26 Common bunker or common room
27 Administrative huts
28 Billets
29 Telegraph Office
30 Mess
31 HQ Führer Escort Command
32 Boiler house
33 Spa House
34 Commander's HQ
35, 36 Wehrmacht Operations Staff
37 Lavatories
38 Guardhouse

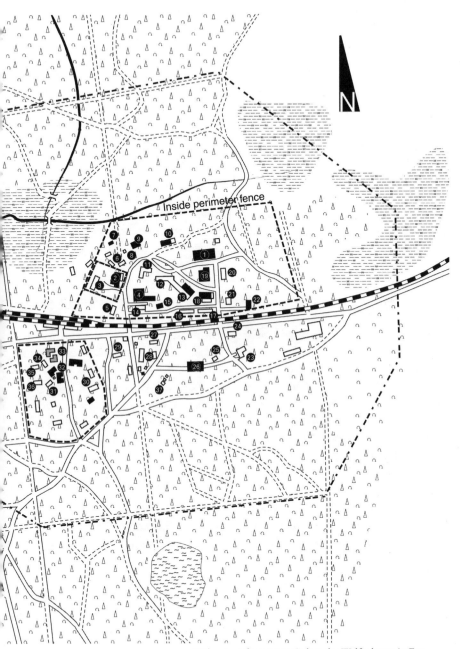

Inside perimeter fence

N

Hitler spent frequent periods at the Wolfsschanze in East Prussia between 1941 and 1944. Massive security precautions such as the many exclusion zones prevented an attempt on Hitler's life until that carried out by Count Claus Schenk von Stauffenberg on 20 July 1944

German troops had abandoned Vilnius, the Lithuanian capital, a few days before. Advance units of Russian tanks were closing in on Siauliai and Jelgava. It was simply not possible to re-erect the German front – everywhere there were yawning gaps. Russian troops were already standing at the borders of East Prussia and a few days before this briefing the Russians had started a massive offensive against Army Group Ukraine. Heusinger began his briefing with the news that the offensive had been launched over a 200-kilometre-wide front. The Russians had been able to hack deep into German defensive positions, including the Prince Eugene position, east of Lvov, and to penetrate it to its entire depth. 'Battles are raging on the roads to Lvov,' Heusinger announced.

At this moment Keitel entered the room in the company of Buhle and Colonel von Stauffenberg.[6] Stauffenberg, who was Chief of Staff to the Supreme Commander of the Replacement Army, Colonel General Fromm,[7] was stationed in the Bendlerstrasse in Berlin, where Fromm's staff was located. He came to Führer HQ only when a report was required on the state of the Replacement Army. Stauffenberg had fought in Rommel's army on the African Front before, where he had been wounded, losing his left arm, an eye, and two fingers on his right hand.

Heusinger continued with his briefing. Hitler was leaning low over the table while he studied the map of the Eastern Front. As became clear later, Stauffenberg had placed a briefcase containing a time bomb under the map table when he came in. He then went out again, saying he had to make a telephone call. Participants in the situation reports could bring their briefcases into the meetings with them without their being searched and freely wander in and out of the rooms.

Heusinger had not finished his briefing when the powerful bomb went off. Günsche and John von Freyend, who had been propping themselves up at an open window, were blown out of the hut by the blast. When Günsche came to, he saw thick smoke pouring from the windows of the conference room and could hear the groans of the people inside. He ran to the entrance. A few SS men from Hitler's bodyguard, who had been at their posts, were also running towards the hut. In the doorway Günsche ran into two swaying figures, blackened by smoke, leaning on one another and looking for a way out. They were Hitler and Keitel. Their clothes hung in tatters. Hitler's hair was wild and singed. There were red splotches on his face, which was covered in soot. Günsche grabbed him under the left arm and cried, 'Heavens be praised, my Führer, you are alive!'

Keitel and Günsche supported Hitler from either side and brought him to his bunker. Hitler had almost completely lost the power of speech.

He fought for breath and croaked, 'What . . . what was that . . .?' In the dining room of the bunker, Keitel and Günsche put Hitler down in an armchair. He groaned, 'An attempt . . . A bomb . . . What was that? What luck! I am alive . . . That was the hand of providence.' In an effusion of joy he kept squeezing Keitel's and Günsche's hands. His second surgeon, Hasselbach,[8] who was standing in for Brandt, hurried into the room. He was followed by Bormann, Morell and Linge. Hasselbach and Morell examined Hitler. They found a contusion to the left arm, damage to the eardrum and light wounding to both legs from wooden splinters that came from the shredded floorboards. Hitler gradually came round. When he had found his voice he expressed the supposition that it had been a time bomb. He was certain that it was one of the workers busy rebuilding the HQ who was after his blood. Fearing that bombs might have been laid in his bunker, he ordered that the floor be pulled up immediately.

Of the participants in the situation report, the following had been injured: Hitler's ADC and Chief of the Personnel Office General Lieutenant Schmundt, the Chief of the Luftwaffe General Staff General Korten, Assistant to the Operations Department of the Army General Staff Colonel Brandt, Hitler Special Appointee for Military History General Major Scherrf, Göring's liaison officer with Hitler General Bodenschatz, Dönitz's representative Vice Admiral Voss, Hitler's army adjutant General Lieutenant Borgmann and the stenographer Berger. They were all taken to the hospital at Karlshof near Rastenburg. Schmundt, Korten, Brandt and Berger died of their injuries. Heusinger, Warlimont, Jodl, Buhle, Fegelein, Puttkamer and Below were only lightly injured.

Thirty minutes after the explosion, Himmler arrived at the Wolfsschanze and heard the reports. About an hour after the attempt on Hitler's life the HQ telephonist, Sergeant Adam, came to see Linge. Those wanting to make telephone calls had to go through him. Adam reported that he had seen Colonel von Stauffenberg come out of the conference room a few minutes before the explosion and get into his car. Linge promptly informed Hitler, who summoned Adam. When Adam repeated his testimony, Hitler asked, 'Who is this Stauffenberg? Where does he come from?' Linge answered that Stauffenberg worked in the General Staff of the Replacement Army with Fromm. When Hitler heard this, he shouted out, 'Stauffenberg is the perpetrator of the attack! Arrest him immediately!'

Now it became clear that Stauffenberg had already left the HQ camp, despite the fact that no one had been permitted to leave after the explosion. Claiming that he had an urgent request to deliver to Fromm from Hitler, he had managed to get out and return to Berlin. Two hours after the attempt, Hitler called Goebbels in Berlin. From him he learned that the government district had been closed off by soldiers and that he could not leave his ministry. While Goebbels was talking to Hitler, Major Remer[9] came into Goebbels's office. He was the commander of the Berlin guard, and it was his soldiers who had sealed off the government district. Remer had come to announce that he had received orders from the Governor of Berlin General Lieutenant von Hase.[10] Hitler called Remer to the telephone and said to him, 'Remer, do you hear, I am alive! Carry out my instructions to the letter!' Hitler commanded Remer to march with his regiment to the staff HQ of Colonel General Fromm in the Bendlerstrasse and to put down the conspiracy. After talking to Goebbels and Remer, Hitler at once appointed Himmler Supreme Commander of the Replacement Army in succession to Fromm. Himmler received orders to fly to Berlin straightaway and flush out the nest of conspirators.

Before Himmler reached Berlin, the Bendlerstrasse was witness to the following drama: Stauffenberg, who had evidently heard the explosion as he was leaving the Wolfsschanze, told his fellow plotters that Hitler was dead. Numbered among the other members of the conspiracy gathered there was General Beck,[11] who had been Chief of the General Staff prior to Halder, General Hoepner, whom Hitler had dismissed from the army after the German defeat before Moscow in the winter of 1941–2, General Olbricht,[12] who had been also placed on the reserve list after the defeat before Moscow, Colonel Mertz von Quirnheim,[13] assistant in the General Staff in the Replacement Army, and General Fromm.

Fromm's staff had issued a report of Hitler's death to all local military commands. At the same time the codeword Walküre had been issued, the signal for the Replacement Army to place the whole of Germany in a state of emergency. Fromm's staff also issued a report to local commands that, in connection with Hitler's death, a new administration was being formed under Field Marshal von Witzleben.[14] Witzleben had commanded the army groups in France until 1941, and Hitler had had a very high opinion of him. He fell into disgrace, however, and the Führer dismissed him. When Hitler heard of the orders issued by Fromm's staff to the local commands he directed Keitel to tell the same commands that he was alive and that they had to obey his orders. With all the contradictory reports and commands that came from the plotters and Keitel, local commands were at a loss to know what to do.

Hitler had trouble assuming the power again to issue orders to troops within Germany. At the time he received great support from Colonel General Guderian, who was then General Inspector of Tank Forces. He instantly placed himself at Hitler's side. In an order to the tank forces of the Replacement Army and the tank school, Guderian condemned the plot against Hitler and instructed that any form of action by units of the Replacement Army should be put down by force.

Among Fromm's staff in the Bendlerstrasse it also quickly became clear that the attempt on Hitler's life had failed. Fromm, who sought to save his skin and cover up his part in the conspiracy, ordered officers on his staff who had remained loyal to Hitler to shoot Stauffenberg, Olbricht and the others. At the time of the shooting Colonel General Beck was in Fromm's office. It later became known that when Beck saw that Fromm had turned his coat he took his pistol from the desk and with the words, 'May I have your permission?', held it to his head and fired. But the pistol failed to go off. Fromm immediately shot Beck himself.* Then he ordered that the bodies be buried in the courtyard of the Bendler building, where his staff was. When Himmler arrived at the Bendlerstrasse, calm had been restored. Himmler arrested Fromm and ordered the bodies of the dead men to be exhumed and photographed. He sent the pictures to Hitler.

Now the mass arrests began. Hitler sent a group of SD men under the command of SS-Hauptsturmführer Hans Bergmüller[15] to the General Staff of Army High Command in Lötzen to carry out arrests. All those departmental heads, generals and officers who were under suspicion of being involved in the plot were arrested and taken to the Wolfsschanze for interrogation. A few generals and officers, Wagner, the General Quartermaster of the General Staff among them, escaped arrest through suicide. The Wolfsschanze investigation was led by Hitler himself, while the interrogations were carried out by the Chief of Hitler's Police Commando, Högl, and members of the SD. Högl reported personally to Hitler with the results and received indications from him as to how to continue and who should be arrested next.

The investigations showed that every departmental head of the General Staff and their closest assistants, with the exception of General Gercke, the head of the Transport Department, and General Heusinger, the Chief of the General Staff, had been initiated into the plot against Hitler.† Heusinger had been injured in the explosion. The prisoners maintained that they had organised the revolt against Hitler because they had come to the conclusion that the war could not be won under his leadership. This

---

*Fromm had been imprisoned by the plotters. He ordered an officer to shoot Beck, who refused. Beck was shot by a sergeant in another room.

†Heusinger knew and approved of the plans. He was arrested in hospital, but no proof was found and he was placed on the reserve list.

assessment of Hitler's capacities as an army leader spread through high military circles and was reflected in the joke that an inscription should be attached to the Hindenburg Monument:

> Step down, noble warrior, rejoin the fray!
> Your corporal has had his day.

After the interrogations the prisoners were transferred to Berlin-Moabit Prison. Those chiefly involved in the plot were arraigned before the court where Freisler, State Secretary in the Justice Ministry, presided.[*] They were condemned to death by hanging. A court of honour had dismissed them from the army. This was presided over by Keitel, Field Marshal Rundstedt and General Reinhardt, who was responsible for National Socialist education in the OKW.[†]

Before their execution the condemned men were allowed to write a final letter. These were opened by the Gestapo and photographed. Hitler received the copies. Among them was the farewell letter to his wife by General Stieff,[16] Chief of the Organisation Department of the General Staff. He wrote that, to save his soul, he had converted to Roman Catholicism before his death. Hitler had a hearty laugh over this; he was happy to give the Pope this 'devil's' black soul but only once he'd been hanged. Hitler called Stieff a 'devil' because of his large, somewhat protruding eyes.

Zeitzler's adjutant, Colonel Smend, had also been sentenced to death. He petitioned Hitler to be allowed to face a firing squad rather than die by the rope, but his request was refused. The condemned were all hanged. They included not just Smend and Stieff but also Field Marshal von Witzleben; the City Commander of Berlin, General von Hase; the General of Signals Regiment, Fellgiebel; the Chief of the Organisation Department of the Wehrmacht Operations Staff, Colonel Meichssner; the Police President of Berlin, SA-Obergruppenführer Count Helldorf; the former Oberbürgermeister of Leipzig, Goerdeler; a few diplomats, including Ambassador von der Schulenburg and Ulrich von Hassell, several priests and other generals and General Staff officers.

They were hanged in the cellars of Moabit prison.[‡] Hitler directed that photographs be taken of the executions and that he should receive copies. For this purpose Hoffmann's photographers travelled up from the Wolfsschanze to Berlin. A picture was taken of each one of them, standing

---

[*] Freisler was now President of the People's Court and Chief Judge of its First Senate.
[†] Not Reinhardt but General Major Hermann Reinecke. The OKW was the Wehrmacht High Command, OKH the Army High Command.
[‡] They were hanged in Berlin-Plötzensee Prison.

on the gallows, as they hanged him, and dangling from the rope. A long iron pylon, in which hooks had been attached, served as the gallows. In the photos Hitler received one could see the pylon with the executed men hanging from it – in convicts' clothes and separated from one another by long curtains.

Together with these executions the Gestapo carried out mass shootings without trial. They shot not only people whom they suspected had been involved in the plot, but also those who were seen as defeatists.[*] Colonel General Fromm was not executed immediately. He remained in custody until April 1945. Only then was he shot on Hitler's orders.[†]

Hitler learned also from Himmler and Bormann that Field Marshal Rommel had made common cause with the plotters. They showed him SD reports and information from the Party boss in Würzburg which proved that Rommel had expressed defeatist remarks and openly stated that the war was lost. Rommel was in his home town of Würzburg at the time, recovering from a slight head injury sustained in a car accident.[‡] Because Rommel was universally loved, Hitler ordered him to be killed in secret, without trial. This order was carried out by General Krebs, who was named Chief of Army General Staff in March 1945. Krebs told Günsche that in October 1944 in Hitler's name he had forced Rommel to take cyanide in his Würzburg flat.[§] The German public was officially informed that Rommel had died of the wounds he had sustained in the car accident. To cover up his murder, he was given a state funeral.

Whenever Hitler spoke about the plot, he always maintained that the instigators had acted not from patriotic reasons connected with the war, but rather because of their personal enmity towards him. He declared, 'Stauffenberg was a tool in the hands of men to whom I had given all: high positions, riches and medals. They supported me in everything and were content as long as they enjoyed my good grace; but now they wanted to

---

[*] More than 7,000 people were arrested and 4,980 of them killed over the next few months. Sixty officers were executed in the OKH, OKW and the General Staff, twenty generals were executed and another thirty-six were condemned by the court for opposition to the regime; forty-nine committed suicide to escape the verdict of the courts. At the fronts another 700 soldiers were executed.

[†] He was executed for cowardice on 12 March 1945.

[‡] His car had been strafed and he badly wounded near Livarot in Normandy. He was recovering at his house in Herrlingen near Ulm.

[§] The commission was carried out by General Wilhelm Burgdorf. When Rommel refused to shoot himself Burgdorf drove him to a nearby gravel pit and handed him the cyanide. Rommel died in minutes. Burgdorf then took him to a hospital in Ulm where he explained that the field marshal had suffered a heart attack.

see the back of me.' He wanted to use the attempt on his life to shroud himself in the aura of a leader chosen 'by fate'. He said, 'Only I am capable of saving the German people. Only I will bring the war to a victorious end.' He told Linge, 'Yes, Linge, I was only saved by a miracle. Providence preserved me for the German people.' At the gathering of National Socialist Party Gauleiters and front officers responsible for National Socialist education specially convened at the Wolfsschanze, Hitler repeated the assertion that providence had saved him to lead the German people to victory.*

To give the attempt on his life an historical dimension, Hitler directed that a special medal be struck and awarded to honour all those injured participants in the situation report. It was conceived after the model of the Wounded Medal. The difference was that in this case it bore the date 20 July 1944 and the name Adolf Hitler. Hitler also awarded one to himself, and several of the medals were laid out in prominent places in his bunker. His own injuries had been insignificant: contusions to his right arm, a few wooden splinters in his legs and slight damage to his ear drums. He had emerged almost untouched because at the moment of the explosion he was leaning forward, studying the map of the Eastern Front and his entire upper body was protected by the table. The table top, made from massive planks of wood, caught the brunt of the explosion.

Hitler's adjutant Schaub desperately wanted to be 'honoured' with the Wounded Medal, even though he had been unhurt. When the bomb went off he was actually sitting in his office, two or three rooms away from that in which the conference was being held. That didn't stop him from telling Hitler's staff and even Hitler himself that his eardrums had been damaged. For several days he pretended he couldn't hear properly and kept putting his hand to his ear. He talked to everyone about his experiences with the bomb. To begin with he thought that Russian aircraft had dropped the bomb. The blast knocked him off his chair and, as champagne bottles tumbled out of the cupboard, he jumped out of the window and hid in the first sanddune. Hitler was ready to honour him with the medal for his 'experiences', but when the other adjutants and the doctors made it clear that he was faking it, he reconsidered.

Sergeant Adam, the telephonist who had revealed that the bomber was Stauffenberg, received a present of 30,000 marks and a large house near Berlin. For interrogating the conspirators in the Wolfsschanze, Högl received the Gold Party Badge. Major Remer, who informed Goebbels of

---

*The speech to the educators took place on 3 August 1944, that to the Gauleiters a day later.

the order to seal off the government district, was immediately promoted colonel and appointed Battle Commander of Hitler's HQ. Hitler introduced this position because the Russians were already at the borders of East Prussia and the Wolfsschanze was now near the front. Colonel Streve, who had commanded HQ up till then, was restricted to administrative duties.

After the attempt, extremely strict security measures were introduced at Führer HQ. Hitler himself dictated the list of permanent delegates to the briefings. These were given to Schädle, the Chief of Hitler's personal bodyguard, and Högl, Chief of his Police Commando, so that they could control access to the meetings. Generals and officers who were not on the list could be given access only when Hitler personally approved an exceptional case. Anyone who came into the conference room – and that included Göring, Dönitz, Keitel, Jodl and Warlimont – had to present his briefcase for inspection. Weapons were to be handed in to the guards. Warlimont, who was particularly sensitive about anything that concerned his person, from now on appeared without a briefcase and with the papers he needed for the briefing in his hand. Even people who had been invited to the HQ to present a special report or to receive the Knight's Cross – which was awarded by Hitler in person – were searched by SD sentries before they could be taken to Hitler.

At the beginning of August 1944 Hitler's health took a turn for the worse, as his fainting fits increased. He was told to keep to his bed for two weeks and was represented by Keitel at the conferences. The 'Lord of the Battlefield', as Keitel was jokingly dubbed by the younger officers on Hitler's staff, thought his moment had come. He tried to imitate Hitler in every possible way. With sweeping movements of his long arms he drew thick blue arrows on the map that were meant to show counter-attacks against Russian breakthroughs at the front. He beat the table with his fist, made unnatural stretching movements and threw threatening glances at those standing around him.

There had been deep-seated changes to military command since 20 July. Even the participants in the situation reports had changed. Guderian was now Army Chief of Staff, having proved himself Hitler's loyal servant after the attempt on his life. His assistant was now General Lieutenant Wenck,[17] who was also Chief of the newly amalgamated Operations Department of the OKH. After the death of Schmundt, General Burgdorf[18] became Hitler's adjutant and Chief of the Personnel Office in his place. After Korten's death the new head of the Air Force General Staff was General Koller.[19]

The 'Lord of the Battlefield' Keitel did not manage to stabilise the Eastern Front, however. The offensive launched by the Russians in the middle of July 1944 in the front sector of Army Group North Ukraine, caused the loss of the cities of Lvov, Przemysl and Jaroslav.[*] Russian troops reached the Vistula south of Warsaw and through a number of smaller bridgeheads on the west bank of the river they managed to create a big one near Sandomierz.[20]

Hitler received the front reports in bed. He spent his evenings with his secretaries, who gathered around him. There was a struggle for power among Hitler's physicians at the time. The doctors treating him and the surgeons Brandt and Hasselbach questioned Morell's methods. They reproached him for the fact that Hitler's body contained too much strychnine, as result of which the patient's general state of health got worse and worse.[†]

Dr Giesing, the ear, nose and throat specialist from Lötzen who had treated Hitler's ears after the bomb plot, openly sided with Brandt and Hasselbach. When the battle came to Hitler's attention, Morell naturally won the day as the Führer could not live without the stimulants and tranquillisers he prescribed. Hitler threw Giesing out, and Brandt and Hasselbach were dismissed, to be replaced by Himmler's personal physician, SS-Obersturmbannführer Stumpfegger.[21]

Hitler urgently needed the attentions of a dentist. His dentist Hugo Blaschke, who had treated him for years, was summoned to the Wolfsschanze.[22] Blaschke had a private practice in Berlin's Kurfürstendamm and was a National Socialist Party member. Before the war Hitler had invested him with the title of professor and he had since been promoted to the rank of SS-Brigadeführer. He was often called to the Reich Chancellery, the Berghof or the Wolfsschanze, where he dealt with the teeth of Hitler, Eva Braun and Hitler's personal staff. The gold that Blaschke used for fillings he received from the reserves of the SS – the Gestapo had taken it from prisoners. Besides this, the SS leadership received crowns, bridges and gold teeth that had been prised out of Russian prisoners of war

---

[*] The offensive started on 13 July 1944. Army Group North Ukraine was torn apart. Of the fifty-six divisions, only twenty-four remained. Eight were completely eliminated. Some 65,000 Soviet soldiers were killed and 224,295 injured.

[†] Hitler was suffering from jaundice. The strychnine was a misinterpretation of the ENT specialist Giesing, who misread the ingredients in packets of Dr Köster's anti-gas pills. Hitler's doctors were alarmed because to have symptoms of poisoning Hitler would have had to have taken around 150 pills daily.

in the camps. This practice was instituted in 1944 on Himmler's secret directive, fulfilling an urgent wish of Hitler's.*

By the middle of August the doctors had restored Hitler's health to the extent that he could take part in the daily briefings again, though he was still very pale and unsteady on his legs. There were dark shadows under his eyes, his left hand shook badly and the right arm that had been injured in the explosion he still carried in a sling. He walked with a worse stoop than ever.

At the first conference after his sickness there were present, besides the usual participants, Bormann, Field Marshal Model, who had replaced Colonel General Reinhardt as Supreme Commander of Army Group Centre, and Gauleiter Koch.† Since the Russians had driven the Germans out of the Ukraine, the 'Emperor of the Ukraine' – as Hitler's staff jokingly named Koch – was back in East Prussia, where he had been given the job of Reich Defence Commissar. The new Chief of the General Staff, Guderian, was dressed in the black uniform of a tank soldier. He explained the position on the Eastern Front. On the sector controlled by Army Group South Ukraine, a major Russian offensive was to be expected in the area of Iaşi–Kishinov. The Romanian divisions on the right wing had no real value in battle, and German divisions had been posted between them to act as 'corset-hooks'. In the sector operated by Army Group North Ukraine, which had been pushed west over the Vistula, no more Russian attacks were expected. German attacks on the Russian bridgehead on the west bank of the Vistula and Sandomierz had yielded no results to date. Hitler interrupted Guderian in a soft voice: 'If we don't manage to remove this bridgehead we will not be able to hold the Vistula when the Russians attack again.' He ordered Guderian to muster all his strength to liquidate the Russian bridgehead and to turn the west bank of the Vistula into a fortified sector of the front.

Guderian continued with his briefing. He described the situation on the East Prussian border, where the Russians had marched up on a broad front. Koch and Model exchanged poisonous looks at this point. Koch suddenly went red and cried out: 'The Wehrmacht is not helping me build defences on the border. Mr Model seems little interested!' Model paid him back in his own coin and shouted in his turn. Koch did as he pleased and was not content to use the pioneers to build defences. Both lost their tempers,

---

*Orders to remove gold teeth had been issued as early as 23 September 1940. This policy was notoriously applied to the Jewish victims of the Final Solution.
†This took place on 15 August 1944.

shouted more and more loudly and hurled unpleasant insults in one another's faces. Hitler had difficulty calming them down.

Since the Russian army had begun to approach the East Prussian border, Koch had assembled hundreds of thousands of inhabitants and Russian prisoners of war to build fortified camps. Apart from the fortified area that already existed in East Prussia known as the Heilsberg Triangle,[23] the Masurian Lakes, which with their natural qualities were relatively easy to defend, had been provided with a thick network of fortified points. On all streets and bridges there was feverish activity building tank traps and ditches. The nearer the Russians got to the East Prussian border, the more refugees streamed out from the areas in immediate danger back towards Germany. It was a completely unknown experience for Germans: for the first time, the war was approaching their own territory.[24] At the end of the briefing the question was aired how women and children could be evacuated from East Prussia to avoid panic. Hitler declared fervently, 'If the Russians should dare to break into East Prussia then they will get to know the German people. They will hold on to their soil with all their strength and fight to their last drop of blood. Then it will be said, the people has risen up.'

The conference had come to an end. As the participants were leaving, Göring arrived unexpectedly, wearing a new parachute regiment uniform and high hunting boots. He propelled himself towards the table where Hitler was still sitting and, panting, he cried out that it would be terrible if the Russians were to march into East Prussia. In Rominten he had already raised the alarm and prepared his hunters for battle. With a sigh he added, 'My poor stags. It is horrible!'

In August Troost's widow, the owner of the Troost Studio in Munich, spent some time at the Wolfsschanze as Hitler's personal guest. Hitler had been a close friend of hers since the founding of the Party. Frau Troost was about forty, a long-time member of the Party and holder of the Gold Party Badge. Her late husband, Professor Paul Troost, had also belonged to the Party for many years, but soon after Hitler assumed power he committed suicide. The Führer had maintained a very close relationship with both for many years. Together they had hatched plans for splendid palaces for the National Socialist Party that Hitler wanted to build once he had achieved power, and Hitler had commissioned Troost to draw up plans from his ideas. Why Professor Troost took his own life remained unclear. In Hitler's circle it was assumed that, when he was granted the opportunity of realising his projects after Hitler came to power, he lost his mind and killed himself. After Troost's death Hitler gave his widow the title of professor and entrusted her with the job of designing the interiors of the Berghof, the Reich Chancellery and several National Socialist Party palaces. That way he kept in contact with her over the years. When he was in Munich he saw Frau Troost almost daily, and Frau Troost visited him regularly at the Berghof and the Chancellery.

This time she had answered Hitler's summons to the Wolfsschanze in order to mate her dog with Blondi. The proceedings took place while Hitler attended the briefing which Guderian explained the situation on the Eastern Front and at which the subject of evacuating women and children from East Prussia had been raised. When Hitler returned with Linge to his bunker after the meeting, he asked him whether the coupling had taken place. 'Yes, my Führer, the state occasion has been completed,' Linge answered light-heartedly.

'How did Blondi behave during the business?'

'Both behaved like debutants.'

'What do you mean?'

'They fell over in the act.'

Hitler had to laugh. Blondi's mating with Frau Troost's dog was a great event for the Führer's staff. Blondi enjoyed a special position with Hitler. Nobody dared touch her. No one could feed her. Blondi would only eat when Hitler was there. When in 1943 she contracted an infectious disease, she was sent to Dr Dopfer's private veterinary clinic in Munich, at 1 Rottmannstrasse. Hitler sent the clinic eggs, meat and cooking fat for Blondi. Every morning a telephone call brought a medical bulletin on her state of health. It was the first thing Linge had to relate to Hitler. When it was not good, Hitler was very worried. It was easier for him to sign a death warrant for an officer convicted of defeatism at the front than it was for him to receive bad reports of the health of his Blondi.

On 20 August 1944 the Russians began their offensive against Army Group South Ukraine in the area of Iași–Kishinev and very soon they had stormed the German–Romanian positions. Kishinev yielded as early as 24 August. A few days later the Russians broke through to the Pruth. When Romania saw itself forced to abandon the war as a result of the Russian offensive,[*] the following reactions were to be observed at Hitler's HQ.

Hitler declared that the Russians would try to use the resulting situation in order to march next into the Balkans and seize the Dardanelles. He concluded that they might postpone their advance westwards. In

---

[*]On 23 August 1944 King Michael of Romania had Antonescu arrested and formed a new government that declared war on Germany on the 28th.

political terms he thought the Russian advance into the Balkans, which the British saw as their sphere of influence, and an attempt to seize the Dardanelles, would increase the tension between the Anglo-Americans and the Russians. To give credence to his view, at the situation reports, Hitler read out reports from British press agencies almost daily, including the London Agency Exchange, which had strong words to say about the Russians. The antipathetic attitude towards the Soviet Union intensified when Russian troops marched into Bulgaria.[*] Hitler believed this to be of extraordinary significance. He paid close attention to the foreign reports of the German News Agency and underlined important passages in red pencil. Before the conference he handed the papers to Günsche and said, 'Don't forget to give me these despatches at the end of the meeting.'

When Hitler referred to the worsening relations between the Western Powers and Soviet Russia, he stressed that now was the moment to gain time. In September 1944, Hitler knew that the Anglo-Americans were ready to sign a separate peace with Germany; but he had to go first. The British demanded the removal of Hitler during talks with representatives of the German Foreign Office in Stockholm, which took place on the initiative of the British. When this was reported to Hitler, he ordered that the negotiations be broken off. Ribbentrop's permanent representative at Hitler's HQ, Ambassador Hewel, expressed his dissatisfaction that the Stockholm discussions had been terminated. In his view the war on the Eastern Front had reached a stage when making peace with the Western Powers had become unavoidable.[†] 'What is the Führer waiting for? He must make up his mind and find a way out,' said Hewel. The way out Hitler was seeking was a conflict between the Western Powers and the Soviet Union. At the end of the situation report he said with emphasis, 'Gentlemen, you will see. I shall be proved right.'

When Romania quit the war, there were many members of Romania's Iron Guard[‡] in Germany who had fled to avoid persecution by the Antonescu regime and been interned with preferential treatment in the concentration camp at Buchenwald. Horia Sima, the leader of the Iron

---

[*] On 5 September 1944. Despite its alliance with Germany, Bulgaria had neglected to enter the campaign against the Soviet Union.

[†] As early as 17 January 1944 *Pravda* had spread the rumour that Ribbentrop was negotiating a separate peace with Britain. Informal contacts with Germany were maintained by Britain, America and the Soviet Union.

[‡] The Iron Guard, formed as the Archangel Michael Legion in 1927, was a paramilitary, Christian-mystical, anti-Jewish organisation that was dissolved in 1937. In various guises it

Guard, was among them. After the fall of the Antonescu regime, Hitler ordered the members of the Iron Guard to be freed. A Romanian puppet government was formed under Horia Sima to act in Hitler's service in the unoccupied parts of Romania. The Russian army advanced so quickly, however, that his 'government' failed to make it to Romania. Sima was then invited to base himself in Vienna and organise sabotage and espionage behind the Russian lines in Romania and to spread anti-Soviet propaganda among the Romanian population. His agents, recruited from among members of the liberated Iron Guard, were equipped with radios and dropped by parachute from German aircraft into Romania.

Hitler had not a nice word to say about his former ally Antonescu. Less than two years before at a conference specially organised for him on the 'alleged position' on the Eastern Front, he had demonstrated that he held him in the palm of his hand. Now Hitler insulted Antonescu because he had failed to deal with King Michael, this 'country bumpkin', and because he had not been able to make the people submissive. 'He is nothing more than a syphilitic!' Hitler said of him dismissively.[25]

At the end of October and the beginning of November, the following situation was unfolding on the Eastern Front. On the northern sector of the front, the Russians had reached the Baltic coast near Memel, and thereby cut off thirty divisions in Courland which were caught in a pincer movement between the towns of Libau and Tukums.[26] The Russians had broken through border fortifications east of the towns of Gumbinnen and Goldap and captured the latter. To make matters worse, East Prussia was threatened on both sides by Russian units standing on the Niemen in the north and the Narev in the south. South of Warsaw the Russians had advanced from the Vistula across a broad front and were heading in the direction of the Upper Silesian industrial region. In the meantime, on the southern sector of the front their troops had crossed the Carpathians and were heading for both Czechoslovakia and Hungary. From the area around Budapest they were threatening Austria and southern Germany. Russian soldiers had already marched into the Yugoslav capital, Belgrade.

carried out terrorist acts including the killing of a Romanian prime minister. The leader, Corneliu Codreanu, was murdered in 1938. His successor Horia Sima participated in the overthrow of Carol II in September 1940 and joined Antonescu's government. After Sima's unsuccessful *coup d'état* in 1941, the SD brought him to Germany, and he was condemned to death *in absentia*. The SS confined him to the camp in Berkenbrück, but he ran away. After he was caught he was a privileged prisoner in Buchenwald because the Germans wanted to keep their options open. His puppet regime began work on 24 August 1944.

The German army had sustained enormous losses in dead and wounded on the Eastern Front. Everywhere the last reserves were being gathered up to be thrown against the Russians. At great speed a Volkssturm, or people's militia, was put together. Its battalions consisted of fifteen- and sixteen-year-old adolescent boys and sixty-year-old men. Activists from the Nazi Party took command, SA men and functionaries from the Hitler Youth.* The Führer Anti-Aircraft Regiment and the Führer Escort Division, which had previously been stationed at the Wolfsschanze, were sent to the Eastern Front. The Escort Division was commanded by the former HQ Battle Commander Remer, who had in the meantime been promoted general major for his services in putting down the plot of 20 July 1944. Only a few companies of guards remained at the Wolfsschanze.

Endless streams of confused and petrified refugees headed west from East Prussia. The war with all its horrors had arrived on German soil.† Hitler's hope that a conflict between the Anglo-Saxons and the Russians would turn the war had yet to be fulfilled. The time in hand which Hitler had reckoned on lost all meaning in the face of the speed with which operations on the Eastern Front unfolded. Hitler was in a tight spot. He could hesitate no longer. So he decided to strike a blow as quickly as possible against the Anglo-American armies in the west, and thereby to lay the keel for negotiations for a separate peace. This is where the idea came from for a German counter-offensive in the Ardennes.

The position on the Western Front had developed as follows after the landing of Anglo-American troops in Normandy on 6 June 1944. The Anglo-American forces gradually established their bridgeheads on the Norman coast, and at the end of July they broke through German lines at Avranches. At the beginning the breakthrough was only a few kilometres deep. German High Command gave Field Marshal von Kluge[27] – who had replaced Rundstedt as the Commander of Army Group West at the beginning of July 1944 – the order to annihilate the advance and re-establish the German line. The planned counter-attack, however, came to nothing as a result of completely unforeseen circumstances. Shortly before the attack was due to begin, Kluge, the Supreme Commander of Army Group West, left his HQ to travel to an unknown destination and disappeared.

---

*The Volkssturm was created on 25 September 1944 on Hitler's orders, and passed on to the Gauleiters to organise, while Himmler's SS was responsible for training and arming the units.
†The great treks to the west started in January 1945 when the Russians began their final assault on Germany.

When Kluge's disappearance was reported to Hitler, he expressed the supposition that Kluge had been a supporter of the 20 July Plot, and had run over to the Americans as a result. He ordered Rundstedt, who had already left on leave, to return immediately to the Western Front, and to reassume command of the army group. After an absence of two days, Kluge reappeared at his HQ. Hitler ordered him to appear before him to explain his conduct. On the way Kluge poisoned himself in his car.*

Both the orderly officer who had accompanied Kluge during his two-day absence from his HQ and his chauffeur testified at their interrogation that the field marshal had been extremely agitated at the time and had driven around in the vicinity of the front line. He had explained his journey to the front line as springing from a wish to see his son, who was serving in a division there. Further information from Himmler and the SD made it clear, however, that Kluge wanted to open the front to the Americans and capitulate, but for technical reasons he could not establish contact with the American High Command. In addition it was shown that Kluge was indeed involved in the 20 July 1944 Plot.[28]

Kluge's disappearance caused chaos in the army group, which was for a long period without orders and direction in the battle and at the same time had to defend itself against the attacking American forces. The loss of time occasioned by Kluge's treachery, the confusion among the German forces, part of which had withdrawn to entirely new positions, and the necessary reformation of the troops which that caused, rendered the planned counter-attack null and void. Now the German High Command was aware that German troops were in danger of being cut off and surrounded at Falaise after further American advances in the direction of Granville and Saint-Lô.[29] Instead of the planned counter-attack Rundstedt received orders to withdraw troops from France and Belgium and reform behind the so-called Siegfried Line.

The Wehrmacht retreated behind the Siegfried Line, fighting light skirmishes on the way.[30] Almost without resistance, Anglo-American troops occupied France and Belgium. The Americans, in particular the Third Army under General Patton, did not even need to exploit the difficult situation the Germans found themselves in as a result of the Kluge Affair. Only because the American military leadership had not fathomed the situation and had therefore hesitated was it possible for the German High Command to rescue its forces and, without heavy losses, bring them in behind the Siegfried Line. Hitler gave a sardonic appraisal of the withdrawal

---

*On 18 August 1944.

of German troops from France and Belgium, suggesting that Eisenhower and Patton would be pretty surprised by their unexpected success. 'These weeds', he said, 'will now take themselves for great strategists thanks to the withdrawal of the armies by the German High Command.' After the German contingents had reached the Siegfried Line there were a few local skirmishes around Aachen in the second half of October. In other parts of the Siegfried Line all was calm.[31]

At the end of October Hitler convened an extraordinary situation briefing among a select circle. The following attended: Keitel, Jodl, Guderian, Christian, Burgdorf, Günsche, Fegelein and General Lieutenant Winter,[32] who shortly before had been named Jodl's deputy in succession to Warlimont. For his part, Warlimont had become Keitel's deputy in the Supreme Command of the Wehrmacht, sitting in Berlin, in the middle of October. The meeting took place in Hitler's bunker, now that its conversion was completed. It began with a briefing by Guderian on the state of the Eastern Front. He reported that in nearly all sectors of the front the battles had abated. Apart from skirmishes here and there, calm reigned over the whole front. He explained that the Russians were currently busy bringing up reserves from behind the lines, and that they would need a lot more time yet before they could begin their new offensive in East Prussia and on the Vistula. At this Hitler decided that the time had come for the planned counter-attack in the West. He gave Jodl the task of working out an immediate plan for a surprise attack on Anglo-American forces in northern France, Alsace and Belgium.*

As Hitler saw it, the main thrust of the attack should come from the Eifel Mountains south of Aachen and be directed against the link between the British and American forces. He wanted to divide them, quickly advance to the Maas, force a crossing of the river and then take Antwerp and its harbour, which was the principal source of supply for the Anglo-American armies.

To carry out these operations it was decided during the meeting to form two Panzer armies: the Fifth under the command of Tank General Manteuffel[33] and the Sixth SS Tank Army under the command of the former chief of SS-Leibstandarte 'Adolf Hitler', Sepp Dietrich, who had now been promoted colonel general. Both these armies should be placed under the overall command of Field Marshal Model and incorporated in

---

*Jodl received instructions to plan an offensive in the Ardennes on 25 September 1944. On 12 October he produced the first plan, Wacht am Rhein, or the Watch on the Rhine.

Army Group West. At the end of the meeting, Hitler stressed once again that the preparation for this operation and the strategic deployment of the forces had to remain top secret. He asked the participants in the discussion to sign a document swearing them to secrecy. The signatures were immediately collected by Hitler's ADC, Burgdorf.

As Hitler wanted to lead the operation himself, he transferred his HQ to the area around Bad Nauheim, in a woody part of the country near the village of Butzbach, fifty kilometres north-east of Frankfurt am Main.* This was the Staff HQ of the Supreme Commander of Army Group West, Rundstedt. Hitler's HQ at Bad Nauheim consisted of six well-camouflaged concrete bunkers. In contrast to the Wolfsschanze the Bad Nauheim HQ was very lightly fortified. In the meantime the Wolfsschanze had been completely evacuated – owing to its proximity to the front, Hitler did not want to go back there any more. Only Guderian remained with his staff at Lötzen in East Prussia.

On the way to Bad Nauheim, Hitler stopped in Berlin for a fortnight. There he spoke to Sepp Dietrich and Manteuffel about the coming operations in the Ardennes. He also received Mussolini's 'liberator', SS-Obersturmbannführer Skorzeny, who was at this time Chief of the Sabotage Department of the Reich Security Main Office (RSHA).† Skorzeny was assigned the task of commanding a unit of captured British and American tanks manned by soldiers dressed in captured British and American uniforms, which would appear behind the lines of the Anglo-Americans and cause panic.‡ Besides this, Skorzeny was to take the most important bridges over the Maas, in order to prevent the enemy from blowing them up before the arrival of the main German army.

Only a few days after his arrival at Bad Nauheim and immediately before the start of the counter-offensive, Hitler summoned the army chiefs concerned – the commanders of the divisions and tank armies, as well as the Supreme Commander of Army Group West, Model – to make clear to them how important the coming operation was§. In a speech lasting around forty-five minutes he explained that the Ardennes operation had

---

*Hitler took up residence on 10 December 1944. It was ten kilometres west of Bad Nauheim.
†He was head of Office VI (the SD's Foreign Department) and the S Department, Sabotage. The RSHA had been formed from a recent merger of the SD and the security police.
‡His unit, called Panzer Brigade 150, had only limited success. They committed a number of solecisms and were shot for contravening the laws of war.
§Hitler spoke on 11 and 12 December 1944 to the divisional and corps commanders of Army Group B.

exactly the same significance as Dunkirk, where the British had been wiped out in 1940. If it was successful, Hitler declared, it would lead to the liquidation of the Western Front and to a fundamental change in the way the war was going. The intention of using this operation to conclude a separate peace with Britain and America was not mentioned to the army leaders.

When the commanders had left the HQ, Hitler, in conversation with his adjutants, expressed the hope for a successful outcome to the operation. If Sepp Dietrich could make it with his army to Antwerp, he would honour him with the Great Cross, because this victory would decide the war. The Great Cross was the highest military order, granted only for a decisive victory at the front. Only Göring had been given this order up to now, despite the fact that his wartime activities had been largely confined to hunting.* Hitler believed that, if German forces took the principal supply depot in Antwerp, the Anglo-Americans would be placed in a hopeless position and would be obliged to make him an offer.

Commenting on the British demands that negotiations for a separate peace with Germany could be carried out only once he himself had stepped down, Hitler pronounced: 'I will show the English gentlemen that peace with Germany can only be achieved with me, and not without me.'

On 16 December 1944 the Germans launched their Ardennes offensive according to plan with an attack from the Eifel Mountains. Dietrich's and Manteuffel's tank armies had no problem breaking through the Anglo-American front line between Liège and Dinant and advancing to the Maas.† A fierce battle ensued.

At this time, towards the end of December, Guderian arrived unexpectedly from East Prussia at the Bad Nauheim HQ and urgently requested permission to report to Hitler. He announced that he had concrete, verifiable information from aerial and ground reconnaissance that the Russians were preparing their forces for new attacks on East Prussia and the Vistula. He said that, in his opinion, a major offensive was to be expected in the next few days. He stressed that it was absolutely necessary to reinforce these sectors of the front. Hitler was angered by Guderian's report and expressed doubts about the veracity of his interpretation.

---

*The Great Cross was created on 1 September 1939 as the highest level of the Iron Cross. Göring was the sole recipient, having been given it on his appointment as Reichsmarschall on 19 July 1940.
†The advance stopped around ten kilometres short of the Maas. The Germans never came near Liège.

One of Hitler's arguments was founded on the weather report supplied by Schuster, the HQ meteorologist, who predicted unfavourable flying weather in the east that was going to get worse. Despite this, Hitler was evidently uncomfortable about Guderian's report. On the very same day he convened an extraordinary situation conference for his closest circle, to which Bormann was also invited. Here Hitler gave a summary of the position on the Western Front, where the counter-attack in the Ardennes was developing successfully. Then he sketched in the situation on the Eastern Front and examined Guderian's prognosis, that the Russians were about to launch an offensive.

Here Hitler showed that Guderian's briefing had completely thrown him off balance. He stressed that a reinforcement of the Eastern Front at this moment would ensure the failure of operations that had already been launched in the Ardennes. Bormann spoke after Hitler. In order not to excite him further, he chose his words very carefully and recommended that urgent steps be taken to reinforce the Eastern Front. He pointed out that a further successful attack by the Russian army would have fateful political consequences for Germany. It could hardly be disputed that a victory for the Russians on the Eastern Front would nullify the success of the Germans in the West.

Hitler reserved his decision, and with that the conference was brought to an end. The next day he convened the same crew. This time he declared that the offensive being prepared by the Russians on the East Prussian border and the Vistula presented, in fact, a very serious danger. 'As a result and with a heavy heart I have decided', Hitler continued in a weak voice, 'to bring the Ardennes offensive to a halt and to transfer Dietrich's Sixth Tank Army, as well as the principal forces of Manteuffel's Fifth Panzer Army, to the Eastern Front.'*

Even before the OKW issued the orders, in January 1945 Hitler commanded Günsche to drive over to Sepp Dietrich on the Western Front. He reiterated to him, 'Tell Dietrich he must withdraw his divisions from the front two at a time. Tell him that I have decided to throw his entire army at the Eastern Front.'

---

*The Ardennes offensive had already been repulsed and the withdrawal of the Sixth Army had no influence on the outcome of the battle. Model had already recognised that he did not have sufficient strength to take Antwerp, and Allied air supremacy played a key role in defeating the German armies. During the Ardennes offensive the Germans lost 17,200 dead, 34,439 wounded and 16,000 prisoners; the Americans lost 29,751 dead and missing, and 47,129 injured.

By the morning of 7 January Günsche was at Dietrich's HQ at Saint-Vith in Luxembourg,* where he communicated Hitler's order. It was as if Dietrich had been struck by lightning. He said everything was ready to force a crossing of the Maas. The Americans had placed a high price on the head of Skorzeny, whose units had caused panic behind the lines and were already approaching the bridges on the Maas. 'The Führer needs to be clear about one thing,' Dietrich continued. 'If my army is withdrawn, then for the British and the Americans the road is open to the Rhine.'

Günsche remained with Dietrich for several days. On 12 January, a few hours before he left, a coded telegram came in to Dietrich's HQ with the order to withdraw the Sixth Army from the front immediately and transfer it to the Eastern Front. That night Günsche returned to Hitler's HQ in Bad Nauheim. To his surprise he found it completely abandoned. Only a few soldier-servants were busy clearing up. They told Günsche that Hitler and his staff had left for the station in Giessen in great haste, from where the Führer was going to take his special train to Berlin. When Günsche arrived in Berlin the next day, 13 January, he learned that, because of the Russian offensive in East Prussia and on the Vistula which had begun on the 12th, Hitler's HQ was now located in the Reich Chancellery.

The Wolfsschanze in East Prussia, where Hitler had whipped up a victorious euphoria at the beginning of the war against the Soviet Union, was blown up on his orders. Berlin was to be the last home to Hitler's HQ.

---

*In Belgium.

13

January – March 1945

Berlin HQ was housed in different places. At first Hitler moved into the old Reich Chancellery on the Wilhelmsplatz. As his presence there remained a secret, no flag flew over the building. Whenever he had come to Berlin in the past, his standard had been raised over the Chancellery by the guard of honour, which would march into the *cour d'honneur* to the sound of drums. Hitler's standard had been made to his own design: a gold-framed white circle was set in a square of red cloth, with a black swastika in the middle. In the four corners were gold-embroidered German eagles, also holding swastikas.[1] For the time being Hitler had allowed only his Leibstandarte to use this flag as their battle standard.

Together with Hitler, the adjutants, secretaries and doctors, Bormann, Fegelein, Otto Dietrich, Hewel and the Führer's personal bodyguard were housed in the building. Keitel and Jodl and their staffs went to Berlin-Dahlem. Guderian moved into the staff HQ in Zossen, thirty kilometres south of Berlin, which had been laid out before the outbreak of war in 1939. Dönitz set up his HQ in Oranienburg, Ribbentrop lived in his own villa in Berlin-Dahlem. Göring repaired to his hunting lodge at Karinhall, which had been constructed shortly after Hitler came to power and which lay in its own game park on the Schorfheide, sixty kilometres north-east of Berlin. The name of the mansion recalled his deceased first wife, the Swedish woman Karin. He lived there now with his second wife Emmy, the former actress Sonnemann, and their seven-year-old daughter Edda. His personal staff was housed with him.

In Berlin Hitler played host to the situation reports twice a day, at 3.00 in the afternoon and at around 12.00 midnight, in the conservatory of the Chancellery. The following people took part: Keitel, Jodl, Guderian, Wenck, Buhle, Koller, Winter, Fegelein, Admiral Wagner from Dönitz's staff, Voss, Bodenschatz, Scherff, Hewel, Otto Dietrich, Christian and Burgdorf, as well as Hitler's adjutants Below, Puttkamer, Borgmann, Johannmeyer[2] and Günsche. In addition there were the officers of the Wehrmacht Operations Staff: Colonel Waizenegger, Major Büchs and naval Captain Assmann, as well as Keitel's adjutant John von Freyend, Fegelein's adjutant Sturmbannführer Göhler,[3] Guderian's adjutant Major von Freytag-Loringhoven,[4] and sometimes also Guderian's orderly officer Captain Boldt,[5] Bormann and his assistant SS-Standartenführer Zander.[6]

It was Hitler's wish that Bormann and Zander should always be present at the situation reports, as Bormann had been given the task of putting together the Volkssturm and evacuating the population from Germany's eastern territories. Göring and Dönitz also took part in almost all the conferences. Guderian or Wenck reported on the situation in the east, and Jodl or Winter on the west. Luftwaffe matters were presented by Christian or Major Büchs from the General Staff of the Luftwaffe, who worked with Jodl in the Wehrmacht Operations Staff. On naval action, the reports were delivered by Admiral Wagner[7] or Captain Assmann.

Fegelein, Hewel and Hitler's adjutants took part in the night conference. The situation at the front was presented in turn by Hitler's adjutants Puttkamer, Below and Borgmann. These were purely information reports and as a rule lasted no more than thirty minutes. Hitler received a short daily front report from the OKW. That arrived at 11.00 a.m., when Hitler was still asleep. Linge laid them on a chair that stood before Hitler's bedroom door, together with the reports from the German News Agency. Hitler collected them from there and took them away.

Besides the OKW reports, Fegelein and Günsche received daily reports on the situation on the Eastern Front from the SS divisions, and these were also relayed to Hitler. They arrived by a tortuous route that avoided the official channels: they were issued by the commanders of the SS divisions and were sent directly to Himmler, who worked on them and sent them on to Hitler. This system of direct reporting by SS divisions was introduced by Hitler in 1942 in order to verify information from the OKW and OKH on the progress of the war on the various fronts. Their practical value was that Hitler was informed of the position at the front before the situation reports came in, provided SS divisions were employed there.

Apart from this Hitler was informed daily after breakfast of the destruction caused to German cities by Anglo-American bombers. The data were collected by Bormann's Party Chancellery from all over Germany, and Hitler was briefed by Schaub. For this reason he earned himself the nickname 'Julius Bombenteppich', or Julius 'Blanketbomb'.

When Hitler moved from Bad Nauheim to Berlin, Eva Braun came too, having been conjured up by the Führer from Munich.* She took up

---

*This had been Eva Braun's decision. Hitler had even begged her to stay in the Berghof.

residence in the Reich Chancellery in the room next to Hitler's apartment. Apart from a two-week stay in Munich in February 1945, she
remained in Berlin with Hitler to the end.

The Russian offensive that began on the Vistula on 12 January 1945 spread
out over the following days to take in the entire front from the Baltic to
the Carpathians. Only a few days later the Polish capital Warsaw fell, which
had been one of the central points of the German defences.*

Soon after the fall of Warsaw the Russians broke through the heavily
manned German defensive system in the south of East Prussia and after
intense fighting occupied the German towns of Allenstein, Tannenberg
and Deutsch-Eylau. At the same time Russian troops overran the German
defences on the west bank of the Vistula at Sandomierz and advanced in
the direction of the industrial region of Upper Silesia.

Guderian was taking this into account when he reported to Hitler that
the Russians had reached the Bay of Danzig and cut East Prussia off,
together with the Third and Fourth Armies of Army Group North. Along
with the Sixteenth and Eighteenth Armies of Army Group Courland,
which had been holed up in the Baltic since the autumn of 1944, the main
force of Army Group North was enclosed in an East Prussian pocket.
Guderian pointed out that they could only be provisioned by sea, and that
with great difficulty. He suggested that units of Army Group Courland
should be evacuated by sea and recommitted against the Russians in
Pomerania.

According to Guderian's plan, the attack on Russian forces should have
been made in a southerly direction from Pomerania. For this he planned
to use Army Group Courland, Sepp Dietrich's Sixth SS Panzer Army −
which had been famously transferred from the west − and the Third Army,
which was already in Pomerania. By this operation Guderian aimed to cut
off the Russian troops before they reached the lower Oder, and to erect a
strong defensive line on the old German−Polish border. In his opinion the
units he had named − which amounted to a total of between forty and
forty-five divisions with 1,600 tanks − would be sufficient for the task.
According to Guderian there was no time to be lost: the Russians had to
be driven out of Germany again as quickly as possible. Hitler had listened
to Guderian's report with increasing impatience. He now responded
shrilly, 'I am well aware that we need to drive the Russians out of Germany,
Guderian. You don't need to tell me that.'

---

*Warsaw fell on 17 January 1945. It was an important victory for Soviet propaganda.

Despite this Hitler categorically rejected Guderian's suggestion that they should fetch Army Group Courland from the Baltic and deliver it to Pomerania. He based this on his premise that it was tying down Russian forces that would otherwise be used for fighting in East Prussia, Poland and Silesia. As early as autumn 1944, when the position on the Eastern Front was more favourable for the Germans, Guderian had suggested that Army Group Courland be brought back from the Baltic and behind the Memel river. Hitler had not agreed then because in his opinion the presence of German troops in the Baltic put pressure on Sweden. He meant that, so long as German troops remained in the Baltic, Sweden would not bow to British pressure and would continue to deliver ore.

This time Guderian would not give in. Against all rules he had brought General Gehlen[8] along to the situation report with him, the Chief of the Department of Foreign Armies East in the OKH. His job was to deal with intelligence observation on the forces of the states of eastern Europe, the Soviet Union included. Gehlen was there to support Guderian's suggestion to make use of Army Group Courland. By using intelligence material Gehlen sought to prove to Hitler that Army Group Courland was not tying down any strong Russian force. Moreover, the Russians had already withdrawn units of considerable strength from this sector which had now been recommitted to the forces attacking near the lower Oder. Gehlen's argument threw Hitler into a rage. He shrieked that he would not tolerate General Staff work of this sort. He forbade Guderian to bring Gehlen with him again or even to mention the withdrawal of the Courland division again. Guderian answered, 'At your command, my Führer,' and fell silent.

When it came to the battle for East Prussia, Hitler declared that every town, village and house should be turned into a fortress, so that the Russians would wear themselves out. He shouted until he was hoarse that the Germans had to fight so hard that the boot was on the other foot, and instead of German troops and civilians being frightened of Russians, Russians would be frightened of them. In fact the fear of the Russians was great. When German troops fled in chaos, the population panicked and ran with their soldiers. A mass migration towards the German heartlands began. The roads and paths of East Prussia were thick with old men, women and children who had turned and run, only to became jammed in the numerous tank traps that offered only a tortuously narrow path. Many – the children in particular – froze to death in the intense cold.

In the next series of battles, the Russians took the towns of Tilsit, Insterburg and Gumbinnen and broke through the heavily manned defensive system around the Masurian Lakes. German troops were herded on to a narrow, sandy strip of land on the Baltic coast and on to the Samland Peninsula. They were now in a hopeless position. When the reports came though to Führer HQ, Hitler's reaction was always the same: 'Hold on and don't retreat!'

When German forces were cut off on the Kurisch Nehrung and the Samland Peninsula, Hitler ordered his army adjutant Johannmeyer to fly to the East Prussian Front in order to make an appraisal and to report back to him. He wanted to check the information he was receiving from the commanders of the German army in East Prussia. In general he would not accept bad news, and on top of this he presumed that the situation was being painted much worse than it was in order to avoid a major battle with the Russians. After his return Johannmeyer confirmed that the troops in East Prussia were in an extremely serious position. He reported that they were pushed on to a narrow coastal strip together with thousands of refugees and cattle where every Russian shell caused enormous loss of life. Hitler countered him: 'I will not withdraw a single solder from there. I must hold Fortress Königsberg at any price. As long as Königsberg is in our hands I can tell the German people, "We still have East Prussia, and the Russians do not."' When Johannmeyer reported that the population was in full flight from East Prussia, which was leading many of them to their deaths, Hitler screamed, 'I can't pay any attention to that!'

At the beginning of April 1945 Königsberg was surrounded by a thick ring of Russian soldiers. Hitler received a report that Russian artillery had set the city ablaze. Despite this, he ordered General Lasch, the commander of Fortress Königsberg, to keep on fighting. On April 9 Königsberg fell to the Russian army and General Lasch went into captivity. Hitler condemned him to death *in absentia*.[*]

On the other hand he did not hold the Party bigwig Koch to account, though he was meant to be the soul of the defence of Königsberg. On the contrary, while the battle raged for Königsberg, Hitler offered Koch the chance to go to Pillau in order to get away from the Russians in time. As Königsberg was already surrounded by Russian soldiers, Koch telegraphed Karl Hanke,[9] the Gauleiter of Breslau, from Pillau to say that he would never yield up Königsberg to the Russians, that the battle for Königsberg would be an example for the struggle of the German people in their unlimited belief in the Führer. Karl Hanke, no less a bigwig than Koch, hurriedly

[*]Königsberg fell on 10 April 1945. Hitler condemned Lasch to death the same day. The family of the General of Infantry were arrested.

sent a telegraph back in the same style: he would likewise never yield up Breslau, which was also already surrounded by Russian forces. To raise the morale of the German people, Goebbels ordered the telegrams of the 'popular leaders' to be read out on the wireless, and thereby to be heard by the public at large. Both Koch and Hanke emerged from the fighting unscathed, while countless German soldiers had to perish in the battles for Königsberg and Breslau.*

Given the catastrophic developments on the Eastern Front at the end of January and the beginning of February 1945, Hitler and Bormann frequently discussed the fate of the Party. Hitler agreed with Bormann's suggestion to withdraw the junior cadre of the National Socialist Party from the Eastern Front – mostly members of the Hitler Youth commanding Volkssturm units – and pack them off to western Germany. The first to be ordered west were pupils at the Ordensburgen and the Adolf Hitler Schools in Pomerania and Silesia. They needed to be prepared for future leadership tasks in the Party – the aim was to preserve them in order to save the Party. Bormann directed them to go underground, to show themselves loyal to the Anglo-Americans and to try to secure posts in the administration. For the time being they should withdraw to the Allgäu, the Bavarian Alps and the region of Bad Tölz–Lenggries. Among those who were to lead the illegal Hitler Youth Organisation in western Germany were the Chief of the Adolf Hitler Schools, Obergebietsführer Petter,[10] and the Chief of Military Training in the Hitler Youth, Schlünder.[11]

At the same time as the junior cadre of the National Socialist Party was being withdrawn to western Germany, Hitler also commanded that Koch, the Gauleiter of East Prussia, Forster, the Gauleiter of Danzig, and Greiser,[12] the Gauleiter of Posen, should make their way there.

There was a secret discussion at the Party Chancellery in the Wilhelmstrasse attended by Petter, Schlünder and Bormann's closest collaborators – State Secretary Dr Klopfer,[13] Friedrichs,[14] the Supreme Commander of the National Socialist Party, and Bormann's personal assistant Müller.[15] At this meeting Bormann referred to the transfer of the Party cadre to western Germany: 'Our salvation lies in the west. There our Party may continue to exist. We guarantee that we will never give up the struggle against Bolshevism.'[16]

---

*Two armies of the First Ukrainian Front surrounded Breslau on 15 February 1945. The city did not capitulate until 6 May 1945. During the fighting 68 per cent of it was destroyed. The number of dead is unknown.

Before his departure for west Germany in March 1945, Oberge-bietsführer Kurt Petter came to say goodbye to Günsche at the Reich Chancellery. Günsche and Petter had been friends since their time together in the Hitler Youth from 1932 to 1934. Petter claimed that the Hitler Youth could provide a future for the Party, as the older generation was too bureau-cratic and hated by the people. Petter drove via Sonthofen to Bad Tölz, in order to take over the leadership of the Hitler Youth groups transferred from eastern Germany.

Almost all Germany's reserves were absorbed in the battles that raged on the Eastern Front – in Courland, East Prussia, Pomerania, Silesia, Bohemia and Hungary – when Anglo-American troops advanced into German ter-ritory in February 1945. The breakthrough took place between Trier and Aachen, that is, in the sector of the front that had been severely weakened by the transfer of Sepp Dietrich's Sixth Tank Army to the east.

The stark contrast between the war in the east and that in the west was once again reflected in Hitler's situation reports. The Führer received Guderian's reports from the Eastern Front stormily and with frequent out-breaks of fury, in contrast to his response to Jodl's from the west. Jodl was able to make Hitler accept the Anglo-American advance as an unavoidable consequence of the weakening of the front resulting from the transfer of forces to the east. The Führer calmed himself with the thought that the Anglo-Americans would be brought to a halt by the natural obstacle of the Rhine. As a result he reacted relatively calmly to Jodl's news that due to the transfer of divisions to the Eastern Front the number of soldiers desert-ing to the Anglo-Americans had grown significantly. When a division was being prepared for departure to the east, it was found that whole platoons, even whole companies, had made for the open and gone over to the enemy.

At the end of every month Hitler received a report from Speer, Minister of Armaments and War Production, or from his deputy Saur, on the pro-duction of weapons and munitions of all sorts. Sometimes these figures were also transmitted by telephone and Hitler entered them personally on to a chart. Most of the time he had one of his adjutants with him, who also listened on the headphones and made notes as well. Then they both verified the figures and compared them to the previous months.

From the reports of January and February 1945 it was clear that the pro-duction of German munitions companies – with the exception of Russian-occupied Silesia – was running at maximum capacity. That was explained by the fact that the Anglo-American bombers concentrated their attacks on companies working for the air industry, on petrol refineries and on airfields. They mounted attacks on the Messerschmitt Works in Augsburg, Focke-Wulf in Bremen-Memelingen, Heinkel in Rostock, the aircraft factory producing jet fighters in Wiener Neustadt, the BMW factory, where aeroplane motors were made, ball-bearing factories in Schweinfurt and Regensburg and small companies that produced planes or plane parts. At Hitler's HQ they were firmly convinced that the Anglo-Americans wanted first and foremost to destroy Germany's air industry, because the Luftwaffe was one of the best ways the Germans had of fighting them. At the same time the Anglo-Americans clearly had no interest in bombing companies that made weapons to be used by German ground troops fighting on the Eastern Front.[*]

All the same, the attacks on German cities by Anglo-American bombers became ever more intense. Hitler seemed rather uninterested that they were being reduced to ruins. Once he said, 'You find better cover in ruins and can defend yourself better.' At another time he said, 'After the war I shall build much more beautiful cities than those that have been destroyed. I actually have to be grateful to the Anglo-Americans that they have saved me the work of pulling down parts of towns I wanted to rebuild.' On the subject of the bombing of Berlin, he remarked once, 'When are they going to bomb Berlin Town Hall! This atrocious building has annoyed the architect in me for years. If the Anglo-Saxons spare it, it is probably to infuriate me.' He said this with a laugh.

In February 1945 Hitler often spoke to Speer about what would happen in the event of an Anglo-American occupation and what they would do with the industrial concerns of western Germany. With the German army's retreat from German areas in the east, Hitler had issued orders to blow everything up so that nothing remained for the Russians. In the west, on the other hand, he gave orders for the complete preservation of industry. On his directives, the industrialists were to remain where they were in the event of an occupation. He thought that if the businesses were to remain in the west it would be a fair assumption that German industrialists could resurrect their friendly relations with Anglo-American industrial magnates. He set much store by this. In his opinion the situation in the east would inevitably lead to a military accommodation between Germany, Britain and

---

[*] Allied bombing destroyed the Krupp works in Essen, the Auto-Union factories in Saxony, and the fuel refineries in Leuna and Zeitz. Attacks on the mines in the Ruhr halved coal production. Continued production is explained by the systematic shifting of industries to underground positions.

America against the danger of Bolshevism. In this the industrialists had an important role to play.

On Speer's suggestion, Hitler directed industrialists in the regions which were being occupied by Anglo-American troops to take away vital parts of their machines to make them unusable. In the course of negotiations with the Anglo-Americans they could have the parts reinstalled and thereby prove their loyalty. With this directive Speer travelled through the western German industrial areas. Hitler advised him to journey accompanied by his loyal disciples – Dr Vögler, the Chairman of the board of the United Steelworks, Dr Rohland, leader of the Main Panzer Committee, and Geilenberg,[17] General Director of the Rhine Metal Works.

By the end of February 1945 the Russians had advanced to the area of Küstrin–Frankfurt–Guben zur Oder, and were now between eighty and ninety kilometres east of Berlin. In the preceding battles the towns and cities between the Vistula and the Oder had been either taken, bypassed or encircled – Thorn, Schneidemühl, Bromberg, Posen and others. These towns lay at important strategic junctions and the Germans had declared them all to be fortresses. All available reserves and forces that could help resist the enemy were now thrown at the Oder in order to hold the Russians at bay. The Replacement Army, sailors from warships and the Volkssturm were sent to the Oder. Special measures were hurriedly implemented to stabilise the front as the precipitate retreat of the German army and the massive blows of the Russians had torn a hole in it and destroyed its High Command. To this end Hitler named Himmler commander of the newly created Army Group Vistula.* He hoped Himmler would succeed in restoring the front between the Baltic and Silesia by his ruthlessness and cruelty.

To stop the flow of fleeing soldiers, SS Special Commandos were set up behind the lines under the command of Police General SS-Obergruppenführer von dem Bach-Zelewski,[18] SS-Obergruppenführer Jeckeln,[19] Skorzeny and others. They shot at soldiers who attempted to run and chased them back to the lines. Officers or Party workers from the Volkssturm who tried to desert were shot on the spot or hanged.

Between the Oder and Berlin heavily manned fortifications with several protective cordons and numerous tank traps were erected at great speed. All inhabitants and Berliners were obliged to play their part. The mobilisation for these works was organised by Stürtz,[20] the Gauleiter of Brandenburg.

---

*On 23 January 1945.

Sepp Dietrich, commander of the Sixth Tank Army, received orders to set up a disruptive radio service in the Fürstenberg–Bad Saarow. At the time his army was in the southern part of the Eastern Front, en route from the Western Front to Hungary. The radio station was established by Dietrich with a number of members of his staff. It emitted fictitious orders and reports from one part of the Sixth Tank Army to another. It was meant to create the impression among listeners that those forces were stationed on the Oder. There was a double intention: to mislead the Russians about the present strength of the troops on the Oder and to conceal the fact that the Sixth Tank Army was being sent to Hungary.

In the middle of February Hitler moved into his air-raid bunker. Eva Braun and Morell also took up residence. Without the latter's injections Hitler could not get through the day. His entire personal staff remained in the Chancellery. Hitler's air-raid shelter, the Führer Bunker, had been built to his specifications in the garden of the Chancellery in 1943.

His first air-raid shelter was under the diplomats' hall of the Chancellery. He had used it until shortly before the air attacks on Berlin started, but it no longer seemed secure enough for him. He wanted to go further under the earth. To this end, the new bunker was dug three metres deeper. From the old bunker into the new there was a stone spiral staircase that led to a small room with an armour-plated door. Behind this was the wide hall of the Führer Bunker, divided in two. In the first half, on the right-hand side, there were several cupboards containing air-defence equipment (gas suits, steel helmets, gas masks, fire extinguishers). A door in this wall led to the machine room and the air-conditioning unit. A second armour-plated door led to six interconnected rooms. This was the telephone exchange with telephone and telegraph connections which was manned by a telephonist from Hitler's bodyguard. Then there was Morell's room, the sick-room, with a bed for Hitler's duty physician Dr Stumpfegger, a bedroom for Linge, another for the soldier-servants and a guest room. Against the left wall in the first half of the hall there was a rectangular table with chairs, and a clock hanging above it. A telephone cabin had been set up here, so that the duty telephonist could announce calls from outside to the attendants at the conference.

A door in the left wall of the corridor led to the lavatories, where a place for Hitler's German shepherd Blondi had been built as well. Her coupling with Frau Troost's male dog had produced nothing. As a result, at the end of January 1945 Blondi was put together with the dog of Reichsleiter Alfred Rosenberg, the ideologist of the National Socialist Party. Hitler had

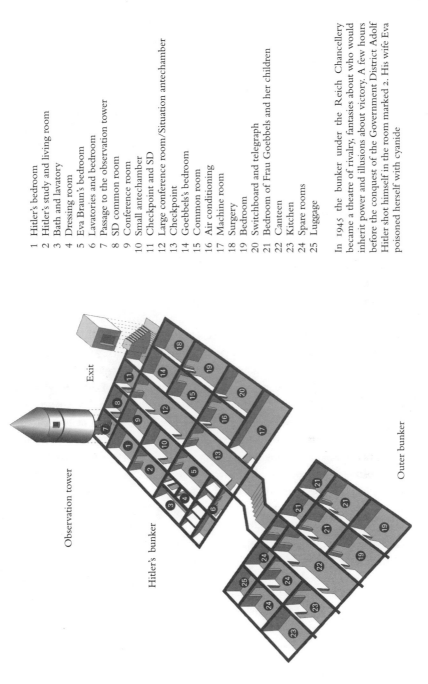

1 Hitler's bedroom
2 Hitler's study and living room
3 Bath and lavatory
4 Dressing room
5 Eva Braun's bedroom
6 Lavatories and bedroom
7 Passage to the observation tower
8 SD common room
9 Conference room
10 Small antechamber
11 Checkpoint and SD
12 Large conference room/Situation antechamber
13 Checkpoint
14 Goebbels's bedroom
15 Common room
16 Air conditioning
17 Machine room
18 Surgery
19 Bedroom
20 Switchboard and telegraph
21 Bedroom of Frau Goebbels and her children
22 Canteen
23 Kitchen
24 Spare rooms
25 Luggage

In 1945 the bunker under the Reich Chancellery became a theatre of rivalry, fantasies about who would inherit power and illusions about victory. A few hours before the conquest of the Government District Adolf Hitler shot himself in the room marked 2. His wife Eva poisoned herself with cyanide

Observation tower

Exit

Hitler's bunker

Outer bunker

Blondi's corner heated by a sun lamp. At the beginning of April the joyful, long-awaited event took place and Blondi gave birth to eight puppies. Three survived. The most robust of them Hitler awarded his own nickname of Wolf. That month he would sit for hours in an armchair and play with his darling Wolf.

The first half of the floor was divided from the second, the so-called situation antechamber, by another armour-plated door. Here stood a sentry, an officer from Hitler's bodyguard. Participants in the conferences waited in the situation antechamber until Hitler arrived. The walls were hung with large, valuable paintings, chiefly Italian landscapes. Along the right wall were twelve to sixteen armchairs opposite an upholstered bench, and in front of a large rectangular table were two more armour-plated doors. The first led into the private rooms of Hitler and Eva Braun, the second into the conference room. Before one reached Hitler's room there was a small antechamber, and behind the door there was a screen, so that those attending the briefing could not see into Hitler and Eva's living space.

Before the double doors of the small antechamber was Hitler's study, which was furnished with a thick, soft carpet. To the right of the door was a big desk and a chair. On the desk was a great bronze lamp, an escritoire, a telephone, an atlas of the world and a magnifying glass. Most of the time Hitler's spectacles were also there. Over the desk hung a portrait of Frederick the Great by Menzel in an oval frame, which Hitler particularly loved. Against the opposite wall was a sofa, and before it a table and three armchairs covered with patterned silk. Over the sofa hung a still-life; to the right of that was a tea-table, to the left a wireless; on the right-hand wall hung a particularly valuable painting by Cranach.

The door next to this led to Hitler's bedroom, which was also carpeted. Apart from the bed there was a night cupboard,[*] a clothes cupboard, a tea-trolley, a safe – in which Hitler kept secret documents – a bookcase and an oxygen canister. On the left-hand side of the study there was a door leading to the bathroom Hitler and Eva shared. From there one had access to Eva's dressing room as well as her bed-sitting room. There was a chaise-longue covered with dark material, a little round table and an armchair. A tall standing lamp cast a muted light over the room. Against the opposite wall was Eva's bed, a cupboard and a basket for her dog. The floor was covered in dark, patterned carpet. Pictures of flowers hung on the wall. Through a second door from Eva's bed-sitting room one reached the small antechamber.

[*] For Hitler's chamber-pot.

On the left-hand side of the big conference room there was a large table with telephones and lamps on it, as well as writing paper, an atlas, a magnifying glass, pencils and Hitler's spectacles. In front of the table several chairs were laid out, and an upholstered foot-rest. The other walls were fitted with an upholstered banquette. To the right of the entrance there was a wireless set and another telephone.

At the end of the large conference room there was the so-called lock with an armour-plated door. From the lock one could reach the Chancellery garden through one of two emergency exits. On the right a spiral staircase with stone steps rose upwards. Over the exit a die-shaped tower had been built with thick concrete walls, where an SD sentry watched over the entrance to Hitler's air-raid shelter. Outside, near the entrance, there was another sentry from Hitler's bodyguard. From the left-hand emergency exit, one reached the outside by means of an iron fire-ladder. It was protected by a cylinder-shaped tower topped by a cupola in which machine-gun nests and observation posts had been built. Here were also stationed SS men from Hitler's bodyguard. The tower possessed a telephone connection to the bunker.

The bunker's floor, ceilings and walls were constructed from best-quality concrete three metres deep. The ceiling had also been reinforced with bulky iron beams. But even then Hitler did not feel sufficiently secure. He ordered the bunker to be roofed with a further layer of gravel secured by a tight steel net one metre thick. Besides this he ordered that the approach from the Chancellery be made in a zigzag form and secured by a heavy, armour-plated door.

Hitler left the bunker only for the daily conference and lunch. When at the beginning of February 1945 the conservatory was destroyed by a bomb, the conferences were transferred to Hitler's study in the New Chancellery, which he reached through the garden. When there was an air-raid warning for Berlin, the conference took place in the bunker. The evening conference was always held there.

After Hitler returned to Berlin from Bad Nauheim on 12 January 1945, he ate only in the company of Eva Braun and his secretaries. Others were no longer invited.

A notable frost entered into the relations between Hitler and Göring, most obvious during the situation reports. The cold shoulder came from Hitler. More and more often he blamed Göring – sometimes at the top of his voice – for the fact that the Luftwaffe had not done its stuff. Hitler could become abusive:

'The Luftwaffe is nothing but hot air!'

'The Luftwaffe ought to be as red as a beetroot that enemy aircraft feel so at home in German airspace!'

'If the Luftwaffe is no longer capable of flying, at the very least they ought to fight on the ground.'

'The figures for the number of shot-down enemy aircraft are false.'

'Many airmen do not deserve their medals.'

Göring held his tongue when these insults were levelled at him. His one reaction was not to wear his medals – at least for the time being. Whenever Luftwaffe operations were being discussed, Göring ostentatiously left the table or the room. At one time Hitler, purple with rage, placed a newspaper article in front of him, which recounted that Göring had been hunting wild boar on the Schorfheide. Hitler shouted at him that if he had nothing to do but hunt wild boar, he could, at the least, ensure that the newspapers didn't write about it. The Führer removed responsibility for building the jet fighter from Göring and entrusted it to Himmler. The engineer SS-Obergruppenführer Kammler[21] took over the task of production.* Since the autumn of 1944 he had been responsible for making rockets and commanded a special unit armed with V1s and V2s.

The more Hitler distanced himself from Göring, the closer Goebbels became. It was not long before the two men enjoyed a special relationship. Goebbels did not take part in the briefings, but Hitler received him daily and discussed every question with him for hours on end. In the last months of the war, Goebbels became the Führer's closest adviser.

At the end of February 1945 Hitler had an operation on his vocal chords, carried out by Professor von Eicken,[22] a specialist in ear, nose and throat diseases. He had identified a polyp, which had developed because Hitler screamed so much. The removal was effected without complications, but the Führer had to keep silent for a whole week, or he risked losing his voice altogether. In this period Hitler's adjutants delivered the briefings from the fronts, and he wrote his orders and directives in the pages of a notebook.

When the Russians facing Army Group Vistula in Pomerania advanced in a broad front towards the lower Oder, there were still around twenty German divisions on a coastal strip some fifty to a hundred kilometres wide between Danzig and Stettin. Hitler gave his opinion of the situation at the front during a briefing at the beginning of March 1945. Although he also saw the situation in Pomerania and on the Oder as extremely critical, he

---

*Kammler assumed control of the project on 27 March 1945.

drew the conclusion that it might be possible to strike a blow against the Russians. He said, 'The Russians won't continue their offensive over the Oder and in the direction of Berlin, because their left flank is threatened by German troops concentrated in Pomerania. As long as this danger remains, there is no danger of an attack on Berlin. That is to say, for the present, important elements of the Russian army are going to be tied down in Pomerania. That allows us the possibility of breaking through Russian positions in the area south of Stettin and attacking the Russians behind their lines in the Oder basin. This operation will create space for German troops in Pomerania, so that they can attack the Russian front south of Danzig, break though and advance in the direction of Schneidemühl–Posen.'

Guderian argued against Hitler's plan. He said that the Russians had already reached the Oder basin and were standing ninety kilometres from Berlin; and that they would seek to take the capital as quickly as they could. Further, the Führer's plan was doomed to failure from the start. All forces needed to be concentrated on the Oder to defend it. Hitler was astounded that someone had contradicted him and fell into a rage, the first time this had happened in Guderian's presence. 'Shut up, Guderian!' he roared. 'The Russians will not be as stupid as we were when we stood before Moscow and wanted to conquer it at once. It was you, Guderian, who wanted to be the first man to march into Moscow at the head of his army. You should know best how these things pan out!'

Guderian went pale. But Himmler, who was to lead the operation according to Hitler's plan, supported Guderian. There was a deathly silence. The only thing one could hear now was how heavily Hitler was breathing. After a short pause he said that his appraisal of the situation was the only one that was correct and that only dilettantes and debutants would judge it otherwise. He ordered the troops from the Oder basin to be withdrawn and made into two attack formations. These were meant to attack in the area south-west of Stettin and from the bridgehead on the east bank of the Oder between Frankfurt and Küstrin. They should break though the Russian lines and push them back. The main attack would be led by the Stettin Group. In later briefings, Guderian repeatedly pointed out that according to German intelligence the Russians had concentrated strong forces in the Oder basin, which attested to the fact that they were going to pursue their attack on Berlin. But Hitler insisted that his plan be carried out.

The counter-attack by German troops, which according to Hitler's plan was to be led from the area around Stettin, was bogged down within days by Russian artillery fire. Hitler was furious. In the presence of everyone at the briefing he tore Guderian off a strip as if he were addressing a school-boy, accusing him of deliberately leading the attack in such a way as to make it fail. He then criticised Himmler for allowing Guderian to talk him round.

When in the following days the Russians did not proceed to Berlin but pursued German contingents in Pomerania instead, Hitler was even more incensed. He insisted that he had been right, that only he had spotted the Russian intentions. To prove it, he had the minutes of the meeting brought in at which they had debated the Russian plans, and gave them to Goebbels so that he could acquaint himself with them. Goebbels took them away and returned them to Hitler later with a note: 'My Führer, why don't you sack these useless generals?'

The relationship between Hitler and Guderian was now irreparably damaged. Moreover, Himmler was replaced as Supreme Commander of Army Group Vistula by Colonel General Heinrici.[23] Angry and upset, Himmler withdrew to the SS sanatorium in Hohenlychen run by SS-Gruppenführer Gebhardt,[24] and had Hitler informed that he was ill. From this point on, SS-Obergruppenführer Kaltenbrunner[25] – who was Chief of the SD and the RSHA – became a permanent feature at the situation reports. He never said a word, but simply listened in silence. Hitler never indicated why Kaltenbrunner was present at the situation reports. In his circle it was presumed that the Führer, who felt increasingly insecure, wanted to issue a warning to those who attended the briefings.

It was the middle of March 1945. In the antechamber to Hitler's study in the New Chancellery the regular participants in the briefings were gathered and were waiting for Hitler to appear. SS soldier-servants served alcoholic drinks and a cold snack. Guderian stood at the buffet and knocked back cognac after cognac. One might have supposed that he felt the need of some Dutch courage before the meeting.

In the meantime Hitler had come through the garden of the Chancellery accompanied by Linge and had gone into his study. He directed Linge to ask the others to come in. The SS men in his bodyguard opened wide the doors to his study. The first to enter was Göring. He was followed by Dönitz, Keitel, Jodl, Guderian, Kaltenbrunner and the rest. Hitler stood at the big marble table and gave each of them his hand. While the maps were laid out by Hitler's adjutant Johannmeyer, Günsche and Guderian's adjutant Freytag von Loringhoven, Guderian said something to Hitler. He smelled strongly of alcohol and had to take a step backwards. Without answering

Guderian, Hitler seated himself at the table with the maps. Thanks to the cognac Guderian was no longer steady on his legs, and held on to the table.

With a slightly heavy tongue he delivered his briefing on the situation on the Eastern Front, beginning with Army Group South. A few of the others exchanged sly grins and nudged one another while they listened to him. He was saying that Army Group South's counter-attack against the Russian bridgeheads on the Danube and the Drau south of Lake Balaton was moving very slowly. He also had information that the powerful Russian attacks on Army Group Centre in Silesia and Bohemia had been contained, up to now, with the exception of a few breakthroughs. Bitter battles were raging, and both sides complained of heavy losses. In the area of Army Group Vistula the Russians had broken through to the Baltic by Köslin and Kolberg and had cut the German forces in Pomerania off from one another. Guderian added that losses were very high and that all the reserves had been thrown into the battle. 'It would be useful', he considered, 'to transfer Army Group Courland to the Oder.'

Hitler jumped up at Guderian's last words, his face as red as a turkey. He swept the map to the floor, pummelled the table with his fists and bellowed that Guderian had been wrong in his appraisal of the Eastern Front for too long. 'You failed to understand the position before Moscow in the winter of 1941!' he screamed. 'You did not know the position on the Vistula at Warsaw in January 1945! Between the Vistula and the Oder you have built fortifications and tied down tens of thousands of soldiers instead of sending them to the front! And finally you have misunderstood the position on the Oder!' Guderian, his face as pale as a corpse, gulped for air and held his hand on his heart. With a faltering voice he began, 'My Führer, you shouldn't speak to me like that. No one has worked so hard to hold the Russians at bay as I have, as far as that was—' Hitler ended the meeting. Everyone left the room. He alone remained.

From this day Guderian was no longer to be seen in Hitler's presence.[*] He was replaced as Chief of the General Staff by General Krebs, who only a few weeks before had replaced General Wenck as Leader of the Operations Department of the OKH, when the latter had been injured in a car accident. Before then Krebs had been chief of staff to Field Marshal Model, whom he resembled in his vivacity and lively gestures. Krebs was a close friend of Burgdorf and later also of Goebbels and Bormann.

[*]He was sacked on 28 March 1945.

14

March 1945

At the beginning of March 1945 Hitler ordered a powerful force to be assembled under the command of General Wöhler[1] in the area of Army Group South. This would include Sepp Dietrich's Sixth Tank Army, which itself comprised such elite SS divisions as the Leibstandarte 'Adolf Hitler', 'Das Reich', 'Totenkopf', 'Wiking', 'Hohenstauffen', 'Frundsberg', 'Hitlerjugend' and others.[*] Hitler was preparing a counter-offensive on Lake Balaton. The strategic objective was to destroy the great Russian bridgehead between the Danube and the Drau, south-west of Budapest, drive the Russian army back over the Danube and retake Budapest. Hitler planned the operation to eliminate the danger to southern Germany and the oil wells of Lake Balaton. This was the last important source of oil available to Germany, leaving aside the small amounts that came from Austria and Germany.[†] Hitler therefore gave orders that the Balaton operation was to be planned with particular care. With this in view he summoned Sepp Dietrich and asked him to lead the operation with total commitment and to crown it with victory, whatever the cost.

The counter-offensive on Lake Balaton was a failure. A few days after the start of the attack the Russians brought the German army to a standstill by delivering heavy blows to the flank, before forcing it back to its points of departure and beyond, even pushing them further to the northwest in the direction of the Austro-Hungarian border and inflicting grievous losses. Hitler instantly dismissed General Wöhler and replaced him[‡] with General Rendulic,[2] an Austrian who had served in that country's army before the Anschluss. Hitler had given him the Gold Party Badge for his unstinting loyalty to National Socialism.

The failure of the Balaton counter-offensive shook Hitler deeply. The hopes he had invested in the SS divisions were now gone. The briefing was

---

[*] 'Frundsberg' was fighting on the Vistula; 'Totenkopf' and 'Wiking' were not under Dietrich's command.
[†] The Red Army captured the oil fields at Nagykanizsa on 2 April 1945.
[‡] On 25 March 1945.

conducted for the first time by General Krebs, who reported on the retreat of Dietrich's army. Stunned, Hitler sat at the table with his head hanging, staring into the middle distance. When a report about Dietrich was given at a later meeting, and reference was made to the fact that his army had lost an enormous number of men and tanks in the bloody fray, Hitler sat up and thundered, 'My SS divisions have forgotten how to fight! They have become cowards!' He fell back into his seat and once more stared dully into the distance, his face twitching. His SS divisions of all people, which he had presented as a model to the whole Wehrmacht and which had been honoured with particular names, now he had to accuse them of cowardice.

After the briefing Hitler called Günsche into his study and asked him whether Dietrich had spoken to him before the Balaton counter-offensive. Günsche said yes. He reported to Hitler that Dietrich had expressed his confidence in the coming operation; he had regretted only that his army was fighting in Hungary and not in Pomerania, as he wanted to fight not for Hungary, but for Germany. Hitler growled, 'Guderian told him to say that. I can imagine.' Then Hitler asked Günsche what he knew of the divisional commanders of Dietrich's army and the regiments of the SS Leibstandarte 'Adolf Hitler'. Günsche stressed that Peiper, commander of the Leibstandarte Panzer Regiment, Hansen of the 1st Motorised Infantry Regiment and Sandig of the 2nd Motorised Infantry Regiment had served with the Leibstandarte since 1933 and had received high honours. Hitler interrupted him: 'Good, good, now leave me alone.'

As it became clear that the counter-offensive on Lake Balaton had finally been defeated, Hitler summoned Günsche again and made him prepare an order for Dietrich, commander of the Sixth Panzer Army, proclaiming that the Leibstandarte no longer deserved to bear the name of Adolf Hitler. Günsche, himself a member of the regiment, sat down dejectedly and reluctantly began to formulate the order while Hitler walked up and down the room. After Günsche had made many attempts and crossed a lot of things out, he finally produced the draft: 'As the Leibstandarte has not carried out my orders and has failed to show the fighting spirit that I expect from it, I command that it is unworthy to carry the name of Adolf Hitler.' In the meantime Hitler had noticed Günsche's reluctance. He walked up to him and said, 'Let it be. I will talk to Himmler myself.'

Himmler, who had not got over being dismissed as Supreme Commander of Army Group Vistula, was still at the SS sanatorium at Hohenlychen. On Hitler's orders he took part in the situation conference the next day. Here Hitler gave free rein to his anger about Dietrich and his army. He fulminated, 'The Leibstandarte exists no longer! It is not worthy of my name! Himmler, you will go to Dietrich in person! I am removing the names from all the SS divisions. Rip off their armbands. Dietrich's too! Tell Dietrich that if the divisions retreat any further, I shall take away all their standards and all the medals from the officers and soldiers!' Himmler answered without expression, 'At your command, my Führer!'*

Göring tried cautiously to make Hitler reconsider his decision. In his opinion the punishment was too severe for the SS divisions, which had shed their blood on the Eastern Front since the start of the war. That made Hitler even angrier. He compared his fate to that of Frederick the Great, who punished several regiments for cowardice during the Seven Years War. 'Frederick the Great removed names, banners and distinctions from his regiments. I shall not be afraid to shoot SS men if they retreat further!'

As Hitler had threatened to take the banners away from the SS divisions, two of Dietrich's officers came to see Günsche at the beginning of April to fetch the battle standard of the Leibstandarte that he was holding in safe-keeping for them in the Chancellery bunker. It was only carried on parade. Günsche handed it over without Hitler's knowledge, and they took it to Dietrich, whose HQ was now located near Vienna.

In the next round of fighting in the southern sector of the Eastern Front, Army Group South – to which the SS divisions of the Sixth Tank Army belonged – was thrown back towards Austria. In Vienna, which Hitler had decreed should be defended to the last man, a revolt broke out against the German administration.[3] Hitler ordered the Austrian-born Kaltenbrunner, who had been Chief of Police in Vienna before being named Chief of the RSHA, to drive immediately to that city and put down the uprising with all severity. On 13 April, however, Russian troops marched into Vienna and rescued the population from Hitler's butcher Kaltenbrunner. Kaltenbrunner meanwhile had driven off in the direction of Vienna to carry out Hitler's orders, but he never came back to Berlin: he simply disappeared. It later transpired that he had made up his mind to clear off to the Anglo-Americans in the west.

When Russian troops reached the Oder in the area of Küstrin–Frankfurt and thereby stood before the gates of Berlin, Hitler became very concerned about whether he was still safe in the Chancellery. Above all he feared possible disturbances or a revolt on the part of the Berlin population. He

---

*Himmler flew to Hungary on 28 March 1945. On 2 April 1945 Dietrich was made battle commander of Vienna. He reacted strongly to Hitler's accusation: 'Hitler calls us cowardly; two-thirds of my men lie under the earth and he calls us cowardly!'

therefore decided to appoint a battle commander for the Chancellery to strengthen the protection provided for the building and for the entire government district. On Burgdorf's suggestion Hitler immediately appointed Lieutenant Colonel Pick[4] to carry out this task. Three weeks later, however, he was replaced by Günsche at Hitler's request. As battle commander of the Chancellery and the government district, Günsche was personally answerable to Hitler. The government district contained the following streets: Unter den Linden, Wilhelmstrasse, Behrenstrasse, Mauerstrasse, Wilhelmplatz, Vossstrasse and the Hermann Göring Strasse as far as the Brandenburg Gate, as well as the Reich Chancellery.

The business of guarding the Chancellery was undertaken by the Guard Battalion of the Leibstandarte, the Berlin Guard Regiment that belonged to the 'Gross-Deutschland' Panzer Division and the SA Regiment 'Feldherrnhalle', as well as forces from the security police and the SD. Besides these Günsche had several Volkssturm companies at his disposal, as well as the Führer Escort Company under the command of SS-Obersturmführer Drobe.[*] The latter, who had been housed until recently in the Lichterfelde barracks of the Guard Battalion of the Leibstandarte, were now relocated to the Reich Chancellery. There they were put up in the diplomats' hall and in other rooms.

On Günsche's orders a defensive ring was thrown around the government district with strongly fortified gun positions. The passage through the Brandenburg Gate was closed off and machine guns were set up under the Quadriga on top. Embrasures were knocked into the garden walls of Goebbels's villa on the Hermann Göring Strasse and machine-gun nests installed. The ruins of the bombed-out AWAG department store opposite the New Chancellery were made impassable with barbed wire and mines.[†] All streets that led into the Wilhelmstrasse were equipped with gun nests and tank traps so that access to the square could be prevented when necessary. There were fortified firing positions in the ruins of houses where the Behrenstrasse met the Mauerstrasse and where Unter den Linden met the Wilhelmstrasse. The roofs of the ministries were given gun nests and the Chancellery was fortified with particular care. The balcony of the Chancellery looking out on to the Wilhelmsplatz, where in his glory days Hitler had received the ovations of Berlin National Socialists, served now as a machine-gun position, because it commanded the whole of Wilhelmsplatz and the Wilhelmstrasse.

[*] Possibly Heinrich Doose.
[†] The former Wertheim had been 'Aryanised' as AWAG.

In front of both the main entrances to the New Chancellery on the Vossstrasse, sandbags and obstacles had been laid out so that they could be closed off. The windows of the building were already barricaded, and they bristled with machine guns. In the garden of the Chancellery there were mortars and stocks of ammunition, while in the garden of the neighbouring Foreign Office a shooting range had been set up for Eva Braun and Hitler's secretaries. They could practise shooting there in case they ever had to join in battle with the Berlin population. The number of sentry posts in the Chancellery was tripled. At every entrance and exit there were ever more men.

With every measure he implemented Günsche was required to report to Hitler. The Führer expressed his satisfaction, but continued to issue fresh orders. Once he had Günsche summoned and addressed him testily, 'My ladies [the secretaries] have complained that they could only come to the tea evening by a tortuous route to the bunker and were held up by a huge number of sentries.' Günsche endeavoured to explain that for reasons of security the watch was reinforced at night-time, but an irritated Hitler interrupted him, 'No one can protect me anyhow. Only providence protects me.' Despite the 'protection of providence' Hitler left everything as it was, however, and gave no orders to reduce the security measures.

While countless resistance nests and support points were set up at the front between the Oder and Berlin, there was feverish work going on to fortify the city. Barricades were built, trenches dug and tank traps laid all over Berlin. The Berlin population was driven out to work.[5] The labour was directed by Goebbels, as defence commissar for Berlin, and by Schach,[6] as assistant National Socialist Party Gauleiter for the capital. There was practically no street without an obstacle created out of the stones of bombed-out houses. A landing strip was created on the east–west axis between the Brandenburg Gate and the Victory Column, and, to make it fifty metres wide, the street lamps on either side had to be removed. Meanwhile the Brandenburg Gate and the Victory Column were equipped with landing lights for aircraft. Columns of soldiers, Hitler Youth and Volkssturm marched out to the city perimeter to take up defensive positions.

While the capital was energetically prepared for defence, Hitler's regime made ready to flee. The signal to evacuate the highest state and Party offices came from Bormann. A long column of big black cars took them to pre-ordained hideaways in the area of Salzburg–Berchtesgaden–Bad Reichenhall in southern Germany. All officers were directed to leave only a skeleton staff of ten to fifteen civil servants behind who could be flown out of the capital at any time. While the Reich administration was being evacuated, Hitler directed his steward, Arthur Kannenberg,[7] to remove all valuables and all his personal possessions from the Chancellery and to carry them to safety. Precious furniture, Gobelin tapestries, carpets and paintings were taken to Schloss Moritzburg, which stood in a range of hills fifteen kilometres from Dresden. Carvings and statues that had been acquired in Italy were brought to the Stuttgart area by Walter Erhardt, an Obersturmbannführer in Hitler's bodyguard. Hitler had Linge transport his own library by train to Bad Aussee near Salzburg, where it was housed in secure bunkers. Here Bormann also lodged the archives of the Munich branch of the Party Chancellery, which had been kept in the Brown House.* Obersturmbannführer Adolf Dirr from Hitler's bodyguard accompanied the library to Bad Aussee. The state porcelain collection, which was worth several million marks and was used for official receptions, Kannenberg transported to Bayreuth in person. He failed to return to Berlin.

In the second half of March 1945 the Russians shattered the German armies in Pomerania and conquered the harbours of Danzig and Gdingen, both of which had been important U-boat bases and supply depots for the Baltic. Only on the Hela Peninsula, a narrow strip of sand jutting out into the Bay of Danzig, were there still a few German units. The German–Soviet front now ran along a line from Stettin to Küstrin, Frankfurt and Guben. In this situation, as Hitler rightly maintained in the course of a briefing, 'Everything depends on how firmly the Oder Front holds.'

Burgdorf encouraged Hitler to drive to the Oder Front and raise the morale among German troops there. But Hitler procrastinated. He felt safer in his bunker. At the end of March he decided to drive to the Oder anyhow, but not to the soldiers in the front line. According to Burgdorf's plan, Hitler should first visit the HQ of the commander of the Ninth Army, Burgdorf's brother-in-law General Busse,[8] in the area of Frankfurt–Küstrin, followed by the HQ of General Huebner.[9] Huebner commanded a People's Grenadier Division that depended on Busse's army. Much propaganda was to be made of Hitler's journey, which was to go out under the slogan 'The Führer in person at the Eastern Front!' Hoffmann's photographers and Frentz, the news cameraman attached to Hitler's HQ, were to be responsible for pictures and newsreel.

*Since 1941 it had been housed in a purpose-built building on the Königsplatz.

Hitler's excursion took place on the morning of 27 March 1945,[*] at a time when no air raids were feared. Hitler left his bunker tired and unsteady on his feet. His face was pale and wrinkled and he had big bags under his eyes. His left hand shook even worse than usual. The blows at the Eastern Front that had begun with the Vistula offensive on 12 January 1945 had had the effect of making him look like a feeble old man. Six great general-purpose vehicles from the Hitler cavalcade had driven up. Bormann, Burgdorf, Fegelein, Morell, Stumpfegger, Hewel, Lorenz and Hitler's adjutants were already waiting by the cars. Hitler shuffled over to them and greeted them with a limp handshake. Then Linge helped him into his enormous and comfortable vehicle. By himself he would not have been able to manage it. Bormann, Burgdorf, Fegelein and Linge got in with him. Bormann, Burgdorf and Fegelein were close friends and in recent times almost inseparable. For this reason they were called the clover-leaf in Hitler's entourage. When Linge got in behind the Führer, the cavalcade started up. Hitler's excursion was kept top secret. The day before, his adjutant Johannmeyer had checked the route. Busse and Huebner had been informed of the visit under the seal of strictest secrecy.

The vehicle's roof was closed. The times were past when Hitler would stand up and drive in an open car in triumph through the streets of Berlin. Now he had the collar of his lined leather coat turned up and he sat as close as possible to the driver. His vehicle was followed by two others containing soldiers from his personal escort commando; behind these were Morell and the adjutants. In the following car sat Stumpfegger, Hewel and Lorenz. The latter was meant to write up Hitler's 'visit to the front' for the press. Right at the end of the convoy was a replacement vehicle. As the column turned into Unter den Linden, crossed the Alexanderplatz and drove though the Frankfurter Allee into the proletarian area of north-east Berlin, Hitler grew increasingly nervous. He fidgeted in his seat and his facial muscles quivered. A deathly silence reigned in the car. Everyone was afraid that Hitler would break out in a tantrum. Suddenly he threw his grey glacé-leather gloves at Linge, who was sitting behind him, and shouted, 'Please give me some better-fitting gloves! These are too tight. They cut off the circulation in my hands!'

Linge handed him another pair of gloves the same size. Hitler put them on and found that they fitted. 'Why did you give me those other ones,' he complained. Then silence fell in the car again. They had an hour and a half's drive ahead of them. When the car drew up in front of a large manor

[*]Actually 3 March 1945.

house that was the HQ of General Busse, commander of the Ninth Army, Linge helped Hitler out of the car. Busse, together with the closest members of his staff, was there to welcome him, arms raised in a fascist salute. Hitler tried to look vigorous as Hoffmann's photographers and Frentz directed their cameras at him, and then shook hands with everyone.

Busse led him into the largest room in the house where a number of staff officers were waiting. Hitler gave them his hand as well. Then he stepped over to a big table where the operations maps for the Eastern Front were laid out, and struck a pose for the photographers, pressing his left arm against his body to stop it from trembling. General Busse stood next to him in order to explain the position in this sector of the front. On the other side Bormann, Burgdorf and Fegelein took their places. Hitler's adjutants, his doctors, Hewel, Lorenz and the SS men from his bodyguard gathered with Busse's staff officers around the table. Everything was arranged for the photographs of Hitler's 'visit to the Oder Front'.

Busse then briefed Hitler, explaining that his position on the heights of the west bank commanded the entire east bank and that his defensive positions were fifteen to twenty kilometres deep. Hitler asked him how much ammunition he had for the artillery and for the ground fighting. He was not happy with Busse's answer and declared that he would look into it, to ensure that this army was provided with the maximum. After half an hour Hitler drove on to Huebner's divisional staff, which was about twenty minutes further on, near Wrietzen. The general briefly outlined the position in his division's sector, but Hitler was not very interested. His main reason for wanting to see Huebner had been to assign to him the task of finding out why the Rhine bridge at Remagen had not been blown up, and why the Americans had been able to stream across it without hindrance.* Huebner was ideally suited to this task as he was known to be devoted to the Führer. Hitler gave him the Knight's Cross and remained with him in his HQ for over an hour. After that he drove back to Berlin and by around 5.00 p.m. was back in his bunker again.

That was Hitler's visit to the front. It made a great propaganda splash in the newsreels and in the papers. Under headlines such as 'The Führer with his troops on the Oder Front', photographs appeared showing Busse's and Huebner's staff officers, the Party bigwig Bormann, the sly fox of the Gestapo Fegelein, the diplomat Hewel, the Kurfürstendamm charlatan Morell, SS officers and soldiers from Hitler's bodyguard and his adjutants.

★

*The Americans crossed the Rhine four days after the visit. Huebner came to the bunker on 9 March, was named head of the court martial there and received his Knight's Cross.

Hitler had commissioned General Huebner to preside over a 'mobile court martial' on the Western Front to find out and punish those responsible for ordering the retreat of the German army and failing to blow up the bridge over the Rhine at Remagen. The report was for Hitler's eyes only. On the Western Front the following situation reigned: on 1 March 1945 the Anglo-Americans reached the Rhine north and south of Düsseldorf. After crossing the Mosel west of Coblenz on 15 March they headed for the Rhine between Coblenz and Bonn. In order to stop them advancing further, all the bridges over the Rhine were blown up. The exception was the bridge at Remagen.

In the course of a briefing Jodl announced to Hitler that the bridge had fallen into the hands of the Americans, and as a result they had marched over to the eastern bank without a fight.* Jodl said that the bridge had been prepared for detonation, but when the Americans approached the electrical fuse failed to work. Hitler, who until then had been calmly listening to him, sprang from his chair at these words and screeched, 'I gave orders to blow up the Rhine bridges in good time! The bridge at Remagen had been intentionally left for the Americans! That is sabotage and treason!'

He hurled furious glances at Jodl. It was the first time he had flown into a rage during one of Jodl's briefings on the Western Front. As Hitler shot up from his armchair, Keitel, who was standing next to him, recoiled in shock. Dönitz, Bormann, Krebs, Burgdorf, Koller, Christian and the adjutants stood around the table in silence. Jodl was about to reply but Hitler turned immediately to Keitel and ordered him to launch an inquiry at once and find out who was guilty of failing to destroy the Remagen bridge. The upshot of the inquiry was that the bridge had apparently not been destroyed because a number of German troops remained on the west bank of the Rhine and were meant to use the bridge in their retreat. While they were being engaged by American forces, however, the electrical fuse failed to work. The commander responsible for blowing the bridge later fell in battle. This was the outcome of the investigation ordered by Keitel.

Hitler did not believe it. He maintained that they were simply putting the blame on the head of the dead bridge commander. For that reason he gave Huebner the task of carrying out a second investigation. The latter

---

*The account is confused. Despite German attempts to destroy it, the Ludendorff Bridge fell to the US army on 7 March 1945. Within twenty-four hours they had established a solid bridgehead of 8,000 men on the eastern bank of the Rhine. The badly damaged bridge collapsed on 17 March.

travelled to the Western Front and soon afterwards reported back to Hitler that his investigation had incontestably concluded that the officers of the pioneer and anti-aircraft units who were meant to defend the Remagen bridge had fled at the approach of the Americans without so much as attempting to blow it up. A few officers had deserted to the Americans. The rest – ten in total – Huebner had condemned to death and had had shot on the spot.

The fact that the Remagen bridge had fallen into the hands of the Americans had a catastrophic effect on the situation on the Western Front. Army Group B under the command of Field Marshal Model had to direct its main forces against the American bridgehead east of Remagen, leaving weak forces for the remaining sectors of the front between Düsseldorf and Bonn. The Americans used the weakening of certain sectors of the front to force a passage over the Rhine at Düsseldorf and elsewhere. The German front on the Rhine collapsed and the Anglo-Americans managed to push deep into Germany without having to put up much of a fight. Model's army group ran the risk of being cut off. On this subject Hitler held a special conference with Keitel and Jodl at which Günsche was present. Keitel thought it was urgently necessary to come to a decision about the Ruhr. Indicating the map of the Western Front, Jodl pointed out that Army Group B was still on the Rhine and actually in danger of being cut off. 'My Führer,' he continued, 'we really must decide now whether Model and his army group should be withdrawn deep into German territory. That would mean giving up the Ruhr.' Hitler hesitated. Then he commanded, 'Model should retreat to the Ruhr and stay there.'

It was unusual that Hitler did not order Model to defend the Ruhr, merely to stay there. In Hitler's entourage it was interpreted as part of his intention to come to a military understanding with the Anglo-Americans against the Russians. For this reason it was important for him to maintain the Ruhr as the industrial base for war production. If Model's forces had fought battles there, the factories might have suffered heavy damage.* Moreover, Hitler wanted to keep Model's army group with its 300,000 to 350,000 men in the west in order to keep another trump card for negotiations with the Anglo-Americans.

Not long afterwards, in April 1945, Model's army group in the Ruhr was surrounded. The field marshal, who, against Hitler wishes, had not wanted to give up the fight, shot himself as the noose tightened around his army.[10] The Anglo-American troops continued their advance north and

---

*The region was already very badly damaged.

south of the Ruhr, crossed the Weser and reached Magdeburg on the Elbe by the middle of April, almost without encountering resistance.

In the middle of March Hitler changed the time of his situation reports to 2.00 a.m. or 3.00 a.m. The reason for this was the nightly air raids on Berlin which generally lasted until around midnight and prevented the staff officers from the OKH and the OKW from coming to the briefing. As the situation at the front became more and more serious the briefings were no longer given by Hitler's adjutants but by the General Staff officers Major Friedel[11] from the OKW and either Lieutenant Colonel von der Knesebeck or Hermani[12] from the OKH.

On 13 or 14 April the following gathered in the antechamber to the conference room in Hitler's bunker: Burgdorf, Zander, Johannmeyer, Günsche, Hermani and Friedel. The bunker was very quiet, as it always was at night. Only the monotonous humming of the ventilators could be clearly heard. Hermani and Friedel were laying out the operations maps for the Eastern and Western Fronts which they had brought with them. The other participants were talking in the antechamber. A few minutes later Hitler emerged from his apartment where he had just eaten in the company of Eva Braun and the secretaries. He exchanged a few words with Burgdorf and went into the conference room. After greeting Hermani and Friedel, he sat down in his chair at the map table.

Hermani began the briefing on the Eastern Front. He reported on Russian preparations for an offensive in the area of Frankfurt–Küstrin, on Army Group Centre's defensive battles in Silesia and Bohemia, as well as on heavy fighting in the area of Army Group South west of Vienna– St Pölten and Brno in Czechoslovakia. Friedel briefed on the Western Front. He reported that the Americans had advanced further into Thuringia and had occupied the towns of Weimar and Jena. Hitler, who had been listening silently and appearing to pay no attention, suddenly asked, 'What happened to the concentration camp at Buchenwald?' (Buchenwald, one of the largest concentration camps in Germany was near Weimar.) Friedel did not know the answer to this question. The others exchanged sly glances and shrugged their shoulders. Hitler stood up. 'Where is Fegelein?' he asked. Günsche replied that Fegelein had already gone to bed. Hitler exploded: 'Gone to bed? He must come here imme-diately, or—' Then he added, 'Let it be. I'll speak to Himmler. Get him on the telephone!'

With a sleepy voice Himmler asked Günsche, 'What's happened?' But Günsche handed the receiver directly to Hitler and picked up the headphones. In an anxious tone Hitler asked Himmler the same question: what had happened to the prisoners from Buchenwald? Himmler replied that the 'most important' prisoners had been shot; for technical reasons the rest of them could not be taken away.* Hitler went even paler. His voice cracking, he asked, 'What, they are still there? Technically impossible? Why were they not liquidated at the right moment? Now they will throw themselves at National Socialists with blind passion!' He added hoarsely, 'Himmler, make sure that your people do not become sentimental! I expected better of you!' With that Hitler slammed the receiver down on the table and left the room.

In the first half of April Hitler's daily schedule was as follows: he was woken by Linge between 1.00 and 1.30 in the afternoon. The Führer had moved into his bunker and did not want to leave it again. The situation reports no longer took place in the New Chancellery for this reason, but in the Führer Bunker. These meetings took place at about 4.00 in the afternoon and continued to 6.00 or 7.00 in the evening. Depending on the length of the air raid on Berlin, the nightly situation reports started between 2.00 and 3.00 a.m. and lasted about an hour. Before them Hitler drank tea with Eva Braun and his secretaries in his study. Two of the four secretaries changed every night in order to allow them to sleep properly. The conversations at tea were all sorts of gossip. They talked about Hitler's adjutants, about Schaub's love affairs, for example, or about Hitler's steward Kannenberg, who was petrified by the air raids. Another theme was recipes for various dishes, and naturally Eva Braun's dog and Hitler's Blondi and her Wolf. As Hitler suffered from insomnia, they sat together until 5.00 or 6.00 a.m.

Hitler looked very old and tired. His hair had turned grey. He had a pronounced stoop when he walked and shuffled his legs. He was unusually nervous and fidgety, was subject to more frequent tantrums than ever and made contradictory decisions. At the beginning of April a new ailment developed alongside his shaky left hand: his right eye began to give him pain. He consulted the well-known Berlin eye-doctor Professor Löhlein.

*Since summer 1944 Buchenwald had been taking in transports from other concentration camps. On 4 April 1945 the SS started trying to evacuate it, and the evacuation got under way on the 7th. More than 28,000 people were sent on death marches, of whom 15,000 died, including 11,000 Jews. Unofficial camp organisations delayed further transports and around 21,000 inmates remained in the camp to be liberated by the Americans on the 11th. Himmler had made it clear on 14 April 1945 that no one in the camp should be taken alive. A few days later he changed his tune in conversation with Count Bernadotte and rescinded the order.

Twice a day Linge had to administer cocaine drops to his eyes to relieve the pain.[13] Hitler commented on this new affliction, 'Now I know how Frederick the Great felt when under the weight of worries his teeth fell out during the Seven Years War. The burden of war has smitten my left hand and my right eye.'

When he came to speak about the war, he always stressed that it was a fight to the finish. He said, 'I am not thinking of bringing it to a halt at the last minute. I am going to fight on.' On the Russian threat to Berlin, he opined, 'In the Seven Years War the Russians reached Berlin, but Frederick the Great fought on despite all that.' In Hitler's entourage neither victory nor defeat was mentioned any more. The general mood could be described as follows: 'Either we win, then everything is all right, or we lose, then – after us the deluge.'

Hitler clung to the hope that the Oder Front would hold. His whole attention was fixed on the strengthening of the front. Under the slogan 'Berlin will be defended at the Oder', which had been dreamed up by him and Goebbels, the last reserve units were cobbled together and hurled at the front. One hundred and twenty heavy anti-aircraft batteries were withdrawn from the defence of Berlin and set down on the Oder, where they were earmarked for ground fighting with the Russians. In his decision to fight the Russians to the end, Hitler felt himself vindicated by the speech President Truman had made on assuming office:[*] he had announced that 'America's theatre was not in Europe, but in East Asia.' Hitler's understanding of these words was that America was not going to stand in his way when he continued to fight against the Bolsheviks.[†]

In the first days of April 1945, Hitler had ordered three Austrian Gauleiters up to Berlin – Hofer from Innsbruck, Uiberreither from Klagenfurt and Eigruber from Linz. Hitler met them with Bormann.[‡] The discussion was about the creation of an Alpine fortress in the high mountains of Austria as a last bastion for the continuation of the war.

The Alpine fortress was going to be close to the Austrian mountains and also convenient for the Salzburg–Bad Reichenhall–Berchtesgaden area. Bormann and Keitel had worked out the technical measures to allow the housing of the entire senior German government apparatus: Hitler's HQ,

---

[*] President Roosevelt had died at Warm Springs, Georgia on 12 April 1945. He was succeeded by his Vice President, Harry S. Truman (1884–1972).

[†] Truman was clear, however, that he was going to deal with Europe first.

[‡] The conversation was on 5 April 1945.

the OKW and OKH, the Party Chancellery, the ministries and the other governmental departments. Bunkers were built, telephone lines laid and subterranean supply depots created. A greater part of Hitler's fleet of cars had already been sent to the Obersalzberg. His special train was in a siding in a wood near Munich. His flight, consisting of fifteen Focke-Wulf 200s and Junkers 52s, was sitting at the ready on Gatow airfield, twenty kilometres west of Berlin.[14] Bormann brought up the subject more and more often, that Hitler's HQ should be transferred to the Obersalzberg as quickly as possible. Hitler refused all suggestions of this sort with the words, 'As long as the Oder Front holds I shall remain in Berlin.'

After the discussion with the Austrian Gauleiters, Hitler spoke to Ferdinand Schörner,[15] the Supreme Commander of Army Group Centre on the Eastern Front, about constructing an Alpine fortress. He was a close friend of Bormann, Burgdorf and Fegelein and unquestioning in his loyalty to Hitler. For this he had received the Gold Party Badge. Hitler referred to him as his best general and listened to his advice. At the above-mentioned meeting the following were present besides Hitler and Schörner: Burgdorf, Fegelein, Günsche and the Chief of the Operations Department on Schörner's staff, Colonel von Trotha.[16] Schörner presented Hitler with a plan for relieving the city of Breslau, which was surrounded by the Russians. Schörner's suggestion put Hitler in a good mood. In recognition of his satisfaction, he slapped the general on the back. Afterwards Hitler spoke to him behind closed doors for three or four hours. In the course of this he promoted him field marshal. Among Hitler's staff it was known that the Führer had used the time to explain to Schörner his plan for continuing the struggle in the Alps. He offered Schörner the position of commander of his last bastion, the Alpine fortress.

In these days it became clear which generals were most loyal to Hitler: Keitel, Jodl, Krebs, Koller, Greim, Wenck, Busch, Kesselring and Dönitz. In the Party leadership his closest Allies were Bormann, Goebbels, Ley and Axmann, the leader of the Hitler Youth.

Bormann held the strings of the Party leadership. The Party authorities, the Reichsleiters and the Gauleiters were personally responsible to him. He maintained his own radio and telegraph connections with Gauleiters in regions of Germany that had already been occupied by the Anglo-Americans. In those areas occupied by the Russians he had no such contacts because, as has already been said, the high Party functionaries had all been moved west. Through these connections Bormann was informed of all political and military proceedings. He alone of all the Party leadership was able to impart this knowledge to Hitler. Reports had come to him from the Anglo-American occupied areas that the armies of occupation would not prosecute members of the Nazi Party and would leave a few of them in place in the administration. When Bormann told Hitler this, he also stressed how important it had been to send the Party's junior cadre west from eastern Germany, because there was a chance of preserving the Party there.

Bormann made every effort to keep all of the leadership of the National Socialist Party in his hands, in order to have a special relationship with Hitler. For this reason he demanded that the Führer's adjutants admit no one from the Party leadership into the Führer's presence without his approval. He justified this by saying that, for the time being, Hitler was too preoccupied with military matters. Bormann was also responsible for the creation of the Volkssturm and for the evacuation of the population from the eastern territories. When he spoke about the end of the war he repeated incessantly that Germany would come to a military understanding with the Western Powers to continue the war against Bolshevism.

Goebbels was the Supreme Propagandist of the National Socialist Party and the Defence Commissar for Berlin. He had enormous influence over Hitler, and in the last weeks of the war enjoyed his unlimited trust. Goebbels was Hitler's loudspeaker when it came to deceiving the German people, mendaciously calling upon them to carry on the war to its victorious end when in truth it was already lost. It was none other than Goebbels who drove the Berlin population out on to the streets at this time – men, women and youths – to build fortifications under threat of severe reprisals. He issued an order that anyone who hung out a white or a red flag when the Russian army appeared on the streets would be shot or hanged.[*] These orders would be carried out in Hitler's name by the Party functionaries of the Volkssturm, who were commanded by Goebbels in Berlin. Among the famished Berliners who had to carry out this forced labour, a bitter joke did the rounds: 'Will swap big Hitler pic for a small Wittler loaf' (Wittler was the owner of a large bakery in Berlin).[17]

At this time Goebbels put on his old worn-out leather coat again, which he had sported in Berlin in the days before Hitler came to power. He wanted to present himself to the Berlin population as a 'man of the people'. He strengthened Hitler's resolve to continue the war come what may. To this end he used risible arguments such as the following: after the presidential elections of 1932 the Nazi Party lost a great many votes and was in

[*]Himmler had issued the 'Flag Order' on 3 April 1945: all male inhabitants of a house displaying a white flag were to be shot.

a critical position, while the communists had increased their share. Despite this, Goebbels said, the Party came to power. In this war too a miracle would occur, and the National Socialists would win. Hitler was impressed by Goebbels's idea. He also constantly repeated, 'I beat the communists in Germany. I shall annihilate the Russian Bolsheviks.' A propos of this, the following joke did the rounds among Hitler's bodyguards: Zarah Leander was invited to the Reich Chancellery so that she could sing 'Ich weiss, es wird einmal ein Wunder geschehn' ('I know, a miracle's going to happen'), a song which she sang in a contemporary German film romance.[18]

Goebbels had no scruples about forcing the German people to shed more blood for this war. He strove to find examples from Napoleon's time to help him. The film-maker Viet Harlan received the commission to make a colour film called *Kolberg*. This film told the story of Kolberg in Pomerania during the Napoleonic occupation, when French troops fruitlessly laid siege to the town for many months. Despite heavy loss of life and horrible deprivations, the Prussian garrison and the civilian population would not give in. This film was meant to show the Berlin population and garrison how they should fight against the storming Russian army.

As the Russians were on the brink of breaking through at the Oder, and Germany on the brink of capitulating, *Kolberg* never reached the screens. Despite this, Goebbels organised a preview for officers of the Berlin Guard and Hitler Youth leaders in his villa in the Hermann Göring Strasse. The latter commanded the Volkssturm units of adolescent boys, the so-called tank-busting squads. Goebbels also invited Axmann, Günsche, the Battle Commander Colonel Streve, as well as Lieutenant Colonel Bärenfänger,[19] the commander of the Berlin region. Altogether some eighty people were present. After the preview, Goebbels delivered a speech on principles. He declared that this film should encourage Berliners to follow the example of Kolberg. Even when no two stones remained cemented together, Berliners must defend their ruins tooth and claw.

Before the film Goebbels provided dinner for his guests. Here he showed his complete mendacity. To demonstrate that he was also hit by shortages in wartime, all his guests had to give in coupons for dinner. As it was written on the invitation, the coupons were to be handed in at the cloakroom. The dinner consisted of a small amount of bread and potatoes and a tiny little piece of meat and ersatz beer of the sort you could buy with coupons. When most of the guests had gone, however, and only his closest circle – Axmann, Streve and Günsche – remained behind, there was a transformation. Goebbels opened up his kitchen and his cellar. In the presence of his wife and Frau von Arendt, the wife of the set designer of the Reichstheater who lived in his villa, all imaginable delicacies were carried to the table together with champagne and cocktails. The earnest expression the Reichskommissar for Defence had put on to receive the invited officers was as if blown away. Goebbels bubbled with wit; there was no more mention of the war.

He told excellent stories of his life before the Nazi takeover. He described for example how, immediately after Hitler took office, he had sacked all the social security officials in Berlin – social democrats to a man – and appointed SA thugs instead. That didn't work. They merely plonked themselves down at the table with a thick cigarette between their lips, flirted with the secretaries and drank schnapps. As far as work was concerned, they offloaded it on to the few remaining elderly employees with threats of beatings if they didn't do it. With a laugh Goebbels recounted that he had watched for a while before he was obliged to step in because the money would have run out had he not. It was not at all easy, however, to remove the SA fellows from their jobs. They were not going to go without a fight. A troop of policemen despatched for this purpose received a horrible drubbing. In the end Goebbels sent a letter of protest with an ultimatum: they must either give up their jobs or receive a beating themselves. If he was made a minister they could be employed by the social security again. Goebbels added, still laughing, that he had finally been able to pacify them by offering them other well-paid jobs that required little work.

In April 1945 Ley also sought to pass himself off as a great leader of men. He appeared on the Oder Front, drove behind the lines, visited small munitions factories and called on local and regional Party bosses to offer tough resistance to the Russians. He formed a troop of women, girls and boys from National Socialist organisations and gave it the sonorous name of the Volunteer Corps 'Adolf Hitler'.[20] He called the Führer frequently and sought him out in the bunker to report on what a 'titanic' labour he was performing to keep the Russians out. Once he even informed Hitler that he knew a man who had discovered 'death rays'.[21] That, however, like all his endeavours revealed itself to be no more than hot air.

The fifty-five year-old Ley actually spent most of his time with his mistress, an eighteen-year-old dancer, in his big, luxurious villa in Dahlem.[22] In the intervals he spared from this dalliance he wrote leaders for the newspapers, in which he called on the German people to risk everything for their Führer and exhorted soldiers to fight to the death against the Russians. Ley had his mistress edit these appeals to the miserable, famished population before they appeared in *Angriff*, the largest National Socialist Party paper in Berlin.

Ley was a professional chemist who had worked for IG-Farben in Leverkusen until Hitler came to power and appointed him head of the so-called Arbeitsfront (Labour Front), which was created to replace the trades unions the National Socialists had smashed. The Führer saw Ley as a gifted union leader, but he knew he was a heavy drinker and a lecher. His first wife divorced him for womanising. The second, who bore him three children, shot herself in 1943 because of his dissipated existence at his manor house at Waldbröl near Essen.[23] Hitler, however, protected him, declaring, 'Ley is the man the workers know and who knows how to treat them.'

In March and April 1945 Hitler grew closer to Artur Axmann, the Reichsführer of the Hitler Youth. Before the accession to power he had led the Berlin Hitler Youth, and in 1940 he replaced Baldur von Schirach at the head of the national organisation. He was a friend of Goebbels and Hitler liked him a lot. In the war he had been with an SS division at the front and had lost his right arm as a result of a severe wound. Axmann was meant to leave, with the junior cadres of the Nazi Party, for British- and American-occupied western Germany, where they were to lead the illegal work of the disparate Hitler Youth groups and connive at the restoration of the National Socialist Party. Instead he remained in Berlin at his own wish, insisting that he would leave only when Hitler went himself.

In March and April Axmann worked intensively on the mobilisation of the Hitler Youth, the Volkssturm and the formation of tank-busting squads made up of youths and destined first for the Oder Front and later for the battle against the Russians in Berlin. He wanted to prove to Hitler that youth was behind him and ready to fight for him. Axmann misled German youth: he made them believe that the lunacy of continuing the war was in the interest of the German people. He tried to convince adolescents that Hitler and the people were one, and that to die for Hitler was to die for Germany.

Axmann took fourteen- to sixteen-year-old boys into the garden of the Chancellery, where he presented them to Hitler as 'warriors',* staging the scene as a mythical spectacle and getting twenty boys to march in military formation. When Hitler came out of the bunker Axmann announced sharply, 'My Führer, your boys present arms.' Hitler took the salute from the boys' squad as if on parade, and with a raised arm cried, 'Heil, boys!' The boys replied, 'Heil, my Führer!'

Hitler gave each of them his hand. Then he delivered a short speech in which he thanked them for their 'active struggle' and claimed that

---

*On 20 March 1945. Twenty boys were decorated, of whom the youngest was twelve. A newsreel was made.

Germany would certainly win. Axmann had lined them up so that the youngest would stand on the left. It was a horrible scene when one considered that these boys with pink cheeks would be sent into the field against Russian tanks, to senseless death. With an extravagant gesture Hitler pinned the Iron Cross on each of their breasts and pinched the cheek of the youngest of them. After that he saluted them again with a raised arm and shouted, 'Heil, boys!' Axmann bellowed, 'Our beloved Führer: Sieg Heil! Sieg Heil! Sieg Heil!' He organised this parade of raw youth in the Chancellery garden in April 1945. Afterwards Hitler went back into his bunker and Axmann packed his troop off to front-line positions.

Another member of the coterie who was close to Hitler at this time was Albert Speer, the Minister for Armaments and War Production. The affinity between Hitler and Speer was above all connected with the Führer's intention of concluding a military alliance with Britain and America against the Soviet Union, thereby using his connections with German industrialists. Speer was also a friend of Eva Braun. He was the only minister allowed to be present when Hitler relaxed with Eva in their apartment. In the last days of April, Speer wanted Hitler and Eva to fly away with him in his Fieseler-Storch, as the city was completely surrounded by the Russian army. On 22 April Speer left Berlin for Hamburg. From there he organised the provision of Berlin's trapped armies with arms and ammunition from the air. Planes landed on the runway that had been laid out on the east–west axis between the Brandenburg Gate and the Victory Column, or dropped their cargo at different points in Berlin.

Hitler's relations with Himmler mirrored the situation on the Eastern Front: they got worse and worse. It began with the defeat in Pomerania, and their relations became even cooler when Hitler rebuked the Sixth Army over the failure of the Balaton offensive. Himmler was at his field command: a special train codenamed Steiermark. The train was in a siding near Hohenlychen in Mecklenburg, a hundred kilometres from Berlin. Himmler appeared before Hitler only when the latter ordered it – of his own volition he would not go at all. Günsche heard that he had several brigades armed with siege guns and reserve regiments at a strength of 15,000 to 20,000 men at his disposal near his field command outside Berlin. By virtue of Hitler's orders, these men should have been on the Oder Front. Günsche reported this to the Führer, who summoned Himmler and screeched at him, 'Himmler, I will not allow you to do what you want! Why do you need a private army? Be so kind as to carry out my orders!' When Himmler left Hitler, he called for Günsche and hissed at him, 'How dare you report that to the Führer. You are lucky that you are not working for me.'

From that moment onwards, Hitler no longer summoned Himmler. Himmler appeared just one more time before the Russians conquered Berlin, on Hitler's birthday on 20 April. Three days before Hitler's suicide, on 27 April, it became known that Himmler had been negotiating with the Swedish count Bernadotte on his own account. Bernadotte was working for the Anglo-Americans. In the preliminary negotiations with Bernadotte Himmler had declared himself prepared to comply with British demands and conclude a separate peace without involving Hitler. He retained the troops at his disposal so that, in the event of a successful conclusion to the negotiations with Bernadotte, he could remove Hitler by force.* Göring only came to the briefings. Hitler did not invite him either, not like the old days.

One evening at the beginning of April Günsche ran into Goebbels in the dining room of the Chancellery. The latter had just spoken to Hitler and was sitting alone over dinner. Looking dejected, he invited Günsche to join him. He then asked him about the security measures that he had made for the government district, and Günsche told him about the various gun emplacements, tank traps and other obstacles that had been built there. Goebbels listened to him attentively and said that he had been pleased to see that his villa had been protected by a number of gun positions. He went on to talk about Berlin's readiness to defend itself and declared with what was for him typical pathos, 'I conquered Berlin in 1933 for the Führer. And I will also defend it.'

Then Goebbels pointed out that many members of the Party leadership were like rats leaving a sinking ship. Göring was one of them.† Goebbels believed that his Luftwaffe bore the main blame for the failure of the German army. Günsche replied that the leadership of the Hitler Youth had inquired on several occasions why Hitler had not replaced Göring. On this question of Göring being Hitler's successor, as ordained by the Reichstag, Günsche informed Goebbels of a letter to Hitler from the regional Hitler Youth leader Kurt Petter. Petter, who was known to be leading illegal troops of Hitler Youth in the Allgäu that had been evacuated from eastern Germany, declared in the name of the Hitler Youth that he would not

---

*This was not mentioned in the discussions with Bernadotte. At the first two talks in March and early April the Swede managed to effect the release of several hundred concentration-camp inmates. The talk on 21 April did not go into political changes. On the 23rd Himmler told the Swede that he thought Hitler was already dead and made an offer of peace with a request that it be taken to Eisenhower. Eisenhower refused and leaked Himmler's treason so that Hitler would learn of it.

†Göring left Berlin on 20 April 1945 and reached the Obersalzberg the next day.

recognise Göring as Hitler's successor. This he expressed in the following words: 'My Führer, I speak in the name of the Hitler Youth and solemnly declare that the Hitler Youth has broken its bond to Göring and no longer accepts him as your successor.' Günsche told Goebbels that he had presented Petter's letter to Hitler. The Führer had read it, but had only waved it aside, saying nothing.

When Günsche had finished his account, Goebbels expressed the opinion that in Göring's case Hitler was too hesitant and would do nothing about him. Günsche replied: if Hitler could not decide whether to get rid of Göring, then the decision should be immediately taken out of his hands. 'Herr Doktor,' Günsche said, 'I think it would be doing the Führer a great service if someone could put a couple of tank mines under Göring's car and blow him sky high.' Goebbels was silent for a while. Then he stood up and replied quietly, 'Herr Günsche, I did not hear that, I don't want to have anything to do with that.' Finally Goebbels shook Günsche's hand warmly and limped slowly out of the room. It was clear that Goebbels had nothing against the murder of Göring, but did not wish to be implicated in it himself.

A notable frost had also entered into Hitler's relations with Ribbentrop. The cause was the following: Hitler had accused Ribbentrop of not pursuing his plan for concluding a separate peace with the British and the Americans as energetically as he might. He opined sarcastically, 'Ribbentrop is already too tired. He is asleep!' It was Ribbentrop's habit, when he was standing talking to someone, to close his eyes and lean his head back as if he were floating in another world. And then he would suddenly come out with 'What did you just say?' It made Hitler maintain crossly, 'He is sleeping on his feet.'

Hitler's accusation that Ribbentrop was incapable of preparing the ground for an alliance with the Anglo-Americans meant that his representative Hewel lost face too. This began with the breaking off of the Stockholm discussions for a separate peace with the British in the autumn of 1944.[*] From then on, Hitler had kept his distance from Hewel. In contrast to the way things had been before when Hewel moved in Hitler's society, frequently lunched with him alone and took part in his tea evenings, now he came only to the situation conferences. At other times Hitler would not let him come near him.

---

[*] A number of feelers had been put out to the Allies via neutral countries, but Hitler did not think they had much chance of success.

15

April – May 1945

On 16 April the night-time situation briefing in Hitler's bunker came to an end at around 3.30 a.m. Lieutenant Colonel von Hermani, who had reported on the Eastern Front, drove from the Reich Chancellery to Zossen and the HQ of the OKH. Major Friedel, who had reported on the Western Front, drove back to Dahlem. As far as the Eastern Front was concerned, Army Group South was involved in intense fighting in Austria, with particularly heavy pressure coming from Russian troops at St Pölten, west of Vienna. There were sustained attacks on the front sector controlled by Army Group Centre at Mährisch-Ostrau and Brno, as well as in Silesia. Hermani said the Oder Front was quiet. There were simply reconnaissance activities to report.

After the evening report, Hitler settled down to evening tea in his study with Eva Braun and his secretaries Frau Christian and Frau Junge. In the smoking room of the Old Reich Chancellery, Burgdorf, Fegelein and Günsche drank vodka and cognac. At around 5.00 a.m. the telephone rang. The Chancellery switchboard informed Burgdorf that 'Maibach' was looking for him everywhere. That was the codename for OKH HQ in Zossen. General Krebs came on the line. It was unusual to receive a call from the Chief of the General Staff so early. Burgdorf's facial muscles tightened, and with a gesture he motioned Fegelein and Günsche to be quiet. He scribbled something on a sheet of paper and shouted in a clipped way into the telephone, 'Where? Küstrin? Where else? On the whole front? I shall report to the Führer at once. When you have a clearer idea, please call immediately. Thanks!' (Burgdorf was on *Du* terms with Krebs.) Burgdorf put down the receiver and turned fretfully to Fegelein and Günsche. 'At around four it started on the Oder: a heavy artillery barrage along the entire front. Russian infantry and tanks have been attacking for the last half-hour.'[1]

Burgdorf picked up the receiver again. He learned from the bunker that Hitler was still sitting at tea. He made his way over to him to deliver Krebs's report in the company of Fegelein and Günsche. The sentries, consisting of Hitler's bodyguard and the SD, were completely amazed to see Burgdorf, Fegelein and Günsche emerge at such a late hour. Burgdorf asked that he might report to Hitler, as he had important information to impart. Hitler immediately came into the antechamber, where Burgdorf, Fegelein and Günsche were waiting. As always when he received an unexpected report, he looked at everyone suspiciously. Burgdorf announced, 'My Führer, I have just had a call from Krebs. At around four the Russians began their offensive on the Oder.' Hitler braced himself. 'Where?' he blurted out.

Burgdorf answered that after a heavy barrage from the Russian artillery powerful infantry and tank formations had gone over to the attack along the entire front. In one or two places they sought to use the cover of darkness to force a passage across the Oder. Major attacks were made from the bridgehead on the west bank of the Oder near Küstrin. Hitler asked for more details, above all whether the troops had been brought away from the Russian artillery fire in time. Burgdorf replied that he did not have detailed information from Krebs yet. Hitler's hands grabbed the back of an armchair. He was trying to conceal his anxiety. His face convulsed. He bit his lips, which for him was a sign of the greatest tension. Then he asked, 'What time is it?' 'Twenty past five,' Günsche replied. Hitler turned to Burgdorf again: 'Give me a report as soon as you hear something new. Even if someone tells you I have retired. I can't sleep anyway. And connect me with Krebs straightaway. I want to speak to him myself.' With that, Hitler went back into his study where Eva Braun and the secretaries were still sitting.

From the reports that came in as the morning developed it was clear that the Russians had attacked in pretty well every sector of the front. There had been a few localised breakthroughs, but for the time being they had been repulsed. Hitler had gone to bed, but did not sleep. He rang for Linge many times and asked him to inquire of Burgdorf or Johannmeyer whether there were any new reports from the Oder. Burgdorf and Johannmeyer, who were in constant telephone contact with Krebs, replied that the picture was still hazy. In a few sectors of the front communications had been severed by Russian artillery and had not yet been reconnected.

On this day, 16 April, Hitler convened the daily conference at 2.30 p.m. In the antechamber of the conference room gathered Göring, Dönitz, Keitel, Jodl, Krebs, Koller, Burgdorf, Buhle, Winter, Christian, Wagner, Voss, Fegelein, Hewel, Lorenz, Hitler's adjutants and several officers from the General Staff. Like some of the generals who were fighting at the front, because of the proximity of the front Keitel was no longer wearing red generals' braid on his trousers. The participants stood around in groups, and spoke in loud, animated voices about the Russian offensive on the Oder which had begun at dawn. Above all they expressed the hope that the Oder Front would be held. Then Hitler came out of his study in the company of Bormann. Everybody went quiet and stood to attention, raising their arms in salute. Hitler quickly gave his hand to Göring, Dönitz, Keitel, Jodl and Krebs. He asked Krebs, 'Do you now have an exact picture of what is happening on the Oder?' Krebs replied, 'Yes, my Führer.'

Hitler just nodded at the others and went with Krebs into the conference room. The rest followed after. Because of the Russian offensive on the Oder, all the participants in the situation briefings had appeared, and the room was so crowded that some General Staff officers and adjutants had to remain outside in the antechamber. The small conference room held a maximum of twenty. Krebs began his briefing with a summary of the situation on the Oder. He reported that the Russian attack had been halted. In heavy fighting the Russians and the Germans had brought thousands of tanks and guns into use. Krebs emphasised that since dawn Russian contingents had received non-stop support from the air. He also reported that in some front sectors the Russians had penetrated the German defences. In those places there had been counter-attacks. The main thrust of the Russians came from their bridgehead on the east bank of the Oder at Küstrin. Attempts by the Russians to cross the Oder and to set up bridges had been stymied by German artillery.

Hitler looked suddenly at Göring, who was leaning over the table to give the impression of looking for a spot on the map. This was how he reacted when Hitler asked about the activities of the Luftwaffe. When Christian noticed Hitler's look, he reported at once that German Stukas had been principally engaged in bombing Russian units that were trying to cross the Oder. He wanted to add something, but Hitler had already turned to Krebs again: 'Go on, Krebs.'

Krebs pointed to the map and explained that after the artillery barrage the Russians had attacked with renewed strength since midday and the German soldiers' predicament, in particular in the sector of the front west of Küstrin, was highly critical. Hitler rose from his chair and announced in a strained voice, 'We have to contain the first Russian attacks, whatever the cost. If the front becomes fluid, then all is lost.'

He ordered Krebs to find out how the fighting near Küstrin was developing. Together with his adjutant Freytag-Loringhoven, Krebs left the conference room to make a telephone call. Loringhoven came back and asked permission to take away the operations map for the Oder Front so that the new positions could be drawn in. While Krebs spoke to OKH

HQ in Zossen, Göring, Dönitz, Keitel and Jodl assured Hitler that the Russian attacks on the Oder would be repulsed. Hitler pointed out that it was especially important to withstand the first day of the attack and inflict heavy losses on the Russians. Keitel and Jodl emphatically agreed. They mentioned examples from the First World War – battles between the Germans and an enemy who was technically very much better equipped – where, because of the doggedness of the German soldiers, the enemy advanced only by metres before eventually petering out.

A few minutes later Krebs and Loringhoven returned to the conference room. Hitler looked at them optimistically. He could hardly wait for the maps to be spread out before he was leaning over them. On virtually the whole of the front line red arrows indicated the Russian attacks. Near Küstrin the Russians had driven deep into German positions, and the situation in this sector of the front was getting worse. The remaining parts of the front stood firm. The Commanding Officer of the Army Group on the Oder, Colonel General Heinrici, believed it necessary to bring the front back west from Küstrin, to prevent the breakthrough from expanding. Hitler's eyes almost popped out of their sockets. On his forehead the veins stood out in anger. He barked, 'No! No, we will not retreat a metre! If we do not hold the Oder, where then? The breakthrough at Küstrin must be liquidated at once! Transmit these orders at once!'

Krebs left the conference room again to transmit the order to the front.[*] Hitler was livid. He railed against Heinrici who, just two days before, within hours of the Russian offensive, had sought permission to transfer his HQ from Prenzlau further west to Neustrelitz in Mecklenburg. Hitler issued a threat: 'From this moment onwards, should anyone so much as dare, whoever they may be, to ask to transfer their HQ to a position further back or to retreat, I shall have them shot on the spot!'

After the briefing Hitler summoned his secretary Frau Christian. He dictated a letter to the soldiers on the Eastern Front. This was written on a so-called Führer sheet. In the right-hand corner of the letter head there was a drawing of a black eagle with a swastika, and under this in capital letters was written 'THE FÜHRER'. The order read as follows: 'Führer Command! To the soldiers on the Eastern Front! Asia's last attack will fail!' The letter went on: 'We knew this attack was coming. Since January this year everything has been done to reinforce the front. The enemy is running into heavy fire from the artillery. The losses incurred by our infantry

[*] The text had already been telegraphed to the army groups on 14 April 1945. On 17th it was printed in the *Völkische Beobachter* and other German dailies.

will be made good by many new formations. Units that have not been used before now, newly formed contingents and the Volkssturm will be despatched to shore up our front. This time the Bolsheviks will suffer the ancient fate of Asia, which means they will and must breathe their last before the capital of the German Reich.'* It added, 'Berlin remains German, Vienna will be German again and Europe will never be Russian.'

With these last words Hitler expressed his conviction that a common front would be created by his Germany together with Britain and America against the Soviet Union. He pinned his hopes on the anti-Soviet tendencies manifest among opinion leaders in Britain and America, which had been growing ever stronger the further the Russians pushed into Germany, the Balkans, Austria and Czechoslovakia. Hitler concluded his command with the words, 'Now that fate has rid the world of the greatest war criminal of all times, there will come a turning in the tides of war.' By that he meant the death of President Roosevelt in April 1945.† In his eyes it had been he who had forever stood in the way of a common front against the Russians. For that reason, with Roosevelt's death 'there would come a turning in the tides of war'.

At the briefing on the night of 16–17 April it was reported that the Russians had thrown the German divisions west of Küstrin even further back. The counter-attack that Hitler had ordered to repair the damage done by the Russian breakthrough had had no success and was to be repeated on the morning of 17 April. That night Hitler sat up until 6.00 a.m. with Eva Braun and the secretaries drinking tea. He declared that the Russians had succeeded in cutting a little slice out of the German defences, but this was just a passing success, a temporary advantage to the attackers.

In the days that followed – 17, 18 and 19 April – the position of the German armies on the Oder became increasingly critical. In the toughest defensive action they retreated under the ever more powerful blows of the Russians. The Russians went over to the attack further south in Silesia, and managed significantly to widen the gap in the front west of Küstrin. Once they had broken through all the defensive cordons they came menacingly

---

*Literally: 'We predicted this advance, and since January this year we have done everything to build up a strong front. The enemy has been met by a powerful artillery. Our shortfall has been made up by countless new formations. Alarm units, new brigades and Volkssturm have reinforced our front. This time the Bolsheviks will experience the fate of Asia, that means they will bleed to death before the capital of the German Reich.'

†When Roosevelt had died suddenly from a brain haemorrhage, Hitler compared the event to the salvation of Prussia in the Seven Years War with the sudden death of the Tsarina Elisabeth in 1762, and her successor's decision to change his alliance.

close to the eastern suburbs of Berlin,* though the German Oder Front still held in the areas of Stettin and Frankfurt. At night the thunder of Russian artillery could now be heard on the streets of Berlin, and Russian reconnaissance aircraft circled over the German capital.

Hitler laid the entire blame for the critical situation at the feet of the Supreme Commander of the Army Group, Heinrici. He called him a vacillating, indecisive pedant who lacked the necessary spark of inspiration. As the battles got closer to Berlin he sacked him as Supreme Commander of the army group that still bore the name Vistula despite the fact that for some time this river had been behind Russian lines. Hitler named no successor to Heinrici, however.† He took over the role of leading the fight for Berlin himself. Although there was no remaining doubt now that the German front on the Oder had collapsed and could not be rebuilt, Hitler pinned his hopes on the sectors that were holding out. He commanded that the Russian advance be liquidated by concentrated blows to the flank.

At the briefing on the afternoon of 19 April, Krebs reported that Russian tank squadrons had advanced yet further and now stood just before Oranienburg, about thirty kilometres north of Berlin. This piece of news exploded like a bomb and threw Hitler completely.

Immediately after the meeting he summoned Linge and complained of acute aches and congestion in his head. Morell had to come and bleed him. Leeches were not applied this time, because he was in urgent need. With Linge's help Morell prepared the instruments on the tea-table in Hitler's bedroom. The Führer took off his jacket, rolled up the sleeve on his left arm and sat on the side of the bed. In a feeble voice he informed Morell that he had had little sleep the last few nights and felt completely crushed. Morell tied a rubber tube around his arm and dug the cannula into his vein. No blood flowed, however. Hitler's blood was very thick; it coagulated immediately and blocked the needle. Morell needed to find a bigger cannula, which with some effort he managed to stick into the vein. Linge held a glass under the syringe, into which Hitler's blood ran in viscous drops. While this was taking place Hitler asked Linge if he could bear the sight of blood. Linge answered, 'Of course, my Führer. SS men are used to it.'

---

*After the Red Army broke through the defensive positions at Seelow on 18 April 1945, their tanks stood before Strausberg a day later. On the 20th the First Belorussian Front had reached a line Bernau–Strausberg–Fürstenwalde. During the night of the 21st the Third Guards Tank Army of the First Ukrainian Front reached the southern perimeter of Berlin.
†Heinrici was replaced by Tippelskirch on 28 April. A day later the latter was replaced by Colonel General Student.

About a water glass full of blood was taken, which coagulated immediately. Linge wanted to show Hitler that he was not frightened of the sight of blood and said as a joke, 'My Führer, now we need to add a little salt and we could offer a "Führer black pudding".' Hitler had to laugh. That evening at tea he told Eva Braun and the secretaries the story.

The optimistic mood that had reigned at the conferences at the beginning of the Russian offensive on the Oder was soon replaced by great anxiety. The participants took Hitler's adjutants aside to find out whether he had said anything about transferring his HQ to the Obersalzberg. During the situation reports an unholy muddle reigned in the conference antechamber and elsewhere in the bunker. Hitler's personal (not military) adjutant Schaub, Albert Bormann, Albrecht, his doctors Morell and Stumpfegger, the secretaries, his pilot Baur and the SS officers of his bodyguard never stopped asking what was happening at the front. Freytag-Loringhoven, who had frequently to go to the telephone from the conference room to make inquiries and to make alterations to the map, was showered with questions: 'Is there any news? Where are the Russians?'

There were constant telephone calls from Ley, Economics Minister Funk, Rosenberg, Speer, Axmann, Ribbentrop and others who were still in Berlin. The questions were always the same: 'How is it going at the front? Where are the Russians? Is the front going to hold? What is the Führer going to do? When is he going to leave Berlin?' Günsche was unmoved in his answers: 'The front on the Oder is holding. The Russians will never reach Berlin. The Führer sees no reason to leave Berlin.' Ley, whose mistress had edited his appeals urging the people to continue the senseless war against the Russians, preferred to move to the west, without saying goodbye to his 'beloved Führer'. At this time both Rosenberg and Funk left, also for the west, without telling Hitler.[*]

As the Russians were coming closer and closer to Berlin, in his role as Battle Commander of the Reich Chancellery, Günsche had a meeting with SS-Brigadeführer Wilhelm Mohnke[2] to discuss measures for reinforcing the defence of the Chancellery and the government district. Mohnke had commanded the SS Leibstandarte 'Adolf Hitler' from August 1944 to the beginning of March 1945 and was presently on leave in Berlin. He offered to make up a battle group of some 3,500 to 4,000 men from members of the Waffen-SS who were then in Berlin: the Guard Battalion, the training company and the convalescent company. Günsche announced the plan to Hitler and he agreed. Thereupon Günsche ordered a massive build-up of

---

[*]Ley, Rosenberg and Funk left Berlin on 21 April 1945.

stocks of weapons and ammunition in the Chancellery. In the bunker in the New Chancellery a huge depot of provisions was completed, and a hospital was set up under the direction of the Chief Physician of the Berlin University Clinic, SS-Obersturmbannführer Professor Werner Haase.[3]

On 20 April Hitler was fifty-six years old. Linge had to think back ten years to the first time he had been present at Hitler's birthday: how very different things were then!

In 1935 all was splendour and magnificence. Already at dawn military bands saluted their 'Supreme Commander in the Field'. The leading lights of industry, the Party, the state and the military made their way to their leader and competed for his favour by bringing him lavish gifts. Then there was the grandiose theatre of the great military parade on the square before the Technical University in Berlin. There, at the end of the war with Russia, would be held a mighty victory parade. Hitler had already designed a gigantic triumphal arch through which the victorious German soldiers would pass on their return to the capital.

And now Russian troops stood before the gates of Berlin and Adolf Hitler was a morally and physically broken man who had crawled into a bunker deep under the earth.

On Hitler's fifty-sixth birthday the Chief of the Reich Security Service, Rattenhuber, showed Linge an SD report which claimed that one of Hitler's soldier-servants was going to murder him on his birthday. From the SD's information the man would apparently be dressed in mufti and had been wounded in the arm at the front. Linge protested that none of Hitler's servants wore mufti or had an arm wound. Nonetheless, Rattenhuber asked him to keep his eyes open.

In years gone by it had been a convention that Hitler's personal staff brought him their best wishes at midnight on the 19th. This time Hitler had already announced that he wanted no birthday greetings. Despite this, at midnight Burgdorf, Fegelein, Schaub, Albrecht, Günsche, Hewel and Lorenz gathered in the small antechamber to congratulate him. He let the gathering know that he had no time. Then Fegelein went to Eva Braun and asked her to intercede and let them give him their birthday greetings. Under pressure from her, Hitler reluctantly came out into the antechamber. He quickly shook everyone's hand so that they could say 'Many happy returns' and then immediately disappeared again. Hitler's pilot Baur, his second pilot Betz, Rattenhuber, Högl and Schädle appeared in the antechamber just before the briefing to congratulate Hitler the moment he left his study to go into the conference room. He gave them his hand in passing. After the meeting, which went off very quickly, he drank tea on his own with Eva in his study.

At about 9.00 on the morning of 20 April Linge woke him at the urgent request of Burgdorf, who had an important piece of news from the front to bring him. Hitler got up and went into his study and through the closed door asked Burgdorf what was happening. Burgdorf reported that at dawn the Russians had broken through the front between Guben and Forst. The breakthrough was not great, and the Germans had gone over to counter-attack. He also reported that the commander of the unit that had let the Russians through had been shot on the spot for failing to fight his ground. Hitler's answer was 'Send me Linge.' Linge was standing next to Burgdorf and announced, 'My Führer?' 'Linge, I have not yet had any sleep. Wake me in an hour, at 2.00 p.m.'

After Hitler got up and had had breakfast in his study, Linge put cocaine drops in his right eye. When the pain had abated a little, Hitler played with his favourite puppy Wolf until lunch, which he ate with Eva and his secretaries. At around 3.00 p.m. a number of delegations appeared in the Chancellery garden to congratulate Hitler: Axmann with representatives of the Hitler Youth; Streve, the Chief of Staff of Army Group Centre* with some officers; and SS-Obersturmführer Doose, the commander of the Führer Escort Company, with some men from his unit. As Hitler was most reluctant to leave the bunker they had been lined up directly in front of the entrance. Hitler went out into the garden with Puttkamer and Linge, the collar of his greatcoat turned up. When the gathering saw Hitler they stood to attention and raised their arms in the fascist salute.

At the entrance into the music room from the garden the following had gathered: Himmler, Bormann, Burgdorf, Fegelein, Hewel, Lorenz, Hitler's doctors Morell and Stumpfegger, and the adjutants Schaub, Albert Bormann, Albrecht, Johannmeyer, Below and Günsche. Himmler walked up to Hitler and wished him a happy birthday. Hitler held out his hand and instantly walked on to greet the others. Then he turned to the delegations. Stooping deeply like an old man and shuffling his legs he slowly inspected the line. The leader of each delegation stepped forward and congratulated him. The officer from Army Group Centre handed him a leather briefcase containing a birthday card signed by Schörner. Axmann congratulated him on behalf of the Hitler Youth.

When Hitler had taken the parade the gathering formed into a semi-circle. They had already been informed that he could not speak loudly, and

---

*At the time the Chief of Staff was General Lieutenant Oldwig von Natzmer.

for this reason he limited himself to a few words. One of them was the stereotypical phrase that victory was coming and that they could say that they had played their part in it. Then Hitler lethargically raised his right hand and withdrew into the bunker. On this day he saw the sky for the last time. He would never leave the bunker again.

Himmler, Bormann, Burgdorf, Fegelein and the adjutants followed him, as the briefing was billed for 4.00 p.m. Twenty minutes before it was due to start Göring, Ribbentrop, Dönitz, Keitel and Jodl arrived to congratulate Hitler. He received every one of them in his study. Linge, who announced each guest and brought them in, heard Göring and Keitel pledge unswerving loyalty and declare their desire to stay at his side until the end; none of them remained long with Hitler. An exception was Ribbentrop, who spent around ten minutes in the study. After the birthday greetings Göring, Dönitz, Keitel and Jodl mingled again with the conference-goers in the antechamber.

Ribbentrop left the Chancellery after his discussion with Hitler. A few minutes later Hitler emerged from his study and saluted the gathering. He thanked them all for their birthday greetings. Then he turned to Krebs and asked for new reports from the Oder Front before going with him into the conference room. All the others followed. The main theme of the meeting was the breakthrough between Guben and Forst. Massed Russian tank squadrons were approaching Berlin and that day they had reached the Spreewald south of the Berlin–Frankfurt motorway. Now the capital was threatened from the south. Russian contingents north of Berlin had already advanced to Oranienburg and in the east they were almost at the city border. The breakthrough between Guben and Forst seemed particularly dangerous because the Russians could cut Berlin off from the south.

The developments at the front seemed so sinister that Bormann made immediate steps to transfer Führer HQ from Berlin to the Obersalzberg. Even during the meeting he left the room in a hurry and called SS-Obersturmbannführer Erich Kempka into the bunker. Kempka was Hitler's personal chauffeur and chief of the Chancellery motor-pool. With Bormann he had brought up a motorised column to take Hitler and his immediate staff to the Obersalzberg. They had assembled fifteen to twenty general-purpose vehicles, several buses and about ten lorries. An armour-plated limousine had been made ready for Hitler. Besides this, Kempka had requested two tanks from the arsenal in Spandau.

Linge arranged that all Hitler's personal belongings were packed, apart from the clothes he wore day in day out. Forty to fifty chests were prepared for transportation to the Obersalzberg. They contained military documents that Hitler had received during the war from the OKW, the OKH, the navy, the Luftwaffe and Speer. They had already been brought from the Wolfsschanze to the Chancellery. On Bormann's instructions Hitler's dietary cook, Constanze Manziarly, packed Hitler's dietary provisions, leaving only a supply sufficient for a few days. Eva Braun's chambermaid, Liesl, continued to pester Linge with the question whether she should pack or not. Hitler was in a meeting again and Eva had no idea. Linge recommended that she make a start in any case, as orders to depart might be suddenly issued. The whole day was filled with preparations for travel. Only Göring wanted to leave that very day. Before the meeting had ended he said goodbye to Hitler with the explanation that he was travelling to southern Germany to gather together the remaining reserves there to throw against the Russians. Towards nightfall Göring and his personal staff drove to the Obersalzberg. His wife and daughter together with all the remaining inhabitants of Karinhall had left for that destination in two special trains many weeks before.

On 21 April Linge woke Hitler as early as 9.30 a.m. and informed him that the Russian artillery was shelling Berlin. Burgdorf and the remaining adjutants were waiting in the antechamber. Ten minutes later an unshaven Hitler hurried out to them. (He always shaved himself. He wouldn't even allow his barber August Wollenhaupt to do it – because, he said, he could not bear the thought of someone holding a razor at his throat.) In the antechamber Burgdorf, Schaub, Below and Günsche were waiting for Hitler. 'What has happened? What is this shelling, and where is it coming from?' he asked in alarm. Burgdorf reported that the centre of Berlin was being shelled by a battery of heavy Russian guns that in all probability were firing from the area north-east of Zossen.* Hitler went pale. He stammered, 'The Russians are already so near?'

Burgdorf continued: Krebs had just reported that about ten Russian tanks were fighting through Baruth in the direction of Zossen and were about ten to fifteen kilometres away from OKH HQ. Hitler went into the conference room with Burgdorf, Below and Günsche and demanded a telephone line to speak to Krebs. Krebs repeated that OKH HQ was under immediate threat from Russian tanks and asked whether he should move

---

*Already at around midday on 20 April 1945 the 136th Cannon Brigade of the LXXIX Rifle Corps, which had reached the northern borders of the city, had opened fire on central Berlin. On the morning of the 21st the 32nd Rifles opened fire from Marzahn in the east.

it to another place. 'No!' Hitler screamed into the receiver. 'Don't get frightened by a few Russian tanks. The OKH remains in Zossen!'

Bormann, Fegelein, Schaub and Johannmeyer rushed into the conference room in a state of excitement. Hitler and the others were conjecturing where the Russian battery might be. The Führer could not sit down. He kept jumping up and issuing orders in a nervous voice that when the position of the Russian battery was fixed it must be bombarded with continuous fire from the 12.5cm anti-aircraft guns in the Tiergarten.[4] They would surely be successful given the great range and accuracy of these guns. At around midday the flak battery in the Tiergarten opened fire in the direction of Zossen; but the Russian battery fired back all day with only occasional interruptions.

At lunch Burgdorf informed the other adjutants that Hitler had ordered preparations to withdraw the German forces facing the Americans between Dresden and Dessau and for them to be thrown against the Russians. On Hitler's orders the HQ of the OKH was to be moved from Zossen to Potsdam-Eiche that very day.

At around 2.30 that afternoon, Dönitz, Keitel, Jodl, Krebs, Bormann, Buhle, Winter, Fegelein, Voss, Christian, Hewel, Koller, Hitler's adjutants and several General Staff officers gathered in the antechamber to the conference room in Hitler's bunker. They were all very agitated. The question kept coming up: 'Is Hitler going to stay in Berlin? Is he going to transfer his HQ to the Obersalzberg? Why is he still here?'

At the meeting Krebs reported that Russian tanks were south of Berlin and had penetrated the Zossen area. German positions to the north of the capital had been overrun and Oranienburg had been taken. In the east the Russians had advanced to the suburbs and in a few places had broken through the defensive ring. Krebs also reported that despite a number of counter-attacks German troops had not managed to plug the Russian breakthrough at the Oder. The situation of the German forces was getting worse by the hour and there was no more hope of resurrecting the front. The Ninth Army looked like being cut off.

For this reason Krebs proposed withdrawing General Busse's Ninth Army, the main force of which was positioned north and south of Frankfurt on the Oder, and bringing it back to defend Berlin. Hitler refused and insisted that the Oder Front be restored, whatever the cost. It was decided not to redeploy the Ninth Army in Berlin, but under the cover of darkness to withdraw all German troops between Dresden and Dessau and throw them into battle against the Russian soldiers attacking in the area between Baruth and Zossen. Dönitz, Keitel, Jodl and Bormann suggested to Hitler that, in the light of the threat to Berlin, he should transfer his HQ to the Obersalzberg. Hitler refused, stating that he saw no immediate danger which called for the withdrawal of his HQ from Berlin.

When the meeting was over the Führer held back Krebs, who had wanted to drive straight back to the HQ of the OKH which had been moved to Potsdam-Eiche, and said to him, 'Krebs, I would like to have you with me permanently.' Krebs stayed and was given quarters in a room in the New Chancellery bunker. From the OKH staff he retained only his adjutant Freytag-Loringhoven and Captain Boldt as his orderly.

After the meeting Hitler went in to lunch. He told Linge that he had heard rumours that he was apparently going to quit Berlin. He had no thought of doing so. When Linge said in riposte that the rumours arose from the preparations for departure to Berchtesgaden that had been ordered by Bormann the day before, Hitler said, 'Yes, of course, all dispensable people should leave Berlin. My personal effects and the military archive should now be taken to the Obersalzberg. Only my immediate personal staff will remain here with me.' Hitler directed Linge to summon Schaub and Below after lunch to receive appropriate instructions. Finally he told Linge that, *in extremis*, he could always leave Berlin in a Fieseler-Storch from the east–west axis. In the days that followed, all the SS men in Hitler's entourage clung to this hope. They thought that Hitler would not insist on remaining in Berlin regardless of the circumstances. When it became dangerous they would be moved to the Obersalzberg.

While the situation report was still in progress Schaub and Below together with Hitler's pilot Hans Baur put together a list of people to be flown to the Obersalzberg. They were to be assigned to aircraft of Hitler's flight commanded by Baur. The four-motor Condor and Junkers planes were standing in readiness on the runway in Gatow. This immediately unleashed an unholy scrimmage around Schaub and Below, who had now become 'almighty' because they were deciding who was to fly to the Obersalzberg. Everyone wanted to go. People kept coming up to announce that they simply had to get to the Obersalzberg because their family was in Bavaria, or because they came from the area and wanted to defend it, and so on. In reality it was only about getting out of Berlin as quickly as possible.

When night fell on 21 April a long convoy of cars and lorries drove through the back gate of the Reich Chancellery into the Herman Göring Strasse and headed off in the direction of Gatow. Between eighty and a hundred people flew to the Obersalzberg including Hitler's personal adjutant Albert Bormann, his naval adjutant Rear Admiral von Puttkamer,

Hitler's dentist Hugo Blaschke, the newsreel reporter First Lieutenant Frentz, the secretaries Frau Wolf and Frau Schroeder and the stenographers. The chauffeurs who came back with the cars from the airport that night reported that there were real fist-fights over seats in the aircraft.

Linge despatched two aircraft to the Obersalzberg. In one of them there were thirty to forty cases of Hitler's personal effects and his dietary products. This was accompanied by Hitler's valet SS-Hauptsturmführer Wilhelm Arndt and two servants. The second plane transported forty to fifty cases of documents from the military archive which had originated in the Wolfsschanze. They were accompanied by men from the SD.[5] During the night a report came in from the Obersalzberg that all the aircraft had landed safely except that bearing Hitler's personal effects. Baur confirmed that it had been caught by American fighters and forced to land near Cologne.[*]

This was the day of universal flight from Berlin. Thousands of people left the city and made for the west by bus, car, horse and cart, bicycle or pram, the vast mass on foot. An unbroken column dragged itself from the city. Civil servants who were still in Berlin also fled – with or without permission and with falsified papers. Even the 'officials' working in the Führer's Chancellery destroyed their Party books and other documents and took French leave from Berlin.

As the capital was under bombardment from the Russian artillery, Günsche in his capacity as Battle Commander of the Reich Chancellery and the government district arranged that the following should move out of the Old and New Chancelleries and take refuge in the New Chancellery bunker: Bormann, Burgdorf, Fegelein, Voss, Hewel, Lorenz, Zander, the adjutants Schaub, Albrecht, Below and Johannmeyer, the pilots Baur and Betz, Rattenhuber, Högl and Schädle, and Hitler's doctor Dr Stumpfegger, as well as those secretaries who had remained in Berlin. Krebs was also given a place.

The New Chancellery bunker had been built in 1938 together with the main building, as Hitler was making rapid preparations for war. With over seventy rooms, it occupied a vast area. It was divided in two by an underground service courtyard. There coal, provisions and the like were delivered. From the courtyard a heavy-duty lorry lift emerged directly on to the pavement of the Vossstrasse. The hole which this made was camouflaged in such a way that uninitiated people would not have noticed it. From the underground service courtyard a concrete corridor about a hundred metres

---

[*]The plane was shot down in Saxony on the night of the 22nd.

long ran under the garden to Hitler's bunker. The telephone exchange of Hitler's HQ was located in the New Chancellery bunker with the code-name Alt 500, together with the radio station, the press office, the office for Hitler's adjutants and Professor Haase's sickbay, as well as the command station for Mohnke's battle group. There were sixty to seventy SD men stationed there under the command of criminal police officer SS-Sturmbannführer Foster, who were responsible for security in the bunker. They searched everyone who went in or out.

On the night of 21 April the Russian artillery went quiet. In exchange German flak began to howl. Russian bombers attacked military targets in Berlin, and bombs also fell in the vicinity of the Chancellery.

On 22 April Russian artillery began a hefty barrage in the morning. It was reported that several heavy batteries were now firing into the centre of Berlin. Russian shells fell in the Tiergarten and in the gardens of the ministries in the Wilhelmstrasse. Hitler was woken at around 10.00 a.m. by the booming of the guns. He dressed, called for Linge and asked agitatedly 'What calibre are the guns?' To comfort Hitler Linge answered that the noise came from the German batteries in the Tiergarten, apart from a few long-range Russian guns. After Hitler had eaten his breakfast in his study he went back into his bedroom, where Morell injected him with stimulants.

The situation report was scheduled for 12.00. Shortly beforehand Dönitz, Keitel, Jodl, Krebs, Burgdorf, Buhle, Winter, Christian, Voss, Fegelein, Bormann, Hewel, Lorenz, Below, Günsche, Johannmeyer, John von Freyend and Freytag-Loringhoven gathered in Hitler's bunker. There followed the shortest meeting of the entire war. Many of them stood around with strained faces. The same question was forever being whispered: 'Why won't the Führer leave Berlin?'

Hitler came out of his apartment, stooping more than ever. After a laconic greeting he settled in his chair, and Krebs began the briefing. He reported that the situation of the German troops defending Berlin had become even worse. In the south the Russians had broken through near Zossen and were approaching the city's boundaries. In the eastern and northern suburbs fierce battles were raging. The situation of the German forces on the Oder south of Stettin was catastrophic. There the Russians had broken open the German front with tanks and driven deep into German positions.

Hitler stood up and leaned over the table. He ran his trembling hands over the map. Suddenly he straightened and threw the coloured pencil away. He was breathing heavily, his face scarlet and his eyes wide open.

He took a step back from the table and cried out in a faltering voice, 'Nothing like this has ever happened before! Under these circumstances I cannot command any more! The war is lost! But if you gentlemen think that I am going to leave Berlin you are making a very big mistake! I'd rather blow my brains out!' Those present stared at him in horror. He raised his hand feebly and said, 'Thank you, good sirs!' With that he turned on his heel and left the room. They all stood around as if struck dumb. Was that the end? Günsche ran after Hitler. From the conference room could be heard his cry of consternation, 'But my Führer . . .'

Günsche caught up with Hitler at his study door. The Führer stopped in his tracks and commanded, 'Get me Goebbels on the telephone at once!' Goebbels was in the air-raid shelter of his villa on the Hermann Göring Strasse. While Hitler was on the telephone to him, the participants in the conference came out of the antechamber looking confused and agitated. Bormann and Keitel ran into Günsche and asked, 'Where is the Führer? Did he say anything else?' Günsche answered that the Führer was presently on the telephone to Goebbels. They all spoke wildly to one another. Keitel waved his arms about. Bormann was completely beside himself and kept stammering, 'That cannot be, that the Führer is serious about shooting himself!' Keitel shouted, 'We must stop the Führer from doing it!' An indescribable chaos ensued. Many of them quickly knocked back a couple of glasses of cognac from the bottle on the table.

A few minutes later, at around 12.30 p.m., Goebbels hurried in. He was limping more heavily than ever. He had rushed over from his villa on the Hermann Göring Strasse in great excitement. 'Where is the Führer?' he asked. He was taken straight into Hitler's study. There they spoke for about ten minutes. When Goebbels re-emerged he was pounced on by Bormann, Keitel, Dönitz and Jodl: 'What did the Führer say?' He was badgered from all sides. Goebbels informed them that Hitler believed the position to be hopeless, and had concluded that the war was lost. Hitler was completely shattered. He had never come across him in such a state. Goebbels added that he was horrified because on the telephone Hitler had requested him in a quavering voice to come over to him in the bunker immediately with his wife and children, because everything had come to an end.

Bormann was so agitated that he could not stand still. He pleaded with Goebbels, Dönitz, Keitel and Dönitz again that Hitler had to be persuaded, whatever the price, to leave Berlin. Goebbels asked Keitel quietly, 'Field Marshal, do you really see no possibility of stopping the Russian advance?' Keitel answered that the last chance would be to withdraw all the forces from the Elbe as quickly as possible – including the most powerful element, Wenck's Twelfth Army – and to throw them at the Russians.* Keitel's proposal was welcomed by all those present with great enthusiasm. Bormann suggested that they inform Hitler. The Twelfth Army, which was called the Wenck Army after the tank general who commanded it, had been created at the beginning of April 1945 by cobbling together elements from the Reich Work Service, together with officer cadets and trainee NCOs. It was based near Magdeburg and had been earmarked by Hitler as a reserve for the OKW. It had yet to fight a battle. The Wenck Army consisted of just four divisions with between 40,000 and 45,000 men, most of whom were poorly trained and scantily equipped. Its artillery consisted of a few batteries of light field guns. It certainly had no tanks or self-propelled guns. These troops faced the Americans across the Elbe.

Keitel, Bormann, Goebbels, Burgdorf and Fegelein asked Linge to allow them to see Hitler. When Linge went in, Hitler was lying completely exhausted on his bed with his jacket undone. He listened to Linge, stood up with an enormous effort and did up the buttons on his uniform tunic. Then he went into his study and said weakly, 'Let them come in.'

Linge asked Keitel, Bormann, Goebbels, Burgdorf and Fegelein to enter Hitler's study. Twenty minutes later Keitel, Goebbels and Burgdorf came out again with confident looks on their faces. The last to appear were Bormann and Fegelein. In the antechamber they asked Linge to pour them a schnapps, which they knocked back in one. Then Fegelein said to Linge, 'Now it will be all right. Wenck is marching on Berlin with his army.' Keitel exchanged a few words with Dönitz in the antechamber and left the bunker with Jodl and his adjutant John von Freyend.

Shortly afterwards, Hitler asked Dönitz to come in for a private chat with him. The Führer received him in the conference room. The result of the conversation was that Dönitz flew up to Flensburg to organise the transfer by plane to Berlin of the so-called death-candidates. These were naval officers and ratings who had been chosen to man special torpedoes (one-man torpedoes) and who were inevitably killed when they went off.[6] Some of them had volunteered for these duties; others had had them thrust upon them. In addition to this task Dönitz was to muster all navy personnel in northern Germany and lead them in person to defend Berlin.†

---

* Wenck's Twelfth Army was meant to have ten divisions and a total strength of 150,000 men. In reality there were but six badly equipped divisions.
† The navy had been fighting on the Oder since March. On 25 April Dönitz received orders to bring Marines to Berlin.

When they had all left, Hitler ordered Field Marshal Schörner, the Supreme Commander of Army Group Centre, to come to him. His troops were bogged down in fierce defensive battles in Silesia and Czechoslovakia. At 6.00 or 7.00 p.m. Schörner arrived in Berlin. His aircraft landed at Gatow, the one Berlin airfield that had not yet been shelled by Russian artillery.

Hitler's adjutant Johannmeyer asked Linge to tell Hitler that Schörner had arrived and was in the old bunker. Hitler ordered him to be brought to the conference room, and then went out into the antechamber himself to receive him. Linge reminded him to bring the marshal's staff with him, because the Führer wanted to give it to Schörner. Hitler waved him contemptuously aside, however, and added, 'That is such a lot of nonsense!' But, as Schörner appeared in Hitler's bunker in the company of Burgdorf, Fegelein and Johannmeyer, Hitler said to Linge, 'All right! Bring the baton into the conference room!'

Hitler greeted Schörner warmly and said to him as they went into the meeting together, 'Schörner, I would like to cut you up so that I had four Schörners.' Schörner responded with a cheerful smile, 'Always at your service, my Führer!' Hitler's discussions with Schörner, in which Bormann, Burgdorf and Fegelein took part, lasted for about an hour. After that Hitler had a conversation with him alone. At around 8.00 p.m. Schörner waved goodbye to the denizens of the bunker with his marshal's baton and drove to the airfield at Gatow, where an aircraft took him back to his HQ.

Schörner's visit had made an impression on Hitler and his entourage. The subdued mood that had reigned that morning in the bunker had to a large extent dissipated towards eventide. Above all Hitler was seized by new strength. He was busy forging new plans. Schörner's army, which was fighting in Silesia, should attack the south flank of the Russian troops that had broken through south of Berlin and fight its way through to the capital. Schörner himself had received orders from Hitler to withdraw his main force to southern Germany and to occupy the Alpine fortress there. A further plan of Hitler's foresaw the linking up of the German armies in Berlin with those in Mecklenburg. To this end on 24 April he gave orders to the commander of the Third Army, SS-Obergruppenführer Felix Steiner, to attack from the area north of Oranienburg and to attempt to cut off the Russian armies that had advanced on Berlin from the north. Himmler's representative Fegelein was supposed to take this order personally to Felix Steiner. He set off on the morning of 23 April.

When Hitler ordered Schörner to withdraw with a part of his army into the Alpine fortress, the hope sprouted among the Führer's entourage that he might leave Berlin at the last moment in order to continue the struggle in the Alpine fortress. This prospect was the pretext for a party. Bormann was once again his old self, and he settled down in the antechamber with Günsche and the secretaries Frau Junge and Frau Christian and they all drank cognac. There he wallowed in oratory about the Wenck and Steiner Armies, and the 'loyal Nazi' Schörner. 'Yes, Schörner is our man,' confirmed the secretary Frau Christian. 'He is a devoted National Socialist.' Bormann raised his glass and offered a toast with the secretaries. 'The day after tomorrow we will be out of danger. Wenck, Steiner and Schörner will not leave us in the lurch. Their armies are coming to Berlin.'

In the evening Linge ran into Ribbentrop in the hall. His former arrogance was nowhere to be seen. With unusual friendliness he inquired of Linge what Hitler intended to do. When Linge replied that he intended to stay in Berlin for the time being, Ribbentrop became markedly nervous and asked whether he might have a private talk with Hitler. Linge announced him, and Hitler promptly received him in his study. After a twenty-minute conversation Ribbentrop left the bunker. That same evening he travelled from Berlin to Hamburg. He did this with Hitler's approval. When Ribbentrop left he said to Linge, 'I don't want to see him around here again.'

On the same day SS-Brigadeführer Mohnke appeared in the Chancellery with the 3,500 men of the battle group he had raised. Hitler ordered him to take over the defence of the whole government district. Mohnke felt flattered and said to Günsche that after the defeat at Balaton 'the Führer didn't want to know about his Leibstandarte, but now we'll show him he still has a Leibstandarte.'

Goebbels with his wife Magda and their five children Hilde, Holde, Helke, Heike and Heiner moved into the New Chancellery bunker.[*] Goebbels's State Secretary, SS-Brigadeführer Werner Naumann, remained at his house together with his adjutant SS-Hauptsturmführer Günther Schwägermann and his valet SS-Unterscharführer Ochs.

On the morning of 23 April Russian artillery began shelling the government district again. The barrage had almost completely ceased during the night. In the *cour d'honneur* of the Chancellery a number of shells hit the tankers that were parked there as well as barrels of benzene. Several soldiers were killed or badly wounded.

Russian bombers thundered over the centre of Berlin and dived low to hit their targets. The Berlin ring – the motorway around the capital – the

---

[*] They were six children, called Helga, Hilde, Hellmut, Holde, Hedda and Heide.

underground railway* and the trams could no longer be used. Empty trams stood on the Leipziger Strasse, the Potsdamer Platz and the Hermann Göring Strasse. Supplies of electricity, gas and water were cut off in almost all parts of the city. Only the Berlin telephone network continued to function.

Hitler was woken once again by the increase in artillery fire. He dressed and called Linge into his study. As he said, he had hardly slept at all that night and he was very pale. He nervously inquired once again what the calibre of the guns was. Then he asked Morell for his injection. When he had gone Linge put the drops in his right eye. Hitler observed that Morell's hand was already shaking from fear. He was glad that Linge was so deft with his drops.

After breakfast at about 12.00 noon Hitler went into the conference. This had now been divorced from the news briefing and took place several times a day at different times and generally lasted no longer than thirty or forty minutes. In the last days before the fall of Berlin the number of participants diminished more and more. Keitel, who had gone to look for the Wenck Army the day before, had not yet returned. He had prudently moved the OKW HQ from Berlin-Dahlem to Krampnitz, twenty kilometres west of Berlin, to escape from the Russian artillery fire. Jodl and Winter, who reported from the Western Front, were not even invited to the meeting. They anyway preferred not to drive to the Führer Bunker, as it meant passing through the Russian artillery barrage. The Luftwaffe's representatives, Koller and Christian, had moved their HQs out of Berlin and installed them in the game park in Potsdam, and for that reason they no longer attended the conferences. They excused themselves by saying they were a long way away. Their reports were telephoned through to the Luftwaffe adjutant Below, who reported to Hitler. The generals Bodenschatz, Buhle and Scherff, who had sworn undying loyalty at Hitler's birthday hardly three days before, had set off towards southern Germany. Göring had been one of the first to leave Berlin, and Himmler likewise no longer appeared in Hitler's bunker.

The only people who came to the briefing now were those who were living in the Chancellery Bunker: Krebs, Bormann, Burgdorf, Voss, Fegelein, Hewel, Below, Johannmeyer, Günsche, Zander, Freytag-Loringhoven and Lorenz. In the last few days Goebbels had also attended

---

*The U-Bahn (*Untergrund*) was principally underground; the S-Bahn was fast (*schnell*). The Kaiser had forced some of the lines underground to prevent the desecration of the Linden and other beauty spots.

the gatherings. Lorenz had shortly before been named Press Chief. Hitler had dismissed Dietrich for 'intransigence' a characteristic which he had just discovered after fifteen years. Dietrich also hurried to join his family in southern Germany. At around 1.00 p.m. Hitler came into the ante-chamber and greeted the participants who were gathered there. He did not ask about the absentees, though he said to Below, 'You are really the only representative of the Luftwaffe now.'

Together with the others Hitler went into the conference room and sank down slowly into an armchair by the map table. Instead of eight or ten maps of the Eastern and Western Fronts there now lay just two small sheets — a map of Berlin and its region and another of the whole of Germany. Maps of the Western Front were not even laid out. Krebs or his adjutant drew in the lines. In his briefing Krebs informed them that it was now clear that the Russians intended to surround Berlin. From the north they were advancing from Oranienburg; in the west they had reached Nauen, thirty kilometres from Berlin. Connection with the outside world was possible only from the north-west. Besides this there was heavy pres-sure on the capital from the south and east. There the Russians had nearly reached the city border. Hitler interrupted Krebs with the question, 'What is happening with the Wenck Army?' Krebs replied that the Wenck Army had been withdrawn from the Elbe the night before. The Americans had not, however, advanced. At the present time the Wenck Army was deploy-ing south-east of Magdeburg.

As Krebs endeavoured to give further details of the Wenck Army the door opened and in came Keitel with his adjutant, John von Freyend. Keitel was unshaven and his uniform was covered with dust. He wanted to show his Führer that he was working on an opportunity that might decide his salvation. Hitler shook him warmly by the hand. When Freyend had laid the map out on the table, Keitel reported that the Wenck Army had withdrawn from the Elbe in full strength and was at present in the process of redeployment. 'All day and all night I have been moving about mobilising the troops for battle. My Führer! Wenck sends his humble greetings and hopes soon to be able to shake your hand in the Chancellery.' Keitel then stood to attention and cried out, 'Now I shall stay with you, my Führer! I could not look my wife and sons in the eye if I were to leave you now.'

Hitler was visibly moved by this new demonstration of Keitel's loyalty. He got up from his chair and placed a few arrows on the map. Next he declared that Steiner's Third Army must attack from the north on 24 April and that the Wenck Army must advance from the south in the direction of

Potsdam, but no later than 25 April. He continued: the goal of the operation was to turn back the immediate Russian threat to Berlin, to break through to the east and to recreate the Oder Front. Naturally nothing came of this ludicrous plan.

Before the meeting came to an end, Keitel asked Hitler for permission to drive out once more to the Wenck Army. In his opinion his presence would strengthen the morale of the troops. Hitler agreed. A few minutes later Keitel left the bunker to drive to Wenck. He never returned from this trip, despite the fact he had just solemnly sworn never to leave him. At the same time Major Lohse, the Chief of the Führer Signal Battalion, disappeared from the Chancellery without leave.[*]

While Hitler was in the meeting, Linge ordered Eva Braun's chambermaid, Liesl, and Hitler's soldier-servant, SS-Unterscharführer Wauer, to clear Hitler's room. The desk in the study Linge arranged himself. On the desk lay a radio message from Göring that had just come in. It read as follows: 'My most beloved Führer! On the way to southern Germany I came to the conclusion that there are not enough forces to continue the struggle from here. For this reason I must urgently beg of you once again to leave Berlin and to come to Berchtesgaden (Obersalzberg), your loyal Göring.'[7]

When the study had been cleaned out and closed up, Eva came out of her quarters with a dog. The shelling of the city centre had slackened off a bit. Eva was looking very pale. She asked Linge to take her out into the garden, so that she might walk her dog. Linge accompanied her and they walked up and down in front of the bunker. With a grave face Eva expressed the opinion that it was all over unless some miracle were to take place. Linge agreed with her, but stressed that the Wenck Army would perform this miracle. As the conversation proceeded Eva remarked sadly that were the miracle not to take place, then death would be the only way out. In that case she had a great longing to die with Hitler as his legitimate wife.[†]

During the meeting Bormann came out into the antechamber with the operations map of the Soviet–German front and spread it out on the table. He examined it together with Zander and Loringhoven. Linge, who was standing by the SS officer's sentry post outside Hitler's apartment, also walked over to the table. Loringhoven showed Bormann that there was still

[*]The Führer Intelligence Department, which was meant to protect information leaving Führer HQ.
[†]Soviet prisoners maintained that Eva Braun was pregnant and that she did not wish to give birth in captivity. The editors of *The Hitler Book* decided not to include this information in the text. See Editors' Afterword, p. 295.

an open path in the direction of Dresden from which one might make it to southern Germany. It was a small strip some fifteen to twenty kilometres wide that might be cut off by the Russians at any moment. Bormann ordered his assistant Zander to use this route to bring all the workers in the Party Chancellery, including his assistant Müller and his six secretaries, out by bus and general-purpose vehicle to the Obersalzberg. Only Zander and the secretary Else Krüger were to stay in Berlin. She was a thirty-year-old woman who was a friend of Eva's and whom Hitler invited to tea in the last days at her own suggestion.

Immediately after the meeting a completely dejected Morell turned up to see Linge. He asked if Hitler had a few minutes to spare to talk to him. Hitler, who had remained alone in the conference room after the others had left, had Morell come in. When Linge brought Morell in, this colossus fell into a chair and wailed like a child. He was a picture of misery. Hitler tried to comfort him, but he carried on sobbing. Hitler became impatient and asked, 'What do you actually want, professor?'

Suddenly Morell blurted out through his sobs, 'My Führer, I simply can't manage it any longer. Please, please, please let me go!' He spoke of heart attacks he had suffered in the last few days. When Linge heard that he closed the door in disgust. Morell came out again soon afterwards. He had received permission from Hitler to fly to the Obersalzberg. In a great hurry he tossed a few largely unintelligible directions to Dr Stumpfegger, who was now in charge of giving Hitler his shots. Sighing and shaking, he left the bunker that evening under cover of darkness and drove to the airfield at Gatow whence a plane took him to the Obersalzberg.

That was Hitler's longstanding personal physician, whom he had granted the title of professor and decorated with the Gold Party Badge and the Knight's Cross. During the war years Morell had bought big factories in Hamburg and in Czech Olmütz, where he had his hormone preparations, his Vitamultin vitamin concentrate and his delousing powder called Russla, made up. The latter Morell had developed specially for the Wehrmacht. He betrayed a particular 'inventive genius' with the name of the potion: Russla was composed from the first syllables of the words *Russische* (Russian) and *Laus* (louse). The soldiers refused to use the powder because it didn't work and because it also smelled disgusting. They joked that the powder increased the number of lice and killed soldiers by its very stench. On Hitler's explicit instructions, however, the Wehrmacht had to adopt the powder, and Morell made millions.[8]

He bought a luxurious villa on the Schwanenwerder on Berlin's Wannsee Lake and another in the resort of Heringsdorf on the Baltic.

He was just in the process of building a third in Berchtesgaden. In 1944 Morell looked into developing a special explosive that was meant to annihilate the Russian army. To do this he demanded an electron microscope of which there were only two or three in Germany, used for atomic research. As his efforts to obtain it were not crowned with success, Hitler waded in and ensured that this valuable instrument was procured for his minion. Morell set the microscope up in his specially constructed laboratory in Berchtesgaden.* Now, however, this war profiteer was running away from the war.

When Morell made for the hills, Goebbels moved into his room, which was directly opposite Hitler's. His wife remained with the children in the old bunker.

That evening Hitler summoned Günsche into the conference room. Goebbels and Bormann were already there. All three were poised over a map of the city of Berlin that was lying on the table. Hitler stared at it darkly. He informed Günsche that he had just been told that people in the northern districts of Berlin and in the working-class area of Weissensee had hung red and white flags out of the windows, that German soldiers in certain places were retreating without a fight and that many had deserted. Hitler ordered Günsche to send in an SS detachment at once and to shoot any fleeing soldiers on the spot. Goebbels immediately added, 'My Führer, I promise you the red and white flags will soon disappear again from the houses. I have ordered that the guilty parties be shot or hanged in the city's public places. That will be a warning to them.'†

Günsche came away from Hitler and promptly put together two mobile squads made up of SS men from Hitler's personal bodyguard and Chancellery drivers and ordered them to proceed to northern Berlin and drive fleeing officers and men back to the trenches. Anyone who resisted had to be brought to the Chancellery. After a while both squads returned with a group of officers and men. They were hanged on Friedrichstrasse station. On their chests they bore a placard with the legend: 'I am hanging here because I did not carry out the Führer's orders!'

At around 5.00 a.m. on 24 April the volume of Russian shelling became audibly greater. Heavy shells exploded in quick succession in the Chancellery and all around. An hour later it became somewhat calmer

---

*There were at least thirty in Germany. The one Morell received was meant for the Academy of Military Medicine.
†Goebbels issued his orders on the 22nd and 23rd.

again. When the barrage abated, Hitler lay down to sleep. At around 10.00 the artillery flared up again. All at once several shells exploded on the roof of Hitler's bunker, and the air conditioning abruptly stopped working. The thunder of the shells woke Hitler. He dressed quickly and rang for Linge. When the latter came into the study, he could see that Hitler shuddered at each detonation and stared anxiously at the ceiling. Linge tried to comfort him with the observation that the noise of the explosion was really proof of the strength of the reinforced concrete that covered the bunker. This morning Dr Stumpfegger administered Hitler's life-enhancing injections for the first time. The situation report was timed for 10.30.

When Günsche entered the bunker at around 11.00 it was already in full swing. Apart from Hitler only Krebs, Burgdorf, Bormann, Goebbels, Johannmeyer, Below and Loringhoven took part. Krebs reported, 'Since this morning Russian soldiers have been attacking Berlin from the north and the south. The circle around the city is almost closed. Only through a narrow passage to the south of Spandau are communications still open to the outside world. It is to be expected that even this will be closed by the Russians. The Steiner Army has not yet come out of the area to the north of Oranienburg. There is no accurate information on Steiner.* Hitler's face tightened in fury. He uttered wild insults against the Steiner Army and called its commander a puffed-up, arrogant general. In recent days he had venerated Steiner, who had graduated from the 5th SS Panzer Division 'Viking' to III German SS Corps, and had only just had been placed in command of the Third Army. Now he issued orders to let Steiner know immediately that he was to attack the next day, the 25th at the latest, and by the evening to restore communications with Berlin.

There was also nothing known about the Wenck Army. The position of the German units that were still on the Oder was becoming catastrophic. Russian troops had broken through and deployed south of Stettin in the area controlled by the Marines.† They had advanced fifty to sixty kilometres to the west. The Ninth Army, which was still near Frankfurt on the Oder, had been surrounded by Russian troops and was now being attacked on all sides. Through his brother-in-law, Burgdorf, and Krebs, its commander, General Busse asked several times for permission to retreat towards Berlin. Hitler, however, refused every time, even though Russian

---

*On 23 April 1945 there was a forty-kilometre-wide gap allowing communications with the west; the next day the passage had been reduced to ten kms. It centred on the Havel bridges, the Pichelsdorfer and the Charlottenbrücke in particular. The Hitler Youth units defending them suffered heavy losses.
†The 1st Marine Rifles was attached to XLVI Army Corps.

contingents were now to be found well behind the Ninth Army lines. He simply wouldn't depart from his view that the old line on the Oder could be rebuilt.

Fegelein, whom Hitler had sent to Steiner the day before, returned on the 24th. He reported to Hitler that Steiner's army could not take action because its forces were too weak. Steiner wanted to wait until he had gathered, with the assistance of recruiting squads, as many as possible of the scattered units that were wandering around. Steiner's hesitancy threw Hitler into a rage: 'Steiner must attack tomorrow at the latest!' he screeched. 'He must be in Berlin by evening!' He ordered Fegelein to return to Steiner immediately and to transmit his command in person. Fegelein started out that same day.

Hitler ate his lunch as usual in the company of Eva Braun and his secretaries. When it was finished he had Schaub summoned. Linge brought Schaub to him in his study and noticed the door to his bedroom was open. Hitler stood in front of the open safe. He told Schaub and Linge that all the remaining documents in the Chancellery were to be burned. Linge had to bring suitcases. When Linge reappeared in the bedroom with some cases, Hitler began to pull documents out of the safe. They were secret papers that he had received from Keitel, Jodl, Dönitz or from the OKH since moving his HQ to Berlin. They included his personal correspondence and several bundles of fifty- or hundred-mark notes. Linge packed them all into four suitcases. Linge, Schaub and the servants who were summoned to help drag the cases out into the park. There the contents were tipped out and sorted into several heaps before being drenched in benzene and set on fire. The flames shot up some ten metres from the emergency exit. Linge waited until every scrap had been burned.

In the meantime Schaub emptied all the safes in Hitler's private apartment in the Old Chancellery. Five in all, they contained political and military papers from the war and before, including draft letters personally corrected by Hitler and sent during the war to Mussolini, Antonescu, Pétain and others; and the replies. With the help of his soldier-servant, Corporal Mandtal, Schaub packed all these into a big suitcase too, had it carried out into the garden by SS men from Hitler's bodyguard and consigned to the flames.

When all the documents found in the Chancellery had been burned, Schaub reported to Hitler in Linge's presence. Hitler commanded Schaub to fly to the Obersalzberg immediately and to burn all the documents he could find in the Berghof as well. In the Berghof there were three big, armour-plated cupboards filled with documents from before and during war. In the bunker there were the collections of minutes from the military situation reports. There was also the military archive that had been taken there from the Wolfsschanze. Hitler decreed that all these papers were to be burned. He handed Schaub the keys to the safes at the Berghof, which he always carried on him. That night Schaub came to bid Hitler goodbye before leaving the bunker together with Corporal Mandtal, who was to accompany him. He told the others who were staying behind, 'In a few days I shall be back!'

No one believed him. He flew from Gatow airfield, which was already being shelled by the Russians and would be occupied by them the next day. Schaub never returned to Berlin. The two remaining stenographers who had taken the minutes during the last briefings and who were not evacuated on the 21st left the capital with him. There was no need for them any more.

That evening in the bunker's spare room, Goebbels dictated an appeal to the people which was copied down by civil servants from the Propaganda Ministry. His appeal appeared in the small-format newspaper *Der Bär*, the only paper still to appear in Berlin, which was printed on the presses of the Propaganda Ministry.[*] When Linge walked through the room to his bed, he heard Goebbels, sitting on the bench beside the table, dictating with his monotonous voice: 'Berliners, stand firm! Defend your capital! Your Führer is working for you in the walls of your city! The Führer has personally taken command of the defence of the capital! Loyalty for loyalty! The enemy may only reach our beloved Führer over our dead bodies![†]

While Goebbels was dictating his appeal, in which he demanded new sacrifices from Berlin's population and maintained that the Führer lived only for the city's defence, Hitler was standing at his safe, pulling out the last documents relating to his time in office and feeding them to the flames, because he did not believe in salvation. After his dictation, Goebbels reported to Hitler that Berlin had sufficient provisions to last two weeks.[‡] All evening new reports came in to Hitler that the situation in Berlin and

---

[*] *Der Panzerbär* ('The Armour-Plated Bear' – the bear was the symbol of Berlin) was printed daily from 22 to 29 April 1945.
[†] On 28 April 1945 Goebbels wrote: '[Hitler] stands with us in the bitter struggle. His orders are still being emitted from Berlin in a battle for freedom that is making world history . . . He is standing on the hottest battlefield man has ever known. And around him have gathered the most fantastic soldiers there have ever been . . .'
[‡] *Der Panzerbär* reported on the 23rd that Berlin had sufficient provisions for another twelve weeks.

round about was getting worse and worse. Among the denizens of the bunker the mood had sunk to rock bottom.

At the beginning it was 'The Russians are advancing down both sides of the Berlin–Zossen road and have broken deep inside Berlin's defensive perimeter.' This was followed by 'Berlin's last airfield, Gatow, has been shelled by Russian artillery. It is no longer usable.' Krebs reported, 'Russian tanks have reached the Berlin–Nauen road.' The next report said, 'The Russians have surrounded Berlin from all sides.' It struck the people in the bunker like lightning. Even the great optimists, who had hoped to get out of Berlin at the last moment, now lost their nerve. Hitler's pilot Baur, who had been wandering in the vicinity of the Führer's rooms all day long, waiting for the order to fly him out on the Condor waiting at Gatow, left the Führer Bunker late that night too. He returned dejected to his quarters.

At dawn on 25 April the capital was undergoing heavy shelling from the Russian artillery. Shells were once again falling on the Chancellery and the ministries near by. In many places fires had broken out, and thick clouds of smoke darkened the skies. At 9.30 a.m. a radio message came in from Keitel: it broke the news that the Wenck Army was on the march. Advance units had reached Treuenbrietzen, forty kilometres west of Potsdam. The news spread like wildfire though the bunker. 'Wenck is on his way, Wenck will liberate us!' Morale soared, and it rose higher when the report came in that the Steiner Army had also fought a battle at Oranienburg in the north, on its way to break the Berlin blockade.

At around 10.30 a.m. Krebs came to Hitler to brief him, though the Führer no longer required this of him. Krebs came when he saw fit, when he had something new to report. The other participants were not even informed. They were in the bunker all the time anyhow and came into the conference room when they saw Krebs go in, to see Hitler with his maps. When Hitler left his apartment and went into the conference room, he found that Krebs, Bormann, Lorenz, Boldt, Loringhoven and Günsche were already there. Goebbels arrived a little late; after him came Below, Hewel, Voss and Burgdorf. Hitler no longer minded that the briefing was constantly interrupted. He looked up only momentarily before returning his gaze to the map. Since the Russians troops had reached the suburbs of Berlin, Krebs used the city plan as an operations map for his briefings. He reported that he had no fresh news from the Wenck Army, or from the Steiner Army which went over to the attack that morning. The Russians were exerting heavy pressure to the south around Tempelhof and also in

A photograph by Heinrich Hoffmann taken at the opening of an exhibition unwittingly points up the irony: Hitler and Göring are at the centre, protected by the Führer Escort Command. The people are held back by the SS Leibstandarte 'Adolf Hitler'

After tough negotiations, the British Prime Minister Neville Chamberlain accepted German territorial demands for Czechoslovakia in the Hotel Dreesen on the Rhine on 23 September 1938. Heinrich Hoffmann was at the ready in the foyer of the hotel as they said farewell: his picture of the two heads of government went round the world, and no article failed to mention the 'peace palm' in the background

Left: Hitler honours his ally Mussolini with a parade. Fascist Italy felt itself ideologically bound to Germany

Centre: Göring also performed ceremonial roles. Here he is on the balcony of the Reich Chancellery. The parade was in honour of the Condor Legion, the air force of which contributed to Franco's victory in the Spanish Civil War

Below: On 29–30 September 1938 the fate of Czechoslovakia was decided by the great powers in Munich – France, Great Britain, Italy and Germany. Hitler appends his signature to the partition agreement. Next to him stands his then personal adjutant, Julius Schaub; behind are the initiators of the talks, Göring and Mussolini

Above: After Georg Elsner's attempt on Hitler's life on 9 November 1939 Gestapo officers comb the ruins of the Bürgerbräukeller

Right: Heinz Guderian was involved in the planning of the so-called Sickle Cut. As a tank general, he led his squadrons to the Channel coast. The photograph shows him in an armoured car in 1940. In the foreground is an Enigma machine

Below: Hitler celebrated Christmas Day 1939 with the SS Leibstandarte in their HQ in Bad Ems

Heinz Linge and Otto Günsche standing up close to the stage of history. *Top*: Linge – on the right – was stationed at the entrance to the railway carriage in Compiègne Forest on 21 June 1940. He is standing next to the French General Huntzinger and Ambassador Noël. *Bottom*: Günsche was posted inside the carriage. He had been told to shoot any French delegate who demonstrated the slightest suspicious movement. The picture shows General Keitel handing the armistice conditions to General Huntzinger

Top: As an enthusiastic amateur pilot, Rudolf Hess kept himself up to date with the production of the latest sorts of aircraft. He is seen here inspecting a Heinkel He 111. For his flight to Scotland he used a converted Messerschmitt Me 110

Centre: The Waffen SS front-line reporter documents its war crimes too. A 1942 photograph shows soldiers from the SS Leibstandarte 'Adolf Hitler' fighting 'partisans' in Russia. A civilian's house is being burned down

Bottom: 1942: the summer offensive looks set to fail. The photograph of a situation conference in June 1942 shows Hitler surrounded by Lieutenant General Adolf Heusinger (foreground), Colonel General Maximilian von Weichs (background, wearing spectacles), Tank General Friedrich Paulus (next to Hitler), Colonel General Eberhard von Mackensen and General Field Marshal Fedor von Bock (right)

Idyll: Adolf Hitler and long-term lover Eva Braun and their dogs Blondi and Stasi at the Berghof in 1942

As it is implied (but not stated) in *The Hitler Book*, Hitler was accurately informed of the murder of the Jews. A group of Hungarian Jews arriving at Auschwitz in 1944

Top: A few days after the attempt on his life Hitler visited the wounded in the hospital in Rastenburg. Here he is standing at the bedside of his naval adjutant, Karl-Jesko von Puttkamer

Centre: At the end of September 1944 the Commander of the Replacement Army, Heinrich Himmler, announced the creation of Volkssturm regiments made up of young boys and old men. Next to him stand Hans Heinrich Lammers, SS Obergruppenführer and Chief of the Reich Chancellery, and Colonel General Heinz Guderian, Chief of the General Staff

Bottom: Hitler made his last appearance for the press photographers on 20 March 1945. The picture shows an image-conscious Führer decorating boy soldiers. His appeal to fight to the last was meant to give the senseless struggle a higher meaning

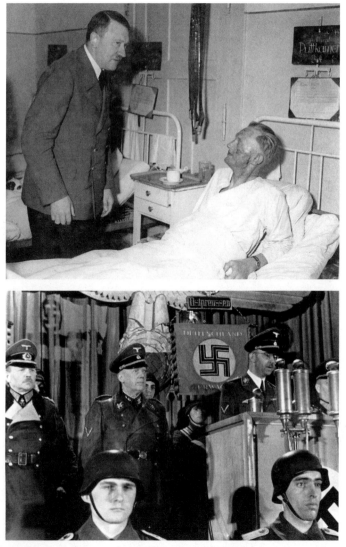

Like all the other corpses of senior Nazis found in Berlin, Body No. 5 was subjected to an autopsy by pathologists belonging to Smersh, or Soviet Military Intelligence, on 8 May 1945. The photograph shows the body of Joseph Goebbels before it was cut open

SS Sturmbannführer Heinz Linge (*below left*) and SS Sturmbannführer Otto Günsche (*below right*) were photographed again in their prison clothes in 1955 shortly before their release

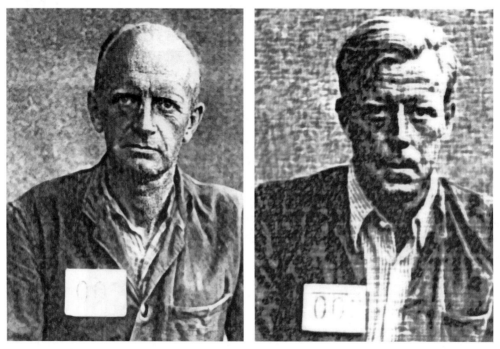

the east and north. The ammunitions dumps, most of which lay around the city perimeters, were lost. There was already a lack of ammunition, particularly when it came to anti-tank grenades.

Krebs reported further on the battles in Berlin: the commander of the 18th Panzer Grenadier Division, who was fighting in the southern part of the capital and had found himself in a difficult situation, had shot himself. Burgdorf remarked, 'His nerve had gone.'* Hitler added, 'At last a general who had found the courage to do what was required of him.' He was, however, an exception. Other generals and many officers who were fighting in Berlin preferred to don civilian clothes and disappear into private apartments. The mobile squads of the SS and the Hitler Youth uncovered many of them and shot them on the spot.

Hitler, who had had his spirits raised by Keitel's radio message, had sunk back into himself. His voice was scarcely audible. The depressed atmosphere was everywhere to be felt. For a while it was deathly quiet in the room and everyone looked mutely at the map. Bormann had not uttered a single word during the entire meeting. He went nervously from one end of the table to the other, left the room and then came back. Even Goebbels was almost completely silent. Only once did he speak, to ask how many kilometres the Wenck Army could cover in a day and when it might be expected in Berlin. After Krebs had finished, Hitler went back into his study. The others also went to their rooms or took themselves off to Hitler's old bunker.

At 2.30 in the afternoon, Bormann, Burgdorf and Krebs came rushing back to Hitler's bunker. They made their way to the conference room, which Hitler was just about to enter. Krebs was distraught. He reported to Hitler that the Russian and American armies had met at Torgau on the Elbe. Bormann blurted out, 'My Führer, it is now really high time you made personal contact with the Americans.' Hitler simply shook his head lethargically and countered: 'I don't have any authority any more. Another person must do that for me. For my own part I must do what I must.'

Hitler left the conference room in silence and went into his study. Bormann, Burgdorf and Krebs walked out of the bunker shaking their heads and shrugging their shoulders. They went back to their rooms.

After lunch Hitler summoned Linge. When he came in, Hitler was sitting at his desk looking completely distraught with his drooping head propped up in his two hands. Linge said, 'My Führer, you called me?' Hitler

---

*The commander of that division, General Major Josef Rauch, had not shot himself; that was General Major Georg Scholze of the 20th Panzer Grenadier Division.

looked at him with tired eyes. Deep in his haggard, waxy face, those eyes were cloudy and staring. He murmured, 'Linge, I would like to let you go to your family—' Linge interrupted him, 'My Führer, I was with you in the good times and I will stay with you in the bad ones.' Hitler sat up and looked straight into Linge's eyes, as if he wished to find out whether it was sincerely meant. Then he said, 'Linge, I have a special task for you.' Hitler had death in his eyes. 'Together with Fräulein Braun I am going to shoot myself in front of the bunker in the Chancellery garden. There is no other way out.' Linge wanted to answer back, but Hitler anticipated him: 'Make sure you have benzene to pour over our bodies and burn us. You must in no circumstances allow my body to fall into the hands of the Russians. They would take delight in having me shipped back to Moscow and putting me on show in a collection of curios. That must not happen.' He was particularly emphatic. Linge could only reply that he would carry out Hitler's orders to the letter.

Hitler added, 'Destroy everything that is in my apartment. Nothing here should remind people of me. This picture' – he pointed to his beloved Frederick the Great which hung over the desk – 'take it out of its frame and give it to Baur. He must carry it to a safe place in Bavaria.' Linge promised Hitler that he would carry everything out as he had ordered, together with his servant SS-Hauptscharführer Heinz Krüger, the commander of his bodyguard SS-Sturmbannführer Franz Schädle and the head of the police squad SS-Obersturmbannführer Peter Högl. Hitler nodded and dismissed him.

From Hitler's chauffeur Kempka, Linge ordered 120 litres of benzene. It was poured into six canisters and put in readiness at the garden exit to the bunker. Then Linge summoned Krüger, Högl and Schädle and initiated them. All three were horrified by what they heard. Like Linge, however, they knew that the Führer was not to be gainsaid. They agreed that Schädle and Linge would burn the bodies and Högl and Krüger destroy Hitler's personal effects in his apartment. When the jobs had been shared out, Linge asked Krüger for a bottle of schnapps, as they needed to wash away the mood that choked them all.

In the evening Lieutenant Kuhlmann reported to Vice Admiral Voss in the Chancellery. He had been sent from Flensburg on a mission by Dönitz with several Ju 52s filled with 'death candidates' from the navy. The planes had landed in the gloaming on the east–west axis between the Brandenburg Gate and the Victory Column, as Gatow airfield had already been occupied by Russian troops. They had landed under fire from Russian artillery. The east–west axis was peppered with shell craters and as a result many planes toppled over when they landed. Among these mariners there were many dead and wounded.[*]

Voss took Kuhlmann to Hitler's bunker and asked Linge if Hitler might see him, as he had only managed to reach Berlin under such adverse circumstances. Hitler lay on the bed in his bedroom. Linge transmitted Voss's request, but Hitler refused. Only when Voss had made a second, more urgent request for Hitler to see Kuhlmann, who had come to Berlin to defend the Führer, did Hitler emerge into the antechamber. When Kuhlmann saw Hitler he stood to attention and raised his arm high before announcing the arrival of his unit. Hitler gave him a limp handshake and said that Kuhlmann would be assigned to Mohnke's battle group defending the government district. Then he disappeared again behind his door. Kuhlmann was briefly introduced to Goebbels and then left Hitler's bunker. He established his quarters with his unit in the cellars of the Foreign Office next to the Chancellery.

That same evening Speer called Linge from Hamburg, to find out Hitler's and Eva Braun's intentions. When Linge told him that both were going to remain in Berlin, Speer replied that he would 'organise' several Fieseler-Storchs and send them to Berlin so that he could at least fly out Eva and Hitler's secretaries.

All that evening, until late into the night, Krebs or his adjutant Loringhoven hurried in and out bringing new reports for Hitler. The situation in Berlin got worse by the hour. The attack launched by Steiner's Third Army became pinned down by Russian artillery fire after an insignificant initial success. Russian tank squadrons had gone well past Berlin and, striking far to the west, had taken Rathenow. The Potsdam Garrison, commanded by General Reymann, had been surrounded and was engaged in desperate defensive battles. In the western districts of Berlin as well, in Zehlendorf, Nikolassee and Dahlem, they were already fighting. Russian troops had broken through at Spandau and had proceeded a long way up the Berlin–Zossen road. They were already close to the great Havel Bridge at Pichelsdorf. To defend this bridge troops from the Hitler Youth had been sent under Axmann's command.

The continued worsening of the situation in Berlin lowered morale yet further in Hitler's bunker. It was once again at rock bottom. In the old

---

[*] After Hitler's directive of 25 April 1945 the Marine Rifle Battalion had flown in. It was immediately brought under the command of the Battle Commander of the Reich Chancellery. The next night naval commandos were also due to land, but that was prevented by heavy artillery fire on the east–west axis.

bunker little groups sat around, drinking schnapps and arguing loudly about whether the Russians could still be held at bay. Others spoke in whispers, and tried to calculate how long Berlin could hold out, and whether there were still ways of leaving the city.

Hitler's unease and nervousness took on threatening proportions. He did not need to be woken in the morning any more. He was tortured by worries and woke very early. In any event, the explosions that went off on the roof of the bunker prevented him from sleeping. As soon as Stumpfegger had given him his shots and Linge his drops he dragged his heels up and down the rooms of the bunker. His hair had become greyer. He looked like an aged man, almost like a living corpse. He couldn't concentrate any more. He would go to the switchboard room, then stand up again and go into the machine room with the air conditioning. He had never looked into these rooms before. Or he would shuffle over to the basket where Blondi lay, take out his beloved Wolf and try to play with him in the hall. He spoke very little.

After lunch he often sat on the banquette in the antechamber. Then he was joined by Bormann, Burgdorf, Fegelein, Frau Christian, Fräulein Krüger and Eva Braun. Eva was drinking a lot of cognac at the time. You rarely heard her laugh any more. She joined in the discussions, mostly instigated by Bormann, Burgdorf, Fegelein or Frau Christian, only when she was drunk on cognac. The others drank a mixture of champagne, cognac and schnapps, without taking any notice of Hitler. Bormann, Burgdorf and Fegelein sprawled wildly in the chairs. Their conversations revolved chiefly around the funnier sides of the lavish existences they had left behind them. They tried to draw Hitler into the conversation. The latter, however, just sat there without participating, staring into space, stroking Wolf or covering him with hysterical caresses.

At the nightly teas which were attended by Eva Braun, the secretaries Frau Christian and Frau Junge, sometimes the diet cook Fräulein Manziarly and Bormann's secretary Else Krüger, Hitler spoke only about the best ways of committing suicide. In the most lurid colours he painted a picture of what would happen to him if he were to fall into Russian hands. He debated in great detail whether it was better to shoot oneself, poison oneself or cut one's wrists. These nightly sessions could drag on until six or seven in the morning. The discussions that were held there drove the secretaries near to real hysteria.

After tea with Hitler, Frau Christian would appear at the telephone switchboard where the SS officers from Hitler's bodyguard sat knocking back champagne. When Linge appeared one morning, Frau Christian suddenly threw a champagne glass at him. Later she apologised and explained that, after listening to Hitler talking about different ways of committing suicide, her nerves were all in. Among the SS men morale was also low. They looked to deaden their gloom in a sea of schnapps and champagne. The only remaining hope was the Wenck Army.

During the night of 25–26 April the Russians cut the last subterranean telephone cable connecting Berlin with the outside world. Now there was just a radio link which was maintained by two 100-watt receivers. Even that was not reliable, as the antennae kept being damaged by exploding ordnance.

At 7.00 a.m. on 26 April Russian artillery launched a firestorm in the government district. The Chancellery and Hitler's bunker were struck by a storm of heavy shells. The roof of the underground passage from the New Chancellery to the bunker was smashed in several places. On the floor of the passageway giant puddles formed that had to be covered with boards. One had to be careful not to lose one's balance when walking on them, lest one fall in. Through the holes in the roof could be seen dark billows of smoke and the burning roof of the Chancellery. The hazy light that filtered through produced an eerie atmosphere in the corridor.

At 9.00 a.m. the artillery fire slackened off a little. Günsche settled down at the telephone switchboard. Goebbels also appeared a little while later. There were red spots on his ashen face, and his eyes glowed like those of a hunted beast. He looked even smaller, weaker and more fragile than ever. He began immediately to talk about the situation in Berlin. He asked Günsche how he saw it, how long Berlin could hold out, whether Wenck would manage to fight his way through, and whether he would come too late. Goebbels had asked these same questions many times over the past two days. You could detect his fear of the end ringing through. He complained angrily about the Nazi Party leaders who had abandoned Hitler to his fate. 'If we ever get out of here I shall clean up the Party, which is as it should be. Many important officials have behaved like cowards and toe-rags.'

Turning to Günsche, Goebbels continued: for a long time – particularly since the start of the war – the Party leadership had been stamped by pettifogging and decay. Before the war senior officials holed up on their estates, went hunting and led the lives of parasites. Why had Hitler protected people like Ley, or the Gauleiters Streicher, Koch and Wächtler? They and many others had caused the Party great harm and brought it down. At Hitler's most difficult moment they showed their real faces. They had all abandoned him: Göring, Himmler, Ribbentrop, Rosenberg, Ley and Funk.

At 10.00 a.m. Krebs appeared to brief Hitler. The only people present were Goebbels, Burgdorf, Lorenz, Günsche and Zander. As the telephone cable had been cut and the radio antenna damaged by artillery fire and not yet repaired, Krebs could give no news of the Wenck Army or of the unsuccessful attack by the Steiner Army. He reported that during the past night the battles in Berlin had cooled off a little, but that they had started up again with a vengeance at dawn. The Russians had overrun German positions once again. In the western part of the city they were in the centre of Zehlendorf and Dahlem. Russian tanks had reached Lichterfelde. In the north-east of Berlin they were on both sides of the Frankfurter Allee and had advanced to the Alexanderplatz.[9] They were dangerously close to the city centre. These reports had a devastating effect on Hitler. While Krebs explained the position, the Führer gazed around blankly.

At around 2.00 p.m. the duty chief intelligence officer in the Chancellery, Sergeant Major Adam (the man who had been the first to denounce Stauffenberg after the attempt on Hitler's life on 20 July 1944) handed Günsche a radio report for Hitler. It came from Göring on the Obersalzberg. Because there was no direct connection any more, it had had to come via a tortuous route through a number of Luftwaffe units. The contents were roughly as follows: 'My Führer, as a result of the encirclement of Berlin you are no longer in a position to exercise total power, and as your liberty to operate is limited I am of the opinion that the moment has come for me – abiding by the decision of the Reichstag of 1 September 1939 which made me your successor – to take over responsibility for the leadership both within and without the German Reich. In the event of my not hearing a negative response from you before 10.00 p.m. today, that is 26 April, I shall take it that you agree.'*

Without announcing himself, Günsche took Göring's radio message directly to Hitler in his study. The Führer was sitting with Eva Braun on the sofa facing the door. When Günsche told him that he must speak urgently to him, Hitler looked at him suspiciously. He nodded at Eva who

---

*The message was sent on the 23rd. The text is as follows: 'My Führer! Are you agreed, after your decision to remain in Fortress Berlin, and in keeping with your decree of 29 June 1941 appointing me your deputy, that I should immediately take over the total leadership of the Reich, with full liberty to act both within and without? Should no answer come in before 10.00 a.m. I shall assume that you have been robbed of your liberty to act, and I will take it that the decree has been enacted and will govern in the interests of the people and the Fatherland. You know what I feel for you in this, the most difficult hour of my life, I cannot express in words. God save you and, despite everything let you come here as soon as you might. Your loyal Hermann Göring.' Hitler issued orders for the SS to arrest him.

immediately left the room. At Hitler's signal Günsche read out the message. He had not come to the end of the first sentence, however, before Hitler jumped up and tore the message out of his hand. With trembling fingers he put on his spectacles. His face puffed up. It turned as red as a turkey from fury. 'Oh this Göring!' he groaned. 'Responsibility of internal and external affairs! To make me an ultimatum!' He crumpled up the radio message in his fist, dropped into a chair and, moaning, covered his face with both hands. A minute later, he blurted out, 'Send a message to Göring at once! Write this down!' Hitler began to dictate in clipped phrases: 'I am as ever in possession of all power and do not feel in any way limited in my freedom of movement. I forbid you to assume power in any way. Adolf Hitler.'* He fell silent and stared into the middle distance.

Günsche said that Göring had made him and the others despair for a long time. He reminded Hitler of the letter from Obergebietsführer Petter, which he had received a little while ago. Feverishly, Hitler commanded, ' Get me Bormann immediately!' Günsche left the study and told Bormann about Göring's radio message. Bormann hurried off to see Hitler, while Günsche went off to the room containing the radio station and ordered Hitler's message to be sent to Göring immediately.

Linge was standing in the antechamber when Bormann, red as a beetroot, tumbled past him and headed into Hitler's study. 'That toe-rag Göring,' he muttered in passing. Bormann stoked up Hitler's anger yet more and drove him to the point of incandescence: 'That pig Göring. He knows full well that your answer cannot arrive before 10.00 p.m.!' he screamed. Hitler threw a tantrum. Pummelling the table with his fists, he yelled, 'Bormann, issue orders to our criminal police on the Obersalzberg to arrest Göring immediately! Send the message at once! If he tries to run away he must be shot on the spot!' Bormann ran out with great zeal. As he dashed past Linge he called out to the duty officer of the bodyguard to send him Högl straightaway. Then he went to Goebbels. When Högl appeared in the bunker, Bormann went with him to the radio station to have Hitler's order transmitted. The commander of the Obersalzberg, SS-Obersturmbannführer Frank, was given the order to arrest Göring.

When Bormann left the bunker, Hitler came out of his study to go to see Goebbels. Goebbels was on his way to see Hitler, so they ran into one another in the antechamber. Goebbels limped up and said − although he

---

*Hitler's answer, dated 23 April 1945, was as follows: 'The Führer Decree of 29 June 1941 is hereby declared invalid. Your behaviour and your measures are treachery against my person and the National Socialist cause. I am completely free to act and forbid any further measures.'

too was simmering with rage – in his monotonous sing-song voice, 'This blow, my Führer, has been inflicted on you by Göring, whom you believed to be the most loyal of the lot.' Hitler went with Goebbels into the conference room, where they remained together for a long time.

Shortly afterwards Eva Braun came out of her room into the antechamber, where Günsche was still on duty. She had no idea what was going on and asked what was happening. Günsche told her about Göring's radio message. Eva observed that she had had a strange premonition on 20 April, when Göring left Berlin. She had spoken to Hitler about it: 'Göring, that renegade, had already deserted the Führer, because he wanted to betray him. The poor Führer . . .' Göring's action was debated in the bunker with great excitement, but soon the unrelenting advance of the Russians reclaimed the complete attention of the inmates.

Together with a few troop units that had retreated into the centre of Berlin in the face of the Russian advance there was a group of BDM* girls in the New Chancellery bunker. That afternoon Linge was summoned to Hitler. When he entered the study Hitler was sitting at the table with Eva Braun. Having trouble forming the words, Hitler said that Eva had seen strange girls in the bunker. Linge reported that they were members of the BDM who had fled from the Russians. Their papers had been examined and they had been put to work performing various tasks in the old bunker. Eva remarked that she had already seen them in Hitler's bunker. Linge replied that they had no doubt come out of curiosity because they wanted to see Hitler. At this point Hitler told Linge, 'The Russians will try anything to capture me alive. They will use every means at their disposal to get what they want. They can also dress girls up in BDM uniforms and give them BDM papers so that they can knock me out with some sort of chemical.' He ordered Linge to throw all these girls out of the bunker.

On that same evening, Colonel General of the Air Force Ritter von Greim[10] landed a Fieseler-Storch on the east–west axis. Hitler had summoned him by radio in order to appoint him to replace Göring as head of the Luftwaffe. The plane, which was piloted by Hanna Reitsch,[11] landed at the Brandenburg Gate under heavy Russian artillery fire. In the course of this Greim's leg was quite badly injured. He was brought to the bunker sickbay where they operated on him and put his leg into a cast. At around 8.00 p.m. Greim was brought on a stretcher into the conference room where Hitler was waiting for him. Hanna Reitsch, a skinny, unprepossessing person with an Iron Cross pinned to her dark-blue dress, walked

*Bund Deutscher Mädel: the female equivalent of the Hitler Jugend or Hitler Youth.

beside the stretcher. When they put Greim down Hitler greeted both, drew up a chair and asked to be left alone with Greim. In the course of their discussion Hitler gave Greim Göring's job and promoted him field marshal.

As early as the autumn of 1944 when Hitler was still in the Wolfsschanze, Greim had been seen as Göring's replacement as Supreme Commander of the Luftwaffe. At that time General Major of the Air Force Peltz, who commanded the German bomber squadrons in the west, and Lieutenant Colonel Baumbach, one of the most famous bomber pilots in the Luftwaffe, had demanded that Göring be replaced on grounds of incompetence. Both these men were highly regarded by Hitler. The proposition had been supported by Hitler's Luftwaffe adjutants Below and by Göring's former adjutant Lieutenant Colonel Boehm-Tettelbach. The latter was the section leader for the Luftwaffe in the OKW. At that time Hitler was unable to bring himself to make a decision.

After his talk with Hitler, Greim remained in the sickbay of Hitler's bunker. Hanna Reitsch, his mistress of many years, was at his side. From his sickbed, Greim sent radio messages in all possible directions and left no stone unturned as he tried to mobilise the last vestiges of the Luftwaffe in the battle for Berlin. In the evening Hanna Reitsch and Goebbels's children sang nursery rhymes and lullabies at Greim's bedside.

On 27 April Greim was supposed to fly to Rechlin in northern Germany to supervise personally the concentration of Luftwaffe forces for the battle of Berlin. But Hanna Reitsch's attempt to take off with Greim failed owing to the heavy Russian artillery fire on the east–west axis. Only on the 28th could she fly Greim out of Berlin.

Hanna Reitsch, who served in the Luftwaffe as a trainer and test pilot, was the only German woman who wore the Iron Cross First Class. She was particularly famous during the war because she flew a plane with a cutting instrument attached to its nose and cut the cables of barrage balloons.[12] A loyal National Socialist, she was highly regarded by Hitler and stayed with him many times. The last time she had visited him was on the Obersalzberg in 1944. Over coffee with Hitler and Below, the conversion turned to Churchill. Hanna Reitsch suggested a plot to kill him in which she would participate. Hitler had answered with a laugh: 'Churchill would not be worse protected than I am.'

The nearer the Russians came to the Chancellery the more nervous Hitler became. In the meantime you had the impression he was losing his wits. At 9.00 in the evening he summoned Günsche and laid into him: 'Where are your troops?'

'Which troops, my Führer?'

Hitler roared even louder: 'Your troops, your 6,000 or 8,000 SS men!'

Günsche replied that he had no such troops: the defence of the government district was in the hands of Mohnke, whose battle group comprised 4,000 troops in total. Hitler, however, raged on: 'Shut up! You are all betraying me! No one tells me the truth!'

When Günsche left the study, Bormann, who had been present the while, caught up with him and also screamed, 'How dare you betray the Führer?' He too was clearly gradually losing his self-control.

Günsche riposted, 'Herr Reichsleiter, what I told the Führer was fact. What do you mean by "betray"?'

Bormann just said, 'Forgive me, but here you can really go out of your mind.'

At around 11.00 p.m. General Weidling,[13] the commander of LVIII Panzer Corps, appeared in the bunker. Günsche took him to Hitler in the conference room. A few days before, the Russians had forced Weidling and the remains of his corps back to Berlin. The unit had suffered the most terrible losses, and their artillery and all their technical support were gone. Because the city commandant of Berlin had been badly wounded on 25 April and there was no successor, Burgdorf had suggested appointing Weidling. When Günsche came in with him Hitler was already there with Goebbels, Bormann, Krebs and Burgdorf. You could read it on Weidling's face that he was not enthusiastic about taking on the command of Berlin in this desperate situation.

He declared that he was entirely conscious of the whole gravity of his task and would assume responsibility only if he alone commanded the Berlin garrison and no one else could meddle in his affairs. Hitler consented. Weidling had hardly been two hours at his command post in the Bendlerstrasse when Hitler began blithely to interfere with his commands. It happened like this: at 1.30 a.m., there appeared in the bunker the commander of a Berlin district, a Lieutenant Colonel Bärenfänger, whose troops were fighting in the Frankfurter Allee and in the Alexanderplatz. He had been summoned by Goebbels and was received by Hitler in the presence of Goebbels and Günsche. His uniform was covered in oil and grime, and he himself was unshaven and black with soot. He had come straight from the fight around his battle position in a U-Bahn tunnel under the Alexanderplatz. He reported to Hitler on the bitter fighting on the streets of Berlin which was being shifted more and more into cellars and U-Bahn tunnels. Horrible scenes were taking place because a large part of the civilian population had taken refuge there.

Hitler interrupted Bärenfänger to ask whether stun gas had been used in the U-Bahn and other underground tunnels. The Warsaw Uprising had mostly taken place in cellars and the use of stun gas against the fighting population had had excellent results.* The effect had been extremely good. Bärenfänger replied that he had no stun gas and complained that his superior officer, a general major, had given him the ridiculous order to abide by the laws of war. At this Goebbels cried, 'My Führer! You must sack the general major forthwith!'† 'He is dismissed, and you, Bärenfänger, have replaced him. I shall promote you to general major!' Hitler declared. He shook the hand of the young officer he had just promoted general major and withdrew into his study to continue drinking tea with Eva Braun and his secretaries and talk about the best way of committing suicide.

Fegelein returned from the Steiner Army that day, landing on the east–west axis in his Fieseler-Storch. He reported to Hitler that the Steiner Army's attack had finally ground to a halt. In his report he laid particular stress on the fact he had sought every possible way of making it succeed and that Steiner had done everything that was humanly possible. But Hitler would not let Fegelein finish and growled, 'Steiner does not want to attack. That's it.'

After Fegelein had delivered his report to Hitler, he told Günsche in confidence that he had gone on from Steiner to see Himmler, whose special train was still stationed west of Hohenlychen in Mecklenburg, and spoken to him. Under an oath of secrecy he told Günsche that Himmler had prevented the Steiner Army from attacking, by which he had sought to drive home to Hitler that there was no hope of breaking the Russian ring round Berlin and that he should finally leave. SS-General Steiner had enjoyed Himmler's protection for a long time and was blindly loyal to him. Günsche said nothing to Hitler about what Fegelein had told him, because he wanted nothing more than that Hitler should leave Berlin.

But Fegelein had lied to Günsche. The real reason why Himmler would not let the Steiner Army attack became clear the next day.

On the morning of 27 April heavy shelling once again to hit the Chancellery. There was a quick succession of explosions on the roof of Hitler's bunker. As soon as the first one went off, Hitler rang for Linge.

---

*The SS and the Wehrmacht had used flame throwers and smoke canisters. They also sprayed targets with the disinfectant creosote which led to asphyxiation when used in concentrated amounts.
†The general was General Major Werner Mummert, commander of the Müncheberg Panzer Division.

Linge found him in the study fully dressed. A strange noise had joined the more usual humming of the ventilators, and Hitler, looking irritably at Linge, asked what it meant. Linge learned from the mechanic Hans Hentschel that the raging fires in the Chancellery garden had caused a wind to blow up that created the noise in the ventilators. The chauffeurs' and servants' wooden barracks were burning. They had been moved there when the HQ took over the Chancellery.

When the hail of shells petered out, Hitler told Linge he wanted to go out into the garden to see how it looked now. Slowly, with his hand gripping the banister, Hitler dragged himself up the steps to the emergency exit. Linge was right behind him, as he was afraid that Hitler, who had grown much weaker of late, might fall backwards. On the last step Linge went past Hitler in order to open the armour-plated door. At that moment a shell landed right next to the bunker. As Linge turned round towards Hitler the Führer had already turned on his heel and was trying to get back to his apartment as quickly as possible. Once he had got there he dropped into an armchair, completely exhausted. In his eyes you could see naked fear. Breathing heavily he said to Linge, 'I have been thinking about things: I shall not shoot myself together with Fräulein Braun in the garden, but here in the bunker. Have some blankets ready to wrap round our bodies, so that we can be carried into the garden and burned there.' Straightaway Linge deposited blankets in the antechamber and in Hitler's bedroom.

Between 10.00 and 11.00 a.m. a message came in from Wenck. He informed them that his advanced units had reached Ferch am Schwielowsee, ten to twelve kilometres west of Potsdam. The news spread like wildfire through the bunker. Everywhere you could hear happy voices and laughter. Maps and street plans of Berlin were brought out to see how far it was again from Potsdam to Berlin. People were slapping one another enthusiastically on the shoulders. Everyone hoped that the Wenck Army would join up with Reymann's corps in Potsdam at midday. From there to Berlin was just twenty kilometres. As is usual in such situations, everybody said what they wanted to hear: 'This evening Wenck will be in Berlin.' Some people laid wagers whether Wenck would reach the Chancellery before nightfall. This time they knocked back the schnapps for joy.

Goebbels came out of Hitler's study and dashed into his quarters, where Naumann was waiting for him. 'The Wenck Army is coming closer and will liberate us. I must now spread the word!' Goebbels shouted to Naumann and began immediately to draft the text for the leaflet. The newspaper *Der Bär* appeared no longer. The leaflet would give the words of Wenck's radio message together with his signature. There would also be a commentary from Goebbels. In lying, hackneyed words he incited Berlin's population to hold out. He wrote that Wenck was already at the gates of Berlin. The moment when the capital would be freed was not long off.

The denizens of the bunker waited impatiently for new reports from Wenck, Hitler included. He went backwards and forwards in his apartment and asked for news from Krebs about Wenck's position every few minutes. At the time Below, Günsche and Johannmeyer were sitting in the conference room, trying soberly to work out the position. On the Eastern Front the Russians had inflicted defeat after defeat on the Germans, despite the fact that they possessed gigantic reserves and had concentrated the entirety of Germany's technical resources there. On the Dnieper, the Vistula, the East Prussian border, the Narew and the Oder they had built mighty fortified positions, but even then German armies shrank back ever further towards the west under Russian blows or in massive battles against the Russians. And now the Wenck Army was to bring the Russian avalanche to a halt!

As the radio transmitter was cut off again that day, no more than fragmentary messages came in from Wenck. Only towards evening was the position clarified a bit. Wenck's attack stopped in its tracks. His army was sitting still north-west of Potsdam, under an onslaught from Russian forces. In the area of Beelitz and Michendorf they were hitting his flank, pushing him on to the defensive and making some of his units retreat.

At around 12.30 p.m. Krebs, Burgdorf, Weidling, Johannmeyer, Loringhoven and Günsche assembled in the conference room. A few minutes later Hitler came in followed by Bormann. He was deteriorating every day. It was an effort for him to move his legs as he walked. He didn't notice any more if someone was smoking in his presence. His handshake was limp. As he sat down on a chair Lorenz walked in, then Goebbels and Naumann, who in recent days had become participants.

Krebs had no new information from Wenck. He asked Hitler's permission to give the order for Busse's Ninth Army to break through to Berlin. It was fighting heavy defensive battles against the Russians in its position west of Frankfurt on the Oder. Hitler, however, ordered that the Ninth Army be directed to join up with the Wenck Army and to break the ring around Berlin together. Those present exchanged astonished looks. The Ninth Army had been surrounded by Russian troops for over a week already and had received no supplies. How was it to break through to the Wenck Army! The soldiers would be able to break out of the encirclement only if they left all their heavy equipment and munitions behind. By doing so their battle worthiness would be reduced to zero. And Hitler wanted to reinforce the Wenck Army's offensive with these soldiers!

After Krebs it was Weidling's turn to report. He described how hopeless Berlin's position was. The Russians had already occupied all the suburbs and peripheral areas of Berlin. In many places the outer defences had been pushed back to the inner defensive ring. In preparation for the defence of Berlin, two defensive rings had been created. The outward one ran around the city border, the inner one around the city centre. In the Tiergarten, the Humboldthain and Friedrichshain well-fortified gun emplacements had been built. Besides these there were flak batteries in the Shell skyscraper and the Tirpitzufer that played an important role in the inner defensive ring and were almost entirely intended for ground battles.

Weidling went on to report that in the north-eastern part of the city Russian troops had advanced to the Alexanderplatz, to the S-Bahn station at Wedding in the north, past Lichterfelde and Zehlendorf in the direction of Steglitz, Wilmersdorf, Friedenau and Halensee in the west. Then he described how heavy the battles in Berlin were. In the air, on the streets, in the U-Bahn tunnels and in the cellars of Berlin houses there were bitter battles raging. Now that the struggle had reached the city centre Russian troops could use the U-Bahn tunnels to emerge behind the backs of German units, which had caused a critical situation. Hitler had listened to Weidling's briefing calmly without making any comment. With an impassive look on his face he now ordered that the locks on the Spree be opened and the U-Bahn tunnels flooded to make them impassable. Hitler was told that the tunnels contained thousands of Berliners and wounded soldiers looking for shelter, and that they would drown if the locks were to be opened. This made no impression on Hitler.*

When Weidling had left, Hitler summoned Mohnke. The protective ring garrisoned by Mohnke's battle group around the government district had been attacked by Russian tanks in several places. They were exerting particularly heavy pressure on the Spree bridges, on the Tirpitzufer and on the Potsdamer Strasse, the Hallesche Tor and the Lustgarten. Hitler ordered Mohnke to blow up the bridges over the Spree.

Axmann arrived to see Hitler after lunch. As the Hitler Youth detachments on the Pichelsdorf Bridge, on both sides of the Heerstrasse and the Olympic Stadium had been surrounded by the Russians, Axmann had established his quarters in the Party Chancellery bunker on the Wilhelmstrasse and now came to see Hitler daily. He had a slight, thirteen-year-old boy with him and reported to Hitler that the boy had ambushed a Russian T-34 tank and destroyed it with an anti-tank grenade. The boy

---

*They were not opened. Occasionally water came in because of an exploding bomb or shell.

was dressed in the tropical uniform of the German Afrika Korps, which was way too big for him. Hitler received him like a worthy general and with a florid gesture pinned the Iron Cross on his chest. Axmann cried out movingly: 'My Führer, you can count on your boys!' Hitler raised his hand in salute and sent this adolescent back into the hell of battle, where he was to continue to fight so bravely. Then he shuffled back in to his apartment.

At around 9.00 p.m. Weidling was back on the spot to inform Hitler of the situation. In the antechamber he told Burgdorf, Krebs, Johannmeyer and Günsche that he had needed half an hour to drive from his command post on the Bendlerstrasse to the Chancellery, a journey that normally took three or four minutes. The streets were covered with bomb craters and ruins and the tram cables were dangling from above. To add to this he had to dodge the continuous fire of the Russian artillery and the attacks of Russian bombers.

Hitler came into the room with his lips pressed tightly together. He was followed by Bormann and Goebbels. He welcomed Weidling then went into the conference room. A bit later Naumann, Axmann and the assistant Gauleiter of Berlin, Schach, appeared. In the last few days Schach had also been invited to hear the situation reports. This time only Weidling spoke. He reported again on the heavy fighting in every district of Berlin. Then he described the terrible position of the Berliners, who had been stuck in their cellars or in the U-Bahn stations for more than a week without food or drink. The hospitals were bursting at the seams with thousands of soldiers and civilians. Because the Russians had occupied the East and West Spree Harbours where the most important supplies of food lay for Berlin's population, there was only enough food left for another two days.

Krebs reported that the Russians had finally beaten off the Wenck Army's attack and that there was now no question of Berlin being relieved. As a result the fall of Berlin was only a matter of days away. Weidling urgently requested that Hitler decide to leave Berlin with the rest of the garrison and to break though in the south-west in the direction of Potsdam, where the Wenck Army was. 'My Führer, I shall answer for this with my head, I will get you out of Berlin safe and sound. That way we can save the capital and its population from its final destruction!' There was a deathly hush in the room. All eyes stared hopefully at Hitler. But he merely hissed through his teeth, 'No!' Weidling sought one more time to talk Hitler round, by explaining his plan for the breakthrough. He proposed that Hitler be put in a heavy tank of the Tiger sort, which would be covered by other tanks of the same type and would take him out of Berlin. Hitler rejoined, however, 'Weidling, I have made my decision. I am staying in Berlin.' And he left the room.

That evening saw the wedding of two SS soldier-servants. At 7.00 p.m. the marriage was celebrated in the common room of the old bunker, where Hitler's bodyguard had their quarters. They were married by the State Secretary in the Propaganda Ministry, SS-Brigadeführer Werner Naumann. The witnesses were Linge and Schädle. Both wore steel helmets and pistols in their belts. The guests at the wedding were Hitler's adjutants, the officers of his bodyguard and the SD as well as the SS batmen. Naumann was also dressed in a steel helmet. He declared solemnly that the exchange of vows was taking place at a memorable time under a hail of shells from the Russian artillery in a Berlin in the throes of battle. But the relief of the capital was nigh, and the young couple had many years of untroubled fortune ahead of them.

After the wedding Linge gave a meal for the newly weds in the old bunker. As the wedding guests sat down at table in the hall of the old bunker, Krebs, Bormann and Burgdorf hurried over to Hitler's bunker. Twenty minutes later they came back at the same speed. They recounted that the Wenck Army had finally been brought to a halt by the Russians. Universal hopelessness reigned. Linge rushed back to Hitler's bunker to find out what the Führer was doing. He saw how he wandered down the corridor with an absent look on his face, hanging his head and staring at the floor. Hitler didn't notice Linge until he addressed him and reported that two servants were enjoying their wedding in the old bunker: didn't he want to congratulate them? Hitler nodded. Linge went back and fetched the young couple, together with the mother of one of the two, and took them into the corridor that connected the old and the new bunkers. Hitler was already standing there. He greeted the newly weds with a limp handshake and said, 'Children, I wish you the very best.' Then he went back.

After the congratulations the mood sank even lower among the guests. Above all it was the women who were shocked by Hitler's appearance. They became silent and pensive. Linge had champagne and cognac brought in. The wedding turned into a drinking bout. Alcohol restored morale. Dancing and merriment continued until the next morning.

On this day a report was picked up on a foreign radio station – if memory serves correctly, Swedish. This maintained that Himmler was carrying on negotiations with the Swedish count Bernadotte to conclude a separate peace with the British and the Americans. Lorenz took this report to Hitler. He had Bormann and Hewel summoned. On the same day the preconditions for the negotiations became known in the bunker: Hitler would be deposed and his place taken by Himmler. The struggle with Soviet Russia would then continue with the support of Britain and

America. Himmler wanted to remove Hitler by force. Now it was clear why Himmler had held the Steiner Army back from attack. He wanted to hold it in reserve in case of a separate peace with the Anglo-Americans. Pressed by Russian forces during the fall of Berlin, the Steiner Army headed west and gave itself up to Anglo-American captivity.

The news of Himmler's negotiations with Bernadotte provoked a terrible tantrum from Hitler. He bellowed, 'They will not push me out so easily!' He immediately sacked Himmler from all his positions and threw him out of the Party. Bormann, who had been a close friend of Himmler's for years and called him *Du*, told Günsche in a lachrymose voice, 'Fate spares the Führer nothing at all: first Göring, then Himmler.'

A little while later Hitler called for Fegelein, but he was nowhere to be found, either in the New Chancellery bunker or in Hitler's. Among the few who still remained with Hitler, the suspicion was instantly aired that Fegelein might have deserted from Berlin. Bormann and Burgdorf, who were both good friends of the missing man, rushed over to Günsche and asked if Fegelein had betrayed any such plans to him. Günsche said no. The Fieseler-Storch that Fegelein had flown into Berlin the day before had been destroyed by a direct hit on the east–west axis. He could not, therefore, have left Berlin by plane. Then Günsche recalled that Fegelein had a flat in the Bleibtreustrasse near the Kurfürstendamm.

That evening a detachment of Hitler's bodyguard under the command of SS-Obersturmführer Hermann Frick was sent to this address. They found Fegelein there. He was dressed in mufti and lying dead drunk on his bed. He had hidden his uniform behind the stove. Also in the flat there was an Obersturmführer from the cavalry division 'Florian Geyer', which Fegelein had commanded. He too was howling drunk, and told them he was Fegelein's orderly officer. There was a suitcase filled with gold watches and other valuable objects in the flat. The night before Fegelein had shown it to Linge and other SS officers in the bunker, and observed that it had been found at the home of the head of the National Socialist Physicians' League, SS-Obergruppenführer Dr Grawitz, who had shot himself and his family in the villa when the Russians appeared in Berlin.*

On Hitler's orders Fegelein and the other officer were brought to the New Chancellery Bunker that same night. The officer immediately admitted under interrogation that Fegelein had planned to flee Berlin. He wanted to wait until the Russians tanks had passed the Bleibtreustrasse

---

*The head of the NS Physicians' League was Leonardo Conti; Ernst Grawitz was the chief SS doctor. It was Grawitz's case.

and then push off to the west. Hitler decreed that Fegelein be punished by being assigned to the Mohnke Battle Group where he should 'prove his loyalty on the battlefield'. Bormann brought Günsche Hitler's order with the task of delivering Fegelein to Mohnke. Günsche was stunned that Hitler should punish the deserter Fegelein with just front-line duty. Only a few days before he had ordered that all deserters were to be hanged, with a placard on their chests inscribed with the legend 'I am hanging here because I did not carry out the Führer's orders.'[14] Now he wanted to let his brother-in-law off as lightly as possible. Günsche told Bormann that he would not carry out the order until he had spoken to the Führer. He immediately went in to see Hitler.

He was sitting with Eva Braun in his study. She was sobbing wretchedly and Hitler was trying to comfort her. When Günsche came in she went into her room. Günsche told Hitler that, if he assigned Fegelein to Mohnke, he would still desert. He tried to convince him not to pack Fegelein off to the Mohnke Battle Group, but to put him before a court martial as a deserter. Hitler was silent for a while. It was clear that he was vacillating and wanted to save Fegelein because of Eva. Then abruptly and with reluctance he said, 'Fegelein to be demoted and put before the court. The president will be Mohnke.' Günsche took the order to Mohnke immediately. With several SS officers Mohnke went to Fegelein, who at his arrest had put on the uniform of a general of the SS. Mohnke tore off his stripes. Fegelein was not wearing medals.

On 28 April Russian multi-barrelled mobile rocket launchers of the Katyusha type began to attack the government district and the bunker.[15] All hell was let loose outside. Hitler jumped out of bed and rang for Linge. As the latter came in, Hitler was crouching by the table in his study and staring with wide, horrified eyes at the ceiling. Once again he asked, 'What is the calibre?' 'They are Stalin Organs.' That is what the German soldiers had baptized the dreaded rocket launchers of the Katyusha type. There had been frequent talk of Stalin Organs during the briefing – Hitler had been specially informed about them many times. It was stressed that the missiles had a devastating effect, that they covered a large area and that they caused inevitable panic among German soldiers. The position of the launchers was hard to determine because they were mounted on lorries and frequently changed position so they could fire from different places.

When Linge spoke of Stalin Organs, Hitler looked at him uncomprehendingly and asked, 'What do you mean, Stalin organs? Something like the colonnade in the New Chancellery?' Plainly his mind was disturbed.

He naturally knew what a Stalin Organ was. Besides which his second question did not follow on from the first – about the calibre of the shell. Linge sought to enlighten him once more what these missile launchers were all about. Hitler said nothing.

At 9.00 Mohnke had Günsche called on the telephone. With a voice cracking with tension he said that the Russians had gone over to the attack at the Hallesche Tor. Fierce battles were raging on the Belle-Alliance-Platz and on the corner of the Wilhelmstrasse. Mohnke added that the telephone connections between his command post and the regiments of his battle group were broken. He had sent out messengers and hoped soon to have a clearer picture of the situation.

Günsche relayed Mohnke's report to Hitler and showed him on the city plan where the battles were currently raging. When Hitler heard that the Russians were getting closer to the Wilhelmstrasse, he started. His eyes positively devoured the map. From the Chancellery there were only 1,200 or 1,300 metres to go. In great excitement Hitler asked if the Russians had already reached the Wilhelmstrasse and what sort of forces Mohnke had at his disposal on the Belle-Alliance-Platz. He walked up and down the room, then slumped into a chair and ordered that Mohnke be called. Mohnke appeared soon after and informed Hitler that they had been able to halt the Russian advance on the corner of the Belle-Alliance-Platz and the Wilhelmstrasse. Now they were advancing in the direction of Gleisdreieck and Anhalt station.

The news of how menacingly close the Russians already were spread quickly through the bunker. The occupants stood around in groups everywhere talking agitatedly to one another. Goebbels went from one group to the next and asked questions. Then he asked Linge too, 'Tell me, is the situation really already so serious?'

That morning Dr Stumpfegger came into Hitler's study and asked him for a signature. Linge was standing next to him when he put the paper down on the desk. It was a request to the hospital in the bunker in the New Chancellery to hand over twelve cyanide pills on Hitler's orders. Hitler signed with a shaky hand. The twelve pills were meant to poison Eva Braun, Hitler's secretaries Frau Christian and Frau Junge, the diet cook Fräulein Manziarly, Bormann's secretary Frau Krüger, Eva's chambermaid Liesl, Goebbels's children and Hitler's German shepherd dog Blondi.

At lunch Hitler was told that the supplies of dietary food had been used up. They could make only a vegetarian soup for him. Did he want to eat the same as everybody else? Hitler replied, 'Soon we won't need to eat anything at all. Bring me soup.'

In the afternoon it was reported that the situation in the outer districts of Berlin was rapidly deteriorating. Because the government district was being constantly shelled Weidling came from his command post in the Bendlerstrasse only once a day to make his report. Any reports that came in the meantime he relayed by telephone to Krebs, who briefed Hitler in turn. Mohnke often came to see Hitler to report to him on the situation in the government district. The immediate danger to the Chancellery now came from the direction of Belle-Alliance-Platz and the Hallesche Tor. Here the Russians had advanced the furthest. The second major threat came from the direction of the Tiergarten and the Zoo.

Weidling reported that Russian tanks had advanced on both sides of the Heerstrasse as far as the street Am Knie and had therefore reached the east–west axis. Charlottenburg was occupied by the Russians. The ring around the government district was being tightened by the hour. No one spoke of the Wenck Army in the bunker any more. 'How long can we hold out? Are there any ways of getting out of Berlin now?' These questions were now on everyone's lips.

At 6.00 Axmann came to see Hitler. He declared in the presence of Bormann and Günsche that he had 200 selected members of the Hitler Youth at his disposal who knew Berlin like the backs of their hands. With their help he could get Hitler out of Berlin safe and sound. As a born Berliner himself he also knew every corner of the capital and would lead the group. Hitler refused Axmann's offer just as he had Weidling's proposition the day before. He shook Axmann's hand and thanked him for his loyalty.

In the evening Bormann wholly unexpectedly informed Linge that Hitler and Eva Braun wanted to be married. The ceremony was to take place in the conference room. Recently the only things heard in the room had been reports of bitter and bloody fighting in and around the streets of Berlin. Here Hitler had issued the order to open the locks in the Spree which would bring death to thousands of soldiers and peaceful citizens. Here he had ordered that Berliners who hung out red or white flags at the Russians' approach were to be hanged. Despite all that, this room was to be the place where Hitler and Eva Braun would seal the knot.

Bormann directed Linge to rearrange the furniture a little. The table on which operations maps were generally laid was moved to the centre of the room. In front of the table four chairs were to be placed: two in the front for Hitler and Eva Braun and two behind for Goebbels and Bormann, who were to be the witnesses. Goebbels called in a civil servant from the Propaganda Ministry who would carry out the civil ceremony. His place likewise was at the table. Bormann them went to Hitler, who was sitting in his study, to tell him that everything was ready for the ceremony.

Hitler and Eva Braun left their apartment hand in hand and went into the conference room. Hitler took each step with a great effort. His face was ashen, his gaze wandered restlessly. He was wearing the crumpled tunic in which nowadays he lay on his bed all day. He had pinned on to it the Gold Party Badge, the Iron Cross First Class and the Wounded Medal of the First World War. Eva Braun, also pale from sleepless nights, wore a dark-blue silk dress under a fleecy grey fur cape. Goebbels and Bormann were waiting for them in the antechamber. The latter had put on the grey uniform of an SS-Obergruppenführer. Goebbels wore the brown Party uniform. In the conference room Hitler and Eva greeted the functionary who had taken up his position at the table. Then they sat down in the first two chairs, and Bormann and Goebbels too went to their assigned places. The door was closed. The ceremony lasted no longer than ten minutes. Bormann opened the door again when Hitler and Eva were signing the licence. Hitler then kissed Eva's hand. She was now his wife. He ordered that the table be laid for a wedding tea in his study. Goebbels and his wife were invited together with Bormann and the secretaries Frau Christian and Frau Junge.

At the same time as Hitler sealed the knot with Eva Braun, another official process was taking place in the New Chancellery bunker – the court martial of Hitler's brother-in-law SS-Gruppenführer Hermann Fegelein, Himmler's permanent representative at Hitler's HQ. Mohnke presided over the bench. The other judges were officers from his battle group: SS-Obersturmbannführer Krause, Sturmbannführer Kaschula and others. Mohnke and his officers sentenced Fegelein to death. Under the pretext that Hitler wanted to see him, Fegelein was led out of the New Chancellery bunker that same night. On the way an SD official despatched him with a bullet in his back.

When the wedding tea was over that night, 28 April, Hitler summoned his secretary Frau Junge to his study. He dictated his will to her. She typed it together with Bormann's secretary, Frau Krüger, on the typewriter in the bunker's common room. Hitler reworked it several times, before ordering three copies to be prepared in the final version. In this document Hitler maintained he had never sought war and that he had dedicated his entire life to the German people. He dictated the composition of the new government. His successor – not as 'Führer' but as 'President' – was to be High Admiral Dönitz, Goebbels was Reich chancellor, Count Schwerin von Krosigk foreign minister, the Gauleiter of Bavaria, Giesler, minister of the interior, and Schörner commander in chief of the armed forces. Bormann was to remain leader of the Party with ministerial rank.*

On Hitler's orders his military adjutant Johannmeyer was to carry a copy of the will to Schörner in Czechoslovakia, another was to be taken by Obersturmbannführer Lorenz to Dönitz in Schleswig-Holstein and the third was to be brought by Bormann's assistant Standartenführer Zander to Giesler in Tegernsee in Upper Bavaria. That night, Johannmeyer, Lorenz and Zander took their leave of Hitler, who told them they would receive copies of the will from Bormann on the morning of 29 April. That day, at 4.00 a.m., Johannmeyer, Lorenz and Zander appeared before Bormann, who was waiting for them with Günsche in the antechamber in Hitler's bunker. All three were wearing camouflage and steel helmets and were armed with machine guns. Bormann gave each of them a white envelope bearing the Führer's seal and containing Hitler's will. They were to break though the Russian lines. Weidling, the commander of Berlin and Mohnke, received orders to let them pass through his units unhindered.

At 5.00 a.m. it was quiet in the bunker. The only thing that could be heard was the hum of the air conditioning and the buzz of the diesel unit in the machine room. Günsche settled into a chair. His peace was short lived. Bormann, sobbing, came into the antechamber with Burgdorf. Krebs followed. All three had had too much to drink. Bormann was waving a bottle of cognac and immediately poured out several full glasses. Hiccuping loudly, he told Burgdorf, 'If the Russians take me alive, I still have my pill.' With a nervous gesture he took a little tube about three or four centimetres long out of his pocket, unscrewed the top and showed Burgdorf an oval glass capsule that was filled with green cyanide.†
Groaning, all three men tumbled into chairs and very soon loud snores were to be heard.

At around 6.00 a.m. a firestorm generated by Russian artillery and mine-throwers suddenly began to rage again over the government district. Shells of every size crashed into the Chancellery and exploded menacingly on the roof of the bunker. Hitler was immediately on his feet and hurrying over to Goebbels. There he also found Goebbels's wife, who had just

---

*The posts were as follows: Reich President, Dönitz; Reich Chancellor, Goebbels; Foreign Minister, Seyss-Inquart; Interior Minister, Giesler; Minister of War, Dönitz; Commander of the Army, Schörner; Commander of the Navy, Dönitz; Commander of the Air Force, Greim; Reichsführer-SS and Chief of Police, Hanke; Economics, Funk; Agriculture, Backe; Justice, Thierack; Education, Scheel. Schwerin von Krosigk was made Foreign Minister in Flensburg.
†Calium cyanide is colourless. The green might have come from the wax seal.

come over from the old bunker where she lodged with the children. Frau Goebbels was weeping copiously and had trouble standing up. A few minutes later the duty officer in Hitler's bodyguard came to see Linge and brought Hitler's order to take his Gold Party Badge and deliver it to Goebbels's room. Linge took the badge from Hitler's tunic and brought it to him. Hitler handed his own badge to Frau Goebbels and told her he was decorating her for her 'brave behaviour'.

At around 10.00 a.m. Russian fire was concentrated in the area of Friedrichstrasse and Unter den Linden. Mohnke rang Günsche and informed him that Russian tanks were advancing into Wilhelmstrasse and towards Anhalt station. Günsche reported this to Hitler, who was sitting with Eva Braun and Bormann on the bench in the antechamber. They all looked at one another silently. No one said a word. Hitler ordered Mohnke to come to him, but would not let him speak. He asked him immediately how long he could hold out. Mohnke hesitated before telling him that he hoped he could manage another day. He had not even left the bunker before new bad news came in: 'The Russians have gone over to the attack on both sides of the east-west axis.' And shortly afterwards: 'Russian tanks are at the Technical University!'

Hitler lay down on his bed fully dressed, but he found no repose. He kept coming out and asking for news, having Mohnke fetched, speaking to Krebs and Burgdorf then going inside. In the afternoon there was a new report: 'The Russians were trying to reach the Chancellery though the U-Bahn tunnel.' Hitler, Eva Braun, Goebbels, Bormann and the secretaries gathered in the antechamber. Hitler played with Wolf to conceal his agitation. Bormann drank schnapps. Goebbels, who by now had turned completely grey, smoked non-stop and stared into the middle distance. Eva occasionally whispered a few words to the secretaries. Suddenly in the corridor: 'The Russians are firing machine guns at the emergency exit door!' 'Russian snipers are sitting on the roofs of the ministry buildings all around!' They all jumped up. The SS men in Hitler's bodyguard and the SD donned steel helmets and ran through the antechamber to the emergency exit.

The excitement in the bunker had reached its high point. Only towards evening did the mood calm down a little. At 8.00 Weidling and Mohnke arrived for the briefing. Their reports were extremely short, as the battles in Berlin were now being played out in a limited area and the German lines were only a few kilometres long. After Weidling and Mohnke had left, Hitler summoned Axmann, who had moved into the New Chancellery bunker that day. In the presence of Bormann, Goebbels and Günsche, he invested him with the German Order Second Class,* which was granted only to the highest officers of the National Socialist Party, and only very seldom, together with the Iron Class First Class. He told Axmann that he was one of the few who had remained loyal to him.

At 12.00 a.m. Hitler went down the underground passage to the old bunker. Here Mohnke and Günsche had formed the secretaries and typists from Hitler's adjutants' pool and Mohnke's command post into a line. Hitler gave each of them his hand and said softly, 'Thank you, children.' Drunken voices could be heard coming from neighbouring rooms. Günsche explained to Hitler that Rattenhuber (the Chief of the RSD) was celebrating his birthday there. Rattenhuber emerged and ran up to Hitler, grabbed his hands and began to kiss them. Hitler stiffly congratulated Rattenhuber on his birthday and shuffled back to his apartment.

The night was spent waiting for the Russians. Everywhere the voice of alcohol could be heard. After midnight the shelling abated a little. In the hall of the bunker Professor Haase was standing with Sergeant Tornow, Hitler's dog handler. Haase was holding a phial of cyanide in one hand and a pair of tongs in the other. Hitler had given him the job of poisoning Blondi. Hitler wanted to try out the cyanide on her. At midnight it was administered to the bitch in the lavatory, Tornow opening her mouth and Haase pushing in the phial with the tongs. The poison had an immediate effect. Shortly afterwards Hitler went into the lavatory to ascertain whether Blondi was really dead. He said nothing, nor did his face express any feeling. A minute later he went back into his study. At this time Günsche and Mohnke were sitting together by the telephone switchboard. They were silent, drank strong coffee laced with cognac and indulged their thoughts.

The Russians in the meantime had advanced from the Zoo into the Tiergarten, and their tanks had reached the Reichstag. On the Prinz-Albrecht-Strasse between the Anhalt station and the Potsdamer Platz they were standing only 300 metres from the Chancellery, while battles were being fought in the Friedrichstrasse, the Prinzenstrasse and the Spittelmarkt. That was how the situation looked in the Chancellery as night fell on 29 April. A decision would have to be made the next day.

What was Hitler waiting for? Günsche asked himself this question more and more. Then he remembered what Hitler had told his field marshals and generals a year and a half before: 'When Germany's last moment sounds, I hope that you, my field marshals, will join me with drawn swords

---

*On 28 April 1945 Axmann received the Golden Cross of the German Order.

fighting on the barricades.'* They were just empty words. Hitler was too much of a coward even to look out of his bunker. In the few hours fate had left for him he was seized by the fear that the Russians could make their way into his bunker.

When it came to the fiasco on the Eastern Front, Hitler had been just as clueless as his generals. During the entire course of the war, right up to the last minute, the generals had done all they could to curry favour with Hitler. Kowtowing one moment, flattering the next, giving only positive reports from the front, never a contradiction, just day in day out the same old song: 'Yes indeed, my Führer!' 'Of course, my Führer!' 'At your command, my Führer!' 'You can rely on me, my Führer!' Gleefully they had received gifts and medals from his hand, but achieving victory over the Russians was beyond their abilities. That Field Marshal von Manstein, who had famously leaped up after Hitler's peroration and had cried out, 'Führer, command and we will obey!', had no problem accepting the highest military distinction, the oak leaves with swords for his Knight's Cross, and a 4,000-mark salary increase.[16] When Hitler dismissed him as Supreme Commander of Army Group South in the summer of 1944 after serious failure in the Ukraine and Crimea he happily went off to his family and his estate.

Goebbels's frail face appeared in the doorway of the telephone exchange. Slowly, limping badly, he approached Günsche and Mohnke and offered them cigarettes. He had become taciturn and spoke very little now. Only a few days before, he had lied to Berliners when he called on them to continue their senseless resistance. Now he asked softly in a distraught voice, 'What do you think, gentlemen? Can I sleep peacefully tonight? Or are the Russians already upon us?'

Even on the night of 29 April, Hitler would not abandon his habit of stretching out his evening tea until morning. On this night Eva Braun, now Frau Hitler, Frau Christian, Frau Junge and Fräulein Manziarly kept him company. It was to be Hitler's last tea evening. At 5.00 a.m. the secretaries and Fräulein Maziarly left Hitler's study with tears in their eyes. Frau Junge reported to Günsche that Hitler wanted to shoot himself that day, because the Russians could force their way into the bunker at any moment. Hitler had finally taken his leave of them. He had also said farewell to Eva, as she wanted to commit suicide as well. Frau Junge recounted that Eva had given her several valuable things – clothes and the fur that she had worn at her wedding. In addition she had made her a present of a little pistol, which Hitler had once given her. Frau Junge handed them over to Günsche.

---

*The Russian editors have garbled the quotation on p. 131.

The rest of the night was spent waiting for the Russians. There were intimations of death everywhere. Bormann, Burgdorf, Krebs, Hewel and Voss lay down in the chairs in the antechamber. The secretaries spent the night on mattresses in the conference room. The rest lay down on their beds fully dressed with loaded pistols at their sides.

At 8.00 a.m. on 30 April Hitler dictated to Bormann in his study the order to the Battle Group Mohnke to break out of the government district. After Hitler's suicide this unit should attempt to escape from Berlin in small groups to join up with German troops who were continuing the struggle. The order was typed out by Bormann's secretary Frau Krüger on the 'Führer sheets' and signed by Hitler. At 10.00 a.m. Hitler summoned Mohnke. When he came out of Hitler's study, radiant with joy, he showed Linge the signed order.

At dawn the hellfire of the Russian artillery had broken out again, crashing down on the Chancellery. It went on all day and sounded like unremitting, heavy thunder. At 2.00 p.m. Bormann emerged into the antechamber from Hitler's study looking pale and confused. He went straight up to Günsche and whispered distractedly in his ear, 'Good that you're here. I wanted to send for you at once.' He told Günsche that Hitler and Eva Braun wanted to bring their lives to an end that day. Their bodies were to be drenched in benzene and burned in the garden of the Chancellery. That was Hitler's categorical order. Under no circumstances should his body fall into Russian hands.

'This is the end then,' thought Günsche, and shuddered: the Führer is to be covered with benzene and burned. He was not so impressed by Bormann's information any more anyway. Hitler was as good as dead. Hitler did not have the courage or the strength to die a soldier's death, which in these last days he had required of German officers and soldiers, even of women and children. Hidden behind the thick walls of his bunker he wretchedly strove to spin out the verdict of fate for as long as he could. Only when the Russians stood on the doorstep of the Chancellery did he attempt an undignified suicide, and not before he had ordered that his body be burned.

Bormann asked Günsche to make sure that everything was made ready for the burning of the body at the top flight of stairs leading to the emergency exit. 'We, the Führer's loyal followers who have remained by his side to the end, will render him this last service,' Bormann declared hypocritically. He left the antechamber, dragging his feet. Günsche remained alone. He immediately called Mohnke and asked him to come to Hitler's bunker. A few minutes later Rattenhuber, Baur and Betz made their way, distraught, into the antechamber. They had just run into Bormann and had learned from him that Hitler wanted to take his own life. Now they assailed Günsche with questions. He was just going to answer when the door opened and Hitler came out. Rattenhuber, Baur, Günsche and Betz shot their hands up in salute. Hitler did not react but in a tired voice merely asked them to come closer. Betz stood a little further away. Hitler turned to him. 'You too, come nearer. You can listen calmly.'

Hitler's eyes, which had once spat fire, were snuffed out. His face was the colour of the earth, and he had dark rings under his eyes. The shake in his left hand seemed almost to have taken over his head and body. The lines came out almost monotonously: 'I have ordered that I am to be burned after my death. Make sure that my order is carried out to the letter. I will not have it that they take my body back to Moscow to exhibit in a cabinet of curiosities.' Hitler traced a lethargic gesture of farewell with his right arm and turned round. Baur and Rattenhuber cried out. Rattenhuber tried to grab Hitler's hand, but the Führer parried him and disappeared behind his study door.

Mechanically but at great speed Günsche set about carrying out Hitler's and Bormann's orders for the burning of Hitler's and Eva Braun's bodies. He summoned Hitler's chauffeur Kempka, who was living in the bunker next to the Chancellery garage in the Hermann Göring Strasse, and asked him to bring ten canisters of benzene to the Führer bunker immediately and to leave it in readiness at the emergency exit to the garden. When that had been done, Günsche informed Kempka of Hitler's intention to take his own life. Then he ordered the SS men of the bodyguard and the Security Service who occupied the little room by the emergency exit to vacate the room and find another place. He even ordered the sentries who stood by the armour-plated door which led from the stairway to the emergency exit to go back into the bunker. Just one man, SS-Untersturmführer Hofbeck, did he leave by the emergency exit with the order to let no one pass. Then Günsche went into the hall of the bunker and took up his position by the antechamber door, while he waited for the fateful shot. His watch read 3.10 p.m.

A little later Eva Braun came out of Hitler's study into the small antechamber. She looked sad as she gave Linge her hand and said, 'Goodbye, Linge. I hope that you get away from Berlin. If you run into my sister Gretl, don't tell her how her husband died.' Then she went to Frau Goebbels, who was in her husband's room. A few minutes later Eva left Goebbels's room and went to the telephone exchange, where Günsche was to be found. She said to him, 'Please tell the Führer that Frau Goebbels has asked him to come to see her one more time.'

Günsche strode to Hitler's study. For the moment Linge was not to be seen, so he knocked and walked in. Hitler was at the table. When he saw Günsche unannounced before him he took fright. 'What is it then?' he growled crossly. Günsche announced, 'My Führer, your wife informs you that Frau Goebbels would like to see you once again. She is with her husband in his room.' Hitler thought for a while then went across to Goebbels's room. At 3.40 Linge came into the telephone exchange where Hitler's servant Krüger was standing with a sentry. Nearby in the common room in front of Goebbels's bedroom Hitler stood with Goebbels, who was trying to convince him for the last time to leave Berlin. Hitler, however, replied in a hysterical voice, 'No, Doctor! You know my decision. It is not going to change!'

Hitler then went into Goebbels's bedroom, where Frau Goebbels and Eva Braun were at the time, and took leave of Frau Goebbels before going back to his apartment. Linge and Krüger followed him. At the door to the study Linge asked him if he might say goodbye to him. Hitler answered him tiredly and dispassionately, 'I have given orders to break out. Try to fight your way through to the west in small groups.' 'My Führer, who should we be fighting our way through for now?' Hitler turned to Linge and stared at him for a while in silence, then he announced pompously, 'For the coming man!' He said goodbye to Linge and Krüger with a limp handshake and raised his right arm. Linge and Krüger stood to attention and raised their arms to salute Hitler for the last time. Then they closed the door to his study and rushed over to the old bunker. 'You have seen and heard nothing,' Linge cried out as they went.

Eva Braun allowed two or three minutes to elapse before she left Goebbels's room. She walked slowly back to Hitler's study. A few minutes later Goebbels came out and headed towards the conference room, where Bormann, Krebs, Burgdorf, Naumann, Rattenhuber and Axmann were gathered.

After a little while Linge returned to Hitler's bunker. In front of the open armour-plated door to the antechamber stood Günsche with SS-Obersturmführer Frick, who was on duty that day. It was now a few minutes to four. As Linge walked past Günsche, he remarked, 'I think it's over,' and quickly went into the antechamber. There he smelled gunpowder, as if from a shot. He rushed out of the antechamber and unexpectedly ran into Bormann, who was standing, with his head hanging, next to the door to the conference room, his hand resting on the table. Linge reported to Bormann that there was a smell of gunpowder in Hitler's antechamber. Bormann stood up straight and together with Linge he dashed into Hitler's study. Linge opened the door and walked in with Bormann. They were presented with the following picture: on the left-hand side of the sofa sat Hitler. He was dead. Next to him was a dead Eva Braun. In Hitler's right temple gaped a bullet wound the size of a Pfennig and two streams of blood ran down his check. On the carpet next to the sofa a puddle of blood the size of a plate had formed. The wall and the sofa were bespattered with blood. Hitler's right hand lay palm uppermost on his knee. The left hung at his side. Next to Hitler's right foot lay a 7.65mm Walther pistol, and next to his left foot a 6.35mm of the same make. Hitler wore his grey tunic emblazoned with the Gold Party Badge, the Iron Cross First Class and the Wounded Badge of the First World War — as he had done constantly in recent days. He was wearing a white shirt with a black tie, black trousers, black socks and black leather slippers. Eva Braun's legs were drawn up under her on the sofa. Her brightly coloured high-heeled shoes lay on the floor. Her lips were firmly pressed together. She had poisoned herself with cyanide.

Bormann rushed out into the antechamber to call the SS men who were to carry the two bodies out into the garden. From the antechamber Linge fetched the blankets he had left there to wrap Hitler up in and spread one of them on the study floor. With the help of Bormann, who had come back again, he laid Hitler's still-warm body on the ground and wrapped him in the blanket.

Günsche now ran into the conference room, throwing open the door so violently that Goebbels, Krebs, Burgdorf, Axmann, Naumann and Rattenhuber took fright. Günsche cried out, 'The Führer is dead!' Everyone rushed into the antechamber. At that moment Linge came out of the study bearing Hitler's body, followed by the SS men Lindloff and Reisser. Hitler's feet, in their black socks and slippers, stuck out from under the blanket as his corpse was carried though the antechamber to the emergency exit and the garden. Goebbels, Burgdorf, Krebs, Axmann, Naumann, Günsche and Rattenhuber, standing in the antechamber, raised their arms in salute. The next to emerge from Hitler's study was Bormann followed by Kempka, who was carrying Eva Braun's corpse in his arms. Goebbels, Axmann, Naumann, Rattenhuber, Krebs and Burgdorf followed Hitler's corpse to the emergency exit. Günsche walked over to Kempka and relieved him of Eva Braun's body, which had yet to be wrapped up, and carried it to the emergency exit. It smelled strongly of cyanide. Günsche sprinted up the steps, past Goebbels, Axmann, Naumann, Burgdorf, Krebs and Rattenhuber, who were standing at the top.

Because of the heavy artillery barrage, they did not go out into the garden. Hitler's shrouded corpse now lay on the ground two metres from the entrance to the bunker. Günsche put Eva Braun down on his right. Bormann bent over Hitler, uncovered his face one more time and stared at him for several seconds. Then he pulled the blanket over him again. Shells were whistling and howling all around as they landed in the Chancellery garden. Thick clouds of smoke hung over the shredded trees. The Reichs Chancellery and the adjoining buildings were burning fiercely.

Bormann, Günsche, Linge, Lindloff, Kempka, Schädle and Reisser grabbed canisters filled with benzene that were standing there in readiness and poured all 200 litres over the corpses of Eva Braun and Hitler. For a long time the benzene refused to ignite, as the strong wind that had been generated by the fires kept blowing out the matches. In the end Günsche grabbed a hand-grenade that was lying in the entrance, in order to light the benzene, but before he could throw it Linge managed to ignite a piece of paper and toss it on to the bodies, thereby setting the benzene alight. Hitler's and Eva Braun's bodies were instantly engulfed in flames. The door to the bunker had to be quickly slammed shut against the encroaching fire. Bormann, Goebbels, Axmann, Naumann, Krebs, Burgdorf, Günsche, Linge, Schädle, Kempka, Reisser and Lindloff lingered awhile at the top of the landing, then went back down into the bunker in silence.

Günsche went into Hitler's study. Nothing had changed. The two pistols still lay on the floor next to the pool of blood. Günsche picked them up and took out the bullets. As he did so he ascertained that the fatal shot had come from the 7.65mm gun. The other one was also loaded, with the safety catch off. Günsche put them in his pocket and later handed them over to Axmann's adjutant, Lieutenant Hamann. He also gave him Hitler's dog-whip. Hamann wanted to keep them safe as relics for the Hitler Youth.

Next Günsche crossed over to the conference room, to which Bormann, Goebbels, Axmann, Burgdorf, Krebs, Mohnke and Naumann had repaired. Decisions had to be taken on what to do next. Bormann, Axmann, Mohnke and Günsche insisted on escaping. Goebbels was opposed. Theatrically he declared, 'I shall now go out on to the Wilhelmsplatz. Perhaps I shall be hit by a bullet!' Bormann was so nervous that he couldn't stand still. He kept calling out, 'Can no one procure me a Storch? I really have to get to Dönitz. It is very important.' One could see naked fear in Bormann's eyes: getting out of this hell – that was his only thought and his heart-felt wish. He was not thinking about Hitler any more. There was just one thing that mattered: 'How do we get out of here?' Finally the new 'Reich Chancellor' Goebbels proposed making contact with Russian High Command and attempting to secure a ceasefire, for a few hours at least. It was clear that Goebbels only wanted to postpone the end for a while, as he could not seriously have believed that such a plan had any chance of success. Krebs's advice was to wait until General Weidling appeared in the bunker — he was supposed to brief Hitler's conference at 5.30. Günsche went to the telephone exchange. He could hear Frau Goebbels sobbing through the half-open door of her husband's bedroom: 'What is to become of me and the children? The Führer should not have done it . . .'

In the meantime Linge had told Krüger and the batman Schwiedel to pull up the blood-stained carpet in Hitler's study. All three looked for the cartridge cases that must have been ejected from the gun when it went off, but they could not find them. They dragged the carpet outside and burned it in the garden. Linge himself burned all the papers that lay on the desk, including the reports from the German News Agency. Hitler's study now contained nothing but the furniture. Linge took the portrait of Frederick the Great that hung over the desk out of its frame and gave it, as Hitler had wanted, to his pilot Baur. Baur hid it under his jacket.

Hitler's dog-handler, Sergeant Tornow, was running around the New Chancellery bunker in a state of total drunkenness shouting, 'The Führer is dead, save yourselves if you can!' Panic broke out among the inmates, particularly the wounded. It became clear that Tornow had just shot Blondi's puppies in the garden, including Wolf, Eva Braun's and Frau Christian's dogs and his own. He was arrested.

At 5.30 Weidling appeared in Hitler's bunker. Goebbels informed him of Hitler's death and of the composition of the new government. Bormann, Goebbels, Axmann, Krebs, Burgdorf, Weidling, Mohnke, Günsche and Naumann took part in the ensuing conference at which they discussed the plans for breaking out of the Chancellery or for asking the Russians for a temporary ceasefire. After much wavering, the second plan was adopted. It was decided that the Head of the Operations Department on Weidling's staff, Colonel Dufving, should be sent as an envoy to the nearest Russian command post.

At 7.30 that evening Dufving left the bunker and passed through the German lines around the Chancellery to the Russians. At around 11.00 he was back. He reported that the Russians would not listen to him as he was not carrying any authority on him. That same night Goebbels and Bormann despatched Krebs to the Russian High Command, where he was meant to negotiate as Chief of the General Staff. His return was impatiently awaited.[*]

When Linge emerged from his billet on the morning of 1 May, he ran into Goebbels in the bunker's antechamber. After they had said hello, Goebbels said in a hoarse voice, 'Tell me, Linge – could you not have stopped the Führer from committing suicide?' Linge riposted, 'Herr Doctor, if you could not manage it, how do you think I would have been able to do so?' Goebbels went on, 'I have had a horrible night. I have also decided to bring my life to an end; but it is a very difficult moment. I have been arguing with myself for ages, but I lack the courage.'

At around midday Krebs returned with the news that the Russian High Command demanded unconditional surrender. At 6.00 p.m. Burgdorf summoned Mohnke and Günsche to the New Chancellery bunker. Weidling and Dufving were already present. When Mohnke and Günsche entered, Weidling was just taking a piece of paper out of his pocket and telling Dufving, 'Oh, before I forget, the Führer had promoted you colonel. Congratulations.' On a little table Weidling laid out a city plan of Berlin. He informed Mohnke and Günsche that the remnants of the Berlin garrison were going to make an attempt to break through the Russian lines and escape from Berlin that evening at 10.00. After he had gone into certain details he asked Mohnke which direction he was thinking of taking with his battle group. Mohnke showed him on the map his planned route to the north-west via Tegel. The meeting then came to an end, and Mohnke and Günsche left the room. From the other side they heard loud hammer blows: the radio station and the telephone exchange of Führer HQ were being destroyed in accordance with instructions.

Mohnke went back to his command post to prepare the order for the break-out. Günsche informed Linge, Schädle, Högl and Kempka that the garrison was planning to escape that evening. He told Bormann, Voss, Hewel and Stumpfegger that they should make themselves ready to depart. He also informed the women – Frau Christian, Frau Junge, Fräulein Krüger and Fräulein Manziarly – who had not taken Hitler's advice to kill themselves. They elected to go with the men.

---

[*]Krebs was the obvious choice, as he had been based in Moscow in 1933. He spoke to the commander of the Eighth Soviet Guard Army, General Vassily Chuikov, at 4.00 a.m. and offered him a truce. Chuikov spoke on the telephone to Marshal Zhukov, who told Stalin. As Krebs had no authority to sign an unconditional surrender there was no result and Krebs returned to the bunker at midday.

At 8.00 p.m. Günsche, Linge, Schädle and Kempka went to Mohnke's command post. The soldiers of the battle group lay in the corridors, passages and rooms of the New Chancellery bunker on chests, on benches or on the ground. They slept in the most unnatural positions with their steel helmets and weapons at their sides, exhausted by the endless heavy fighting. Between them lay the wounded, groaning. At short intervals, when Russian artillery fire slackened off, the latter were carried off in stretchers to the hospital that had been set up in the cellar of the half-bombed-out Hotel Adlon on the Linden. Those who had already expired from their wounds were carried into the Chancellery garden to be buried. The stream of wounded men never ceased. Wild screams of agony and groans rang out in all the rooms. Tobacco smoke, sulphur, carbolic and the stench of overflowing lavatories mixed with the stale air. It was enough to make one throw up.

Axmann, Naumann, Albrecht, Rattenhuber and several officers from the battle group had already made their way to Mohnke's command post. Mohnke read out the order to escape, which also decreed by what stages the Chancellery was to be evacuated. The first group was to be commanded by Mohnke himself. It was to be composed of Günsche, Hewel, Voss, Frau Christian, Frau Junge, Fräulein Krüger and Fräulein Manziarly, as well as Hitler's Escort Company under the command of Obersturmführer Doose. The second group, under the command of Naumann, was to comprise Bormann, Schach, officials of the Berlin Nazi Party and a Volkssturm battalion from the Propaganda Ministry. The third group, headed by Kempka, was made up of Linge, the soldier-servants, Hitler's bodyguard and the Chancellery drivers. A fourth group was commanded by Hitler's personal adjutant, Brigadeführer Albrecht, and consisted of the staff of Hitler's adjutants. The fifth group under Rattenhuber was made up of Baur, Betz, Högl and the members of the SD. The sixth group led by Axmann was composed of 200 Berlin boys whom he had brought into the bunker a few days before to get Hitler out of Berlin. When Hitler had refused their services, Axmann kept them on for his own use.

The break-out was to go ahead according to the following plan: after leaving the Chancellery the six groups were to take the U-Bahn tunnel to Kaiserhof station, and from there proceed as far as possible towards Wedding. In small groups they could use the side streets to get past the Stettin station and Tegel and move in a north-westerly direction to reach the German forces fighting there.

Günsche left Mohnke's command post to inform Linge, Schädle, Kempka and Högl of the details of the escape plans. At 10.00 p.m. Günsche said goodbye to Hitler's ADC Burgdorf and the Chief of the General Staff, Krebs. They did not wish to take part in the escape attempt, but preferred to shoot themselves in the *cour d'honneur* at the moment the Russians came in. Burgdorf explained, 'As a young officer in 1918 I lived through the defeat of Germany in the First World War. I was young then and full of strength. Now I am too old and too dispirited.' Then Günsche took his leave of the Gestapo Chief, SS-Gruppenführer Müller, who told him that he was going to shoot himself in the Chancellery, as he had no desire at all to fall into Russian hands alive.

Günsche next went to Goebbels to say a last adieu to him and his wife. Frau Goebbels was sitting in a chair in the depths of despair. She just stretched her hand out silently to Günsche and withdrew into Goebbels's bedroom. Goebbels's face was ashen. He was almost inaudible when he spoke: 'I am going to shoot myself with my wife here in the bunker. I hope that you get out of Berlin safely.' Goebbels took out a cigarette, gave Günsche his hand and likewise disappeared into his bedroom.

Now Günsche went across into the New Chancellery bunker. The groups had assembled there at 9.30 for the break-out. At 10.00 Goebbels's adjutant Schwägemann and the valet Ochs came from Hitler's bunker to join their group. They told Linge the following: Goebbels and his wife had shot themselves a few minutes before in the bunker. Naumann, Schwägermann, Ochs and others had soaked the bodies with benzene in Goebbels's bedroom and set fire to them.[*] After that they had problems getting out of the bunker themselves as the fierce draught that had been unleashed by the flames had made the armour-plated door slam shut.

A few hours before, at 4.00 p.m., when Linge was still in Hitler's bunker, Hitler's doctor Stumpfegger had performed the task assigned to him by Goebbels and had killed his five children, mixing poison into their coffee. Frau Goebbels waited for Stumpfegger outside the door. When he came out, he nodded to her as a sign that the children had been poisoned. She fainted and two SS men from Hitler's bodyguard carried her back to her husband's bedroom.[†]

Around 2,000 people left the Chancellery. Most of them were armed with machine guns, automatic pistols, revolvers and anti-tank weapons. They left with the Mohnke Battle Group, which was composed of some

---

[*] Others maintained that they shot one another in the garden. This version was accepted by Soviet Military Counter-Intelligence.
[†] There are other versions of the killing of the children. In one Stumpfegger gave them a sleeping draught and later poisoned them with Magda Goebbels.

3,000 men and several Tiger tanks, self-propelling guns, anti-tank guns, mine-throwers and heavy machine guns. The hospital remained in the New Chancellery bunker under the direction of Professor Haase.

Shortly after 10.00 p.m. the first group left the bunker under Mohnke's orders. Besides eighty to a hundred soldiers there were Günsche, Hewel, Voss, the secretaries Frau Christian, Frau Junge and Fräulein Krüger, the diet cook Fräulein Manziarly and several officers from the Mohnke Battle Group. In small parties they crossed the New Chancellery's *cour d'honneur* and went out on to the Wilhelmsplatz through the great arch before running to Kaiserhof U-Bahn station. From there they reached Friedrichstrasse station through the tunnel. The tunnels, and the stations above all, were crammed full of soldiers and civilians. Weeping children and hysterical, screaming women were everywhere, along with soldiers either uttering curses or giving orders. The situation at Friedrichstrasse station was particularly chaotic. Here the tunnels had been barricaded up and rendered impassable. One could get out only in small groups, as the exits were covered by Russian mortars.

One part of the Mohnke group was lost in the crowd. Mohnke with some of his people managed finally to leave the U-Bahn and get across the Weidendamm Bridge to the other side of the Spree. From there they made it through the courtyards of the Charité Hospital and, via connecting cellars, on to the Chausseestrasse. From there they passed the Maikäfer Barracks and arrived at Wedding station. The group had been reduced to twenty to twenty-five persons, including – besides Mohnke himself – Günsche, Hewel and the four women, Frau Christian, Frau Junge, Fräulein Krüger and Fräulein Manziarly. The streets were deserted and many houses were burning. This part of the city had suffered little shelling up to now. They unexpectedly ran into a brace of T-34 tanks which were controlling a crossroads and which fired on them with their machine guns, forcing them to retreat. They tried to negotiate the back streets, but without success. The little group was becoming noticeably smaller. In the end only Mohnke, Günsche, Hewel and the four women remained.

Before noon on 2 May they reached the big air-raid shelter next to the brewery on the Schönhauser Allee. This contained several hundred German soldiers from every sort of unit. The cellar housed the command post of divisional commander General Major Rauch and the commander of the Parachute Division, Colonel Herrmann. Together with Rauch and Herrmann and a few other officers, Mohnke and Günsche tried to redeploy the soldiers and continue the break-out. Gradually more and more officers and men from Mohnke's battle group turned up, plus

SS officers from Hitler's bodyguard and the SD as well as several members of Hitler's personal staff who had left with other groups. Among them was the head of the SD, Rattenhuber, who had been slightly injured in the leg.

At 3.00 p.m. Russian units approached the air-raid shelter in the Schönhauser Allee. Russian officers came to Rauch's and Hermann's command post and declared that the Berlin garrison had capitulated the night before.[*] In order to avoid further bloodshed, they requested that the Germans lay down their arms and give themselves up. They asked Rauch and Hermann to accompany them to the nearest Russian staff post, where Berlin's capitulation would be confirmed. Günsche advised Hitler's secretaries and Fräulein Manziarly to leave the air-raid shelter and to break through on their own. They agreed and Mohnke gave Frau Christian a little sack filled with diamonds. The gems had been intended for the making of important medals, and it had been Burgdorf's job to look after them. He had handed them to Mohnke when his group left the Chancellery.

At 4.00 p.m. Mohnke, Rauch and Günsche drove with one of the Russian officers to Russian army HQ. There a Russian general confirmed to them that Berlin's Commandant, General Weidling, had capitulated during the night of 1 May. The general declared, 'Now this horrible war has come to an end. We should all rejoice in that.'

Mohnke, Rauch and Günsche returned to the air-raid shelter escorted by the same officer. It was now 10.00 p.m. The remaining German officers and men had already given themselves up. The air-raid shelter and a few adjoining rooms were now occupied by the Russians. As Mohnke, Rauch and Günsche went in, they ran into Hewel, SS-Standartenführer Professor Schenck, a lieutenant colonel and several young officers who had hidden from the Russians in another room. Mohnke told them it was all over. Russian officers came in and demanded that they lay down their arms and follow them. At that moment Hewel whipped out his pistol and shot himself. The others handed over their weapons and followed the Russian officers.

The third group to break out, the one to which Kempka and Linge belonged, left the New Chancellery bunker at 10.30 p.m. It contained more SS men from Hitler's bodyguard as well as his drivers and soldier-servants.

When Linge and Kempka and the group emerged into the Vossstrasse, the government district was being subjected to a continuous Russian

---

[*]A truce had entered into force on the morning of 2 May. A few hours later General Weidling signed the order for unconditional surrender.

artillery barrage. In the darkness only ruins were to be seen. Everywhere half-destroyed façades pointed up to the skies. Thick clouds of smoke billowed out of dark window-frames. On streets pitted by bombs and shells lay beams, bricks and pieces of masonry. The skies were bright from the reflections of so many fires. Linge, Kempka and the others ran past the ruins to the Wilhelmplatz U-Bahn station. From there they followed the tunnel to Stadtmitte station, before running across the ruined Friedrichstrasse to the station of that name. At the other end of the Weidendamm Bridge soldiers of the Mohnke Group were fighting the Russians, who were pinning them down with fire from houses in the Chausseestrasse. The German soldiers were trying to get through with the help of tanks, but they did not succeed.

Linge saw from the other side of the bridge how Bormann and Naumann jumped on to a German tank that was driving by, in order to get through the Russian lines. He also saw that a grenade was thrown at the tank. At the same time Albrecht, Högl and many members of Hitler's adjutants' pool were killed on the Weidendamm Bridge. Linge lost Kempka in the confusion and joined the rest of a troop of Mohnke's battle group, which together with a hundred civilians managed to get through the U-Bahn tunnel from Friedrichstrasse to Seestrasse. Among them was the Assistant Gauleiter of Berlin, Schach.

On the morning of 2 May Russian soldiers informed this group too that Berlin had capitulated during the night. They requested that they give themselves up. Schach shot himself on the spot.* Linge and the other members of the group went into captivity.

On 8 May Germany capitulated. Here ended the epoch of the Third Reich, which according to Hitler should have lasted a thousand years. When he came to power he had promised the German people, 'If I remain in power for ten years, you will no longer recognise Germany.' And that was true: after Hitler's rule Germany was no longer the same. It lay in ruins. Hitler himself had ended his life in suicide in terror of the Russians.

---

*This is false. Schach went into captivity and after his release lived in Lower Saxony.

Editors' Afterword

The Hitler Book was put together in the years 1948 to 1949. Since then more than a thousand biographies of Hitler have been published, as well as more than 10,000 works on the National Socialist regime, on the genocide of European Jews and on the Second World War. With Ian Kershaw's detailed 1998 biography of the German dictator, research on Hitler the man came to a temporary halt.[1] There have been many biographies published on the Soviet autocrat and both lives were compared by Alan Bullock in 1991.[2] That there are still details of Hitler's life that remain to be researched has been demonstrated by Anton Joachimsthaler in several books.[3] More revelations are to be expected from research in Russian archives, which contain not just the documents of the Soviet ministries, the secret police and the armed forces, but also large collections of plundered German archives. Access to the Russian archives is nonetheless limited: Western historians usually find that they are not permitted to carry out research on their own. But it was information from the Soviet secret police in 1945 and 1946 that gave rise to the compilation of the NKVD dossier, *The Hitler Book*. This volume therefore offers a glimpse of the conclusions reached by the 1945–6 Russian investigations.

Adolf Hitler, Führer and Chancellor of the German Reich, killed himself on 30 April 1945 at around 3.30 p.m. by shooting himself in the right temple. Joseph Vissarionovich Stalin, General Secretary of the Communist Party of the Soviet Union, President of the State Committee for Defence and President of the Council of the People's Commissars, received the news some thirteen hours later, on the morning of 1 May. At around 5.05 a.m. local time, his personal secretary Alexander N. Poskrebyshev received the following telegram: 'Urgent, Top Secret! From General Zhukov to Comrade Stalin. The Chief of the General Staff, Infantry General Kreps [sic], appeared at the HQ of the 8th Army and declared the following: on 30 4 at around 15.50 Berlin time Hitler ended his life by suicide.'[4] Five hours after this first report, Marshal Georgi Zhukov transmitted further details together with an offer to open peace negotiations by the new Reich Chancellor Joseph Goebbels. Stalin refused: it was not enough, and he demanded unconditional surrender. On the death of his enemy, he apparently remarked, 'It is therefore all over for him. What a pity that we didn't get him alive. Where is Hitler's corpse?'[5] Stalin received no further information until four days later. The GRU, or Soviet military intelligence, had captured and interrogated General Helmuth Weidling, Hitler's naval liaison officer Vice Admiral Hans-Erich Voss and Hitler's chief pilot Hans Baur. All three testified that Hitler was dead, and that his body had been burned in the Reich Chancellery garden.

The head of the military intelligence service, Colonel General Fyodor F. Kuznetsov, informed Stalin immediately afterwards in a five-page briefing 'on the fate of Hitler, Goebbels, Himmler and Göring'. According to the prisoners, Hitler and Eva Braun had first poisoned themselves and then shot themselves. Immediately afterwards both bodies were burned in the Chancellery garden. Goebbels, his wife and their six children were also dead and had been identified by Vice Admiral Voss. Their bodies were being held by the 39th Rifles. No details were known of the fates of Himmler and Göring. Kuznestov informed Stalin, however, of the peace negotiations between the SS-Führer and the Western Allies and of the fact he had been thrown out of the Nazi Party. Göring, the report continued, had sought to remove Hitler from power. The German dictator had taken measures against him immediately afterwards, but nothing more about this was known for the time being.

That same day, 5 May, officers from another Russian secret-service contingent dug up the mortal remains of Hitler and his wife. Soldiers from the Military Counter-Espionage Department – Smersh* – belonging to LXXIX Rifle Corps of the Third Assault Army had already discovered the bodies the day before. As they believed that the remains of Hitler and Eva Braun were still lying in the Chancellery building, however, they reburied the corpses. On the morning of 5 May the intelligence men realised their mistake and quickly dug 'two badly burned bodies' and the bodies of two dogs out of a bomb crater some three metres from the emergency exit of the bunker. The remains were wrapped in blankets and packed into two ammunition cases. The Smersh men secretly smuggled the corpses to their new HQ in Berlin-Buch, as the duty of guarding of the Chancellery had

---

*The name Smersh derives from the Russian words *Smert' shpionam*, which mean 'death to spies'. The organisation reported to the People's Commissariat of State Security, or NKGB, headed by Viktor S. Abakumov. Another, rival secret police organisation was the People's Commissariat of Internal Affairs, or NKVD, headed by Lavrenti Beria. The military GRU was a further rival.

in the meantime been taken over by the Fifth Assault Army and they wanted no valuable trophies to fall into its hands.

Three days before, on 2 May, the Red Army in Berlin had captured more members of Hitler's immediate entourage. SS-Sturmbannführer Otto Günsche, personal adjutant to the Führer since February 1944, gave himself up to Soviet forces at the Schultheiss Brewery on the Prenzlauer Berg. To begin with, the SS man claimed that he was the adjutant to the former Battle Commander of the Chancellery, SS-Brigadeführer Wilhelm Mohnke. A few days later the truth came out. On 6 May Soviet officers discovered his real identity and removed him from the other prisoners. The first interrogations by members of the GRU military intelligence began at once. Only two days later GRU chief Kuznetsov told the head of the NKVD, Lavrenti Beria, that they had made their first interim report about this questioning of Günsche.

On the same day, at the field surgical hospital No. 496 in Berlin-Buch, an autopsy was carried out on a total of eleven human corpses and the bodies of two dogs by a medical commission led by the chief coroner of the 1st Belorussian Front, Lieutenant Colonel Faust I. Shkaravsky. Those eleven corpses were the already clearly identified remains of General Krebs, Goebbels and his wife and six children as well as the presumed remains of Adolf Hitler and Eva Braun. In their report the coroners maintained that, in respect of all the bodies, the probable cause of death was 'poisoning by cyanide.' Only the dogs' bodies showed clear signs of shooting, though in one animal they had nonetheless discovered evidence of cyanide.[6]

Smersh's officers vacillated when it came to transmitting the autopsy results to the Soviet leadership. The autopsy, the circumstances surrounding the discovery of the bodies and the statements of the witnesses were contradictory, because the overwhelming conclusion was that Hitler had shot himself. The counter-intelligence officers therefore interrogated more witnesses. They were faced with the problem, however, that all the people they had been able to find up to now from Hitler's closest entourage knew the facts from hearsay. The Smersh officers were unable to present real eye-witnesses to the suicide. So they waited for the dental examination of the two bodies that had yet to be positively identified. On 11 May the dentist Professor Hugo Blaschke and the dental technician Käthe Heusermann stated that the bodies in question were those of Hitler and Eva Braun. The head of military counter-intelligence on the 1st Belorussian Front, Lieutenant General Alexander A. Vadis, informed Stalin only on 27 May of the results of the autopsy that had been carried out on the 8th. Smersh informed the Soviet dictator that Hitler and Eva Braun had clearly committed 'suicide by swallowing cyanide compounds'.

One should add that when the NKVD chief Beria forwarded to Stalin Vadis's letter, he did so without attaching a covering note. He evidently feared that he would be directly associated with the results of the Smersh investigation carried out by his rival Viktor S. Abakumov. The disparities between the report of the autopsy carried out by Shkaravsky, the verdicts of the resulting coroners' commission and the witnesses were all too obvious. No one concluded that the death had been caused by gunshot.

When on 16 June Stalin finally received the minutes of the autopsy and the coroners' analysis of the tests on the organs, Beria decided to interfere with the evidence in the investigation. In order to prevent the Soviet dictator from learning of the disparities, he removed from the dossiers two analyses that had been carried out by the 291st Medical and Epidemiological Front Laboratory in June. The chemists had examined a total of thirty organ and twelve blood samples for cyanide and alkaloids from the autopsy carried out in Berlin-Buch on 8 May. The tests on organ material from the autopsies numbered 1 to 11 – that is, the Goebbels family, General Krebs and the dogs – revealed significant traces of Prussic acid, but 'in the material relative to the minutes of Nos 12 and 13 no cyanide compounds were discovered'. And the autopsy reports Nos 12 and 13 probably relate to the corpses of Adolf Hitler and his wife. In order to maintain the theory of cyanide poisoning which had been accepted up to now, documents that contradicted that theory were not shown to Stalin for the time being. Shooting was considered the honourable way out; poison was for dogs. As a result the dictator showed himself satisfied with the results of the Smersh investigation.

By this time Günsche had already been transferred to the NKVD's Main Administration for Prisoners of War and Internee Affairs (GUPVI). The first to interrogate him in the middle of May was assistant head of the GUPVI, Lieutenant General Amayak S. Kobulov, and the head of his operations, Lieutenant Colonel Fyodor K. Parparov. The statements given by Günsche and by the head of the RSD, SS-Gruppenführer Johann Rattenhuber, who was interrogated at the same time, went directly to Beria. As these statements had not yet been verified, he hesitated to forward them to Stalin. On 18 and 19 May there were more interrogations conducted by Kobulov and Parparov. Once again they dwelt on the question of Hitler's death: 'When did he decide to die?', 'Who determined he was dead?', 'Who poured the benzene over the bodies, and who lit it?' A little while later Günsche was flown to Moscow and taken to the NKVD's prison, the Butyrka, where it dealt with POWs and internee affairs.

In the meantime SS-Obersturmbannführer Heinz Linge, head of Hitler's personal household, had arrived in Moscow. On the night of 2 May Soviet soldiers had captured him in the U-Bahn station Seestrasse after the break-out from the Chancellery. He was brought unrecognised to the POW camp near Posen, where his true identity was uncovered. A little later the NKVD transferred him to the Lubyanka in Moscow, where the first interrogations began in November 1945. As in the Günsche case, what the secret police wanted to ask him about was Hitler's death.

A month before, the leadership of the Soviet secret police had begun to have its first doubts about the version of Hitler's suicide that they had accepted up till now. The British and American intelligence services had handed over their own research material to Colonel General Ivan A. Serov, the representative of the NKVD in the Soviet Zone of occupied Germany in mid-November 1945, which pointed clearly to death by gunshot. At the same time the Western Allies requested access to the results of the Soviet investigation. While Beria and his assistants Sergei N. Kruglov, Vsevolod N. Merkulov and Bogdan S. Kobulov were in favour of making the Soviet material available to the British and Americans, the Smersh chief Abakumov raised serious objections and asked for a personal talk with the head of the NKVD. For Abakumov it seemed perfectly clear that the Western Allies would immediately spot the weak points in what was chiefly his investigation, and this would cast serious doubts on the version fed to Stalin of how the German dictator had committed suicide. Beria now saw his chance to cause trouble for a rival in the struggle for access to Stalin. So in December 1945 the NKVD chief ordered fresh inquiries into the exact circumstances of Hitler's suicide.

At the end of 1945 new interrogations were carried out to establish the background to Hitler's suicide. His former chief pilot Hans Baur had been questioned. Beria wanted to be sure above all that the dictator was actually dead, as there were still rumours that he might have escaped the clutches of the Russian army at the last moment and been whisked abroad. At the same time Beria hoped to learn how Hitler had actually killed himself. The interrogations of Linge and Günsche, as well as comparison with the testimonies of people imprisoned by Smersh who had belonged to Hitler's immediate circle, led the NKVD leadership to instigate the operation codenamed Myth at the beginning of 1946. The goal of the operation was to conduct an 'accurate and strict investigation of all the factors' involved in Hitler's suicide on 30 April 1945.

Beria commissioned the GUPVI to undertake Myth. In the middle of February 1946 they presented a 'plan for agent-investigation measures for the elucidation of Hitler's disappearance'. The plan required, first, all those in NKVD custody who had belonged to Hitler's immediate circle to be transferred to the Butyrka and, second, the formation of a five-man special commission under the presidency of Lieutenant Colonel Julius K. Klausen. That meant that Linge, Baur and the latter's cellmate Rochus Misch, the former Chancellery telephone operator, were transferred from the Lubyanka to NKVD custody elsewhere.* The purpose of these measures was to compare all the interrogations and statements, given that the various reports had served up so many contradictions about the circumstances of Hitler's death. The prisoners were kept rigorously apart. Their interrogation was only a part of the plan – the GUPVI had also suggested that 'each prisoner subject to investigation be provided with a cell agent'. What this unwieldy bureaucratic terminology signified was a common or garden stoolpigeon. So as not to rely only on statements, every cell was fitted with listening devices. Also the other individual departments for POWs and Internee Affairs received orders to hand over to the special commission all the information they had gathered so far on Hitler's suicide. At the same time the POW camps around Moscow were directed to find more prisoners who had been part of the garrison of the Führer Bunker in the last days of the Third Reich. In POW camp No. 297 in Mozhaisk they managed to track down SS-Untersturmführers Hans Hofbeck and Josef Henschel, former members of the Reich Security Service (RSD) who had belonged to the Chancellery Guard. They were immediately transferred to the Butyrka. The search for other witnesses in the camps controlled by the GUPVI, however, proved fruitless.

It remains striking that the NKVD made no attempt to contact their rivals, Smersh or the GRU. Nor did GUPVI ask the People's Commissariat for State Security (the NKGB) to interrogate the witnesses they had in custody, such as Hans Rattenhuber, nor did they ask for the transfer or copies of the documentary material assembled by the GRU on the Hitler case. Only Beria would have had access to all the material.

There are two features here that are of particular importance for the later *Hitler Book*. The first is the strict secrecy surrounding the entire investigation. Besides Beria the only people who had any knowledge of Myth were the Minister of the Interior, Kruglov, the Soviet NKVD chief in the Russian Zone, Colonel General Ivan A. Serov, the head of GUPVI, Lieutenant General Michael S. Krivenko, his assistant Amayak Kobulov and the head of the Operational Administration of GUPVI, General Major

---

*Baur had been badly injured in both legs. Misch had been ordered to assist him.

Viktor A. Drosdov. As far as the rest were concerned it demonstrated the strict separation and rivalry among the institutions of the Stalinist dictatorship. In the interests of his compartmentalised rule Stalin made sure that his secret services avoided all contact with one another and that the quasi-totality of intelligence was concentrated in him.

The NKVD interrogations were set for the middle of February, and were accompanied by the usual techniques of torture – beatings, sleep- and food-deprivation, threats against families – and simultaneously offers of reward for co-operation. The initial resistance on the part of the witnesses was quickly broken. The most effective means by far was the removal of the prisoners' POW status on 27 February 1946 and their classification as war criminals. After being robbed of their uniforms and dressed in the standard prisoners' clothing, with their rations reduced to the appropriate Soviet levels, most of them submitted. The use of stoolpigeons as cellmates proved just as effective. With the usual German efficiency, they provided the NKVD interrogators with useful information, and observed extremely accurately the effects of the interrogators' methods of intimidation. Thus Agent 'B-III' gave the following information on Baur on 20 February 1946: 'He is very frightened of reprisals and expects to have a hard time with the interrogations. At the same time his injured leg gives him discomfort, as does the fate of his family and the question of how long he will have to stay in prison. When he thinks he will be tortured he regrets that he did not kill himself.' It is hardly surprising that Baur was beaten by an interrogation officer a few days later.

Linge's cell stoolpigeon 'Bohemia' made an attempt at a psychological interpretation: 'Linge has a good memory and is simply playing the role of someone who is sick with nerves, of a naïve person. During the interrogations he is sloppy and maintains that there is only one person who can substantiate what he says, and that is Bormann.' Only the next day the stoolpigeon asked the interrogation officer to go on with his hard line as it was having an effect: 'Linge is now getting cold feet. If he could be interrogated roughly for a few days, he will come out with a more truthful statement.'

Only in Günsche's case was the stoolpigeon unable to work his way into the prisoner's trust. The SS officer distrusted his cellmate deeply, with the result that the man was scarcely able to make worthwhile reports. During the interrogations that were carried out between mid-February and the end of March 1946 the NKVD officers were primarily interested in the circumstances surrounding Hitler's death and in any information they could glean on his personal life and leadership style. They had little interest in the political victims of the National Socialist regime, the breaches of international law during the military campaigns and the systematic murder of the Jews. They did not look into figures for the German armaments industry and completely ignored the jet fighter, the V-weapons and the research on the German atomic bomb. Instead, the secret policemen wrote in the minutes of the interrogations and the summaries of agent reports that 'Hitler has many international friends, in Argentina, for example', that women had played 'a great role in his life' and that the dictator had directed those he trusted to 'destroy his remains'.

For a while the interrogators seemed to accept the theory that Hitler took poison and shot himself at the same time. To clarify things, a site inspection was carried out in the spring of 1946. At the same time the officers working on Myth planned a new autopsy on the body Smersh had found. In order to examine more closely the statements made in Moscow, the Butyrka inmates were also taken to Berlin.

In May 1946 the members of the Myth team arrived in the former Reich capital. While the prisoners were interned in the NKVD prison in Lichtenberg and subjected to further questioning, a special commission examined the Chancellery bunker and garden again. As well as Klausen, the members included Militia Colonel N. F. Osipov and the coroner Piotr S. Semenovsky. The last two named were responsible for carrying out the first forensic examination of the circumstances of Hitler's 'disappearance'. Particular care was taken by the criminologist and the coroner to analyse the bloodstains in the dictator's study and on the stairs leading out to the garden.

Their analysis was categorical: 'On the basis of the great number of streams and spots of blood on the sofa it must be concluded that the wound was accompanied by a profuse shedding of blood, which was as good as life threatening. At the moment of the wounding the person in question was sitting in the right-hand corner of the sofa, next to the arm . . . Such a quantity of blood spots and rivulets, as well as the characteristic appearance, indicate that the wound was confined to the head, and not the chest or stomach . . . The damage to the head resulted from a gunshot wound and not from a blow to the head with a heavy instrument. Proof of this is to be found in the fact there are no bloodstains on the back of the sofa, the sofa itself or on the back frame. After the head wound the wounded man lost consciousness and remained motionless for a while, sitting with his head inclined towards the right arm of the sofa.'

This report was confirmed on 30 May 1946 by further digs in the Chancellery garden. In the spot where a year before Smersh men had dug

up the bodies of Hitler and Eva Braun, the coroner discovered two frag-
ments of a male skull, from the left and right parietal bones. The left-side
one betrayed an injury that, according to the coroner Semenovsky, suggested the exit hole of a bullet. He further affirmed that 'the shot was
directed from the bottom upwards and from right to left, and from the
back'. Therefore Hitler had shot himself, as the witnesses Linge and
Günsche had stated.

To test conclusively the theory that there had been a simultaneous intake
of cyanide, however, a new autopsy had to be performed on the corpses.
This Smersh refused to allow. Despite making strenuous efforts, the
Myth special commission did not manage to persuade military counter-
intelligence to give up the already dissected bodies of Hitler and Eva
Braun. This made the NKVD officers reluctant to commit themselves, so
they renounced the opportunity to inform Stalin of the results of their
investigation. This allowed further speculation about Hitler's death to arise,
ranging from 'exclusively suicide by poison' to a *coup de grâce* (administered
by either Linge or Günsche, depending on whether one accepted the con-
jectures of Rattenhuber or Voss).

New versions of Hitler's fate were presented by the Soviet Union
according to the political needs of the moment. In the years immediately
after 1945 it was maintained that he was not dead, but had fled and was
being sheltered by Moscow's former allies in the West. To support this
theory the Soviet authorities even produced a Hitler 'double'. Lev
Besymenski, the leading protagonist of the poisoning and *coup de grâce* theories who published successful books on the death of Hitler in 1968 and
1982,[7] excused himself in 1995 for having told 'deliberate lies'. Now he
was doing 'penance', the Russian historian wrote, though this meant he
was still shirking responsibility. In the Soviet Union access to archives was
politically controlled, and his texts had been dictated by informants from
the KGB. Besymenski had ignored serious historians in Great Britain, the
USA and West Germany anyway. *The Hitler Book* compiled for Stalin was
also based on the 1946 investigation. Why should the editors of Linge's and
Günsche's testimony lie?

After Operation Myth was put on hold in summer 1946, nothing further was done until March 1948. That month Amayak Kobulov learned
that the German officer Gerhard Boldt had written a book entitled *The
Last Days in the Reich Chancellery*.[8] Kobulov requested that Lieutenant
Colonel Klausen organise the material from Operation Myth and send it
to the KI (that is, the Information Committee, which had co-ordinated
Soviet secret-police work since 1947). At the same time he proposed that

Baur, Günsche and Linge should be put together in a cell and invited to write a comprehensive document of the last days of Hitler.

The idea of *The Hitler Book* had now been born, but the MVD (or Ministry of Internal Affairs, as the NKVD had now become) could not be certain that this initiative would find favour with the Politburo of the Communist Party, the only possible authority for a project of this sort. On 27 April 1948 they sent up the first 'test balloon'. Stalin, Molotov, Beria, Zhdanov, Malenkov, Mikoyan, Kaganovich, Voznesenski and Bulganin, the inner circle of the Soviet leadership, received a document prepared by Günsche on the Ardennes Offensive and the German attempts to reach a separate peace with the former Western Allies. The Soviet dictator seems to have read the document with interest, for he had it placed not in the Party Archive, but in his personal files at the Kremlin.

It was decided soon afterwards to withdraw Baur from the 'writing programme' and to put just Linge and Günsche to work on the book. As Baur maintained in his memoirs, first published in West Germany in 1956, he could not offer much of a statement on the deaths of Hitler and Eva Braun. Nor was his knowledge sufficient for a detailed account of Hitler's policies.[9]

For their work on *The Hitler Book* Linge and Günsche were moved to a special department of the Butyrka Prison hospital. For reasons of secrecy, in August 1948 they were transferred to 'Special Object No. 5 of the MVD' – a villa near Moscow – where they were supposed to continue their 'writing activities'. In this 'Special Object' of the Soviet secret police the two SS officers had to supply written and spoken information over many months: first about the last days of Hitler, then increasingly about his private life, and finally about his political and military decisions. The interrogators worked from 1945 backwards to 1935, the year when Linge entered the Führer Escort Command. In due course the years 1933 and 1934 were filled in, although neither Linge nor Günsche had any first-hand information relating to that period. Eventually a detailed biography of Hitler was produced that, in the view of the MVD officers, would fulfil Stalin's expectations.

In charge of the editing were the MVD officers Lieutenant Colonel Fyodor Parparov and Major Igor Saleyev.[10] They oversaw the work in progress, asked the key questions and contributed explanations or background information. As has already been explained, they had carried out interrogations between 1945 and 1946; they spoke excellent German and translated the statements of the prisoners into Russian. When it was finished they took over the detailed editing of the text to make it properly readable.

снаряд стал известен впоследствии под названием "ФАУ-2".
Доклад Брауна держался в строгом секрете. На доклад, который
состоялся в помещении кино ставки "Вольфшанце", были допуще-
ны Кейтель, Иодль, Буле, Шмундт, Гюнше и другие ад"ютанты
Гитлера. Здание кино было оцеплено эсэсовцами из личной ох-
раны Гитлера. Браун иллюстрировал свой доклад световыми кар-
тинами. Они изображали огромную ракету, взлетавшую на высо-
ту 80-ти километров. Этот снаряд, наполненный тонной взры-
вчатого вещества, обрушивался с колоссальной скоростью на
цель в 200-300 километрах от места вылета. Силой взрыва
снаряд мог разрушить целый городской квартал, не оставляя
ничего живого.

Во время доклада Гитлер горячо аплодировал и с упоени-
ем описывал те ужасные сцены, которые могут разыграться при
взрыве снаряда среди населения. Он был в восторге от доклада, тут же дал Брауну звание профессора и обещал посетить
его экспериментальные лаборатории, находившиеся у Пенемюнде.

В эти же дни Гитлер вызвал к себе Кейтеля и Гиммлера и
Гитлер дал им директиву неуклонно следить за выполнением его
приказа все разрушать на пути отступления немецких войск в
Советской России. Гитлер подчеркивал, что русским войскам
нужно оставить выженную землю и безлюдную пустыню. Он счи-
тал, что это должно явиться одной из преград наступлению
русских. Гитлер затронул также вопрос об усилении репрессий
в оккупированных еще немцами русских районах. В связи с этим
Гитлер предложил Гиммлеру ввести более широко применение
закрытых автомашин с газовыми камерами. Он говорил, что не
надо тратить патроны на расстрелы русских, патроны нужны войскам...

Гиммлер, ссылаясь на доклад группенфюрера СС и началь-
ника полиции в Ростове Гейнеке, доложил Гитлеру, что опыт
применения газовых камер вполне оправдывает себя.

Цинично смеясь, Гиммлер сказал, что этот способ убийст-
ва "деликатнее" и "бесшумнее", чем расстрелы.

Гитлер в свое время лично интересовался вопросом изго-
товления газовых камер. Он тщательно изучал проекты их кон-

A page taken from the last version of the manuscript – from the end of 1949. The markings are
those of the main Russian editor of the text, Lieutenant Colonel Fyodor Karpovich Parparov.
The page describes Hitler asking Himmler about the gas chambers

-330-

Линге, пробыв несколько минут в старом бомбоубежище, вернулся в бомбоубежище Гитлера. У раскрытой бронированной двери в приемную стоял Гюнше с дежурным оберштурмфюрером СС Фриком. Оставалось несколько минут до четырех. Линге проходя мимо Гюнше, сказал:

— Я думаю, что все уже кончено, — и быстро прошел в буфетную . Там Линге сразу почувствовал запах пороха, как это бывает после выстрела, и тут же снова вышел в приемную. Там неожиданно оказался Борман. Он стоял, опустив голову и опершись рукой о стол, около самой двери в комнату для совещаний . Линге доложил Борману, что в буфетной чувствуется запах пороха. Борман выпрямился и вместе с Линге поспешил к кабинету Гитлера. Линге открыл дверь и вошел вместе с Борманом в комнату. Им представилась следующая картина: на диване слева сидел Гитлер. Он- был мертв. Рядом с ним-мертвая Ева Браун. На правом виске Гитлера зияла огнестрельная рана величиной с монету, на щеке -следы скатившейся двумя струйками крови. На ковре около дивана была лужица крови величиной с тарелку. На стене и на диване виднелись брызги крови. Правая рука Гитлера лежала на его колене ладонью вверх. Левая-висела вдоль тела. У правой ноги Гитлера лежал револьвер системы "Вальтер" калибра 7,65 мм, а у левой ноги- револьвер той же системы, калибра 6,35 мм. Гитлер был одет в свой серый военный китель, на котором был золотой партийный значок, железный крест I класса и значок за ранение в первую мировую войну, который он носил все последние дни. На нем была белая рубашка с черным галстуком, черные брюки навыпуск, черные носки и черные кожаные полуботинки.

Ева Браун сидела на диване, подобрав ноги. Ее светлые туфли на высоких каблуках стояли на полу. Губы ее были крепко сжаты. Она отравилась цианистым калием.

Борман снова выбежал в приемную и позвал эсэсовцев, которые должны были вынести трупы в парк. Линге вышел в буфет-

A page taken from the document in the Russian State Archive of Contemporary History (RGANI), describing the death of Hitler

The MVD officers could be particularly confident of Linge's collaboration in this project. Although he stressed in his later memoirs that he had not been very co-operative,[11] this Soviet assessment suggests otherwise: 'During this work Linge was always positive and offered admissions of his own free will. From one or two checks it was established that Linge hoped thereby that he might play down his responsibility for his service within Hitler's closest circle and effect his release from captivity. His writings Linge characterised as "his salvation".'

Günsche on the other hand was unforthcoming: 'Günsche is very negative about the work. He is reluctant to give truthful information and tries to bring Linge round to his point of view, and in this respect he is not afraid to use threats.' In the judgement of Parparov and Saleyev, Günsche was 'A convinced Hitlerite and a potential enemy of democracy and the Soviet Union.'

Work on the MVD Hitler biography lasted more than a year and a half, not least because the interrogators and the prisoners could not agree on how to handle certain matters, such as the co-operation between the German Reich and the Soviet Union in the years from 1939 to 1941. The one-time SS officers did not always have an answer to the questions either. In the end the interrogators altered the concept of the book. To begin with the MVD officers had thought of providing a general description of German policy and conduct of the war under the title 'Castles in the Clouds'. In Soviet eyes the phrase was a metaphor for the ambitions of Hitler's regime: Russian 'castles in the clouds' are much the same as German (and English) 'castles in the air'. The title appealed because of the German dictator's pompous residence. The Berghof was not only as large as a castle, it had the infrastructure of one too – and that is leaving aside the New Reich Chancellery. But that title seemed too lyrical, and the volume that finally emerged was not a survey of German policy but a text about Hitler – a biography of the German dictator from 1933 to 1945.

Stalin received *The Hitler Book* on 29 December 1949 from his Minister of the Interior, Sergei Kruglov – a single copy of the 413-page report. The other members of the Politburo were not given copies, though a few told Stalin that they had had a look at the document. Although the Soviet dictator did not mark the book himself and refrained from writing in the margin,[12] it is possible to reconstruct from other sources what might especially have interested him. For example he was profoundly mistrustful of his entourage. On 22 June 1945 he had been given a translation of one of Bormann's notebooks and had above all marked the passages concerning the dismissal of former Party comrades and close associates of Hitler: '29 March . . . Guderian sent on leave!', '30 March . . . Dr Dietrich sent on leave by the Führer!', '25 April Göring expelled from the Party!', '28 April . . . Fegelein demoted', '29 April . . . wedding of Adolf Hitler + Eva Braun . . . The traitors Jodl, Himmler and Gen[erals]', '1 May attempted break-out!'[13]

After the book was finished, Linge and Günsche were kept for the time being at Special Object No. 5 to be ready to answer further questions. After the MVD had decided they had no further use for them they were condemned on 15 May 1950 by a military tribunal in the Ivanovo area to twenty-five years in a labour camp for participating in war crimes. The sentences were to begin on 6 April 1950, the day of their transfer to Prison Camp No. 48 at Ivanovo in the Moscow region. A little later the MVD transferred Linge to Punishment Camp No. 476 near Sverdlovsk whence he was released to West Germany in October 1955. Günsche had also been packed off to this camp, but he showed himself much more refractory than Linge and during his time in captivity he had to serve many additional punishments for anti-Soviet propaganda and refusal to work. The MVD finally transferred Günsche in December 1955 to the East German Ministry of the Interior and left it to them to decide what to do with him.

MVD officers were well schooled Marxist-Leninists and had strict ideas about how history was to be interpreted. In the composition of *The Hitler Book* they relied on the statements of people who did not share their ideology. Moreover they were also obliged to pander to the voyeurism of their patron Stalin. Despite bringing to their task therefore a vision of the National Socialist dictatorship and the Second World War that had been impaired in these three different ways, it can be said unhesitatingly that the authors' collective of the Soviet state security sought to record history as it actually happened.

The satisfaction of special interests was not necessarily damaging to the search for truth, nor does the selection of themes designed to appeal to Stalin clash with the interests of contemporary readers. It was only because Stalin was forever gathering personal information about his opponents that certain details were sought for *The Hitler book*.[14] In the study of Hitler as a private man three things come to the fore: his eating and drinking habits, his health and his life with Eva Braun. Describing these aspects is not just interesting in itself but helps track his progressive mental and physical collapse. He was a non-smoker and abhorred tobacco smoke in his presence.[15] In the book this is mentioned only in a scene in the Führer Bunker in Berlin at a time when he was barely registering what was going on around him. His extreme reservations about alcohol are not especially noted in *The Hitler Book* either. In truth, before 1931 Hitler drank a good deal of beer at Party gatherings – as much as seven litres – but more usually a glass or two with his dinner. As a digestive he occasionally drank a bitters, a brandy or a fruit schnapps. The authors of *The Hitler Book* indicate this reservation only at the point when he abandons it. They quote a statement of Linge's that after the Battle of Stalingrad he drank a 'considerable quantity of schnapps or cognac' at 'every lunch and dinner'. They do not say, however, that he never lost control when he drank and quickly put his glass down again.[16]

Hitler's vegetarian diet is likewise only touched upon,[17] although that must be seen as a cause of his frequent illnesses, and moreover the MVD and Stalin took great interest in it. The MVD officers often noted the quick change from restraint to gluttony in Hitler's eating habits, which struck other contemporaries as well. Friedelind Wagner reported that Hitler ate noodle soup every day for lunch in Bayreuth, and sometimes for dinner as well. On the other hand he ate daily up to two pounds of pralines.[18] Supported by Linge's statements more and more dizzy spells and illnesses are described. The MVD officers relay over and over again the impressions that document Hitler's accelerating physical decline. His personal physician, Theodor Morell, the MVD officers roundly characterise as a 'charlatan', and looking at the extensive evidence for the misuse of medicaments that are advanced by *The Hitler Book*, this opinion does not seem far fetched.

The prescription of eye-drops containing cocaine cannot actually be called an error of practice or drug abuse, as is suggested in *The Hitler Book*.[19] The same cannot be said, however, of the frequent use of 'injections of stimulants'. Morell injected Hitler with his own preparation, Vitamultin which contained an extremely high quantity of Pervitin and caffeine. If Hitler regularly received this stimulant, up to four injections in one day, one must speak of a dependency. His extremely rapid bodily and mental decline between 1942 and 1945 might also be attributed to this misuse of drugs.[20] However the SS doctor Ernst Günther Schenck, who worked in the hospital beneath the Reich Chancellery in the final days and who also wrote a medical life of Hitler, came to the conclusion that Hitler's decline 'was not due to the Pervitin dependency, but more a sign of a completely exhausted, worn-out man'.

In addition Schenk suggests that Hitler was suffering from incipient Parkinson's disease. The cause is generally given as cerebral arteriosclerosis and not generally as the use of psychotropic drugs or amphetamines – in

Hitler's case Pervitin.[21] The psychiatrist Fritz Redlich, who had fled from Vienna in 1938 and later taught at Yale, states 'categorically' in his medical biography of Hitler that he was suffering from Parkinson's disease, but he does not attribute the cause to the use of amphetamines. Redlich made a detailed study of the psychic and physical consequences of the long-term abuse of Pervitin and came to the conclusion that it had made Hitler more aggressive but that the sickness was not the cause of his criminal policies. Hitler's personal physician, Morell, accepted the diagnosis of Parkinson's disease only at the beginning of 1945. Morell's chronic misdiagnoses were not helped by Hitler's uncooperative behaviour. Only then did the dictator receive medication that was designed to slow down his mental and physical collapse. It is, however, possible that Morell had hoped to improve Hitler's bodily and mental decline by giving him amphetamines.[22] No less than the prisoners in Soviet captivity who gave their testimony in *The Hitler Book*, Redlich came to the conclusion in his diagnosis that at the end of the war neither Hitler's intelligence not his memory was impaired. On the basis of eyewitness accounts, the biographer Werner Maser judged that Hitler's mind was 'was captivatingly clear and nimble to the end of his days'.[23] This view has remained unchallenged for years, despite the fact that it owes much to the unconditional loyalty of his followers. The statements of Linge and Günsche in this matter are very clear, however. There is frequently evidence of Hitler's mental absence, even disorientation, and of his complete indifference to his surroundings. According to *The Hitler Book* a few of the dictator's alleged tantrums never actually took place.[23]

But such scenes provide spectacular cinema and necessarily made their way into Bernd Eichinger's Oscar-nominated 2005 film *Downfall*. An eloquent example of this is the alleged tantrum that was caused by Fegelein's treachery. The cinema-goer hears Hitler, beside himself with fury, bellowing 'Treachery!', 'Fegelein! Fegelein! Fegelein!', and the script emphasises, 'Each time Hitler beats the table with his fist. His face is so red that it is fit to explode.' In reality Hitler had to be told by Günsche, the Battle Commander of the Government District, to hand his brother-in-law over to the court martial. Other scenes in the film are either pure invention or stem from unreliable witnesses. The last visit of Speer's was clearly less emotional than its depiction in the film; and the secretary Traudl Junge was not, as is shown in the film, saved by a boy but raped many times and was for several months the 'personal prisoner' of a high-ranking officer in Soviet intelligence. Time and again the chronology of the film fails to match historical reality. Hitler appears as the driving force of everything that happens, but the Wenck and Steiner Armies were summoned not by

Hitler, but by Keitel, Krebs and Burgdorf: it was generals in Hitler's entourage who were running the war at the end, not Hitler himself.

As early as autumn 1945 the Soviet interrogators questioned the prisoners from Hitler's entourage about his sexual behaviour. Linge in particular was required to give details in this respect. So too, however, were Baur and Günsche. The NKVD officers quickly stumbled on the relationship between Hitler and Eva Braun. Without beating about the bush the files refer to her as Hitler's 'lover' or 'bedfellow' – and this finds its way into *The Hitler Book* – supported by Linge's graphic descriptions of enjoyable evenings with champagne, pralines and stimulants. It also seemed plausible that Hitler kept quiet about the relationship from political considerations. His marriage to Eva Braun at the end of his life confirmed this for them. Speculations about the nature of their relationship were otiose.

From a Soviet point of view Hitler's chance remark about homosexuals in the SA was an indication that his sexuality was 'normal', as were the highly informal life in the Berghof and the gossip about his niece Angela Raubal. The fact that many of the descriptions were based on hearsay was taken into consideration, such as the mistaken use of the pet-name 'Nicki' rather than 'Geli' for Angela. One piece of information that rested on the 'agent report' of Baur's cell-sneak 'Hunter' was not transferred to the dossier prepared for Stalin. On 25 December 1945 'Hunter' told his spymaster on the record, 'At the end of the war, Eva was expecting Hitler's child.'

The proponents of the thesis that Hitler was homosexual – albeit repressed or merely latent – will not be deflected by the information in the Russian files. They have already rejected the evidence of witnesses to his former lovers as unbelievable and cast doubt on the research of other Hitler biographers. On the other hand Baur's remark about Eva Braun's pregnancy is not incontrovertible proof of a sexual relationship with Hitler or of his potency; and the historian Anton Joachimsthaler, who has researched Hitler's personal circumstances in detail, considers sexual relations between Eva Braun and her brother-in-law, the SS officer Hermann Fegelein, to be possible, perhaps even probable.[24] Other things being equal, if you accept the results of German historical research or the contemporary evidence of German and Russian sources, there is much to be said for the argument that Hitler was reserved in his sexual behaviour or that his sexual desires had withered away,[25] but there is little credence to be given to the idea of homosexual tendencies.

Stalin and the Soviet intelligence services were interested in Hitler's private life, but they also examined his methods of rule. Stalin behaved within his closest circle in accordance with the motto 'You can change convictions, but the fear remains.' Hitler shared this view when it came to the nations he ruled, but he saw his personal entourage as faithful, or at least loyal. Not least for this reason, the MVD officers took pains to point out that in the end Hitler was disappointed in this respect. Passages on the apparent treachery of Wehrmacht generals and SS leaders loom large. Just as incomprehensible in the eyes of the Soviet editors was the magnanimity with which Hitler treated the army leadership. 'Hitler always maintained that the generals were alone responsible for his defeats,' they wrote, 'but he called none of them to account.' The MVD officers could not fathom why he pensioned them off and also invested them with high honours. During the purges of 1937–38, on the other hand, Stalin had had thousands of high-ranking officers executed and in that way had enforced loyalty. Even during the war he had generals executed whom he felt had failed.

The specifically Soviet viewpoint is reflected over and over again in the frequent naming of the Nazi Party's supporters. That big industrialists have a substantial role attributed to them in this way does not seem at all false in retrospect, but the editors of *The Hitler Book* resisted applying this viewpoint throughout the book and stuck to the historical facts. Armaments Minister Albert Speer often stressed that the great industrialists had not ruled the state, and judged in retrospect, 'A few of them certainly helped him, but they were never more than helpers.'[26] The subordinate role played by the industrialists is also shown in the fact that not one manager featured in Hitler's immediate circle, as was also true of high-ranking officers and civil servants. At the Führer HQs or the Berghof, Albert Speer, Heinrich Himmler or the General Staff Chiefs were often to be found, but with the exception of Speer contacts were confined to working relationships. The informal circle was composed exclusively of old Party comrades, the adjutants of the various branches of the Wehrmacht, the secretaries and the leaders of the Party Chancellery, Hess and later Bormann.

It is noteworthy that people who had been close to Hitler before 1933 were progressively elbowed out. Increasingly he surrounded himself with people who were neither his intellectual equals nor the occupants of responsible positions. In *The Hitler Book*, the Berghof appears overwhelmingly as the place for private parties and not as a governmental seat. Hitler's irregular working hours strengthen this impression, but despite his Bohemian nature he ordered his daily tasks in a disciplined way and dealt with his administrative demands sometimes to the point of exhaustion.

The Soviet editors chose from Linge's and Günsche's writings representative political statements by Hitler. For example, they presented

Stalin with Hitler's reaction to the Naval Agreement of 1935, his reflections on the split between the French and British allies in 1940 and the dictator's view of other heads of state. The selection was decided by the important political constellations of 1948 and 1949. From Stalin's point of view, the countries of interest were those in which the Soviet Union was acting offensively, Hungary or Romania for example, or those in which the future path had yet to be decided – for example, Italy.[27] An evaluation of British appeasement policy provided real meaning with the dawn of the Cold War. Stalin observed with suspicion his former Allies reversing their policies and as a result the Soviet intelligence men who edited the book laid great stress on a selection of episodes that outlined British and German co-operation or which showed the half-hearted war leadership of the British. These include not just the Munich Agreement for the partition of Czechoslovakia in 1938 and the failed British landing in Norway, but also Himmler's dealings with British negotiators for a separate peace and the 'treachery' of SS-Obergruppenführer Felix Steiner, which appeared to be somehow connected.

There is a particularly detailed account of Hitler's reaction to Rudolf Hess's flight to Scotland. It also contradicts the version given by Linge. In the memoirs he published in West Germany, Linge wrote that Hitler was already dressed and shaved and came out soon after he knocked.[28] This description also made its way into academic literature on the subject. In *The Hitler Book* the scene is very different. Hitler replied with a 'sleepy voice' and emerged 'unshaved'. The fact that he was dressed explains why he needed 'a few minutes' to leave the study, which adjoined his bedroom. The thesis that he was complicit in Hess's alleged mission thereby loses one of its more important foundations.

The interrogators were interested in the tense relations between Hitler and his commanding generals. After their interrogations of Linge and Günsche, they reached conclusions similar to historians in the West. The Soviet officers observed that the temporary alliance between the National Socialist regime and the Prussian-dominated officer corps became more fragile with each defeat. They interpret the attempt on Hitler's life of 20 July 1944 as striking testimony to a departed loyalty.[29] The state security interrogators, who were themselves survivors of Stalin's Purges, wanted to measure the scale of the conspiracy in *The Hitler Book*. They kept asking Linge and Günsche who had stood loyal to Hitler and who had been involved in the preparation of the plot. They were not surprised that high-ranking officers had taken part in the conspiracy. In the Soviet Union even members of the Communist Party Politburo had been designated 'enemies of the people' and executed. The text as Stalin received it clearly suggests a contempt for Hitler because he had not taken measures to purge the officer corps. The MVD officers also could not resist repeating Hitler's words that he had been saved by 'providence'.

The Hitler Book paints a vivid picture of the dictator as a military leader. There are detailed evocations of Hitler's reaction to particular events in the war – for example, the Battles of Stalingrad, the Kursk Salient and the Oder. Virtually none of the minutes relating to the situation conferences alluded to in the text have survived, so Günsche's reports are the only source. Given that we have had more than fifty years of continuous and intense research on all aspects of the Second World War, it would, however, be perverse to suggest that *The Hitler Book* calls for a comprehensive new appraisal.

A proper assessment of Hitler as a warlord rests on consideration of certain events and decisions. The readiness with which he declared war on the USA, and in a strategically very uncertain situation, was extraordinary. Just as astonishing was his unreflective reaction to the Allied landings in Normandy, and his relationship with the Supreme Commander of the Luftwaffe, Hermann Göring – unbroken until the last days of the war. In contrast to this indifference are the frequent changes of mood following victory and defeat on the Eastern Front, which show that he was in no condition to provide the leadership which the national predicament required. After the defeat at Stalingrad, at the latest, as is evident from *The Hitler Book*, he lost his objective view of the strategic problem and placed tactical success in the foreground.

These writings also echo what is in retrospect a remarkable lack of realism: clearly he believed that the battalions, regiments and divisions whose movements he followed on the staff maps disposed of the same fighting strengths as at the beginning of the war. He attributed the failure of the attacks, counter-attacks and pincer movements that he ordered to the incompetence of commanders and staff officers. Frequently he accused them of inaction or cowardice, occasionally even of sabotage. The dismissals of the responsible military leaders succeeded each other at ever shorter intervals, and were often accompanied by angry outbursts on Hitler's part. A few of these arguments between Hitler and high-ranking officers are memorably described in *The Hitler Book*, such as the dismissal of Guderian as Chief of the General Staff.

The argument that the Western Allies' bombing campaign might have had a decisive effect on the war was denied in 1948 to 1949 from considerations of contemporary politics: from Stalin's and the Soviet officers' point of view it would have diminished the value of the victory of the Soviet army. It was therefore out of the question to treat the targeted bombardment of the German arms industry as effective. Yet after 1943 combined air and land operations by German forces were hardly possible any longer, and owing to Allied air superiority, the Germans could win neither the Normandy campaign nor the Ardennes offensive.

The authors of *The Hitler Book* are not entirely wrong in placing the accent on the German–Soviet war. German historians too have come to the conclusion that the Second World War was decided on the Eastern Front, a conclusion supported by the number of casualties. The latest figures cited by Russian historians give 11.27 million military dead on the Soviet side. Of the 4.2 million German soldiers who died before 31 January 1945, some 1.83 million fell on the Soviet front. Before 9 May 1945 a further 1.4 million members of the Wehrmacht and SS were killed in combat with the Soviet army. Another 3.1 million Germans went into Soviet captivity between 1941 and 1945.

These figures attest to the pitilessness of the German–Soviet war. Despite the focusing of *The Hitler Book* on personalities, it can be seen here too. On the other hand it is mentioned only in a few places that the campaign against the Soviet Union was also a racially motivated war of annihilation, which claimed the lives of 18.4 million civilians. This war of annihilation was carried out above all by the SS, but a politically indoctrinated Wehrmacht played its part.

In the last months of the war German propaganda made use of the crimes committed against German soldiers and civilians for an effective mobilisation of all reserves. On 28 February 1945 Propaganda Minister Joseph Goebbels made a speech on the wireless calling people to battle against 'an enemy thirsting for blood and sick with revenge [!]'. Hatred such as had never been known before had to harden in German hearts. *Der Panzerbär*, touted as 'Battle News for the Defenders of Greater Berlin' and printed in the Propaganda Ministry, contained appeals to carry on the struggle reinforced by lies about the actual progress of the war. Berlin was the 'breakwater for the Russian flood', *Der Panzerbär* reported on 25 April 1945. Printed in bold on page one was a quotation from Ulrich von Hutten beneath the headline 'The call of iron': 'I can perish, but slave I will never be, nor Germany enslaved can I see!' The reduction of the poetic works of Ulrich von Hutten to a slogan would have been a trifle had a 'people's grenadier division' not received the name of the humanist a few days before. The Volkssturm, which had been formed on 26 September 1944, recruited all men aged between sixteen and sixty, of whom 200,000 died or were reported missing. In *The Hitler Book* the Volkssturm was morally condemned and, in retrospect there can be no doubt of the military sense-lessness of this last German contingent.

Despite their miserable equipment, these doomed squadrons held up the Red Army for weeks. The Hitler Youth, too, like those members deco-rated by Hitler with the Iron Cross in the Chancellery garden on 20 March 1945, were similarly filled with Goebbels's will to hold out. A great many of them doubted neither the truth of the propaganda nor the strength of Hitler's leadership. The older soldiers also fought on until Hitler's suicide, even though they were disillusioned and believed the war was lost. They fell into the moral trap of exaggerated patriotism for which a line from Heinrich Lersch's poem 'Soldier's Song' of 1914, inscribed on countless monuments to the dead of the First World War, served as a motto: 'Germany must live, even if we all must die!'

For this reason it is not possible to pronounce on whether the protag-onists of *The Hitler Book* actually felt the repugnance over senseless exhor-tations to defence that they express in the text. In 1961 the historian Percy Ernst Schramm, co-author and editor of the OKW War Diaries, gave the verdict of history which concurs with the verdict of the survivors: 'Hitler knew earlier than anyone on earth that the war was lost . . . he thereby brought down inextinguishable guilt upon himself that he stretched it out longer.'[30] One of the initiators of the desperate last battle seemed to think the countless martyrs justified, even decades later. It was not about keep-ing Adolf Hitler alive for another three days, said former Reich youth leader Artur Axmann, 'but that loyalty should not be denied the world.'[31]

Hitler was adept at using the mental character of the German people and mobilised large parts by appealing to burning political issues, whether real or imaginary. As an orator, he possessed both in private conversation and at mass meetings a suggestive power. His voice spoke directly to the emotional centres of perception and, with his rudimentary means of mass communication, the show he offered was astounding. Stalin on the other hand possessed no personal charisma, and his appeal was systematically manufactured through the cult of personality. In order not to draw atten-tion to the differences between the two dictators, the state security men edited Linge's and Günsche's texts so that Hitler's talent for mass leadership was hardly detectable. The countless mass rallies of the Nazi Party were scarcely touched on and Hitler's effect on the masses airbrushed out.

Over and over again the Soviet editors include the passages, obviously written by Günsche, on the SS Leibstandarte 'Adolf Hitler', who clung fast to their unconditional loyalty to their Führer, even after Hitler divested them of his name following the failure of the Balaton Offensive at the end of March 1945. In this context the stubborn reaction of Wilhelm Mohnke, the last Battle Commander of the government district, seems remarkable. In April 1945 he told Günsche, 'The Führer didn't want to know about his Leibstandarte, but now we'll show him he still has a Leibstandarte.' The way Hitler inspired this loyalty was not investigated by the NKVD/MVD, however.

These lacunae in *The Hitler Book* are explicable and certainly forgivable. But it seems outrageous that the NKVD interrogators made no effort to find out the causes of the murder of the Jews in the German-controlled area. In the parts of the Soviet Union controlled by the Wehrmacht 2.1 million Jews were killed between 1941 and 1945, while the total number of Jewish victims of National Socialist rule comfortably exceeds five million. When those who died in ghettos and camps from hunger and poor sanitation are taken into account, the victims of the Final Solution total more than six million. Despite that, the Soviet interrogators sought neither to reconstruct Hitler's directives for the murder of the Jews nor to describe his anti-Semitic ideology. Both Linge and Günsche could easily have given details. Only in one place was Hitler connected with the building of gas chambers. In *The Hitler Book* it is shown that he took a 'personal' interest in the construction of the gas chambers. He had approved the models shown him by Himmler and ordered that their constructor 'should be given comprehensive support'. Up to now research has proceeded from the standpoint that Hitler had commissioned the SS to carry out the genocide, but wanted to know as few details as possible.

The explanation for the silence over the Final Solution in *The Hitler Book* is self-evident. Both before and during the Second World War the organs of the State Security murdered many Jews or had them executed on trumped-up charges. The numbers must total tens of thousands, but the exact figure has not been settled. After 1947 the persecution, which had previously been limited, grew in intensity and scale. It was no longer politically motivated, but had now acquired a clear anti-Semitic orientation. The NKVD's successor, the MVD, was responsible for the reprisals. The cases against Zionists and cosmopolitans were assembled by officers of the state security who also carried out killings without sentences from the courts, just on the directives of Stalin. *The Hitler Book* was compiled at the height of the anti-Jewish policy of the Soviet Union. Given Stalin's manifestly anti-Semitic views, no attempt was made to examine the murder of Jews.

Clearly the German–Soviet alliance of 1939 to 1941 was also taboo. In *The Hitler Book* only a part of this partnership was mentioned, the

Non-Aggression Pact. Neither its inception not its consequences are discussed. In the description of the German Polish campaign, the Soviet editors do not acknowledge that their country was also waging a war against Poland. The original working plan for *The Hitler Book* envisaged discussion of this theme, but the idea was thrown out again by the MVD officers responsible for the book, Lieutenant Colonel Parparov and Major Saleyev. Both men knew only too well what was politically opportune in the highest circles of the Soviet leadership, partly as a result of their own experiences of repression during the Stalinist Purges.

The German attack on the Soviet Union was also preceded by a number of errors on Stalin's part. As a result the events of the summer 1941 are presented only summarily in *The Hitler Book*. All the same the authors from state security refrained from repeating the propaganda formula of a 'treacherous attack'. They understood very well that Stalin had known the date of the invasion in the early summer of 1941. He threw out intelligence reports, however, covering them with unflattering marginalia about disinformation. Instead the Soviet Union drew up its own plans for an offensive, overestimating its potential possibilities and underestimating that of their German enemies. The question whether it can be seen as a preventative war from the German point of view has been extensively discussed and as often accepted as rejected. After the division of power in 1939, two heavily armed world powers with diametrically opposed imperial designs stood facing one another across the border. The Soviet Union and the German Reich were ideologically stamped totalitarian states which had in recent years carried out aggressive wars and which saw a conflict as unavoidable. Both sides worked out detailed plans of attack and tried to get the better of the other. The concept of preventative war seems, all the same, to be politically motivated and is an unfitting characterisation for the German–Soviet war.

Hitler had been pushing heavily for the conquest of European Russia and the creation of a colonial empire since 1933, irrespective of any tactical considerations. The conquest of 'living space' in the east was a central plank in his ideology. As early as 1927 he had described Russia in *Mein Kampf* as a future area of settlement and the Bolshevik regime as 'ready to collapse'.[32] Despite a strategic need brought about by the course of the war, the campaign against Soviet Russia was in the end a war of conquest.

Just as the Soviet editors abbreviated the statements of Linge and Günsche on the beginning of the campaign, they also fall tellingly silent about the initial success of the Wehrmacht in the USSR. Even though the Soviet army was vastly superior in numbers and very well armed, before the end of 1941 around 3.8 million of its soldiers ended up in German captivity. More accurate accounts of the conduct of the war and the activities of Hitler as Supreme Commander of the Wehrmacht enter *The Hitler Book* only at the point where the German offensive grinds to a halt. The reactions to the defeat before Moscow and the unsuccessful blockade of Leningrad are evocatively described. In the ensuing descriptions, however, it seems over and over again that whole episodes relating to the success of German arms have been crossed out. Until the Battle of Stalingrad the text seems episodic.

Irrespective of what in contemporary eyes seem to be false interpretations and politically motivated lacunae, *The Hitler Book* gives us a powerful portrait of the German dictator and offers a remarkably detailed chronicle of his policies and his military actions. Hitler's absolute unscrupulousness and his unbounded desire to exterminate are clearly shown. The chapter covering the last days in the Führer Bunker is shocking in its depiction of his attempts to spin out his life to the last possible moment, even though that would lead the German people into catastrophe. That *The Hitler Book* was specially written for the Soviet dictator Stalin does not detract from its vividness.

Acknowledgements

We would like to thank the staff of the various archives we have used in Germany and Russia for their professionalism and readiness to be of help. In particular we are indebted to Natalia G. Tomilina, the Director of the Russian State Archive for Contemporary History (RGANI) and Mikhail Y. Prosumenshchikov, Director of the Publication Department of RGANI, as well as Berit Pistora at the Federal Archives in Koblenz.

A special word of thanks too to Professor Vladimir N. Chaustov, who verified and guaranteed the authenticity of *The Hitler Book* against the deposits in the Archives of the President of the Russian Federation, which was not accessible to us.

We are grateful to Helmut Ettinger for successfully rendering the amorphous text into German, to our agent Thomas Karlauf for his wise counsel and to Elmar Klupsch and his professional editorial team at Gustav Lübbe Verlag.

Last but not least we owe a debt to our colleagues at the Institut für Zeitgeschichte in Munich and Berlin, and the Martin Luther University in Halle and Wittenberg, who gave us their support in so many ways.

Henrik Eberle and Matthias Uhl
January 2005

The author and publishers would like to thank the following for permission to reproduce illustrations: Plates 1, 2, 5, 6, 7, 8, 9, 18, 19, 20, 22, 23, 25, 26, 27, 28, 29, 30, 31, 32, 33, 34, 35 and 38, Bundesarchiv Koblenz; 4, 21 and 37, Bayerische Staatsbibliothek, München; 10, Bundesarchiv Berlin; 11, 12, 13, 14, 15, 17 and 24, Heinrich Hoffmann, Bundesarchiv Koblenz; 36, Europapress, Bundesarchiv Koblenz; 39 and 40, Russisches Staatliches Militärarchiv Moskau.

Table of comparative Third Reich military ranks and British/US equivalents

Army	Luftwaffe	Kriegsmarine	Waffen-SS
Leutnant	Leutnant	Leutnant zur See	SS–Untersturmführer
Second lieutenant	*Pilot officer*	*Acting sub-lieutenant/ Ensign*	
Oberleutnant	Oberleutnant	Oberleutnant zur See	SS–Obersturmführer
Lieutenant	*Flying officer*	*Sub-lieutenant/ Lieutenant junior grade*	
Hauptmann	Hauptmann	Kapitänleutnant	SS–Hauptsturmführer
Captain	*Flight lieutenant*	*Lieutenant*	
Major	Major	Korvettenkapitän	SS–Sturmbannführer
Captain	*Squadron leader*	*Lieutenant commander*	
Oberstleutnant	Oberstleutnant	Fregattenkapitän	SS–Obersturmbannführer
Lieutenant colonel/ Major	*Wing commander*	*Commander*	
Oberst	Oberst	Kapitän zur See/Kommodore	SS–Standartenführer SS–Oberführer
Lieutenant colonel/ Major	*Group captain*	*Captain*	
Generalmajor	Generalmajor	Vizeadmiral	SS–Brigadeführer
Brigadier/ Brigadier general	*Air commodore*	*Vice admiral*	
Generalleutnant	Generalleutnant	Konteradmiral	SS–Gruppenführer
Major general	*Air vice-marshal*	*Rear admiral/ Commodore*	
General der . . .	General der . . .	Admiral	SS–Obergruppenführer
Lieutenant general	*Air marshal*	*Admiral*	
Generaloberst	Generaloberst	Generaladmiral	SS–Obergruppenführer
General	*Air chief marshal*	*Admiral*	
Generalfeldmarschall	Generalfeldmarschall	Grossadmiral	Reichsführer-SS
Field marshal/ Five-star general	*Marshal of the RAF*	*Admiral of the Fleet/Fleet admiral*	

Notes

FOREWORD BY RICHARD OVERY

1. J. Stalin, *Works*, 13 vols, Foreign Languages Publishing House, Moscow, 1952–5, vol. xiii, 118, 'Talk with the German author Emil Ludwig', 13 December 1931.
2. V. M. Berezhkov, *At Stalin's Side: Memoirs of an Interpreter*, Carol Publishing Corp., New York, 1994, 10.
3. Cited in R. H. McNeal, *Stalin: Man and Ruler*, Macmillan Press, London, 1988, 237.
4. F. Genoud (ed.), *The Testament of Adolf Hitler*, Cassell, London, 1960, 100, entry for 26 February 1945.
5. See R. J. Overy, *Interrogations: The Nazi Elite in Allied Hands*, Allen Lane, London, 2001, 215–84 for Speer's lengthy account of Hitler's personality. Much of the material was recycled in Speer's own memoirs, *Inside the Third Reich*, Weidenfeld & Nicolson, London, 1970; see also U. Schlie, *Albert Speer: Alles was ich weiss*, Herbig, Munich, 1999.
6. W. C. Langer, *The Mind of Adolf Hitler*, Basic Books, New York, 1972.
7. K. Heiden, *Der Fuehrer*, Houghton Mifflin, New York, 1944, republished as *The Führer*, Constable, London, 1999. See too K. Heiden, *One Man Against Europe*, Penguin, London, 1939.
8. See D. Rayfield, *Stalin and His Hangmen*, Viking, London, 2004, 15–24.
9. A. Resis (ed.), *Molotov Remembers: Inside Kremlin Politics*, Ivan R. Dee, Chicago, 1993, 180.
10. G. K. Zhukov, *Reminiscences and Reflections*, 2 vols, Progress Publishers, Moscow, 1985, vol. ii, 226.
11. See J. Harris and M. J. Trow, *Hess: The British Conspiracy*, André Deutsch, London, 1999; M. Allen, *The Hitler/Hess Deception*, HarperCollins, London, 2003.
12. On Soviet attitudes to the Holocaust Z. Gitelman (ed.), *Bitter Legacy: Confronting the Holocaust in the USSR*, Indiana University Press, Bloomington, IN, 1997; L. Dobroszycki and J. Gurock (eds), *The Holocaust in the Soviet Union: Studies and Sources on the Destruction of the Jews in Nazi-Occupied Territories of the USSR 1941–1945*, M. E. Sharpe, New York, 1993.

13. A. Joachimsthaler, *Hitler's Ende: Legende und Dokumente*, Weltbild, Munich, 1999; T. Junge, *Until the Final Hour: Hitler's Last Secretary*, Weidenfeld & Nicolson, London, 2003; J. Fest, *Inside Hitler's Bunker*, Macmillan, London, 2004. On Soviet versions of Hitler's last days see L. Bezymenski, *The Death of Adolf Hitler: Unknown Documents from the Soviet Archives*, Michael Joseph, London, 1968 and A. Petrova and P. Watson, *The Death of Hitler: The Final Words from Russia's Secret Archives*, Richard Cohen, London, 1995.

14. Zhukov, *Reminiscences and Reflections*, vol. ii, 390.

TRANSLATOR'S PREFACE BY GILES MACDONOGH

1. See Editors' Afterword, p. 294.
2. Albert Speer, *Spandau: The Secret Diaries*, trans. by Richard and Clara Winston, Collins, London, 1976, 41.
3. See below, p. 279.
4. Hugh Trevor-Roper, *The Last Days of Hitler*, 7th edn, Macmillan, London 1995, 29.
5. All except Günsche, who was released into East German captivity.
6. Trevor-Roper, *Last Days of Hitler*, Introduction to the Third Edition, xliv.

CHAPTER 1: SUMMER 1933 – SUMMER 1934

1. Originally a troop of 120 armed men whose first duty was the personal security of Adolf Hitler, but who also performed ceremonial roles. In 1938 they were brought up to the strength of a motorised infantry regiment through their merger with the SS-Verfügungstruppe/Emergency Troops based in Berlin-Lichterfelde. After the Polish campaign they were incorporated into the Waffen-SS; in 1940 they rose to brigade strength, and in 1941 they became a division. In October 1943 they were reformed as 1st SS Panzer Division and took part in numerous war crimes. After the failure of the Balaton Offensive in 1945 they retreated to Austria, where they surrendered to the Allies at the beginning of May.
2. Wilhelm Brückner (1884–1954), until 1940 Hitler's chief adjutant.
3. Julius Schaub (1898–1967), chief adjutant in succession to Brückner.
4. Otto Dietrich (1897–1952), Hitler's press chief until April 1945.
5. Heinz Linge (1913–80), formerly with the Leibstandarte. Linge was Hitler's soldier-servant from 1935 and personal servant from 1939, and one of the principal sources for *The Hitler Book*.
6. Despite his much-vaunted fondness for Wagner, Hitler liked to listen to popular music. Lehar is often cited as his favourite. The SS man Rochus Misch, who was with him in the bunker to the last, remembers seeing him

sunk in sadness listening to 'Dein ist mein ganzes Herz' from Lehar's *Im Lande des Lächelns* (*Süddeutsche Zeitung*, 29 April 2005).

7. The main offices of the Secret State Police Office (Geheimes Staatspolizeiamt, or Gestapa) were to be found in the buildings of the former School of Applied Arts (Prinz Albrecht Strasse, 8). The Hotel Prinz Albrecht (Prinz Albrecht Strasse, 9) was the headquarters of the SS leadership. The Gestapo, the Secret State Police (Geheimes Staatspolizei), was created in 1933 and functioned until 1945 as the political police of the Reich. It was initially under the control of Hermann Göring, but in 1934 it was transferred to Heinrich Himmler. From 1939 the Gestapo was active in German-occupied areas.

8. Hitler often threatened to put people into the camps, but he seldom did in fact.

9. A former military lock-up, it was used as a 'wild' or unofficial concentration camp from 1933. Infamous as a centre for torture, it was closed in 1936 and demolished in 1938. During its three years' service around 8,000 people were detained here by the SA and the SS.

10. Edmund Heines (1897–1934), SA leader in Silesia, killed in the Night of the Long Knives.

11. The Leibstandarte killed fourteen people in Lichterfelde, including the SA leader for Berlin and Brandenburg and his adjutant.

CHAPTER 2: SUMMER 1934 – FEBRUARY 1936

1. He died on his Neudeck estate on 2 August 1934. The Minister of War, Blomberg, now ordered that the Reichswehr swear the oath of allegiance to the 'Führer of the German Reich and People, Adolf Hitler'.

2. Sales of *Mein Kampf* for 1930 were 54,000; 1931: 50,808; 1932: 90,351; 1933: 854,127. In 1933 Hitler declared an income of 1,232,335 marks, half of which he tried to pass off as professional expenses. In the following years the Eher-Verlag paid him between a million and two million marks in royalties, but Hitler did not collect them all. In 1944 they amounted to a backlog of 5,525,811 marks.

3. By 1944 the Nazi Party's own Standarte GmbH and Herold press, to which Eher also belonged, controlled around 90 per cent of the German press and a large part of the book market.

4. Gotthard Färber, (1896–?) administered the Nazi Party's property holdings.

5. The Soviet editors mean the various funds available to the Reich President. From 1935 there were no further audits carried out and Hitler used this purse to reward or corrupt civil servants and officers.

6. Between 1933 and 1937 the Nazi Party bought fifty-four plots on the Obersalzberg, totalling 2,900,000 square metres. Hitler himself bought 80,000 square metres and the Administration of the Bavarian Forests ceded the Kehlstein area with around 6,700,000 square metres. Fifty houses were torn down. Their owners were paid off, but were put under considerable pressure to sell. Later some were threatened with concentration camps if they refused.

7. Six thousand workers were involved. At first they were German, but after the start of the war skilled Czechs and Italians. They were not forced labourers but they were housed in huts and a strict discipline was imposed. Any infringement was met with punishments: fines, reduction of rations and cigarette cards, and confinement. During the building work a total of fourteen people died accidental deaths.

8. Possibly Christine Almer, an antique saleswoman in Munich.

9. Karl Haberstock (1878–?), antique salesman and Party member in Berlin.

10. Heinrich Hoffmann (1885–1957), early Nazi, procureur who profited from his exclusive right to photograph the Führer. Imprisoned by the Americans after the war.

11. Heinz Posse, from 1939 in charge of the special project for Linz. He selected paintings for Hitler's residences as well as the planned museum in Linz. His staff plundered works of art from museums in occupied countries and acquired works from Jewish collections for a fraction of their actual worth.

12. The total cost of the Kehlstein House was 29.6 million marks.

13. The speech has been abridged for ideological reasons. Hitler spoke openly of rearmament on 16 March, 4 April, 21 May and 16 September 1935 (the last being the 'Day of the Wehrmacht').

14. Alfried Krupp von Bohlen und Halbach (1907–67), Nazi fellow traveller, served brief sentence after the war; Hermann Röchling (1888–1981), manager of the Bochum steelworks and Party member; Emil Kirdorf (1847–1938), coalmine proprietor, early Nazi; Albert Vögler (1877–1945), steel king, committed suicide at the end of the war in American captivity; Ernst Poensgen (1871–1949), Chairman of the United Steelworks; Hugo Stinnes jnr (1897–1982), chairman of numerous companies involved in the exploitation of occupied areas; Kurt Freiherr von Schröder (1889–1966), member of the famous Hamburg and London banking family, Party member; Robert Pferdmenges (1880–1962), banker and businessman, co-founder of the CDU and adviser to Adenauer after the war.

15. For example the *Admiral Hipper* of 18,200 tons, where only 17,500 were permitted under the agreement.

16. Hans Baur (1897–1993), Hitler's pilot; captured by the Russians, he was a secondary source for the information in *The Hitler Book*.

17. Anni Winter (née Schuler) (1905–70) ran Hitler's Munich household from 1929 to 1945. Interned.

18. Christian Weber (1883–1945), one of the first Nazis. Died in a road accident being transferred from one Allied camp to another.

19. Julius Streicher (1885–1946), schoolmaster, early Nazi and rabid anti-Semite. Hitler later distanced himself from Streicher, who was nonetheless hanged after the war.

20. Two temples of honour had been built on the eastern side of the square to the designs of Paul Ludwig Troost.

CHAPTER 3: MARCH 1936 – OCTOBER 1937

1. The Treaty of Locarno had been signed by Belgium, Germany, France, Great Britain, Italy, Poland and Czechoslovakia. These discussions took place on 12 February 1936. Military commands were ready on 2 March 1936.

2. The Foreign Office also raised doubts, seeing possible negative repercussions. Goebbels mocked them as worriers in a speech on 6 March 1936.

3. Friedrich Carl Rabe von Pappenheim (1894–1977), military attaché in Brussels and Budapest, ended the war as a general lieutenant in Soviet captivity. Released 1955.

4. Frederick Elliot Hotblack (1887–1979) was military attaché in Berlin 1935–7. He had won the Military Cross in the First World War.

5. Truman Smith, 1935–9 US military attaché in Berlin and 1939–45 German specialist in US Military Intelligence and personal adviser to General George C. Marshall.

6. Two brigades of gendarmes were already in the Rhineland. On 8 March they were officially incorporated into the Wehrmacht.

7. In 1935 Hoffmann bought the house at Wasserburg Strasse, 12 for 35,000 marks on Hitler's behalf. Eva Braun took up residence in 1936. It was transferred to her name in 1937 or 1938.

8. Theodor Morell (1886–1948) was a specialist in skin and sexual diseases. There is no written evidence that he prescribed Hitler sexual stimulants, as is suggested here. Briefly imprisoned by the Americans and died soon after.

9. On 30 May 1937 Hitler opened an exhibition of the Reich Provisions Department.

10. Alwin-Broder Albrecht (1903–45), Hitler's liaison officer to the navy from 1938 and later personal adjutant. Killed trying to escape from the bunker. It was not, however, Albrecht who brought Hitler the news that day, but Karl-Jesko Otto von Puttkamer.

11. Erich Raeder (1876–1960), from 1935 to 1943 Supreme Commander of the Navy. Sentenced to life imprisonment in 1946, released in 1955.

12. On 29 May 1937 two Spanish aircraft bombed the *Deutschland* after she had opened fire on them. The attack cost the lives of thirty-one German sailors; a further seventy-five were wounded.

13. Captain Paul Fanger. He was relieved of his command and appointed governor of the fortresses of East Friesland.

14. On 31 May 1937 the German warship *Admiral Scheer* and four torpedo boats opened fire on the port of Almería: twenty-one Spaniards were killed and seventy-one injured.

15. Wilhelm Faupel (1873–1945), Ambassador – or rather military adviser – in Franco's HQ. Retired in August 1938.

16. Winifred Wagner, née Williams (1897–1980), English-born wife of Wagner's son Siegfried. As an orphan she was adopted by a Berlin piano

teacher. Joined the Nazi Party in 1926. Unrepentant at the end of her long life.

17. Johannes Graf von Welczeck (1878–1972), later Ambassador to Paris. Settled in Spain after the war and died in Marbella.

18. Hugo Sperrle (1885–1953), First World War flying officer. In the Second World War commanded the Luftwaffe in the Battle of Britain.

19. Erwin Jaenicke (1890–1960), later Colonel General and Supreme Commander of the Seventeenth Army in the Caucasus and the Crimea. Sacked for suggesting an evacuation of Sebastopol. Released from Soviet captivity in 1955. The discussion leading to the creation of the 'Special Staff W' took place on 27 July 1936.

20. Germany was forbidden aircraft, tanks, anti-aircraft guns and heavy artillery under the terms of the Treaty of Versailles. Within the framework of military co-operation between the Red Army and the Reichswehr, these weapons had been tried out in Russia during the Weimar Republic.

21. The visit took place on 26 September 1937. The guests witnessed a simulated attack by two tank brigades supported by several bomber squadrons.

CHAPTER 4: NOVEMBER 1937 – FEBRUARY 1939

1. Paul-Otto Schmidt (1899–1970), career interpreter with the German Foreign Office. Joined the Nazi Party in 1943. Imprisoned after the war, he remained wedded to right-wing politics to the end.

2. On his return journey Halifax noted that he thought he had seen a general desire for rapprochement with Britain – from Hitler to the ordinary man in the street.

3. Wilhelm Keitel (1882–1946), the most pliant of Hitler's field marshals, and known behind his back as 'Lakeitel' or 'lackey'. He signed Germany's unconditional surrender on 8 May 1945, and was hanged by the Allies the following year.

4. Franz von Papen (1879–1969), former royal page and Chancellor of the Weimar Republic who served Hitler as Ambassador to Vienna then to Ankara. Imprisoned after the war, he was released in 1949.

5. Sir Nevile Henderson (1882–1942), British Ambassador to Germany 1937–9. Famously encouraged the government's policy of appeasement.

6. Walther von Brauchitsch (1881–1948), from 1938 Supreme Commander of the Army; 1940, field marshal. Removed after the failure of the Russian offensive. Died in British captivity.

7. Arthur Seyss-Inquart (1892–1946), Austrian Minister of the Interior who replaced Schusschnigg as Chancellor in March 1938. Joined the Nazi Party and the SS that year 1940; Reich Commissar for Occupied Holland. Sentenced to death and hanged at Nuremberg.

8. Fedor von Bock (1880–1945), promoted field marshal after the Fall of France, dismissed in 1942. Killed in an air raid.

9. Theodor Innitzer (1875–1955), Archbishop of Vienna from 1932 to 1955, cardinal from 1933. Misjudged Hitler at first. Later active in protecting non-Aryan Christians.

10. Wilhelm Ritter von Leeb (1876–1954), Bavarian staff officer, already commanded an infantry division in 1930. Dismissed over the Fritsch Affair in February 1938, but brought back in October that year. Promoted field marshal after the Fall of France. Spent three years in prison after the war.

11. Alexander Freiherr von Dörnberg zu Hausen (1901–83), former Freikorps soldier and career diplomat. Joined the Nazi Party in 1934. Protegé of Ribbentrop's; high SS rank; on Himmler's staff. Cleared by a Bavarian court in 1948.

12. Rudolf Schmundt (1896–1944), from 1938 Hitler's chief Wehrmacht adjutant; from 1942 chief of personnel; died of the wounds received on 20 July 1944.

13. Walther Hewel (1904–45), early Nazi; spent time in England and the Dutch East Indies as a planter; with Ribbentrop from 1937; 1938, accorded diplomatic rank and named Foreign Office representative on Hitler's staff; expressed his reservations about the drift into war; 1943, promoted Ambassador on special duties; shot himself on 1 May 1945.

14. Friedrich Gaus (1881–1955), jurist and diplomat who worked on the Treaty of Locarno and the German–Soviet Non-Aggression Pact.

15. Johanna Wolf (1900–85) joined the Party in 1929; moved to Berlin in 1933; served in different Führer HQs; allowed to leave the bunker 22 April 1945. Interned until 1948.

16. Between 1936 and 1938 the Czechs had built a line of fortresses along their German and Polish frontiers with French help.

17. Wilhelm Keppler (1882–1960), engineer and businessman; joined the Nazi Party in 1927 and created the 'friends' circle that sought business backing for Hitler; joined the SS in 1933; leader of the economic section of the Nazi Party from 1934; on the boards of several companies; 1936–45, member of the Council of Ministers for the Four Year Plan; 1938–45, State Secretary in the Foreign Office; sentenced to ten years in 1947. Released in 1951.

18. Albert Speer recalled that Hitler intended to live in the building for ten or twelve years before he moved into his new palace.

19. On 13 March 1939 Hitler had put pressure on Tiso to declare Slovakian independence the next day.

20. On 2 October 1938 the Poles occupied Teschen in the wake of the German invasion. On 14 March 1939 the Hungarians marched into the Carpatho-Ukraine, formerly part of Czechoslovakia.

21. Hácha had arrived in Berlin and had been accommodated at the Hotel Adlon. Hitler had him wait until 1.00 a.m. before he would receive him.

22. Wilhelm Stuckart (1902–53), former Freikorps soldier; early Nazi; dismissed as a judge for membership of the Nazi Party; after 1933 State Secretary in the Prussian Culture and Reich Interior Ministries; helped frame the Nuremberg Racial Laws; 1936, joined the SS; involved in the plans to annex foreign territories; participated in the Wannsee Conference on the Final Solution of the Jewish Problem on 20 January 1942; arrested in 1945 and released three years later; active in the politics of German refugees; died in a car accident.

23. Possibly August Körber, a member of Hitler's Escort Command from 1933. Hermann Bornhold (1908–76) was a loyal SS man who had joined the Nazi Party in 1929; Max Hansen (1908–90) was a member of the Leibstandarte who rose to command the 1st Panzergrenadier Regiment in the Battle of the Ardennes.

24. Karl Hermann Frank (1898–1946), Sudetener; initially in local government, then a bookkeeper; ran a bookshop; 1935, joined the Sudetendeutsche Party; member of the Czech parliament; 1938, Nazi Party; 1938–40, assistant Gauleiter of Sudetenland; 1939–45, senior SS and Police Leader in Bohemia and Moravia; 1944, General of the Waffen-SS; 1943–5, Minister of State for Bohemia and Moravia; 1945, fled to Bavaria; 1946, handed over to the Czechs; sentenced to death.

25. Wilhelm Frick (1877–1946), lawyer; from 1919 chief of the Munich political police and later head of the criminal police; arrested after the Hitler Putsch; 1924–45, member of the Reichstag; 1925, joined the Nazi Party; 1930–1, Minister of the Interior in Thuringia; 1933–45, Reich Interior Minister; August 1943–5, Reich Protector of Bohemia and Moravia and Reich Minister without Portfolio; 1946, sentenced to death.

CHAPTER 5: MARCH – NOVEMBER 1939

1. The treaty had been signed by the Foreign Ministers of Germany and Lithuania on the night of 22 March 1939. Hitler was on board the warship *Deutschland* at the time, on his way to Memel. He landed on the afternoon of the 23rd. Memel and the surrounding area had belonged to the German Reich until 1919. In 1921, 90 per cent of the population voted for the establishment of a free state on the Danzig model. Lithuania occupied the territory in 1923. There had been frequent conflicts between the German majority and the Lithuanian Governor.

2. Erich Koch (1896–1986) worked in railway administration until joining a Freikorps in 1919; 1922, became a member of the Nazi Party; as a Nazi official in the Ruhr he was arrested many times by the French; 1928–45, Gauleiter in East Prussia; 1933–45, Governor of East Prussia and from 1939 Reich Defence Commissar; 1942–4, Reich Commissar for the Ukraine; 23 April 1945 flight to Flensburg; disguised himself as a farm worker until 1949; delivered to Poland in

1950; sentenced to death in 1959, but the verdict was commuted the following year. Died in prison.

3. Albert Forster (1902–54) first joined the Nazy Party in 1923; wrote for Streicher's anti-Semitic paper *Der Stürmer*; 1926 joined the SS; 1930–45, member of the Reichstag; 1930–9, Gauleiter of Danzig; 1939–45, Gauleiter of West Prussia; March 1945, fled to Schleswig-Holstein; arrested and handed over to the Poles, who sentenced him to death. It is not clear when the sentence was carried out.

4. Gerda Daranowski (1913–97), from 1937, secretary to Hitler's adjutants in various HQs; 1943, married Eckhard Christian; 1 May 1945, successfully made it through the Russian lines to the west. Christa Schroeder (1908–84), from 1930, typist with the Nazi Party; Party member; 1933–9, secretary to Hitler's personal adjutants and secretary to Hitler in various HQs; flight to Bavaria, 22 April 1945; arrested and imprisoned. Released 1948; thereafter secretary in various industrial concerns.

5. The hymn of Hitler's Germany was named after the pimp and SA man Horst Wessel, who was well known as a murderer of communists. Workers from Berlin-Wedding killed him shortly before Hitler came to power. (Russian note.) The fanatical National Socialist's lover prostituted herself out of financial necessity. Wessel was not her pimp but received support from her to continue his studies. He was killed by her former pimp who had been released from prison and was angry that the woman had fallen in love with Wessel. The former pimp was a member of the Red Front Fighter Union, which enabled both the communists and the Nazis to treat the death as political. He was sentenced to imprisonment for manslaughter and in 1933 was murdered by the Nazis.

6. A distance of around 3.5 kilometres.

7. Leni Riefenstahl (1902–2003), originally a dancer, but from 1926 switched to acting; made her first film in 1932; in the 1930s mostly documentaries for the Nazi Party: *Triumph des Willens* (1934), *Fest der Völker, Fest der Schönheit* (1936) on the Olympiad of that year; thereafter fictional films, even on occasion using gypsies who were taken to a concentration camp once the filming was ended. Arrested and denazified; became a much admired photographer for her work in Africa and the Indian Ocean.

8. Sophie Stork (1903–81), artist and craftswoman and sometime lover of Wilhelm Brückner; joined the Nazi Party in 1931; friend of Eva Braun; decorated the Berghof; financially supported by Hitler; briefly interned after 1945.

9. The British Ambassador Nevile Henderson was personally received by Hitler in the Reich Chancellery at 7.00 p.m. on 29 August 1939, when the latter handed him a note that amounted to an ultimatum to Poland. This led to an exchange during which Henderson bellowed louder than Hitler. Henderson later told Chamberlain that he had told Hitler he would not accept that sort of language from anyone.

10. The sessions of the Reichstag were held in the Kroll Opera House because the National Socialists had provocatively set fire to the Reichstag in 1933 in order to smear the German Communist Party. In connection with this, Dimitroff was tried on trumped-up charges in Leipzig. (Russian note.) There is is no proof that the Nazis started the Reichstag fire. The perpetrator was the mentally disturbed Dutch communist Marinus van der Lubbe.

11. The Führer's Special Train served as HQ during the Polish campaign because Hitler was expecting an attack from France in mid-September and wanted to be ready for a rapid transfer of his command post.

12. Fifty kilometres north of Schneidemühl, now Pila in Poland.

13. Case White was mostly Brauchitsch's work, with some assistance from Franz Halder (1884–1972), Chief of the General Staff in succession to Beck, and a general who shared the latter's anti-Hitlerian views. Arrested after 20 July 1944, he was sent to Dachau. In May 1945 he was interned again by the Americans, but released in 1947. From 1946 to 1961 he worked in the Historical Division of the US Army.

14. Peter Högl (1897–1945), former miller and policeman; 1932, in the criminal branch; 1933, assigned to Hitler's protection; 1934, joined the Nazi Party; died in the break-out from the bunker.

15. Ludolf von Alvensleben (1901–70), scion of one of Prussia's oldest families; fought in a Freikorps; entered the Nazi Party; in 1929; 1933–45, Reichstag deputy; joined SA in 1934 and then the SS; 1938 to January 1941, chief adjutant to Himmler; from October 1941, Chief Police and SS Leader in southern Russia; similar functions in the Ukraine; arrested in 1945, but managed to escape to Argentina with the help of the Evangelical Church; condemned to death by a Polish court *in absentia*.

16. Hans Frank (1900–46) with the Freikorps Epp; studied at Munich University with Karl Haushofer; 1923, entered Nazi Party; took part in the Putsch; qualified as a lawyer; head of the Party's legal department; head of the National Socialist Lawyers' League; 1930–45, member of the Reichstag; Bavarian Minister of Justice until 1934, then Reich Minister without Portfolio; 1939–45, Generalgouverneur in Poland; arrested 1945 and hanged at Nuremberg the following year.

17. The Phoney War or 'Sitzkrieg' ('Drole de guerre' in French) lasted until the German attack in the West on 10 May 1940. There was almost no military activity apart from occasional reconnaissance probes, exchanges of artillery fire and leaflet drops.

18. Willy Liebel (1897–1945), former personal assistant to General Erich Ludendorff, printer and publisher; 1925, joined the Nazi Party; 1933–45, Mayor of Nuremberg; from 1936, member of the Reichstag; worked as an assistant to Speer until 1944; April 1945, committed suicide.

19. Benno Martin, (1893–1975) with Freikorps Epp; doctorate in law; senior policeman in Nuremberg; 1933, joined the Nazi Party and became Police

President in Nuremberg; 1934, entered the SS; SS general; indicted and cleared of deporting Franconian Jews.

20. Johann Georg Elser (1903–45) had worked as a clockmaker in Germany and Switzerland. Had been a member of the Red Front Fighters' Association and was a pacifist opposed to the Nazi Party. Had already been arrested trying illegally to cross the border near Constanz. The police found a postcard of the Bürgerbräukeller on him, notes on the making of explosives and some remarkably odd-looking pieces of metal. When they received the report of the plot, they made the connection to Elser. He was kept in Sachsenhausen pending a show trial, and transferred to Dachau at the end of 1944 or the beginning of 1945 where he was killed on orders from Berlin.

21. The radio contact between SD-Ausland and MI6 had begun in October. The capture of Richard Stevens and Sigismund Payne Best is known as the Venlo Incident and had wide-ranging repercussions when it came to future German attempts to contact the British. From then on the policy was 'absolute silence'.

22. Payne Best and Stevens were kept in Sachsenhausen.

CHAPTER 6: DECEMBER 1939 – MAY 1941

1. Walther Funk (1890–1960), journalist; 1922–30, editor of the *Berliner Börsenzeitung*; 1931, entered the Nazi Party; active in Nazi economic policies; 1933–8, Press Chief and State Secretary in the Propaganda Ministry; from 1938, Reich Minister of Economics and from January 1939 President of the Reichsbank; sentenced to life imprisonment in 1946 but released in 1957.

2. Fritz Todt (1891–1942) joined the Nazi Party in 1922; on Röhm's staff; head of the Main Office for Technology; from July 1933, Inspector for Roads; 1938, placed in charge of fortress construction; founder of the Todt Organisation using foreign and slave labour for major building works; from 1940 also Reich Minister for Armaments; died in a plane crash.

3. Josef 'Sepp' Dietrich (1892–1966), coachman, hotel buyer; policeman in Bavaria and briefly in Freikorps Oberland; 1923, entered the Nazi Party; took part in the Putsch that year; 1928, joined the SS; 1930–45, member of the Reichstag; given the job of forming the Leibstandarte 'Adolf Hitler'; 1934, SS-Obergruppenführer; 1941 SS general; Supreme Commander of the Fifth and later Sixth SS Panzer Army; taken prisoner in Austria; tried and imprisoned for life for atrocities committed at Malmédy; released in 1955; tried again for murders during the Röhm Putsch and sentenced to a further eighteen months; released in 1959.

4. Nikolaus von Falkenhorst (1885–1968), general staff officer and military attaché in Prague; 1937 general lieutenant; 1940, infantry general; assigned command of the Scandinavian campaign; colonel general; condemned to death by a British Norwegian court for shooting British commandoes;

commuted to twenty years; released in 1953. Hitler gave orders for 'Weser Practice' on 1 March 1940 – the occupation of Denmark and Norway.

5. Apart from the Battle of Jutland in 1916 (Skagerrak in German), the German surface fleet was scarcely used in the First World War, even if submarine warfare was fully developed.

6. Dr Kurt Diesing of the Reich Weather Service.

7. The planned Adlerhorst HQ near Bad Nauheim was not ready. Felsennest lay on a hill in the village of Rodert near Bad Münstereifel, twelve kilometres from Euskirchen.

8. Alfred Jodl (1890–1946) originally gunner and staff officer; seconded to the Turkish Army; from August 1939 Chief of the Wehrmacht Operations Staff; his duties were to direct the war in the west; 1944, colonel general; signed unconditional surrender; arrested and sentenced to death.

9. The so-called Sickle Cut: the advance of powerful German tank units through the Ardennes, which had been seen as impassable, to the Channel coast. It was a modified version of the Schlieffen Plan that the German General Staff had presented in October 1939. The Panzer squadrons of Army Group A covered 250 kilometres in six days and cut off forty-two divisions of Allied troops in Belgium and northern France. Army Group B went north and Army Group C advanced to the West Wall and the Upper Rhine. The violation of Belgian neutrality made the senior army staff unhappy, but their qualms were pushed aside by Hitler and the authors of the Sickle Cut.

10. The Luftwaffe underperformed at Dunkirk. Despite Göring's boasts that he would prevent the evacuation, the British escaped with relatively small losses: around 7,000 soldiers were killed and seventy-two ships sunk.

11. SS-Obersturmführer Hans Bastians shot himself on 14 June 1940. It was the first death at Führer HQ.

12. Max Amann (1891–1957), NCO in the 'List' Regiment; 1921, joined the Nazi Party and became its manager; publisher of the *Völkischer Beobachter*; and from 1922 to 1945 manager of the Eher Publishing Group; took part in the Putsch and was imprisoned; 1932; entered SS; 1933–45, Reichsleiter for the German press; arrested in 1945 and released in 1953.

13. Fritz Wiedemann (1891–1970), staff adjutant in the List Regiment; various business ventures; from 1934, worked with Hess; 1935–9, Hitler's personal adjutant; unofficial diplomatic missions to Austria and London; 1938, Member of the Reichstag; dismissed as adjutant for pessimism; 1939–41, Consul General in San Francisco; from 1941, Consul General in Tientsin in China; arrested by the Americans and released 1948.

14. Eberhard von Stohrer (1883–1953), career diplomat; 1936, appointed Ambassador in Madrid; retired in 1943.

15. Kurt von Tippelskirch (1891–1957), in French capitivity during the First World War and later interned in Switzerland; language student; later military interpreters' school in French, Italian and English; staff officer during the

Weimar Republic; 1940, general lieutenant; 1942, infantry general; commanded XII Army Corps; July 1944, injured in a plane crash; commanded First Army and Fourteenth Army; led his troops into British captivity. Released in 1948.

16. Henri Philippe Pétain (1856–1951), French field marshal and politician, Minister President of France in June 1940, head of the Vichy government from July 1940. Interned by the Germans in 1944, fled to Switzerland in April 1945 but returned to France of his own free will. Sentenced to death, but this was commented to life imprisonment. Died on the Ile de Yeu.

17. Hubert Lanz (1896–1982), staff officer specialising in mountain warfare; general of mountain troops; sentenced to twelve years for war crimes; released in 1951.

18. The 21cm K 12 V was mounted on a railway carriage. It cost about 1.5 million marks from Krupp. The 33-metre gun fired a 107.5kg shell a distance of up to 115 kilometres. The barrel wore out quickly; after ninety discharges. In the whole course of the war it was used to fire only seventy-two shells at the British coast.

19. Hitler signed directive no. 21 for Case Barbarossa after the meeting with Franco. It began with the words: 'The German Wehrmacht must be prepared to defeat Soviet Russia in a quick campaign even before hostilities have ended with England [sic].' Preparations for the campaign were to be finished by 15 March 1941.

20. Before mid-September the navy had assembled 168 troop transports, 1,975 barges, 100 coastal motorboats, 420 tugs and 1,600 motorboats. In three waves they were to ferry 260,400 men, 34,200 vehicles and 61,983 horses to the British Isles. On 12 October 1940 Sea Lion was postponed to 1941 and on 10 January 1941 finally scrapped.

21. Albert Kesselring (1885–1960), Bavarian artillery officer; 1933, transferred to the Luftwaffe; 1936, general lieutenant; in 1938, Chief of Air Fleet 1; 1940, Air Fleet 2; 1943, field marshal; and return to the land army; Supreme Commander in Italy; sentenced to death in 1947, he was released in 1952.

22. The Luftwaffe received instructions to destroy the RAF on 1 August 1940. On the 'Day of Eagles' – 13 August – the Battle of Britain began. It did not succeed in significantly weakening British air defences and due to heavy losses the Luftwaffe went over to bombing in September. In May 1941 the campaign was abandoned due to the battles in the Balkans and the forthcoming attack on the Soviet Union. The Luftwaffe had already lost 1,142 bombers, 802 fighters, 330 fighter-bombers and 128 dive-bombers over Britain.

23. Albert Bormann (1902–89), Martin Bormann's younger brother; worked in a bank in Munich; 1927, joined the Nazi Party and the SA; from 1931, involved in Party finance; 1933–45, head of Hitler's private chancellery; 1934, adjutant; April 1945, flew to the Obersalzberg; worked on the land under the assumed name of Roth; gave himself up, interned and released, all in 1949.

24. Karl Heinz Pintsch (1909–?), entered the Nazi Party in 1925; 1934, adjutant to Rudolf Hess; cashiered and put in a punishment detachment for his knowledge of Hess's flight; 1944, promoted lieutenant; captured by the Russians and released in 1955.

25. Albrecht Haushofer (1903–45), historian and geographer; geopolitician; taught at Berlin University; foreign political adviser to Hess; arrested after 20 July 1944. Wrote the Moabit Sonnets in prison; murdered by the Gestapo as the Russians entered Berlin.

26. Ernst-Wilhelm Bohle (1903–60), born in Bradford in England; attended school in South Africa; represented British and American firms in Germany as an importer (Chrysler); 1932, joined the Nazi Party; 1933–45, in the Reichstag; 1934–45, head of the Party's foreign organisation; 1936, entered SS; sentenced to five years, released in 1949. Eberhard von Jagwitz (1887–?), businessman in Argentina; 1933, entered the Nazi Party; represented the Party in Spain; departmental chief in the Ministry of Economics and Under State Secretary. Karl Haushofer (1869–1946), father of Albrecht; professional soldier and military historian; general major in Bavarian Army; taught geography at Munich University where he became Hess's mentor; killed himself to escape arrest by the Allies. Alfred Hess (1897–1963), born in Egypt like his brother where his father was a businessman; 1920, entered the Nazi Party; represented the Party in Egypt; outside trade office of the Party in Berlin; assistant chief of the Party foreign organisation.

CHAPTER 7: JUNE 1941 – JANUARY 1942

1. The order to build the Wolfsschanze was given immediately after the visit of the Soviet Foreign Minister Molotov in November 1940. Work was meant to be finished by April 1941. During his visit Molotov presented a catalogue of territorial demands that made a future conflict inevitable for the German leadership. They included the Bosporus and the Balkans as a Russian sphere of influence. This would have endangered Germany's provision of Romanian oil.

2. The Focke-Wulf 200 had a range of 4,400 kilometres. It had been launched as a passenger plane in 1937.

3. Karl Rudolf Gerd von Rundstedt (1875–1953), staff officer in Turkey and France in the First World War; 1928, general major; 1932, general of cavalry; 1938, colonel general; 1940, Supreme Commander, Army Group A and field marshal; dismissed for retreating in Russia; brought back in March 1942 as Supreme Commander in the West; President of the Court of Honour after 20 July 1944 that stripped officers of their rank, thereby allowing them to appear before Freisler's People's Court; released from prison in 1949. Ewald von Kleist (1881–1954), scion of one of Prussia's great military dynasties; cavalry officer; general staff; 1931, commanded an infantry regiment; 1932, general major;

1933, general lieutenant; 1938, retired; 1939, brought back; 1940, colonel general; 1943, field marshal; 1944, dismissed March; taken prisoner by the British who handed him over to the Yugoslavs, who handed him on to the Russians. Died in captivity in a Soviet camp. Alexander Löhr (1885–1947) entered service with the Austrian army in 1906; staff officer with air department; 1933, commander of the Austrian air force; 1939, colonel general; sentenced to death for the bombing of Belgrade.

4. Gerhard Engel (1906–76), from 1938, adjutant to Hitler; finished the war as general lieutenant and commander of the People's Grenadier Division 'Ulrich von Hutten'. Briefly imprisoned by the Americans.

5. The Corpo di Spedizione Italiani in Russia was composed of three divisions and around 62,000 men. It was later expanded to ten divisions. Most of the men perished on the Don during the winter offensive of 1942–3.

6. Heinz Guderian (1888–1954), intelligence then staff officer in the First World War; responsible for the development of armoured warfare in the Weimar army; 1935, commander of 2nd Tank Division; 1938, commanded a corps; 1940, 2nd Panzer Group – Panzer Army from 1941; dismissed in 1941 for suggesting a withdrawal before Moscow; brought back in 1943; filled in as Chief of the General Staff after 20 July 1944; dismissed 28 March 1945 for suggesting negotiation with the west. Released from American captivity in 1948.

7. Erich Hoepner (1886–1944), cavalry officer; general staff; 1936, general major; 1938, general lieutenant; 1941, colonel general; dismissed for 'cowardice and disobedience'; had contacts with Beck before 1938, and later with Olbricht and Stauffenberg. Condemned and executed after 20 July 1944.

8. Franz Schädle (1906–45), 1930, entered the Nazi Party; head of Hitler's Escort Command; committed suicide.

9. Walter von Reichenau (1884–1942), staff officer with leanings towards Nazism; 1940, field marshal; turned a blind eye to the atrocities carried out around him.

CHAPTER 8: FEBRUARY 1942 – FEBRUARY 1943

1. Walter Rohland (1888–1981), 'Panzer-Rohland'; academic engineer; 1933, entered the Nazi Party; Chief Executive of the Bochum Steelworks; entrusted with the tank-building programme by Todt; Assistant Chairman of the United Steelworks; on the boards of other industrial concerns. Erich Müller (1892–1963), 'Cannon-Müller'; engineer; started work with Borsig before going to Krupp; study journeys to the USA; 1933, joined the Nazi Party and SA; from 1936, at Krupp where he headed the artillery section; on the board from 1938; sentenced to twelve years, released in 1951. Paul Pleiger (1899–1985), engineer; 1932, entered the Nazi Party and SA; Party official; given the job of running the Hermann-Göring-Werke; 1942, Reich

Plenipotentiary for the Eastern Economy; tried and sentenced to fifteen years. Released in 1951.

2. Romania had provided twenty-seven divisions for the Eastern Front. They had been incorporated in Army Group B.

3. On 30 August 1940 in Vienna, Romania had been forced by Germany and Italy to cede the northern Siebenbürgen and the Szepler Mountains to Hungary. Romania lost 43,500 square kilometres and 2.5 million inhabitants. The Germans and Italians then issued Romania with a guarantee for the rest of its territory. At the end of the Second World War the Soviet Union initiated a new border change. As compensation for the cession of eastern Moldavia Romania received northern Siebenbürgen back.

4. It was originally called Eichenhain.

5. Kurt Thomas (1896–1943), originally pioneer, later cavalry officer; 1940, commander of Hitler's Escort command, then Commander of Führer HQ; promoted general major and sent to Africa; killed when his plane was shot down; posthumously appointed general lieutenant.

6. Johann Rattenhuber (30 April 1897–1957), Freikorps Epp; Bavarian police; adjutant to Himmler; 1935, chief of a special department of the Reichssicherheitsdienst (RSD); taken prisoner by the Russians, released 1951.

7. Wilhelm Kube (1887–1943), journalist; founder of the German Conservative Party, member of DNVP, then the Freiheits Partei – all nationalist parties of a more traditional nature; 1928, joined the Nazi Party; from 1933, SS; General Commissar for White Russia; killed by partisans. Hinrich Lohse (1896–1964), bank clerk; 1924, joined the Nazi Party; 1932, member of the Reichstag; 1933, Oberpräsident of Schleswig-Holstein; 1941–44, Reich Commissar in 'Ostland'; took over from Kube in White Russia after his death; sentenced to ten years by a German court and released in 1951. Herbert Backe (1896–1947), farmer; from 1922, SA; 1933, State Secretary in the Reich Ministry for Food and Agriculture; replaced Darré as minister in 1942. Albert Ganzenmüller (1905–96) took part in the Hitler Putsch; engineer; 1931, entered the Nazi Party; worked for the railways; concerned with the railways in the east; 1942, assistant director of the German Railways and responsible for the railway transport of Jews to the extermination camps; arrested in 1945 but fled to Argentina two years later; returned to West Germany in 1955; 1960, case presented accusing him of being an accessory to thousands of deaths; the case dropped for reasons of health.

8. Fritz Sauckel (1894–1946), sailor; interned by the French until 1919; from 1922, SA; technical studies; 1923, entered the Nazi Party; 1927–45, Gauleiter of Thuringia, and Minister President from 1933; he was accorded huge powers to recruit forced labour in the occupied countries of the east; arrested by the Americans and hanged.

9. Friedrich Paulus (1890–1957), Badenese infantry officer; served under Guderian; 1939, general major; 1940, general lieutenant; capitulated at

Stalingrad 30 January 1943, the day he was promoted field marshal; released from prison into the East Germany in 1953.

10. Wilhelm List (1880–1971) Bavarian artillery officer; staff officer; 1940, field marshal; 1942, sacked; tried by the Americans for killing partisans; released 1952.

11. The climb was nonetheless seen to have propaganda value.

12. List was relieved of his command on 9 September 1942, Halder two weeks later.

13. By the English poet Robert Graves. Hitler's obsession with flies bears a similarity to the Emperor Domitian in Suetonius' *Twelve Caesars* – also translated into English by Robert Graves.

14. Walter Scherff (1898–1945), staff officer; in February 1941 made Chief of the War History Section of the OKW; Scherff destroyed a very large part of the records of the war before giving himself up to the Americans.

15. Wilhem Zeitzler (1895–1963), started as an officer in the pioneers; Freikorps Torgau; staff officer, was Chief of Staff to XXII Corps at the beginning of the war; April 1942, general major; 24 September 1942, Chief of the General Staff in succession to Halder; July 1944, colonel general; sent on leave and dismissed after his heart attack.

16. German defences on the Atlantic and Channel coasts. Despite 1,200 bunkers, gun towers and so on, the defences were patchy and failed to stop the Allied landings in June 1944.

17. 'What we have acquired, we shall actually seize so firmly that the places where we stand in this war will never be penetrated by another.'

18. Karl Heinrich Bodenschatz (1890–1979), Bavarian officer; flier from 1916; 1933, joined the Luftwaffe as Göring's adjutant; ministerial appointments; 1938–9, liaison officer at Führer HQ; 1941, general; severely wounded, 20 July 1944. Theodor Krancke (1893–1973), officer on torpedo boats in First World War; served in Weimar Navy; 1937, captain; 1939–40, commanded the heavy cruiser *Admiral Scheer*; helped plan the invasions of Denmark and Norway; January 1942–February 1943, liaison officer and Supreme Naval Commander at Führer HQ; thereafter commanded Western Fleet from Paris; at the end of the war in Norway. British captivity. Karl Wolff (1900–84), First World War officer; Freikorps; in banking and advertising; 1931, entered the Nazi Party and SS; on Himmler's staff from 1933 and his chief adjutant from 1935; from August 1939, SS liaison officer with Hitler; 1942, SS general; for a while co-ordinated the deportations of Jews to extermination camps; from February 1943, Chief SS and Police Officer in Italy; from February 1945, secret negotiations with the Allies; in custody with the British; released in 1949; in 1962, indicted as an accessory in the killing of at least 3,000 people; in 1964, sentenced to fifteen years. Released in 1969.

19. Karl Brandt (1904–48), Alsatian doctor; 1932, joined the Nazi Party; 1934, SS; physician in Hitler's Escort Command; service with the Leibstandarte;

involved in the murder of the mentally ill; initiated the experiments on humans in the concentration camps; sacked after a conflict with Morell; Hitler ordered his arrest on 16 April 1945 for taking his wife and child out of Berlin; sentenced to death then released; fled to Flensburg; arrested by the Allies; 'doctors' trial': executed.

20. Gertraud Junge, née Humps (1920–2002), Bavarian; secretary in a law firm then on a magazine; from September in the Reich Chancellery; November 1942, summoned to the Wolfsschanze, and 30 January 1943 became Hitler's secretary; in the bunker until the break-out of 30 April 1945; captured by the Russians; lived with a Russian officer for a year; fled to Bavaria and arrested again. Her memoirs formed the basis for the feature film *Der Untergang* or *Downfall* of 2004. Johanna Wolf (1900–85), Bavarian secretary; 1929, joined the Nazi Party; secretary to Hess; 1933, moved to Berlin and to Hitler's adjutants; served in various HQs; ordered to leave on 22 April 1945.

21. Walter Warlimont (1894–1976), Bavarian artillery officer; army civil service appointments; 1929, observer with the US Army; 1936–7, posted to Franco's staff; 1939, office of Chief of Wehrmacht Operations Department; involved in the plans for the invasion of Soviet Russia; 1942, general lieutenant; tried in 1948 and sentenced to eighteen years. Released in 1957.

22. Göring had bought Rominten from the former Kaiser for 700,000 RM.

23. Walter Buhle (1894–1959), Swabian infantry officer in First World War; in the 1920s, seconded to operations; 1937, staff officer; 1938, Chief of Operations at OKH; 1940, general major; finished the war as the head of the Wehrmacht Armaments Section.

24. Hans Jeschonnek (1899–1943), flying officer from West Prussia; involved in the secret air force; 1935, adjutant to Milch; 1939, Luftwaffe Chief of Staff; committed suicide after the heavy raids on German cities.

25. Eckhard Christian (1907–85), Berliner; 1926, entered the navy; 1934, transferred to the Luftwaffe; general staff office and representative of Jodl in Führer HQ. Married Gerda Daranowski.

26. Nikolaus von Below (1907–83), from old Mecklenburg noble family; trained as a civil pilot; 1929, in Reichswehr; 1933, Luftwaffe; 1937, captain and adjutant on Hitler's staff; 1944, colonel.

27. Gerhard Engel (1906–76), 1925, Reichswehr; 1938, adjutant to Hitler; commanded infantry regiments; 1944, general major; 1945, general lieutenant.

28. Karl-Jesko von Puttkamer (1900–81), from an old Pomeranian noble family; 1917, joined navy; 1935, second naval adjutant with Hitler; 1939, principal naval adjutant; 1941, captain; 1943, rear admiral.

29. Erhard Milch (1892–1972), from 1915, artillery officer and pilot; airborne police and civil pilot; 1923, with Junkers; 1926, Lufthansa; 1933, State Secretary in the Air Ministry; 1938, General Inspector of the Luftwaffe; 1940, field marshal; sentenced in 1947 to life imprisonment, released 1954.

30. Hans-Valentin Hube (1890–1944), regular army officer from Prussian Saxony; instructor at war school in Dresden; 1935, commander of the Dresden Infantry Academy; 1940, general major and divisional commander; general lieutenant and commander of the XIV tank corps; surrounded at Stalingrad, escaped by air; returned to Stalingrad and escaped a second time; fruitless bid to make Hitler approve an attempt to break out; commanded First Tank Army; killed in a plane crash.

31. Walter von Seydlitz-Kurzbach (1888–1976), descended from the family of Frederick the Great's most famous cavalry general; 1939, general major; Paulus relieved him of his command on 26 January 1943 after his repeated requests to surrender; after the capitulation vocal in the Free Germany movement; condemned to death in Germany *in absentia*; 1950, condemend to death by the Soviets; 1955, released – alive – to the west.

32. Karl Strecker (1884–1973), infantry officer; staff officer; policeman in Weimar Republic; 1935, returned to the army and general major; 1940, general lieutenant; captured at Stalingrad; Free Germany Committee; released 1955.

33. XI Corps were the last to surrender. Between 90,000 and 130,000 German and Romanian troops went into captivity, of these 6,000 eventually came home. 146,000 had already fallen. Soviet losses in the battle amounted to 474,871 killed and 974,734 wounded. There are no figures for civilian losses.

CHAPTER 9: FEBRUARY – SUMMER 1943

1. Hitler's intestinal cramps were caused by his vegetarian diet and his lack of exercise. Added to this his intestinal flora had been eradicated by frequent prescriptions of Ultraseptyl. Morell built it up again with a bacterial preparation called Mutaflor. The vitamin preparation he injected Hitler with – Vitamultin – he combined with glucose injections, which were presumably mixed with the stimulant Pervitin. He administered the calmative opium derivative Eudokal and the cramp relaxant Eupaverin six times in 1943, and not at all in the second half of 1942.

2. On 2 February 1943 the Red Army began its two offensives on the Don: Star and Leap. Star was meant to advance to Kursk, while Leap was aimed at the capture of Kharkov.

3. Führer Command No.4 of 16 February 1943 had directed that 'any structures or buildings of value or use to the enemy' had to be 'destroyed or burned down'. He also commanded that the mass of the people be brought with the retreating armies and put to work. The abandoned villages were 'then to be destroyed'.

4. Maximilian Freiherr von und zu Weichs an der Glon (1881–1954), Bavarian General Staff officer on the eve of the First World War; taught tactics at the War School in Dresden in the 1920s; 1933, general major; 1935, general lieutenant; 1939, commanded second Army; 1940, colonel general; 1943, field

marshal; he commanded the remains of Army Group B until it was reassigned to Manstein; pensioned off in March 1945.

5. Walter Brugmann (1887–1944), architect and member of the Nazi Party (1933), commissioned by Speer to undertake the building work for the Party stadium at Nuremberg; Speer's man in Russia.

6. Wolfram Freiherr von Richthofen, (1895–1945), officer from an old Silesian noble family; flier from 1917 in the Richthofen Squadron; 1923; returned to the Reichswehr; qualified engineer; 1932, military attaché in Rome; 1934, transferred to Luftwaffe; 1936–8, Condor Legion in Spain; 1940, air marshal; 1943, field marshal; died following an operation on his brain.

7. Rainer Stahel (1892–1955), officer in First World War; fought in Finnish army where he ended up commanding a corps; 1933, German Luftwaffe; commanded anti-aircraft regiment; 1943, commanded a fighter group; commandant in Vilna; general major, commander in Rome who ordered the defence of the Vatican; Luftwaffe commander in Romania; commandant in Bucharest; 1944, general lieutenant. Died in Soviet captivity.

8. Erwin Rommel (1891–1944), officer on the Isonzo Front in the First World War; taught tactics at the Infantry School in Dresden; 1939, commander of Führer HQ at the invasion of Czechoslovakia and general major; commander of the 7th Panzer Divsions; commander of the Afrika korps; 1942, colonel general; 1943, Supreme Commander of Army Group B in north Italy; end of 1943, Inspector of the Coastal Defences in France; increasingly critical of the leadership, requested that Hitler end the war on 15 July 1944; 17 July 1944, injured in a bomb attack; because of his contacts with the men of 20 July 1944, forced to take poison.

9. Eberhard von Mackensen (1889–1969), cavalry officer before First World War; General Staff; Reichswehr Ministry; 1933, to the Cavalry Corps; 1940, general of cavalry; 1942, Supreme Commander First Panzer Army; 1943, colonel general and Supreme Commander Fourteenth Army. Rommel was succeeded as Commander in Chief of the Africa Korps by Colonel General Hans-Jürgen von Arnim, not Mackensen. Sentenced to death by the British, but sentence commuted and released in 1952.

10. Werner von Braun (1912–77), rocket engineer; 1940, joined the Nazi Party and SS; shifted rocket production to the concentration camp at Dora-Mittelbau in the Harz Mountains; 1945, fled to Bavaria; taken to USA and set to work; 1955, US citizen; active in the development of US rocket programme.

11. Mobile gas chambers had been used first around Posen in the summer of 1940 for the killing of mental patients. Carbon-monoxide canisters were employed. From September 1941 the exhaust gases were fed directly into the wagons and used by the SD in occupied areas in the Soviet Union. The first proved use occurred in the regions of Poltava in November and Kharkov in December 1941.

12. Paul Hennicke (1883–1967), railway administrator; 1920, took part in the Kapp Putsch; 1922, joined the Nazi Party; 1929, SS; 1937–42, Police President

in Weimar; police chief in Rostov and Kiev in occupied Russia; despite repeated trials served only one year in prison after the war.

13. The first gas chambers were set up in connection with the killing of mentally ill patients at six clinics in Germany at the beginning of 1940. Between March and October the SD ordered gas chambers to be set up in the extermination camps at Belzec, Sobibor and Treblinka in the Generalgouvernement and later in other concentration and extermination camps. In occupied Russia there were none.

14. Günther Korten (1898–1944), officer in First World War; pioneer; 1933, Luftwaffe; 1939, Chief of Air Fleet 4; 1940, general major; Chief of the General Staff of the Luftwaffe; killed on 20 July 1944.

15. Ernst Udet (1896–1941), second most important flying ace of the First World War; founded an aircraft-construction business; test pilot; appeared in numerous films; 1935, in Air Ministry; 1939, general major; 1940, colonel general; suicide following an argument with Göring.

16. Walter Frentz (1907–2004), UFA cameraman who worked for Leni Riefenstahl; from 1939, newsreel cameraman at Führer HQ. Resumed work as a photographer after the war.

17. Marion Schönmann (1899–1981), née Petzl, friend of Hoffmann's wife Erna and a frequent guest at the Berghof between 1935 and 1944. In 1937 she married Fritz Schönmann.

18. Margarete Braun (1915–87), worked for Hoffmann in Munich; studied photography; 3 June 1944, married Hermann Fegelein; bore him a posthumous daughter on 5 May 1945; remarried in 1954.

19. Kastrup, Eva Braun's companion. No details known.

20. Manja Behrens played in a number of UFA films before the war and continued her career after 1945 with DEFA. She died in 2003.

21. Edgar Feuchtinger (1894–1960), artillery officer in the First World War, born in Lorraine; taught at the artillery school in Jüterbog; 1939, commanded an artillery regiment; 1943, 1st general major and commander of 21st Panzer Division; general lieutenant; 5 January 1945, sentenced to death for corruption and deserting his post (at the time of the Allied landing in Normandy he was in bed with his mistress in Paris); Hitler pardoned him and had him sent back to the front as a gunner, but he escaped to the British lines; after his release lived in Krefeld and worked in the chemical industry; recruited by Soviet Intelligence; delivered Bundeswehr and Nato secrets to the Soviets; died during a meeting with his contact officer in East Berlin.

22. Verena Wagner (1920–), Wagner's granddaughter; trained as a nurse; married the Nazi Party official Bodo Lafferenz; 1949, excluded from decisions in the family opera company.

23. Otto Meissner (1880–1953), jurist; civil servant in the Weimar President's office; 1935, Chief of the Chancellery; 1937, minister; acquitted at the Wilhelmstrasse Trial.

24. Walter Model (1891–1945), infantry officer in the First World War; staff officer; 1932, lieutenant colonel; 1939, general major 1940, commanded 3rd Panzer Division; 1942, colonel general and Supreme Commander of the Ninth Army; 1944, Supreme Commander of Army Group North and field marshal; 16 August 1944, Supreme Commander in the West; committed suicide to avoid surrender. Hermann Hoth (1884–1971), 1904, commissioned; 1932, colonel; 1938, general major; 1942, commanded Fourth Panzer Army; sacked for defeatism; sentenced to fifteen years by the Allies; released 1954.

25. The 'Fritz Todt' Battery contained four 38cm guns with a range of fifty-four kilometres which had originally been called 'Siegfried' on Cap Gris Nez. The name had been changed after Todt's death.

CHAPTER 10: SUMMER 1943 – FEBRUARY 1944

1. Prince Philipp of Hessen (1896–1980), officer and architect, and, with Karl Edouard of Coburg, one of the most National Socialist of the German princes; joined the Nazi Party in 1930 and the SA in 1931; Oberpräsident of Hesse-Nassau; informal ambassador for the regime; on 9 September 1943 thrown into Flossenbürg concentration camp; later transferred to Dachau. After the war he lived mostly in Italy. His wife Mafalda, daughter of the Italian King, Vittorio Emanuele III, was put into Buchenwald on the same day as Philipp was sent to Flossenbürg. She died as a result of injuries sustained during an Allied raid on the camp.

2. Otto Skorzeny (1908–75), qualified engineer; 1930, joined the Nazi Party; 1939, entered Leibstandarte 'Adolf Hitler' later with other SS divisions; 1943, transferred to the department of foreign sabotage; liberated Mussolini; in 1944, arrested the Hungarian regent Horthy; active in the Battle of the Bulge; briefly in American custody; escaped to Spain; involved in right-wing politics.

3. Kurt Student (1890–1978), Prussian officer; flier from 1916; remained with aeronautical warfare until 1928; 1930, Major; 1933, commanded Technical School in Jüterbog; returned to Luftwaffe; 1938, commander of the Parachute Forces; 1940, general lieutenant; severely wounded in Holland; 1941, masterminded the invasion of Crete; together with Skorzeny liberated Mussolini; in the last days of the war Supreme Commander of Army Group Vistula; sentenced to five years' imprisonment by the Allies, but did not serve it all.

4. Originally the SD had had a more ambitious plan to arrest all those who had been responsible for deposing Mussolini. Operation Alarich was abandoned in September.

5. Theodor Wisch (1907–95), 1930, joined the Nazi Party and SS; 1933, Leibstandarte; 1942, commanded the motorised SS regiments; 1943, commander 2nd Panzer Grenadier Regiment of the SS Leibstandarte 'Adolf Hitler'.

6. In northern Italy and southern France 330,000 of the 480,000 Italian troops were interned and mostly turned over to forced labour. In central and southern Italy the Germans disarmed 300,000 troops and interned 2,000. In the Balkans and the Aegean around 380,000 Italians were disarmed and interned.

7. The German answer to the Soviet T-34. It weighed 45.5 tons and had a 7.5cm cannon. The Type IV was the standard Panzer of the Wehrmacht; 8,000 were made. It had a 7.5cm cannon and weighed around 25 tons. It proved its worth until 1940 but it was not up to the T-34.

8. Fieseler-Storch STOL aircraft of the type Fieseler 156, used above all for reconnaissance; it could take off in sixty-five metres and land in twenty.

9. Gustav Krupp's mind was not wholly on the front. He was busy working out plans to turn his company over to his successor by dispossessing the shareholders. Hitler overruled German law in order to allow him to carry this out.

10. Schacht does not mention this letter in his memoirs. His last conversation with Hitler had taken place in February 1941 when Hitler had asked him about America's response to an attack on the Soviet Union. In August 1943 Schacht asked Lammers if he might write him a memorandum on the political situation. His request was refused, but he wrote the memorandum anyway. Schacht was arrested on 23 July 1944 as he had contacts with the men of 20 July 1944. As there was insufficient evidence to condemn him he was put in Sachsenhausen concentration camp, where he received special treatment.

11. Around 100,000 men belonging to General Otto Wöhler's Eighth Army and Hans Hube's First Panzer Army had been surrounded. On 17 February 30,000 men managed to break through their lines, leaving 55,000 dead and 18,000 prisoners. The Soviet forces lost 270,200 dead and 839,330 wounded.

CHAPTER 11: FEBRUARY – JUNE 1944

1. Herta Schneider (1913–94), née Ostermeier, a school friend of Eva Braun's.

2. Hans Erich Voss (1897–1987), Prussian naval officer; fought in the First World War; 1939 captain; 1942–3 commanded the heavy cruiser *Prinz Eugen*; from 1943, at Führer HQ; 1944, vice admiral; captured by the Russians and released in 1955.

3. Gustav Streve (no dates), commander of Führer HQ before and after Remer.

4. Heinrich Borgmann (1912–45), 1932, Reichswehr; 1935, lieutenant; 1940, rose from first lieutenant to battalion commander in 46th Infantry Regiment; end of 1942, major in the 3rd Luftwaffe Field Division; 1943, GSO2 of the 327th Infantry Division; September, Wehrmacht adjutant with Hitler; injured 20 July; returned to Führer HQ in January 1945; killed in the Battle of Berlin.

5. The Berghof and the neighbouring administrative buildings were reduced to rubble by the RAF on 25 April 1945.

6. It survived, one of only a handful of buildings to do so in a long street. It is still an Italian restaurant and has its original decorations dating from the first years of the twentieth century.

7. Allach, based at Dachau, was 100 per cent owned by the SS company Deutsche Wirtschaftsbetriebene GmbH.

8. Helmut Schreiber (1903–63), 'Kalanag', practised as a magician in Munich from 1919 and organised the first worldwide magicians' congress; 1939 joined the Nazi Party; performed all over the world after the war; his wife Gloria wrote his scripts and assisted him on stage.

9. Goebbels announced total war on 18 February 1943. Six hundred thousand new recruits were found among the young and elderly. Those born in 1926 or 1927 were called up to work on air-raid batteries.

10. Hitler ordered some 200,000 Luftwaffe personnel to be delivered to the army. Göring thwarted him by creating twenty-one 'field divisions'. The inexperienced troops did badly in the war. In March 1945 just five divisions remained.

11. The First Ukrainian Front offensive opened on 4 March 1944 against the First and Fourth Panzer Armies of Army Group South.

12. Created 6 March 1943, it suffered great losses retreating from the Dnieper to the Dniester. In August 1944 it was surrounded in the area of Kishinyov and destroyed.

13. The hill of Monte Cassino was the lynchpin of the Gustav Line that was formed to halt the Allied advance. The Allies started their attempts to break through in October 1943, but it took four battles before they broke through on 13 May 1944. Allied casualties ran to 12,000 dead and wounded; on the German side there were 20,000. On the summit of Monte Cassino was the Benedictine monastery of that name, the oldest in Europe. The order to destroy it was given by the British, who considered the intact building bad for morale. The Germans occupied Monte Cassino only after the Allied bombing.

14. The Polish Volunteer Army had been formed in the Soviet Union at the end of 1941. Originally made up of 70,000 men, it fought in Iraq, then in North Africa and Italy, where it stormed the ruins of Monte Cassino. In February 1945 Anders received the supreme command of Polish forces in the West with an army of nearly 200,000 men. More than 80 per cent refused to be repatriated to Poland after the war.

15. Günther Smend (1912–44), Westphalian officer; 1934, lieutenant; front experience in the infantry, France and the Soviet Union; 1942, General Staff; 1943, adjutant to Zeitzler; had contact with the Plotters of 20 July 1944; executed.

16. Adolf Heusinger (1897–1982), lieutenant in the First World War; staff officer from 1929; 1934, commander company in an infantry regiment; 1936, GSO to 2nd Division; 1937, Operations Department; 1940 colonel and Head of Operations; 1941, general major; 1943, general lieutenant; from June 1944,

stood in as Chief of the General Staff; after 20 July in Gestapo custody; POW until 1948, then rejoined the army; 1955, general lieutenant in the Bundeswehr; 1957, General Inspector of the Bundeswehr.

17. Hermann Fegelein (1906 –45), Bavarian police and show jumper; 1931, joined the Nazi party 1933, SS; 1935, founded the SS riding school in Munich; 1939, Waffen-SS as Obersturmbannführer; 1943, commanded the SS Cavalry Division 'Florian Geyer'; injured in the Pripet Marshes and after his recovery posted to Führer HQ as Himmler's liaison man; 3 June 1944, married Gretl Braun; 21 June 1944, promoted general lieutenant of the SS; 27 April 1945, deserted; tried, and shot in the Chancellery garden.

18. Ilse Braun (1909–79), 1937, secretary to Albert Speer; 1941, *Deutsche Allgemeine Zeitung*.

19. Waldemar Fegelein (1912–2000), vet; 1933, join the Nazi party and SS; war service in Poland; commanded 2nd Regiment of the 8th SS Cavalry Division.

20. Ernst Busch (1885–1945), 1904, lieutenant, 1912–13, War School in Cassel; Freikorps; staff officer; 1928, General Staff; 1930, battalion commander; 1932, colonel and regimental commander; 1935, general major and divisional commander; 1938, commander VIII Army Corps; 1940, colonel general and Supreme Commander of the sixteenth Army; 1943, field marshal; placed on the reserve list then reactivated 20 March 1945; died of a heart attack in Aldershot, England.

21. The Dnieper Line was not strong enough to hold off the Russian attacks.

CHAPTER 12: JULY 1944 – JANUARY 1945

1. Georg-Hans Reinhardt (1887–1963), Saxon officer; 1907, lieutenant; adjutant in First World War, then sent for staff training; staff appointments during the Weimar years; lectured on tactics at the Infantry School in Dresden; 1931, battalion commander; 1933, GSO to the 4th Division; 1934, colonel; 1938, general major; commanded the 4th Panzer Division in the Polish campaign; 1939, general lieutenant; 1940, commander XLI Panzer Corps; 1941, Supreme Commander Panzer Group 3; colonel general; 1944, Supreme Commander of Army Group Centre; sacked after losing East Prussia; sentenced to fifteen years in 1948, released in 1952.

2. Ernst John von Freyend (1909–80), 1936, reserve lieutenant; 1941, captain; 1942, adjutant to Keitel; lieutenant colonel; arrested 1945.

3. Herbert Büchs (1913–96), Silesian; studied economics; 1935, joined the navy; transferred to Luftwaffe; 1941, Air War Academy; March 1943, GSO1 VIII Air Corps; August 1943, GSO1 in 1 Air Corps; from November 1943, in Wehrmacht Operations Staff; joined the Bundeswehr 1957; brigadier general; Chief of Staff; major general; general lieutenant; retired 1974.

4. Heinz Assmann (1904–54), 1922, entered navy; 1926, lieutenant; 1938, corvette captain; 1942, First Officer on the *Tirpitz*; 1943, captain; Wehrmacht Operations Staff from August 1943.

5. Franz von Sonnleithner (1905–81), Austrian diplomat; legal studies; Police Commissioner in Vienna and Salzburg; arrested as a Nazi activist; 1938, in the Foreign Office in Berlin; on Ribbentrop's personal staff; 1943, Foreign Office representative at Führer HQ; prisoner of the Americans until 1949.

6. Claus Schenck Graf von Stauffenberg (1907–44), 1927, lieutenant; 1934, captain; took part in the Polish and French campaigns; 1940, major; January 1943, with Africa Corps; 7 April 1943, badly wounded; colonel and Chief of Staff to General Olbricht; involved with planning 20 July 1944 plot; 1 July 1944, Chief of Staff to General Fromm in the Replacement Army. Executed 20 July 1944.

7. Friedrich Fromm (1888–1945), commander of the Replacement Army, ordered the execution of the Plotters on 20 July 1944, but was unable to prevent his own execution in March 1945.

8. Hans-Karl von Hasselbach (1903–88), surgeon; 1933, entered the Nazi Party; 1934, SS; 1935, escort doctor to Hitler; 1939, with the Wehrmacht; from September 1942, with Hitler's permanent staff; discharged 9 October 1944; ran field hospital on the Western Front; imprisoned by the Americans.

9. Ernst Otto Remer (1912–97), 1935, lieutenant; 1941, captain; battalion commander in the Panzer Regiment 'Gross-Deutschland'; appointed colonel for his role in putting down the 20 July Plot; August 1944, commander of the Führer Escort Brigade; 30 January 1945, general major; active in extreme right-wing politics after the war; denied the mass murder of the Jews; fled to Spain and died in Marbella.

10. Paul von Hase (1885–1944), Governor of Berlin; executed after the 20 July Plot.

11. Ludwig Beck (1880–1944), 1935–8, Chief of the General Staff, resigned his command and tried to influence other generals to do the same. Involved in various plots to remove Hitler. On 20 July 1944 in the Bendlerstrasse HQ where he tried to take his own life; he was finished off by an NCO on Fromm's orders.

12. Friedrich Olbricht (1888–1944), Saxon staff officer; took part in the Polish campaign; 1940, general lieutenant; headed the replacement office at OKW; involved in planning the July Plot; shot on Fromm's orders on 20 July 1944.

13. Albrecht Merz von Quirnheim (1905–44), 1923, entered Reichswehr; general staff, friendly with Stauffenberg; 1942, lieutenant colonel; involved in planning the July Plot; shot on Fromm's orders.

14. Erwin von Witzleben (1881–1944), Silesian officer; staff officer in First World War; 1931, colonel; 1934, general major; 1938, Supreme Commander of Group Command 2; already involved in plans to remove Hitler with Beck; 1939, commander Army; 1940, field marshal; March 1942, placed on reserve list; sentenced to death after 20 July 1944.

15. Johann Bergmüller (1894–?), Bavarian policemen; 1933, on Himmler's staff; 1934, SS; 1937, Nazi Party; sentenced to three years' imprisonment in 1940 for drunken excesses, but sentenced deferred; ejected from SS and Nazi Party; June 1944, allowed back; after 20 July 1944 entrusted with the interrogation of the plotters; released from Soviet captivity in 1949.

16. Helmuth Stieff (1901–44), Prussian gunnery officer; War Academy; GSO1 Fourth Army; December 1942, Chief of the Organisations Department of the General Staff; contract with Henning von Tresckow; involved in the July Plot; sentenced to death.

17. Walther Wenck (1900–82), Freikorps; 1923, lieutenant; 1934, captain; War Academy; 1939, GSO1 1st Panzer Division; 1942, Chief of Staff of LVII Panzer Corps; 1943, general major; April 1944, general lieutenant; finally Supreme Commander of the Twelfth Army.

18. Wilhelm Burgdorf (1895–1945) officer in the First World War; taught tactics at the Dresden School of War; began Second World War in command of an infantry regiment; 1942, general major; 1944, Head of Personnel and successor to Schmundt in Führer HQ.

19. Karl Koller (1898–1951), Bavarian flier in First World War; policeman; 1935, Luftwaffe; 1936–8, Air Academy; 1941, colonel and Chief of Staff of 3rd Air Fleet; November 1944, Chief of Staff of the Luftwaffe.

20. This provided the cue for the Warsaw Uprising, which nonetheless received no support from Stalin. The Poles gave up on 2 October 1944, but they were recognised as prisoners of war. During the battles they had lost 16,000. At the same time 166,000 inhabitants of the city lost their lives and 70,000 were committed to forced labour. Hitler gave orders that Warsaw was to be levelled.

21. Ludwig Stumpfegger (1910–45), SS doctor; 1937, joined the Nazi Party; worked in the SS hospital in Hohenlychen; Himmler's personal physician; October 1944, duty doctor to Hitler; poisoned himself with Bormann.

22. Hugo Blaschke (1889–1951), studied in Philadelphia and London; from 1911, dental practice in Berlin; Göring's dentist and, from 1933, Hitler's; 1931, joined the Nazi Party; 1935, SS; high SS rank.

23. Built in 1918 between the Alle and Passarge rivers.

24. A secret Nazi Party report announced moves to evacuation the population of East Prussia. These were not followed up.

25. He does not appear to have had any evidence for this diagnosis.

26. Thirty-three Divisions were cut off and all means of evacuation by sea denied them. Eventually 208,000 men went into Soviet captivity.

27. Hans Günther von Kluge (1882–1944), 1901, lieutenant; 1908–11, War Academy; 1912, General Staff; 1918, GSO1 in 236th Infantry Division; 1927, lieutenant colonel; 1933, general major; 1934, general lieutenant; 1935, commander of VI Army Corps; 1940, colonel general and field marshal; 1941, Supreme Commander of Army Group Centre; 1943, placed on the reserve

list; July 1944, Supreme Commander in the West; contacts with the military opposition; poisoned himself near Metz.

28. Kluge had wavered many times, particularly after the attempt, when he knew Hitler was still alive.

29. The Germans were finally cut off on 20 August 1944. Around 50,000 men had already escaped; 50,000 or so were captured and around 10,000 killed.

30. Before September 1944 the Wehrmacht lost more than 414,802 in casualties on the Western Front. The Allied figures are 40,000 dead, 164,000 wounded and 20,000 missing.

31. The Allies lost around 17,000 men in Operation Market Garden in Holland at the end of September, while the Canadians lost about 13,000 on the Scheldt Estuary between October and November.

32. August Winter (1897–1979), Bavarian intelligence officer; from 1934, taught at War Academy; from 1937, OKH; 1940, on General Staff of Army Group A; 1943, Chief of Staff of Panzer Army; 1944, general lieutenant; Jodl's assistant in the Wehrmacht Operations Staff.

33. Hasso von Manteuffel (1897–1978), scion of a great Prussian military dynasty; served as a hussar officer in the First World War; Freikorps; involved in motorised warfare; 1937, on the staff of the Inspector of Panzer Warfare; 1939, taught at tank school; 1941, commander 7th Panzer Division; 1943, Manstein Division in Tunisia; 1943, general major; 1944, general lieutenant and commander of the Panzer Grenadier Division 'Gross-Deutschland'; commander of the Fifth Panzer Army in the Ardennes; taken prisoner by the British; member of the Bundestag; 1959, sentenced to two years' imprisonment.

CHAPTER 13: JANUARY – MARCH 1945

1. Later oak leaves were introduced in the borders and in the claws of the eagles.

2. Willy Johannmeyer (1915–?), 1933, SS; entered army; 1938, infantry lieutenant; 1943, battalion commander; April 1945, replaced Albert Bormann as adjutant and took Hitler's will to Ferdinand Schörner; imprisoned by the Americans.

3. Johannes Göhler (1918–?), Saxon SS man; 1937, joined the Nazi Party; commanded a squadron of SS Cavalry; SS-Sturmbannführer; adjutant to Fegelein.

4. Bernd von Freytag-Loringhoven (1914–), 1934, entered the Reichswehr; 1937, lieutenant; 1942, captain in 2nd Panzer Regiment; 1943, major in 3rd Infantry Division; 1944, adjutant to Guderian and Krebs in the Operations Department; left the bunker to make contact with Wenck; captured by the Americans; 1956, Bundeswehr; general lieutenant; retired in 1973 and lives in Munich.

5. Gerhard Boldt (1918–?), 1937 cavalry officer; 1944, Guderian's orderly officer and later performed the same duties for Krebs; after the war worked for Gehlen in intelligence.

6. Wilhelm Zander (1911–74), timber trader; 1931, joined the Nazi Party and SS; on Himmler's staff; after a duel transferred to Hitler's and Bormann's service; alternating political and military functions in the SS and Nazi Party; brought a copy of Hitler's will to Bavaria.

7. Gerhard Wagner (1898–1986), Mecklenburger; navy from 1916; 1925, commanded a torpedo boat; 1931, Naval Academy; 1936, Spanish Civil War; 1937, commanded the destroyer *Leberecht Maass*; 1940, captain; 1941, Chief of Operations and liaison officer to the Naval High Command; 1956, rejoined the navy and rear admiral; 1961, Nato command for North Central Europe based in Kiel; 1962, vice admiral.

8. Reinhard Gehlen (1902–79), 1933–5, War Academy; various staff jobs; at the beginning of the war on the staff of 213th Infantry Division; from 1942, Foreign Armies Department in the General Staff; 1944; general major; built the Gehlen Organisation for the Americans; 1955, BND – German Intelligence organisation that was made part of the Bundeswehr; general lieutenant; pensioned off in 1968 after the BND was infiltrated by the East German MfSS or Stasi.

9. Karl Hanke (1903–45), miller; member of a number of army organisations; taught trades in Berlin; 1928, joined the Nazi Party; 1932–45, member of the Reichstag; ran Goebbels's secretariat; 1934, SS; 1935–7, on Himmler's staff; 1938, State Secretary in the Propaganda Ministry; volunteer in the Polish and French campaigns; 1941, first lieutenant in the Wehrmacht; cooling of relations with Goebbels due to his relationship with Magda; 1941, Gauleiter for Lower Silesia; Reich Defence Commissar and various offices within his *Gau*; the force behind the declaration of Breslau as a 'fortress'; caught by Czech partisans and presumed shot.

10. Kurt Petter (1909–69), medical doctor; 1930, joined the Nazi Party; 1934, Reich Youth Office; 1937, inspector of the Adolf Hitler Schools; commander of the Academy for Youth Leadership in Brunswick; Leader of the Reich Führer School for Hitler Youth in Potsdam; war service as a medic; official in the Nazi Party from November 1943; worked with Baldur von Schirach in Vienna. Worked as a paediatrician in Hamburg after the war.

11. Ernst Schlünder (1898–?), officer in the First World War; studied economics; sports teacher; 1933, joined the Nazi Party; on various bodies promoting sport and physical exercise; in the office of the Hitler Youth chief; 1944, entered SS; served in the SS Panzer Division 'Hitler Youth'; commanded the Hitler Youth's last stand on the Pichelsdorf Bridge; civil servant after the war.

12. Arthur Greiser (1847–1946), co-founder of the Stahlhelm veterans' association after the First World War; 1929, joined the Nazi Party and SA; 1930, SS; President of the Danzig Senate and Gauleiter of the Warthegau; 1943, SS general. Organised the clearance of jews from the Warthegau and Lodz. Surrendered to the Americans in the Bavarian Alps. Sentenced to death and publicly hanged by the Poles after being paraded around Poznan in an iron cage.

13. Gerhard Klopfer (1905–87) lawyer; 1933, joined the Nazi Party and SA; 1934, Gestapo; 1935, on Hess's staff; 1941, close colleague of Bormann; took part in the Wannsee Conference; practised as a lawyer in Ulm after 1945.

14. Helmuth Friedrichs (1899–1945), officer in the First World War, POW in Britain until 1920; 1929, joined the Nazi Party; from 1942, close colleague of Bormann; 1936, SS; presumed dead fighting with the Volkssturm.

15. Henrich Müller (1896–1945), lawyer; 1921, joined the Nazi Party; civil servant; 1933–4, Interior Minister in Hessen; Mayor of Darmstadt; personal assistant of Martin Bormann.

16. The evacuation plans for the ministries were worked out at this meeting, under the codename Thusnelda.

17. Edmund Geilenberg (1902–64), engineer; managed the Hermann Göring Works; director of the Brunswick Steelworks; head of the ammunition committee in the Armaments Ministry; involved in the plans to accommodate industry in subterranean sites and staff them with slave labour.

18. Erich von dem Bach-Zelewski (1899–1972), Pomeranian soldier; 1916, lieutentant; Freikorps; varied existence in the 1920s including spell as taxi-driver and farmer; 1931, joined the Nazi Party and SS; rose quickly through the ranks of the SS; 1936, Gestapo in Königsberg; 1938, Police Chief in Breslau; 1941, general lieutenant of the police; November 1941, general; 1942, dealt with partisans behind the German lines; 1944, general of the Waffen-SS; led the suppression of the Warsaw Uprising; led various SS corps until his capture; evaded prison until 1951; released 1958; 1962, sentenced to life and died in a prison hospital.

19. Friedrich Jeckeln (1895–1946), officer in the First World War; farmer then engineer; 1929 joined the Nazi Party; 1930, SS; policeman; 1941, general of the police; 1944, general of the Waffen-SS; sentenced to death in Riga.

20. Emil Stürtz (1892–1945), sailor in the First World War; metalworker and driver; 1925, joined the Nazi Party; 1930–45, member of the Reichstag; 1936, Gauleiter of Kurmark; 1937, Oberpräsident of Brandenburg.

21. Hans Kammler (1901–45), Reichswehr and Freikorps in 1919; technical studies; qualified as an engineer; 1932, joined the Nazi Party; 1933, SS; various portfolios involving building, air travel and race; after 1941, involved in the planning and building of concentration camps in Majdenek and Auschwitz; later responsible for the development of Mittelbau-Dora; directly answerable to Himmler; given responsibility for the V-weapons and the jet fighter; thought to have committed suicide.

22. Carl von Eicken (1873–1960), ENT specialist, Professor of Medicine at Giessen and Berlin; director of the ENT Clinic at the Charité.

23. Gotthard Heinrici (1886–1971), staff officer in the First World War; 1930, battalion commander; 1933, colonel; 1938, general lieutenant; 1944, commanded First Panzer Army. Replaced Himmler as Supreme Commander of Army Group Vistula on 22 March 1945.

24. Karl Gebhardt (1897–1948), surgeon and assistant to Ferdinand Sauerbruch, the most famous German surgeon of his day; 1933, joined the Nazi Party; led the SS clinic at Hohenlychen; instigated the experiments on concentration camp inmates. Sentenced to death and executed.

25. Ernst Kaltenbrunner (1903–46), Austrian lawyer; 1930, joined the Nazi Party; 1931, SS; imprisoned for illegal membership; State Secretary for Public Security after the Anschluss; January 1943, head of the SD; February 1944, head of the Abwehr; arrested by the Americans and executed.

CHAPTER 14: MARCH 1945

1. Otto Wöhler (1894–1987), ended the First World War as a battalion commander; staff appointments during Weimar; 1935, lieutenant colonel; 1936, GSO1 VIII Army Corps; 1939, Chief of Staff of XVIII Army Corps; 1942, general lieutenant; 1943, commander 1 Army Corps, general of the infantry; sentenced to eight years, released 1951.

2. Lothar Rendulic (1887–1971), 1917, captain in the Imperial Army; 1929, lieutenant colonel; 1933, Austrian military attaché in Paris and colonel; 1935, dismissed for contacts with the Nazi Party; 1938, colonel in the Wehrmacht; 1939, general major; 1944, colonel general; sentenced to twenty-five years but released in 1951.

3. The officers who planned it were betrayed. On 8 April 1945 three of them were publicly hanged.

4. Gerhard Pick (1910–1987), commander of the 577th Infantry Regiment of the 305th Infantry Division; 1945, lieutenant colonel.

5. The order was given by the commander of the Defensive Area of Berlin – Lieutenant General Hellmuth Reymann – on 9 March 1945. Reymann made it clear that it would not be an open battle, but fought in streets and houses. He was accepting a high number of civilian losses from the start.

6. Gerhard Schach (1906–72), textile salesman in Berlin; 1928, joined the Nazi Party; Party functionary in the Berlin area; 1933–45, member of the Reichstag; 1944–45, assistant Gauleiter of Berlin; in *The Hitler Book* falsely said to have died.

7. Arthur Kannenberg (1896–1963), cook, waiter, cooper, bookkeeper; ran his father's restaurant; in 1930 he was running a pub where Göring and Goebbels met; 1931, ran the mess in the Brown House; 1933, majordomo in the Reich Chancellery; after the war, ran a pub in Düsseldorf.

8. Theodor Busse (1897–1986), Prussian officer in the First World War; 1929, staff officer; 1939, lieutenant colonel; 1940, GSO1 in Second Army; 1942, GSO1 in Army Group Don, later South; 1944, Commander 1 Army Corps and general of the infantry.

9. Rudolf Huebner (1897–1965), born near Posen; volunteer in the First World War; dentist; 1935, captain; 1940, major; 1942, commanded an infantry

regiment as lieutenant colonel; 1943, colonel; wrote the text of 'Why are we fighting?' In April 1944, in the National Socialist Operations Staff with the Wehrmacht; August 1944, Chief of the National Socialist Operations Staff with the Wehrmacht; 1 February 1945 commanded the 303rd Infantry Division 'Döberitz' – a well-equipped unit cobbled together from Luftwaffe ground crews and the survivors of shattered divisions; Commandant of Munich, where he sentenced 200 'rioters' to death; later sentenced to four years for his unjust treatment of those who failed to blow up the bridge at Remagen.

10. The US First and Ninth Armies joined up at Lippstadt on 31 March 1945. On 14 April they managed to split the pocket in two. The smaller half capitulated on 16 April, the larger one a day later, and 325,000 German soldiers went into captivity. Model shot himself on 21 April in a copse near Duisburg.

11. Friedel was a major on the General Staff who witnessed the signing of the capitulation in Rheims. Nothing else is known about him. Lieutenant Colonel von der Knesebeck is also obscure.

12. August Hermani (1911–?), 1934, lieutenant; 1940, transport chief in the General Staff; 1934, GSO1 XLII Army Corps; 1944, lieutenant colonel and GSO1 in 26th Infantry Division; 1944, in Operations Department of the General Staff; entered Bundeswehr in 1956.

13. Manfred Löhlein (1882–1954) was professor at Berlin University and the Chief of the eye clinic at the Charité. He was a member of the Nazi Party. The drips he prescribed contained no cocaine, but Morell had used a solution containing 1 per cent for conjunctivitis.

14. The Junkers 52 was the standard transport plane of the Luftwaffe. At the end of the war Hitler's flight consisted of forty aircraft of the types Fiesler 156, Focke-Wulf 200, Heinkel III, Junkers 52, Junkers 290 and Siebel 204.

15. Ferdinand Schörner (1892–1973), Bavarian officer in the First World War; had briefly studied philosophy and modern languages; Freikorps Epp; staff officer during Weimar; 1937, regimental commander; 1940, commanded the 6th Mountain Rifles Division; fought in Greece and the Soviet Union; 1942, general lieutenant; 1944, colonel general; May 1944, Chief of the National Socialist Operations Staff; 5 April 1945, field marshal; released from captivity in the Soviet Union in 1955. Imprisoned in Munich in 1957 for manslaughter. Released 1960.

16. Ivo Thilo von Trotha (1905–98), 1937, War Academy; 1941, GSO1 in 267th Infantry Division; October 1942, GSO1 in Fourth Army; 1943, colonel; October 1944, Chief of Staff in the First Panzer Army; March 1945, Chief of Operations in the OKH; 1 April 1945, general major.

17. Founded 1898. During the war it supplied the Wehrmacht.

18. *Die Grosse Liebe* of 1942.

19. Erich Bärenfänger (1915–45), 1941, lieutenant; 1942, captain; 1943, major and regimental commander; 1944, lieutenant colonel; commanded defensive section A in Berlin and was promoted from lieutenant colonel to general major; killed himself in Prenzlauer Berg station.

20. It is difficult to estimate the size of this organisation now. Some units were attached to the Twelfth Army during the Battle of Berlin. In Munich they shot and hanged several dozen people after the revolt of the resistance group Freedom Action Bavaria.

21. Experiments of this sort had been carried out by all the main powers in the war. In the Tyrol there had been tests of killer soundwaves.

22. The Estonian singer and dancer Madeleine Wanderer.

23. Gut Rottland near Waldbröl was a former convalescent home belonging to the Protestant Church in Cologne. In 1945 Ley had the SS destroy the model estate he had created.

CHAPTER 15: APRIL – MAY 1945

1. The Soviet Oder offensive, which led to the final battle for Berlin, began on 16 April 1945 at 3.00 a.m. with a twenty-five-minute artillery barrage. The Soviet army numbered 2.1 million men, with 41,600 artillery pieces, 6,250 tanks and 7,500 planes. They were faced by a million Germans armed with 10,400 artillery pieces, 1,500 tanks and 3,300 planes. In the course of the battle 80,000 Russians were killed and 280,000 wounded. German casualties are not known.

2. Wilhelm Mohnke (1911–2001), 1931, SS; 1933, Leibstandarte; various campaigns; 1943, Obersturmbannführer and commander of the Panzer Grenadier Regiment; 1945, Brigadeführer; appointed 23 April 1945 to defend the government district of Berlin; captured, and released from Soviet Russia in 1955.

3. Werner Haase (1900–50), surgeon; 1933, joined the Nazi Party and SA; 1935, SS attached to Hitler's staff; taught at Berlin University; Professor of Surgery; April 1945 in charge of the hospital under the New Reich Chancellery; died in the Butyrka Prison.

4. There were six Luftwaffe flak towers in Berlin: two in the Tiergarten, two in Humboldthain and two in Friedrichshain. The forty-metre-high towers had been erected in 1940 and were each armed with four 12.8cm twin anti-aircraft guns. The towers also provided air-raid shelter for up to 15,000 people.

5. The aircraft containing the minutes of the situation conferences arrived in Reim near Munich at six in the morning of 23 April. The documents were stored in the Berghof and on the 25th burned on the instructions of Bormann's assistant Senate President Müller. The military historian Scherff approved destruction of the papers, which meant there would not be an objective account of the history for decades to come. A few charred papers were published in West Germany in 1962.

6. Called 'Nigger torpedoes' after their inventor, Richard Mohr (the name translates as 'Moor'), a manned torpedo led one filled with explosive. They were first successfully used at the Allied landings at Anzio. The second trial was in the Seine basin, when they sank a British cruiser and a few other craft. Beause of heavy losses as a result of technical drawbacks, the 'Niggers' were no longer used.

7. The text has not survived.

8. The active ingredient was Xanthogenat and it was a development from a Russian anti-louse soap.

9. The 'Alex' is just under a kilometre from the former Royal Palace and a little over two kilometres from the former Reich Chancellery.

10. Robert Ritter von Greim (1892–1945), Bavarian flying officer in the First World War; studied law; trained the Chinese air force; 1928–34, ran the flying school in Würzburg; 1934, lieutenant colonel in the Luftwaffe; 1937, Chief of Personnel; 1939, commander of the 5th Flying Division; 1940, general lieutenant; 1941, commander of the Luftwaffe Command East; 1943, colonel general and Supreme Commander of the Air Fleet 6; 26 April 1945, appointed successor to Göring; arrested by the Americans. Committed suicide.

11. Hanna Reitsch (1912–79), studied medicine without qualifying; 1934, established world record for long-distance flight by a woman; 1937, flight captain; 1939, test pilot for the Luftwaffe. Mistress of Ritter von Greim; interned in 1945 and released a year later; continued winning prizes as a pilot.

12. In 1940–1 Hanna Reitsch had flown Heinkel III and Dornier 17 planes to test whether the steel guys of British barrage balloons could be cut with an apparatus mounted on the plane's nose. She received the Iron Cross for this, although the experiment was only partially successful.

13. Helmuth Weidling (1891–1955), Zeppelin officer in the First World War; served in the artillery; 1922, captain; 1935, lieutenant colonel and commander of 56th Artillery Regiment; 1942, general major and divisional commander; 1943, general lieutenant and leader of XLI Panzer Corps; general of the artillery; reserve list; 12 April 1945 commander of LXI Panzer Corps and Battle Commander of Berlin. Died in Soviet captivity.

14. Contemporary sources tell of 10,000 or so 'deserters' killed in this way.

15. These had a range of 2,500 to 8,400 metres. They were not particularly accurate but they caused terror by the volume and speed of their discharge and the large area they struck. They were called 'organs' because of the wailing noise they made.

16. Field marshals received, in addition to their monthly salaries of 2,000 marks, special bonuses of 4,000 marks and 400 marks.

17. Heinrich 'Gestapo' Müller (1900–45); Bavarian policeman; placed in the political department to observe the communists; 1933, criminal inspector; 1934, SS and SD; 1939, joined the Nazi party; 1941, general lieutenant of police; his end is the subject of much speculation.

EDITORS' AFTERWORD

1. Quotations will be from the two-volume paperback edition.

2. Alan Bullock, *Hitler and Stalin: Parallel Lives*, HarperCollins, London, 1991.

3. See Anton Joachimsthaler, *Hitlers Liste. Ein Dokument persönlicher Beziehungen*, Herbig, Munich, 2003. Anton Joachimsthaler, *Hitlers Ende. Legenden and Dokumente*, Herbig, Munich, 2004.

4. Quoted in Lev A. Besymenski, *Operazija 'Mif' ili skol'ko ras choronili Gitlera* [The Operation Myth, or how often Hitler was buried], Moscow 1995, 105.

5. Antony Beevor, *Berlin: The Downfall, 1945*, Viking, London, 2002; Georgi Zhukov, *Errinerungen und Gedanken*, Deutscher Militärverlag Berlin, Stuttgart, 1969, 604ff.

6. The minutes of the coronary investigation are printed in Lev Besymenski, *Der Tod des Adolf Hitler*, Herbig, Munich, 1982, 321–51.

7. Hitler had had to be 'shot down like a dog', according to Besymenski. See *Der Tod des Adolf Hitler* (Wegner, Hamburg, 1968) and – heavily altered, but in its substance the same – *Der Tod des Adolf Hitler* (1982); for a critique see Joachimsthaler, *Hitlers Ende*, 266.

8. Gerhard Boldt, *Die letzten Tage in der Reichskanzlei*, ed. Ernst A. Hepp, Rowolt, Hamburg and Stuttgart, 1947.

9. The real reasons are nonetheless unclear. For one thing Baur refused to make any more statements and went on hunger strike. For another he had been designated a source of the 'second rank'. After 1948 he was dragged through a number of camps, sentenced to twenty-five years' imprisonment and then in 1955 released to West Germany. See Hans Baur, *Hitler at My Side: The Memories of Hitler's Personal Pilot 1932–1945*, M.S. Trading, London, 1958.

10. In addition to Parparov – who spoke fluent German and was experienced in intelligence work – and Salayev – who had a doctorate in social sciences and had been active in Germany – the NKVD team comprised the Estonian Lieutenant Colonel J. K. Klausen, the Latvian Jan W. Schweyzer, a member of the state security organs since 1925, and the historian W. S. Stern, later the Chief of the Military History Institute in East Germany, as well as the non-German-speaking Lieutenant N. M. Smirnov and a women interpreter from Leningrad.

11. See Heinz Linge, *Bis zum Ende, als Chef des Persönlicher Dienstes bei Hitler*, ed. Werner Maser, Herbig, Munich, 1980, 307 passim.

12. This is not particularly astonishing as Stalin mostly only marked and commented on documents of a strategic character, or papers that dealt with the arrest, interrogation or torture of particular people.

13. A copy of the German original is in Lev Besymenski, *Die letzten Notizen von Martin Bormann. Ein Dokument und sein Verfasser*, Deutsche Verlags-Anstalt, Stuttgart, 1974.

14. He was interested not least in being able to support his prosecutions during the purges, but the gathering of information on those who were dependent on him was motivated by the exigencies of power. With time political calculation was turned into uncontrolled paranoia.

15. Largely for financial reasons, Hitler gave up smoking in his youth. Only later did he develop an hostility to smoking that was strengthened by the deaths of

members of his circle and by popular science. He forbade it in his entourage and supported non-smoking campaigns and medical research on this 'poison', but for political reasons he did not ban it. The testimonies of witnesses and early research were discussed by the SS-doctor Ernst Günther Schenck see *Patient Hitler. Eine medizinische Biographie*, Bechtermuenz Verlag, Augsburg, 2000, 32–8.

16. See *ibid.*, 32.

17. He was a vegetarian from 1931, the year his niece Geli Raubal died.

18. See Friedelind Wagner, *Nacht über Bayreuth*, Ullstein Taschenbuchvig, Munich, 2002, 121.

19. Morell's eye-drops were a solution containing 1 per cent cocaine, a quantity which is not sufficient to cause addiction.

20. Also to be considered are the effects of the attempt on his life of 20 July 1944 in which Hitler was more seriously injured than the regime's propaganda claimed.

21. Schenck, *Patient Hitler*, 203.

22. Fritz Redlich, *Hitler: Diagnosis of a Destructive Prophet*, Oxford University Press, Oxford, 1999.

23. Werner Maser, *Adolf Hitler, Legende, Mythos, Wirklichkeit*, Bechtle Verlag, Esslingen, 1971, 485.

24. Joachimsthaler, *Hitlers Liste*, 475–82.

25. Schenck, *Patient Hitler*, 122–30.

26. See Albert Speer, *Spandauer Tagebücher*, Ullstein Verlag, Frankfurt am Main, Berlin, Vienna, 1975, 122.

27. In Soviet eyes Hungary and Romania were on the brink of going over to socialism, while in Italy the Communist Party was still included in the executive. Georgi Dimitrov's Bulgaria was solid with the Soviet Union, while Tito's Yugoslavia had already taken the path to confrontation. As a result neither Yugoslavia nor Bulgaria was much mentioned in *The Hitler Book*.

28. Linge, *Ende*, 142. It is unclear whether the editor was responsible for this.

29. The idea that the military resistance had always wanted to kill the dictator is without foundation. Even in 1944, only a small number of people in positions of responsibility were ready to sacrifice themselves. Not even the conspirator Stauffenberg, who was firmly decided, trusted his co-plotters. That more than 7,000 people were executed or murdered after the plot was due to the desire of the Nazi Party to persecute and owed nothing to the scale of the resistance.

30. Percy Ernst Schramm, ed., *Kriegstagebuch des Oberkommandos der Wehrmacht (Wehrmachtführungsstab) 1940–1945. Studienausgabe in 8 Bänden,* Bernd and Graefe, Frankfurt, 1961–65, vol.

31. Artur Axmann, *'Das kann doch nicht das Ende sein'. Hitlers letzter Reichsjugendführer erinnert sich*, Bublies, Koblenz, 1995, 560. Axmann, who with good anti-communist slogans sent thousands of Hitler Youths to senseless deaths, later founded a firm that did good business trading with East Germany and the Soviet Union.

32. Adolf Hitler, *Mein Kampf*, Zentralverlag der NSDAP, Munich, 1940, 743.

Select Bibliography

UNPUBLISHED SOURCES

Russian State Archive of Contemporary History (RGANI)
  5/30/462a
Reports from the Archive of the President of the Russian Federation (AP RF)
  3/58/530
  3/58/531
  3/58/532
State Archive of the Russian Federation (GARF)
  9401/2/96
  9401/2/97
  9401/2/199
  9401/2/236
  9401/2/550
  9401/2/551
  9401/2/555
Russian State Military Archive (RGVA)
  460/1878 (Trial/Urteil Günsche)
  460/1871 (Trial/Urteil Linge)
Institute of Contemporary History (Institut für Zeitgeschichte [IfZ])
  Fa 74 Günsche, Otto, Akz. 2108/57
  Fa 74 Linge, Heinz, Akz 2108/57
  F 135/1, Akz 6714/83

PUBLISHED WORKS

Allen, Martin, *The Hitler/Hess Deception*, HarperCollins, London, 2004
Applebaum, Anne, *Gulag: A History of the Soviet Camps*, Allen Lane, London, 2003
Arendt, Hannah, *The Origins of Totalitarianism*, André Deutsch, London, 1986
Aronson, Shlomo, *Hitler, the Allies, and the Jews: The Multiple Trap*, Cambridge University Press, Cambridge, 2004

Baur, Hans, *Hitler at My Side: The Memoir of Hitler's Personal Pilot 1932–1945*, M. S. Trading, London, 1958

Beevor, Antony, *Stalingrad*, Viking, London, 1998

——, *Berlin: The Downfall, 1945*, Viking, London, 2002

Below, Nicolaus von, trans. Geoffrey Brooks, *At Hitler's Side: The Memoirs of Hitler's Luftwaffe Adjutant*, Greenhill Books, London, 2001

Benz, Wolfgang, and Pehle, Walter H., *Encyclopedia of German Resistance*, Continuum, New York, 1997

Blandford, Edmund L., *Hitler's Second Army: The Waffen SS*, Airlife, Shrewsbury, 1994

Boldt, Gerhard, *Hitler's Last Days: An Eye-witness Account*, Barker, London, 1973

Breitman, Richard, *The Architect of Genocide: Himmler and the Final Solution*, Harvill Press, London, 1994

Browning, Christopher R., *Nazi Policy, Jewish Labor, German Killers*, Cambridge University Press, Cambridge, 2000

——, *The Origins of the Final Solution: The Evolution of Nazi Jewish Policy, September 1939–March 1942*, Heinemann, London, 2004

Bullock, Alan, *Hitler and Stalin: Parallel Lives*, HarperCollins, London, 1991

Burdick, Charles, and Jacobsen, Hans-Adolf (eds), *The Halder War Diary, 1939–1942*, Presidio Press, London, 1988

Burleigh, Michael, *The Third Reich: A New History*, Pan, London, 2001

Butler, Rupert, *SS-Leibstandarte: The History of the First SS Division 1933–1945*, Staplehurst, 2001

Churchill, Winston, *The Second World War*, 6 vols, Penguin, London, 2005

Domarus, Max, *Hitler: Speeches and Proclamations, 1932–1945: The Chronicle of a Dictatorship*, I. B. Tauris, London, 1990

Fest, Joachim, *Hitler*, Weidenfeld & Nicolson, London, 1987

——, *Inside Hitler's Bunker: The Last Days of the Third Reich*, Macmillan, London, 2005

Finkelstein, Norman G., and Birn, Ruth Bettina, *A Nation on Trial: The Goldhagen Thesis and Historical Truth*, Metropolitan Books, New York, 1998

Fleming, Gerald, *Hitler and the Final Solution*, Hamish Hamilton, London, 1985

François-Poncet, André, *The Fateful Years: Memoirs of a French Ambassador in Berlin 1931–1938*, trans. Jacques LeClercq, Gollancz, London, 1949

Friedländer, Saul, *Nazi Germany and the Jews: Years of Persecution, 1933–39*, Weidenfeld & Nicolson, London, 1997

——, *Extermination of the Jews*, HarperCollins, London, 2005

Gassert, Philipp, and Mattern, Daniel S., *The Hitler Library: A Bibliography*, Greenwood Press, Westport, CT, 2001

Germany and the Second World War, ed. Militärgeschichtiches Forschungsamt, Freiburg, Oxford, 1990–

Goebbels, Joseph, *Diaries*, ed. Hugh Trevor-Roper, Secker & Warburg, London, 1978

Gorodetsky, Gabriel, *Grand Delusion: Stalin and the German Invasion of Russia*, Yale University Press, New Haven, CT, 1999

Haffner, Sebastian, *The Meaning of Hitler*, Weidenfeld & Nicolson, London 1999.

Heiber, Helmut, and Glantz, David M. (eds), *Hitler and His Generals: Military Conferences from Stalingrad to Berlin, 1942–1945*, Greenhill Books, London, 2002

Heinsohn, Gunnar, *Lexikon der Volkermorde*, Rowohlt, Reinbek, 1998

Hillgruber, Andreas, *Germany and the Two World Wars*, Harvard University Press, Cambridge, MA, 1981

——, *Hitlers Strategie: Politik und Kriegführung 1940–1941*, Bernard und Graefe, Munich, 1982

—— (ed.), *Staatsmänner und Diplomaten bei Hitler, 1 Teil: Vertrauliche Aufzeichnungen über Unterredungen mit Vertretern des Auslandes 1939–1941*, Bernard und Graefe, Frankfurt, 1967

——, *Staatsmänner und Diplomaten bei Hitler, 2 Teil: Vertrauliche Aufzeichnungen über Unterredungen mit Vertretern des Auslandes 1942–1944*, Bernard und Graefe, Frankfurt, 1970

Hitler, Adolf, *Mein Kampf*, trans. Ralph Manheim, Pimlico, London, 1992

——, *Hitler's Table Talk*, ed. Hugh Trevor-Roper, Enigma Books, London, 2000

Hobsbawm, Eric J., *Age of Extremes: The Short Twentieth Century, 1914–1991*, Abacus, London, 1994

Hoffmann, Peter: *The History of the German Resistance, 1933–1945*, McGill Queen's University Press, Montreal, 1996

——, *Hitler's Personal Security*, Da Capo Press, London, 1979

Höhne, Heinz, *Der Orden unter dem Totenkopf: Die Geschichte der SS*, Orbis Verlag, Bindlach, 1990

Irving, David, *The War between the Generals*, Focal Point Publications, Harmondsworth, 1982

Ishoven, Armand van, *The Fall of an Eagle: The Life of Fighter Ace Ernst Udet*, William Kimber, London 1979

Joachimsthaler, Anton, *The Last Days of Hitler: The Legends, the Evidence, the Truth*, Caxton Editions, London, 1996

Johnson, Aaron L., *Hitler's Military Headquarters: Organization, Structures, Security, and Personnel*, R. James Bender, San José, CA, 1999

Junge, Traudl, *Until the Final Hour: Hitler's Last Secretary*, Weidenfeld & Nicolson, London, 2003

Kater, Michael H., *Hitler Youth*, Harvard University Press, Cambridge, MA, 2004

Keegan, John, *The Second World War*, Pimlico, London, 1989

—— (ed.), *The Times Atlas of the Second World War*, Times Books, London, 1989

—— (ed.), *Who's Who in World War II*, Routledge, London, 2001

Keitel, Wilhelm, *Mein Leben, Pflichterfüllung bis zum Untergang*, ed. Werner Maser, Edition q, Berlin, 1998

Kershaw, Ian, *Hitler 1889–1936: Hubris*, Allen Lane, London, 1998

——, *Hitler 1936–1945: Nemesis*, Allen Lane, London 2000

——, *The Nazi Dictatorship: Problems and Perspectives of Interpretation*, Hodder Arnold, London, 2000

——, *The 'Hitler Myth': Image and Reality in the Third Reich*, Oxford Paperbacks, Oxford, 2001

——, and Lewin, Moshe (eds), *Stalinism and Nazism: Dictatorships in Comparison*, Cambridge University Press, Cambridge, 1997

Kolpakidin, Alexander I., and Prochorov, Dimitriy P., *Vneschnaya rasvedka Rossii*, St Petersburg, 2001

Kopperschmidt, Josef, and Pankau, Johannes G. (eds), *Hitler der Redner*, Wilhelm Fink, Munich, 2003

Koslov, Vladimir A., *'Gde Gitler?' Povtornoe rassledovanie NKVD–MVD SSSR obstoyatel'stv istschesnoveniya Adol'fa Gitlera 1945–1949*, Moscow, 2003

Lang, Jochen von, *Bormann: The Man Who Manipulated Hitler*, Weidenfeld & Nicolson, London, 1979

Lehmann, Armin D., and Carroll, Tim, *In Hitler's Bunker: A Boy Soldier's Eyewitness Account of the Fuhrer's Last Days*, Mainstream Publishing, Edinburgh, 2003

Liddell Hart, Basil. H., *History of the Second World War*, Papermac, London, 1992

Lilla, Joachim, *Statisten in Uniform: Die Mitglieder des Reichstages 1933–1945, ein biographisches Handbuch*, Droste, Düsseldorf, 2004

Linge, Heinz, *Bis zum Ende: Als Chef des Persönlichen Dienstes bei Hitler*, ed. Werner Maser, Herbig, Munich, 1980

Lucas, James, *Hitler's Elite: Leibstandarte SS 1933–1945*, Macdonald, London, 1990

Lukacs, John, *The Hitler of History*, Weidenfeld & Nicolson, London, 2000

Lustiger, Arno, *Stalin and the Jews: The Red Book – The Tragedy of the Jewish Anti-Fascist Committee and the Soviet Jews*, Enigma Books, New York, 2003

Machtan, Lothar, *The Hidden Hitler*, Basic Books, New York, 2001

Macksey, Kenneth, *Guderian: Panzer General*, Greenhill Books, London, 2003

Magenheimer, Heinz, *Hitler's War: Germany's Key Strategic Decisions, 1940–1945*, Cassell, London 2002

Manstein, Erich von, *Lost Victories*, Presidio Press, London, 1982

Maser, Werner, *Hitler*, Allen Lane, London, 1974

——, *Hitler's Letters and Notes*, Bantam Books, London, 1976

——, *Nuremberg: A Nation on Trial*, Viking, London, 1979

Morell, Theo, *Adolf Hitler: The Medical Diaries*, ed. David Irving, Focal Point Publications, London, 1983

Müller, Rolf-Dieter, and Ueberschär, Gerd R., *Hitler's War in the East, 1941–1945: A Critical Assessment*, Berghahn Books, New York, 2002

Neufeld, Michael J., *The Rocket and the Reich: Peenemünde and the Coming of the Ballistic Missile Era*, Simon & Schuster, New York, 1995

O'Sullivan, Donal, *Stalins 'Cordon sanitaire': Die sowjetische Osteuropapolitik und die Reaktionen des Westens 1939–1949*, Schoeningh, Paderborn, 2003

Overy, Richard J., *The Air War 1939–1945*, Brassey's, London, 1980

——, *Why the Allies Won: Explaining Victory in World War II*, Jonathan Cape, London, 1996

——, *Russia's War*, Penguin, London, 1999

——, *Interrogations; The Nazi Elite in Allied Hands, 1945*, Allen Lane, London, 2001

——, *The Dictators: Hitler's Germany, Stalin's Russia*, Penguin, London, 2004

Pauley, Bruce F., *Hitler, Stalin, and Mussolini: Totalitarianism in the Twentieth Century*, Harlan Davidson, Wheeling, IL, 2003

Perrett, Bryan, *Encyclopedia of the Second World War*, Longman, Harlow, 1989

Pressac, Jean-Claude, *Les Crématoires d'Auschwitz: la machinerie du meurtre de masse*, CNRS Editions, Paris, 1993

Rayfield, Donald, *Stalin and His Hangman: An Authoritative Portrait of a Tyrant and Those Who Served Him*, Viking, London, 2004

Read, Anthony, *The Devil's Disciples: The Lives and Times of Hitler's Inner Circle*, Jonathan Cape, London, 2003

Redlich, Fritz, *Hitler: Diagnosis of a Destructive Prophet*, Oxford University Press, Oxford, 1999

Rees, Laurence, *Auschwitz: A New History*, PublicAffairs, London, 2005

Reuth, Ralf Georg: *Goebbels*, Constable, London, 1993

Rhodes, Richard, *Masters of Death: The SS-Einsatzgruppen and the Invention of the Holocaust*, Perseus, Oxford 2002

Roewer, Helmut, Schäfer, Stefan, and Uhl, Matthias, *Lexikon der Geheimdienste im 20. Jahrhundert*, Herbig, Munich, 2003

Rossiya i SSSR voynach XX veka, Statistitscheskoe issledovanie, Moscow, 2001

Ryan, Cornelius, *The Last Battle*, Wordsworth Editions, New York, 1965

Schenck, Ernst Günther, *Das Notlazarett unter der Reichskanzlei: Ein Arzt erlebt Hitlers Ende in Berlin*, Ars Una, Wiesbaden, 2000

——, *Patient Hitler: Eine medizinische Biographie*, Bechtermuenz Verlag, Augsburg, 2000

Schirach, Henriette von, *Der Preis der Herrlichkeit*, Herbig, Munich, 2003

Schmidt, Matthias, *Albert Speer: The End of a Myth*, Macmillan, London, 1985

Schramm, Percy Ernst (ed.), *Kriegstagebuch des Oberkommandos der Wehrmacht (Wehrmachtsführungsstab) 1940–1945. Studiendausgabe in 8 Bänden*, Bernard und Graefe, Frankfurt, 1961–65

Schroeder, Christa, *Er war mein Chef*, ed. Anton Joachimsthaler, Langen Müller, Munich, 1985

Shirer, William L., *Berlin Diary: The Journal of a Foreign Correspondent, 1934–1941*, Johns Hopkins University Press, Baltimore, 2002

Siegmund, Anna Maria, *Die Frauen der Nazis*, Heyne, Vienna, 1998–2002

Skorzeny, Otto, *Skorzeny's Special Missions: The Memoirs of the Most Dangerous Man in Europe*, Greenhill Books, London, 1997

Smelser, Ronald M., *Robert Ley: Hitler's Labor Front Leader*, Berg Publishers, Oxford, 1988

——, and Zitelmann, Rainer (eds), *The Nazi Elite*, Palgrave Macmillan, New York, 1993

Smersch, *Istoritscheskie otscherki i archivnye dokumenty*, Moscow, 2003

Snyder, Louis L., *Encyclopedia of the Third Reich*, Wordsworth Editions, London, 1998

Sofsky, Wolfgang, *The Order of Terror: The Concentration Camp*, Princeton University Press, Princeton, NJ, 1997

Speer, Albert, *Inside the Third Reich: Memoirs*, Simon & Schuster, New York, 1997

Suvenirov, Oleg F., *Tragediya RKKA 1937–1938*, Terra, Moscow, 1998

Le Tissier, Tony, *The Battle of Berlin 1945*, Jonathan Cape, London, 1988

——, *The Third Reich: Then and Now*, After the Battle, London, 2005

Trevor-Roper, Hugh (ed.), *Hitler's War Directives 1939–1945*, Birlinn, Edinburgh, 2004

Ueberschär, Gerd R. (ed.), *Das Nationalkomitee 'Freies Deutschland' und der Bund Deutscher Offiziere*, Fischer Verlag, Frankfurt, 1996

——, *Hitlers Militärische Elite: Vom Kriegsbeginn bis zum Weltkriegsende*, 2 vols, Primus Verlag, Darmstadt, 1998

——, *Der Nationalsozialismus vor Gericht: Die alliierten Prozesse gegen Kriegsverbrecher und Soldaten 1943–1952*, Fischer Verlag, Frankfurt, 1999

Ueberschär, Gerd R., and Vogel, Winifred, *Dienen und Verdienen: Hitlers Geschenke an seine Eliten*, Fischer Verlag, Frankfurt, 2001

Unknown Pages of the History of World War II: Hitler. Documents from KGB secret archives, Moscow 1995 (CD-ROM)

Van der Vat, Dan, *The Good Nazi: The Life and Lies of Albert Speer*, Weidenfeld & Nicolson, London, 1997

Van Pelt, Robert Jan, *The Case for Auschwitz: Evidence from the Irving Trial*, Indiana University Press, Bloomington, IN, 2002

Volkogonov, Dmitrii A., *Stalin: Triumph and Tragedy*, Weidenfeld & Nicolson, London, 2000

Wagner, Friedelind, *Heritage of Fire: The Story of Richard Wagner's Granddaughter*, Harper & Brothers, New York, 1945

Wallach, Jehuda L., *The Dogma of the Battle of Annihilation: The Theories of Clausewitz and Schlieffen and Their Impact on the German Conduct of Two World Wars*, Greenwood Press, London, 1986

Wegner, Bernd, *The Waffen-SS: Organization, Ideology and Function*, Blackwell Publishers, Oxford, 1990

Die Wehrmachtsberichte 1939–1945, 3 vols, DTV, Cologne, 1989

Weihsmann, Helmut, *Bauen unterm Hakenkreuz: Architektur des Untergangs*, Promedia, Vienna, 1998

Weinberg, Gerhard L., *A World at Arms: A Global History of World War II*, Cambridge University Press, Cambridge, 1994

——, *Germany, Hitler, and World War II: Essays in Modern German and World History*, Cambridge University Press, Cambridge, 1995

——, *Visions of Victory: The Hopes of Eight World War II Leaders*, Cambridge University Press, Cambridge, 2005

Weitz, John, *Hitler's Banker: Hjalmar Horace Greeley Schacht*, Time Warner Paperbacks, Boston, 1999

Wistrich, Robert S., *Who's Who in Nazi Germany*, Routledge, London, 1995

Witte, Peter (ed.), *Der Dienstkalender Heinrich Himmlers 1941/42*, Christians, Hamburg, 1999

Zitelmann, Rainer, *Hitler: The Politics of Seduction*, London House, London 1999

Index